# THE STATE
# AND NATURE

# THE STATE AND NATURE

## VOICES HEARD, VOICES UNHEARD IN AMERICA'S ENVIRONMENTAL DIALOGUE

**Jeanne Nienaber Clarke**
*The University of Arizona*

**Hanna J. Cortner**
*Northern Arizona University*

Prentice
Hall

Upper Saddle River, NJ 07458

Library of Congress Cataloging-in-Publication Data

The state and nature : voices heard, voices unheard in America's environmental dialogue
/ [edited by] Jeanne Nienaber Clarke, Hanna J. Cortner.
    p. cm.
  Includes bibliographical references.
  ISBN 0-13-028908-6 (pbk.)
    1. Environmental policy—United States—History.  I. Clarke, Jeanne Nienaber, (date).  II.
  Cortner, H. (Hanna), (date).

GE180 .S72 2002
363.7'05'0973—dc21

                                                                                    00-140091

VP, Editorial Director: Laura Pearson
Senior Acquisitions Editor: Heather Shelstad
Assistant Editor: Brian Prybella
Editorial/Production supervision
  and interior design: Mary Araneo
Director of Marketing: Beth Gillett Mejia
Editorial Assistant: Jessica Drew
Prepress and Manufacturing Buyer: Ben Smith
Cover Art Director: Jayne Conte
Cover Designer: Bruce Kenselaar
Cover Photo: La Jolla, California, Luke Suttile, 1998

This book was set in 10/11 Palatino by A & A Publishing Services, Inc.,
and was printed and bound by Courier Companies, Inc. The cover was
printed by Phoenix Color Corp.

© 2002 by Pearson Education, Inc.
Upper Saddle River, New Jersey 07458

Printed in the United States of America

10  9  8  7  6  5  4  3  2  1

ISBN   0-13-028908-6

PRENTICE-HALL INTERNATIONAL (UK) LIMITED, London
PRENTICE-HALL OF AUSTRALIA PTY. LIMITED, Sydney
PRENTICE-HALL CANADA INC., Toronto
PRENTICE-HALL HISPANOAMERICANA, S.A., Mexico
PRENTICE-HALL OF INDIA PRIVATE LIMITED, New Delhi
PRENTICE-HALL OF JAPAN, INC., Tokyo
PEARSON EDUCATION ASIA PTE. LTD., Singapore
EDITORA PRENTICE-HALL DO BRASIL, LTDA., Rio de Janeiro

To the memory of Aaron Wildavsky:
Teacher, Scholar, Friend, Mensch
(JNC)

And for Barbara  J. Rothgeb
(HJC)

# Contents

# Introduction

The *State and Nature* traces a two-hundred year history of environmental policy, broadly conceived, in the United States. It does this through a selection of original readings, accompanied by substantial editorial comments designed to make explicit the link between the readings and what was occurring in the country at the time of the writings.

The readings have been selected in this manner: First, we relate intellectual thought with political action. A basic premise is that ideas matter in politics and policy making, although there may well be a substantial time differential between the occurrence of an idea and its application in the public sector. Further, it is usually a case of accretion; it takes a number of writings, over time, on a given subject before politicians and policy makers take notice and act.

Second, the selection of readings is premised on the belief that a fundamental relationship exists between the state, its political institutions and processes, and the natural environment in which it is, literally, grounded. To put it another way, physical space and political space are interconnected, although not in a narrow, deterministic manner. Most physical locations allow for the appearance of a rather wide array of social organizations. But clearly such basic natural phenomena as mountains, coast lines, rivers, degree of rainfall, nature of soil, and so forth, act as constraints on economic, political, and social behavior. In the opposite direction, the impact of the state on its natural underpinnings also can vary extensively. A society's footprints can leave traces on nature that range from negligible to destructive.

Third, the readings have been selected to provide a historical dimen-

1

sion to understanding contemporary environmental politics. This, we believe, is essential: History matters. Exploring Thomas Jefferson's philosophy about democracy and human connections does more than shed light on the personality of one of the founding fathers and the nation's third president: Jefferson's land policies shaped the nation. His exaltations of the virtues of the yeoman farmer are embedded in American political consciousness; the image of the small family farm is the referent that frames many issues even as farming and ranching wear a more corporate face. And today in public meetings and ad-hoc community forums around the country, citizens can be heard debating the merits of Jefferson's ideal of participatory democracy versus Madison's representative republic, as they grapple with the challenge of designing new approaches and new institutions for resolving resource-management conflicts. Moreover, many modern debates have antecedents in historical debates. Yesterday's debate about dam construction on the Snake River is today's debate about dam removal. Today's debate over teaching evolution versus the biblical version of creation has deep roots in prior social and legal battles about the roles of science and religion in American life. The existing framework of environmental policy—including laws, administrative organizations, interest groups, public attitudes and behavior, and the roles of science, ethics, and economics—can thus only be understood fully by examining its evolution. For example, virtually all informed commentary on the current political situation notes how extremely difficult it is to get anything done. Frustration is endemic, as is apathy among a large number of citizens. Adjectives such as gridlock, deadlock, stalemate, and status quo are used to characterize current policy making. Why?

A major reason is that America, since the New Deal of the 1930s, has witnessed an explosion in interest group formation and its attendant lobbying (Lowi 1979; Berry 1989, 1999; Clarke and McCool 1996). This has occurred at all levels of government, from the local to the transnational. In one sense, such an increase in political action can be viewed as an indicator of a healthy polity. But the downside is that it is possible to have too much of a good thing. The substantial increase in the variety and number of groups in America has produced a condition approaching political paralysis. Moreover, the explosion in special interests, and in what is called single-issue politics, have occurred at the same time as millions of Americans have turned off to politics. This latter group, perhaps constituting a numerical majority, has come to believe that political participation on its part is futile, precisely because it sees politics as controlled by special interests.

What many people think is needed at this juncture is a political movement, and strong leadership, to break what scholar James MacGregor Burns called in 1963 the "deadlock of democracy." Centrifugal forces always have been strong in the United States, but from time to time political leaders and movements have emerged to provide the centripetal force necessary to check the forces of disintegration and fragmentation that have always been with us. This occurred, for instance, at the beginning of the twentieth century with President Theodore Roosevelt, who championed both political reforms and the progressive conservation movement.

In this evolutionary context, it is also important to note the gradual widening of the debate in America over environmental policy. As the legal scholar Christopher Stone noted in his book, *Should Trees Have Standing?*(1972), the history of law in western societies has been in the direction of according the same rights to individuals, groups, and entities that once belonged to a few. In the same way, over the space of two hundred years there has been a marked increase in the voices heard in the environmental policy arena. With the introduction of new voices there comes a different conception of nature, or at least different beliefs of what is important and what is not. And, while the extension of democracy in this manner is generally considered a positive development, it is possible to have too much group identification and not enough community spirit. We believe that this is the political condition facing the United States in the twenty-first century.

It is these two enduring features of American politics—group activity as the engine driving *most* policy making and periods of inspired national leadership that stress Americans' common purpose amidst their great diversity—which provide the basis for the readings. In other words, this book documents a history of "punctuated equilibrium" in American politics and environmental policy making. A political theory of punctuated equilibrium seeks to more thoroughly explain what historians and other scholars have long known about the episodic nature of American politics: The country enjoys long periods of relative quiescence, followed by the build-up of political "anomalies," which then get resolved by a creative outburst in the political arena. Interestingly, social scientists have borrowed the theory from the field of evolutionary biology, and especially from the well-known work of Stephen Jay Gould.

This book casts a broad net in order to document the diverse nature of environmental and resource issues. The readings cover such topics as public lands, air and water pollution, property rights, energy, toxics, and population control. We are purposefully avoiding the overworked dichotomy wherein environmental policy is treated as pollution-control policy, with the Environmental Protection Agency as the major focus, and natural-resources policy is treated as public-lands policy, with the U.S. Forest Service, Bureau of Land Management, and the National Park Service as the primary foci. In addition, we want to emphasize the point that environmental policy can be as much about how humans treat one another as it is about how they treat nonhuman flora and fauna. Racism, for example, squanders both natural and human capital; resources often become pawns in games to gain ascendance over others, with devastating impacts upon physical landscapes as well as democratic principles. If humans cannot learn to treat different races, ethnicities, and genders with respect, it is unlikely that our relationships to nonhuman objects will ever be one of stewardship and community.

The readings are organized into seven historical eras. Admittedly, we had to omit a number of seminal essays and authors to keep this book to an acceptable length. The choices were especially difficult for the last two historical eras, roughly 1961 to the present, because of the virtual explosion of scholarship and political action in the environmental arena during these years. We preface the readings in each section with commentary describing the evolving American state and intellectual thought relating to resource use and preservation during that period. Each specific reading also is preceded by a short biographical sketch about the author as well as discussion of the author's overall influence. Finally, we are keenly aware that many think history is only tangentially related to current policy issues. To add to the relevance of the readings, discussion questions at the end of each section are designed to provoke instructor and student discussions about the link between contemporary issues and the evolution of political and intellectual approaches to the state and nature.

Many individuals had a hand in seeing this effort to completion and deserve our thanks. Joel Rayan and Laura Tanzer, graduate students in the Department of Political Science and the School of Renewable Natural Resources at the University of Arizona, performed various research tasks. Val Catt did invaluable work in initial manuscript preparation. James Clarke and Richard Cortner read portions of the manuscript and made numerous helpful suggestions along the way. Finally, we wish to thank Rachel Dorushka and Beth Gillett Mejia of Prentice Hall and production editor Mary Araneo for their encouragement and support in turning project concept into publication reality.

# PART I

## "The Land Was Ours Before We Were the Land's"*
### FORMATION OF THE REPUBLIC, 1780–1840

History is a seamless web, so any beginning must be somewhat arbitrary. But one has to start somewhere, and so this narrative on the relationship between the American state and nature begins in the late eighteenth century. The reason is clear: The drafting and passage of the Constitution marks a new beginning in the New World. With the establishment of a more powerful union in 1789, America was off on a new trajectory. It was one which would have profound impacts not only on the natural environment in which the new nation was embedded, but also on relationships among the various peoples living on the continent. One hundred years later, with the advent of "The American Century," the impacts would be felt worldwide.

Still, by 1789 Europeans had been on this continent, living in close proximity with the original inhabitants, the Indians, for over two hundred years. These Americans, as they called themselves, already had an established order. They built villages, towns, and cities up and down the Eastern seaboard, and even far inland; they constructed land- and water-based transportation routes; some had farmed the land for generations; and there was an embryonic industrial base. Americans had taken advantage of the abundance of resources found in the New World—wood, water, land, and wildlife—and had passed laws addressing localized resource shortages and the occurrence of natural disasters, such as fire. There were regulations concerning trade, and there was a well-established system of rights in property,

---

*Robert Frost, from the poem, "The Gift Outright."

including the right to own slaves. Also, by 1781, Americans had written a Declaration of Independence, successfully overthrown English rule in the thirteen colonies, and approved the nation's first constitution, the Articles of Confederation.

The shift from Indian to European dominance in the New World largely institutionalized the idea and practice of treating natural resources as commodities. This not only had profound effects in the political realm but also on the physical environment, as the new settlers prodigiously transformed what they found around them into economic wealth. Following the Declaration of Independence in 1776, the original states ceded their claims to western lands to the national government. This created a *national* interest in the lands and resources lying to the west of the existing states, and it enabled the Congress to pay off Revolutionary War debts by disposing of much of this "surplus" land. At the same time, Indian tribes, either by negotiation or by force, ceded some of their lands to the new governments.

Despite these augmentations in political power and natural resources, the alliance of states that existed during the Revolutionary War and under the Articles of Confederation proved too weak to hold the new nation together. The Constitutional Convention was convened in Philadelphia in 1787, for the purpose of creating a stronger national system of government. Following ratification of the Constitution, the new government took office in 1789.

The period between the establishment of the first colonial settlements in the sixteenth century and the drafting of the Constitution in the eighteenth certainly was significant. A new political culture, with definite ideas about property, commerce, participatory forms of government, and individualized rights, had been created. By the time the framers of the Constitution began their important work, much institution building had already taken place. Yet, there was an insufficiency of power at the national level, and so the Constitution drafted in 1787 and approved by the states in 1788 marks a critical juncture in the nation's history.

Separation of powers, checks and balances, federalism, a bicameral legislature, an independent chief executive and an independent judiciary, a bill of rights—these fundamental principles of the Constitution are well known. Less appreciated, however, are what can be called the environmental aspects of the Constitution. What constitutional principles and theories connect the political state to the natural state? For instance, how is property defined? What groups have control over water, land, and other natural resources essential to life, liberty, and the pursuit of happiness? How do the aboriginal peoples, the Indians, fare when a new government is superimposed on what had been their lands and their cultures? Finally, what attitudes will an enslaved people, defined as property, have about the land?

The Constitution is a succinct document in which little is explicitly said about these issues. Nevertheless, there is enough written down so as to form the foundation for much of the subsequent history of environmental policy making in the United States to this very day. The Constitution frames the debate and therefore needs to be carefully considered. And, what the document itself doesn't say, others in this formative period have said, including icy of generous public land disposal. The General Land Office sold it to pay Revolutionary War debts; it gave parcels to the new states to benefit public education; it granted land to both states and private interests such as the railroads to encourage settlement and infrastructure development; and it donated it to landless settlers. Each new land disposal policy, however, was rife with problems—speculation, squatters who neglected to pay, and widespread corruption.

American beliefs concerning the state and nature also reflected the Enlightenment doctrine of natural law that reigned supreme among American thinkers and statesmen in the late eighteenth century. Nature was perceived as an awesome, divinely ordered entity, whose laws should extend to civil society. Thus, the "good society" was one that conformed as far as possible to natural law. But what, one may ask, *is* natural law? The Declaration of Independence, with its self-evident truths that all men are created equal, and that all men have a right to life, liberty, and the pursuit of happiness, serves as a prime example of Enlightenment thinking in the New World. So does the Constitution, with its carefully considered balance of powers and its Bill of Rights.

It was Chief Justice John Marshall, however, who positioned the federal courts to play a pivotal role in giving life to the abstract principles of natural law and fundamental rights. Marshall, who had been appointed to the Supreme Court by President John Adams in 1801, seized every opportunity to take what looked like a mundane and straightforward case and to use it as a tool to elaborate on his philosophy of natural law as well as to build a stronger national government. When Marshall and the Court held part of the Judiciary Act of 1789 unconstitutional in *Marbury v. Madison* (1803), the Court became more than a passive player in public policy. By claiming for the Court the power to review acts of Congress and declare them unconstitutional (judicial review), Marshall helped secure for the Court (and the judiciary in general) a major voice in ensuring the flexibility, durability, and scope of the Constitution. Marshall's court also expanded the powers of the national government in cases such as *McCulloch v. Maryland* (1819), which gave the Court a role in supporting the supremacy of national law as well as giving Congress greater power to legislate using implied powers under the necessary and proper clause, and in *Gibbons v. Ogden* (1824), which interpreted the commerce clause and provided the basis for national regulation of the economy.

Perhaps there has never been a stronger voice on the Supreme Court. During Marshall's long, 34-year tenure, he personally wrote 519 of the Court's 1106 opinions, which included almost all of the Court's historic opinions on constitutional interpretation. He established the Court as the ultimate interpreter of how the abstract principles of Enlightenment thinking and constitutional law would be applied to everyday life.

Enlightenment thinking which, on the one hand, provided the liberating force to move humans toward creating a modern state embracing liberty, equality, and individual rights, also, on the other hand, provided justification for attitudes and behavior that subjugated nature to human domination. The English philosopher John Locke, whose *Two Treatises of Civil Government* deeply influenced the thinking of the founding fathers, viewed land as inert and useless until human labor converted it into something valuable. Thus nature is devoid of meaning independent of its meaning as property and its immediate utility to humans. The new nation's founders generally subscribed to Locke's, and others' utilitarian view of the environment. However, they also believed that republican government was dependent upon a broad distribution of property. Because "power follows property," it was necessary to ensure that wealth did not become concentrated among a small group, and so the abundance of land in the New World again provided the necessary physical foundation for building a democratic society. But it meant also that "Nature" became "Property" and put in active service of the state.

Finally, in terms of eighteenth century attitudes concerning the state and nature, there existed (among whites, of course) the widely held belief in the natural superiority of their race. Indians and Negroes, and their respective cultures, were thought to be at a much lower stage of development. Therefore, they did not enjoy the same rights and privileges that "American citizens" enjoyed. Indian tribes constituted a semisovereign nation, with some rights, while Negroes in servitude had no rights. They were, in fact, considered property; and so the voices of Negro slaves were even more silent than those of the Indians in this early period. From the very beginning of the new American republic, the position of Indians and Negroes vis-à-vis the state was that of the "other." For generations, their voices generally were lost, or had to be interpreted by whites to have legitimacy.

The framers of the Constitution expected the political system to work without political parties, believing that in their form of republicanism the people's representatives could set aside individual interests in favor of the common good. However, divisions within George Washington's administration and within Congress became apparent in his first term as president. Competing factions started forming into "parties." There were domestic disagreements over Secretary of the Treasury Alexander Hamilton's fiscal policies, particularly his proposal to charter a national bank. There were also foreign policy disagreements, which came to a head with Jay's Treaty of 1795 (an attempt to resolve issues between Britain and the United States left unresolved by the treaty ending the Revolutionary War). Two of Washington's most powerful cabinet members, Hamilton and Jefferson, emerged as leaders of two broad factions. By the time he gave his farewell address in 1796, a dispirited President Washington was warning Americans about the "baneful effects of the spirit of party."

Opposition to the Alien and Sedition Acts—repressive laws that had been provoked by the war with France in 1798—heavily contributed to the "Revolution of 1800." This so-called revolution consisted of the electoral defeat of the Federalist faction and the election of the Democratic-Republican, Thomas Jefferson, as President. That election represented the nation's first transfer of power from one political group to another, but it wasn't until Andrew Jackson's election in 1828 that parties truly emerged as that necessary, extraconstitutional device for giving voice to opposing interests in their struggle to control the machinery of the state.

More eloquently than any of his contemporaries, Thomas Jefferson explored the relationship between the agrarian way of life and democracy. He argued for the centrality of the small farming family in maintaining the civic virtues necessary for a decentralized and democratic state. The original "small is beautiful" theorist, Jefferson's voice remains today one of the most powerful and influential in American political thought. Thus, it is ironic that this agrarian democrat, who philosophically and emotionally loved the small scale, would, as president, help set in motion a quite opposite force, that of Manifest Destiny.

Jefferson's presidency boasts numerous accomplishments, but the one that stands out above the rest is the 1803 Louisiana Purchase. Historians consider it to be one of the ten most fateful presidential decisions ever made. Despite concerns about the constitutional authority to do so, Jefferson proceeded with the purchase. In one fell swoop, the land mass of the United States was doubled. That natural divide—the Mississippi River—no longer marked the western boundary of America. The great westward migration began.

But what kind of land, with what climate, and with what amount of water, had the U.S. purchased from France? Apart from some vague rumors about a Great American Desert, nobody knew. To find the answers to these questions, President Jefferson directed two captains, Meriwether Lewis and William Clark, to head an expedition through the new territory. Thus, in 1803, a year after Congress established a corps of engineers to explore and to keep open the nation's waterways, Jefferson launched one of the most famous expeditions in all of recorded history. In his instructions to Lewis and Clark, Jefferson stated that the object of the mission would be to "explore the Missouri river, & such principal stream of it, as, by its course & communication with the water of the Pacific Ocean may offer the most direct & practical water communication across this continent, for the purposes of commerce." Reflecting his deep interest in nature and the unknown political territory he had just brought into the United States, Jefferson also asked the explorers for extensive documentation of the flora and fauna they discovered, and information about the Indian tribes they encountered. Lewis and Clark followed the president's orders, and their accounts of the amazing journey continue to be read in the twenty-first century.

Not only did the Louisiana Purchase and the great migration westward transform American society and its political institutions, it spelled doom for the Native American way of life. Always a latent problem, the "Indian problem" became manifest in the 1820s and 1830s. Land-hungry frontiersmen demanded that Indians be pushed further and further to the West, and states such as Georgia, where gold recently had been found on Cherokee lands, passed laws imposing state jurisdiction over Indian lands, thereby opening those lands to white settlement. To deal with this problem Congress passed, and President Andrew Jackson aggressively implemented, the Indian Removal Act (1830), which allowed the president to reserve public lands west of the Mississippi for Indian occupancy and to use military force to relocate the tribes to their new reservations. Astonishingly, noted de Tocqueville, Indian removal was accomplished in the name of morality.

At the same time as President Jackson was sending messages to

Congress justifying the policy of Indian removal, the artist George Catlin was traveling in the West and witnessing the unfolding tragedy. Catlin is often credited with having first conceptualized the idea of a "national park," but his vision for the western territories was much more radical and encompassing than even that unique notion. He hoped that the federal government would set aside a vast tract of land in what became Wyoming, Montana, the Dakotas, and Nebraska to allow Indians to live as they had lived, in close contact with nature, and without continued threats—and contaminating influences—from whites for their lands. Catlin's 1832 vision was for a Great Plains "Buffalo Commons," which recently has been revived by some environmentalists.

When Lewis and Clark set out on their expedition in 1803, nothing moved faster on land than a horse. A mere thirty years later, when de Tocqueville visited the United States, steamboats were moving commerce and railroad tracks were extending in all directions. Each year the frontier pushed seventeen miles further west, thereby intensifying conflicts between the original inhabitants and the new settlers. Land was being cleared, and resources used, as if there was an inexhaustible supply.

And there were more than two million people in bondage. Debates over slavery and the other great differences between the North and South dominated the national agenda. Southerners like John Calhoun argued for state sovereignty and for the rights of nullification and secession, while the abolitionist movement in the North slowly gathered momentum. Immeasurably contributing to that movement were the voices and experiences of individuals like Frederick Douglass, who escaped from slavery in 1838, and who spent the rest of his life writing and speaking out against the evils of slavery. It is little wonder that the slave's view of the state and nature were radically different from that of the dominant group, but these views usually are underappreciated, even today.

To conclude: During America's formative period there is much to celebrate. Americans had crafted a Constitution built upon Enlightenment principles of popular sovereignty, liberty, and individual rights, and they had begun establishing a democratic polity. America as "the last, best hope on earth" was not only a nineteenth-century belief but one that still resonates around the world today. But there is also much to lament in this formative era. We had fashioned a nation that tolerated the domination of one group of humans over other groups, including Indian tribes and Negro slaves. These early Americans also had "objectified" nature, treating it overwhelmingly as commodity, property, and something to be transformed from its original, wild state. So nature, too, was subjugated. The subsequent history of democracy in America, and the state-nature relationship, necessarily involved significant redefinition and reformulation of some of these original realities.

# 1
# James Madison (1751–1836)

James Madison is often referred to as the "father of the Constitution." The most learned and best prepared of the delegates to the Constitutional Convention, he came to this fateful meeting in Philadelphia strongly influenced by the writings of John Locke. It was Locke who argued that government must ultimately rest upon the consent of the governed and that individuals living in civil society possessed natural rights that could not be infringed upon by government.

While waiting for a quorum to arrive in Philadelphia, Madison drafted the Virginia Plan, which was adopted for the purposes of discussion, thereby shifting the agenda away from the more limited task of amending the Articles of Confederation toward the more ambitious one of drafting an entirely new constitution. He took copious notes, a task which he later declared "almost killed him," and his *Notes of the Debate* serve as the most complete record of the convention and the intentions of the framers.

In addition to his pivotal role in drafting the Constitution, Madison was instrumental in securing its ratification. Madison authored some of the most significant of the papers that he, Alexander Hamilton, and John Jay wrote under the pseudonym Publius, in order to sway citizens to ratify the Constitution. The 85 essays—contributed to New York newspapers during 1787–1788 and collected in book form as *The Federalist*—remain the most thorough and important explication of the philosophy underlying the Constitution and American democracy. At first unpersuaded by the need for a separate statement of individual rights, Madison nonetheless prudently recognized that the promise of a bill of rights was required to secure state ratification of the Constitution. When the first Congress assembled in 1789, he assumed principal responsibility for authoring those amendments. Appointed Secretary of State in Jefferson's administration, he succeeded him as the nation's fourth president in 1809.

Madison and the other framers feared "the masses." Consequently, the Constitution created a republic and not a genuine democracy. The framers assumed that men of property would rule with the consent of the governed; therefore they limited the opportunities for direct citizen participation. In *The Federalist No. 10*, which appeared in *The New York Packet* on November 23, 1787, Madison discussed how a geographically extensive republic would diffuse power among the groups and interests that might form to control government, and why small, direct democracies could not be held as a cure for the "mischiefs of factions." Madison rationalized the framers' choice of a republic over a direct democracy based on his view of the pernicious effects of group activity. From the outset, then, questions about the role and influence of groups in the political life of the nation have been of profound interest to politicians, citizens, and students of American democracy.

# "THE MISCHIEFS OF FACTION"*

To the People of the State of New York:

Among the numerous advantages promised by a well-constructed Union, none deserves to be more accurately developed than its tendency to break and control the violence of faction. The friend of popular governments never finds himself so much alarmed for their character and fate, as when he contemplates their propensity to this dangerous vice. He will not fail, therefore, to set a due value on any plan which, without violating the principles to which he is attached, provides a proper cure for it. The instability, injustice, and confusion introduced into the public councils, have, in truth, been the mortal diseases under which popular governments have everywhere perished; as they continue to be the favorite and fruitful topics from which the adversaries to liberty derive their most specious declamations. The valuable improvements made by the American constitutions on the popular models, both ancient and modern, cannot certainly be too much admired; but it would be an unwarrantable partiality, to contend that they have as effectually obviated the danger on this side, as was wished and expected. Complaints are everywhere heard from our most considerate and virtuous citizens, equally the friends of public and private faith, and of public and personal liberty, that our governments are too unstable, that the public good is disregarded in the conflicts of rival parties, and that measures are too often decided, not according to the rules of justice and the rights of the minor party, but by the superior force of an interested and overbearing majority. However anxiously we may wish that these complaints had no foundation, the evidence of known facts will not permit us to deny that they are in some degree true. It will be found, indeed, on a candid review of our situation, that some of the distresses under which we labor have been erroneously charged on the operation of our governments; but it will be found, at the same time, that other causes will not alone account for many of our heaviest misfortunes; and, particularly, for that prevailing and increasing distrust of public engagements, and alarm for private rights, which are echoed from one end of the continent to the other. These must be chiefly, if not wholly, effects of the unsteadiness and injustice with which a factious spirit has tainted our public administrations.

By a faction, I understand a number of citizens, whether amounting to a majority or minority of the whole, who are united and actuated by some common impulse of passion, or of interest, adverse to the rights of other citizens, or to the permanent and aggregate interests of the community.

There are two methods of curing the mischiefs of faction: the one, by removing its cause; the other, by controlling its effects.

There are again two methods of removing the causes of faction: the one, by destroying the liberty which is essential to its existence; the other, by

---

*James Madison. 1787. *The Federalist No. 10.*

giving to every citizen the same opinions, the same passions, and the same interests.

It could never be more truly said than of the first remedy, that it was worse than the disease. Liberty is to faction what air is to fire, an aliment without which it instantly expires. But it could not be less folly to abolish liberty, which is essential to political life, because it nourishes faction, than it would be to wish the annihilation of air, which is essential to animal life, because it imparts to fire its destructive agency.

The second expedient is as impracticable as the first would be unwise. As long as the reason of man continues fallible, and he is at liberty to exercise it, different opinions will be formed. As long as the connection subsists between his reason and his self-love, his opinions and his passions will have a reciprocal influence on each other; and the former will be objects to which the latter will attach themselves. The diversity in the faculties of men, from which the rights of property originate, is not less an insuperable obstacle to a uniformity of interests. The protection of these faculties is the first object of government. From the protection of different and unequal faculties of acquiring property, the possession of different degrees and kinds of property immediately results; and from the influence of these on the sentiments and views of the respective proprietors, ensues a division of the society into different interests and parties.

The latent causes of faction are thus sown in the nature of man; and we see them everywhere brought into different degrees of activity, according to the different circumstances of civil society. A zeal for different opinions concerning religion, concerning government, and many other points, as well of speculation as of practice; an attachment to different leaders ambitiously contending for pre-eminence and power; or to persons of other descriptions whose fortunes have been interesting to the human passions, have, in turn, divided mankind into parties, inflamed them with mutual animosity, and rendered them much more disposed to vex and oppress each other than to co-operate for their common good. So strong is this propensity of mankind to fall into mutual animosities, that where no substantial occasion presents itself, the most frivolous and fanciful distinctions have been sufficient to kindle their unfriendly passions and excite their most violent conflicts. But the most common and durable source of factions has been the various and unequal distribution of property. Those who hold and those who are without property have ever formed distinct interests in society. Those who are creditors, and those who are debtors, fall under a like discrimination. A landed interest, a manufacturing interest, a mercantile interest, a moneyed interest, with many lesser interests, grow up of necessity in civilized nations, and divide them into different classes, actuated by different sentiments and views. The regulation of these various and interfering interests forms the principal task of modern legislation, and involves the spirit of party and faction in the necessary and ordinary operations of the government.

No man is allowed to be a judge in his own cause, because his interest would certainly bias his judgment, and, not improbably, corrupt his integrity. With equal, nay with greater reason, a body of men are unfit to be both judges and parties at the same time; yet what are many of the most important acts of legislation, but so many judicial determinations, not indeed concerning the rights of single persons, but concerning the rights of large bodies of citizens? And what are the different classes of legislators but advocates and parties to the causes which they determine? Is a law proposed concerning private debts? It is a question to which the creditors are parties on one side and the debtors on the other. Justice ought to hold the balance between them. Yet the parties are, and must be, themselves the judges; and the most numerous party, or, in other words, the most powerful faction must be expected to prevail. Shall domestic manufactures be encouraged, and in what degree, by restrictions on foreign manufactures? are questions which would be differently decided by the landed and the manufacturing classes, and probably by neither with a sole regard to justice and the public good. The apportionment of taxes on the various descriptions of property is an act which seems to require the most exact impartiality; yet there is, perhaps, no legislative act in which greater opportunity and temptation are given to a predominant party to trample on the rules of justice. Every shilling with which they overburden the inferior number, is a shilling saved to their own pockets.

It is in vain to say that enlightened statesmen will be able to adjust these clashing interests, and render them all subservient to the public good. Enlightened statesmen will not always be at the helm. Nor, in many cases, can such an adjustment be made at all without taking into view indirect and remote considerations, which will rarely prevail over the immediate interest which one party may find in disregarding the rights of another or the good of the whole.

The inference to which we are brought is, that the *causes* of faction cannot be removed, and that relief is only to be sought in the means of controlling its *effects*.

If a faction consists of less than a majority, relief is supplied by the republican principle, which enables the majority to defeat its sinister views by regular vote. It may clog the administration, it may convulse the society; but it will be unable to execute and mask its violence under the forms of the Constitution. When a majority is included in a faction, the form of popular government, on the other hand, enables it to sacrifice to its ruling passion or interest both the public good and the rights of other citizens. To secure the public good and private rights against the danger of such a faction, and at the same time to preserve the spirit and the form of popular government, is then the great object to which our inquiries are directed. Let me add that it is the great desideratum by which this form of government can be rescued from the opprobrium under which it has so long labored, and be recommended to the esteem and adoption of mankind.

By what means is this object attainable? Evidently by one of two only. Either the existence of the same passion or interest in a majority at the same time must be prevented, or the majority, having such coexistent passion or interest, must be rendered, by their number and local situation, unable to concert and carry into effect schemes of oppression. If the impulse and the opportunity be suffered to coincide, we well know that neither moral nor religious motives can be relied on as an adequate control. They are not found to be such on the injustice and violence of individuals, and lose their efficacy in proportion to the number combined together, that is, in proportion as their efficacy becomes needful.

From this view of the subject it may be concluded that a pure democracy, by which I mean a society consisting of a small number of citizens, who assemble and administer the government in person, can admit of no cure for the mischiefs of faction. A common passion or interest will, in almost every case, be felt by a majority of the whole; a communication and concert result from the form of government itself; and there is nothing to check the inducements to sacrifice the weaker party or an obnoxious individual. Hence it is that such democracies have ever been spectacles of turbulence and contention; have ever been found incompatible with personal security or the rights of property; and have in general been as short in their lives as they have been violent in their deaths. Theoretic politicians, who have patronized this species of government, have erroneously supposed that by reducing mankind to a perfect equality in their political rights, they would, at the same time, be perfectly equalized and assimilated in their possessions, their opinions, and their passions.

A republic, by which I mean a government in which the scheme of representation takes place, opens a different prospect, and promises the cure for which we are seeking. Let us examine the points in which it varies from pure democracy, and we shall comprehend both the nature of the cure and the efficacy which it must derive from the Union.

The two great points of difference between a democracy and a republic are: first, the delegation of the government, in the latter, to a small number of citizens elected by the rest; secondly, the greater number of citizens, and greater sphere of country, over which the latter may be extended.

The effect of the first difference is, on the one hand, to refine and enlarge the public views, by passing them through the medium of a chosen body of citizens, whose wisdom may best discern the true interest of their country, and whose patriotism and love of justice will be least likely to sacrifice it to temporary or partial considerations. Under such a regulation, it may well happen that the public voice, pronounced by the representatives of the people, will be more consonant to the public good than if pronounced by the people themselves, convened for the purpose. On the other hand, the effect may be inverted. Men of factious tempers, of local prejudices, or of sinister designs, may, by intrigue, by corruption, or by other means, first obtain the suffrages, and then betray the interests, of the people. The question resulting is, whether small or extensive republics are more favorable to the election of proper guardians of the public weal; and it is clearly decided in favor of the latter by two obvious considerations:

In the first place, it is to be remarked that, however small the republic may be, the representatives must be raised to a certain number, in order to guard against the cabals of a few; and that, however large it may be, they must be limited to a certain number, in order to guard against the confusion of a multitude. Hence, the number of representatives in the two cases not being in proportion to that of the two constituents, and being proportionally greater in the small republic, it follows that, if the proportion of fit characters be not less in the large than in the small republic, the former will present a greater option, and consequently a greater probability of a fit choice.

In the next place, as each representative will be chosen by a greater number of citizens in the large than in the small republic, it will be more difficult for unworthy candidates to practise with success the vicious arts by which elections are too often carried; and the suffrages of the people being more free, will be more likely to centre in men who possess the most attractive merit and the most diffusive and established characters.

It must be confessed that in this, as in most other cases, there is a mean, on both sides of which inconveniences will be found to lie. By enlarging too much the number of electors, you render the representative too little acquainted with all their local circumstances and lesser interests; as by reducing it too much, you render him unduly attached to these, and too little fit to comprehend and pursue great and national objects. The federal Constitution forms a happy combination in this respect; the great and aggregate interests being referred to the national, the local and particular to the State legislatures.

The other point of difference is, the greater number of citizens and extent of territory which may be brought within the compass of republican than of democratic government; and it is this circumstance principally which renders factious combinations less to be dreaded in the former than in the latter. The smaller the society, the fewer probably will be the distinct parties and interests composing it; the fewer the distinct parties and interests, the more frequently will a majority be found of the same party; and the smaller the number of individuals composing a majority, and the smaller the compass within which they are placed, the more easily will they concert and execute their plans of oppression. Extend the sphere and you take in a greater variety of parties and interests; you make it less probable that a majority of the whole will have a common motive to invade the rights of other citizens; or if such a common motive exists, it will be more difficult for all who feel it to discover their own strength, and to act in unison with each other. Besides other impediments, it may be remarked that, where there is a consciousness of unjust or dishonorable purposes, communication is always checked by distrust in proportion to the number whose concurrence is necessary.

Hence, it clearly appears, that the same advantage which a republic has over a democracy, in controlling the effects of faction, is enjoyed by a large over a small republic,—is enjoyed by the Union over the States composing it. Does the advantage consist in the substitution of representatives whose enlightened views and virtuous sentiments render them superior to local prejudices and schemes of injustice? It will not be denied that the representation of the Union will be most likely to possess these requisite endowments. Does it consist in the greater security afforded by a greater variety of parties, against the event of any one party being able to outnumber and oppress the rest? In an equal degree does the increased variety of parties comprised within the Union, increase this security. Does it, in fine, consist in the greater obstacles opposed to the concert and accomplishment of the secret wishes of an unjust and interested majority? Here, again, the extent of the Union gives it the most palpable advantage.

The influence of factious leaders may kindle a flame within their particular States, but will be unable to spread a general conflagration through the other States. A religious sect may degenerate into a political faction in a part of the Confederacy; but the variety of sects dispersed over the entire face of it must secure the national councils against any danger from that source. A rage for paper money, for an abolition of debts, for an equal division of property, or for any other improper or wicked project, will be less apt to pervade the whole body of the Union than a particular member of it; in the same proportion as such a malady is more likely to taint a particular county or district, than an entire State.

In the extent and proper structure of the Union, therefore, we behold a republican remedy for the diseases most incident to republican government. And according to the degree of pleasure and pride we feel in being republicans, ought to be our zeal in cherishing the spirit and supporting the character of Federalists.

PUBLIUS.

# 2
# Thomas Jefferson (1743–1826)

The Virginia farmer and third president of the United States, Thomas Jefferson, loved nature, especially as it manifested itself in his native state. Whether in the role of disinterested natural scientist, recording his *Notes on the State of Virginia*, or as an American president giving his inaugural address, Jefferson always had in mind nature and what constituted the good society.

The ideal society and the one best suited for America, Jefferson believed, was that of an "agrarian democracy." Jefferson spoke eloquently on how the rural way of life—the life spent close to nature, in constant communication with the land, the seasons, the climate—inculcates the values essential to fostering and maintaining democracy. Jefferson's yeoman farmer would have an abundance of civic virtues, including: an appreciation for hard work and a sense of pride in a job well done; an intimate knowledge of nature and her processes; a sense of proportion; self-reliance; a love of family; and a community-based spirit. The bedrock of the republic would reside in its agrarian population.

Jefferson's *Notes on the State of Virginia*, the only full-length book he wrote, is a detailed commentary about the institutions and resources in one American state—which at that time, it must be remembered, claimed territory embracing approximately one-third of the American continent. In addition to detailed commentary about physical geography, climate, and flora and fauna, the book sets forth Jefferson's political philosophy on subjects ranging from representative government, to separation of church and state, to slavery. Written in 1781, in the midst of the Revolutionary War, and in response to the semiofficial inquiries of a French diplomat residing in Philadelphia, the notes were eventually published in 1787.

Jefferson's First Inaugural Address is clearly conciliatory in tone, seeking to allay the fears of the Federalists about the transition of power to the Jeffersonian faction. It also succinctly sets forth his views on the essentials of American democracy. Jefferson feared strong executive power, believed states should be the primary jurisdiction for domestic affairs, favored strict construction of the Constitution, and advocated the use of frequent constitutional amendment or entirely new constitutions to reflect the will of emergent majorities.

Yet, Jefferson's high ideals often conflicted with his actions. Today, some consider him a racist, for he owned slaves and thought blacks were inferior (even though it is highly likely that he fathered children with his slave mistress Sally Hemings). He stretched the bounds of executive authority (e.g., with the Louisiana Purchase), and he was essentially an imperialist who sought to create an "Empire of Liberty" spread across the American continent. Despite these contradictions, Jefferson's faith in the people and his concepts of a more participatory democracy still epitomize the spirit of American democracy.

Jefferson retired to Monticello in 1809. Deeply in debt, he sold his library, which became the foundation of the Library of Congress. He directed that three accomplishments be engraved upon his tombstone: author of the Declaration of American Independence, author of the Statute of Virginia for Religious Freedom, and father of the University of Virginia. Conspicuously absent was mention of his tenure as the nation's third president or of the many other political offices he held. He died on July 4, 1826, Independence Day, the same day that his friend, fellow revolutionary, and fellow president, John Adams, died.

---

# "AN IMMENSITY OF LAND"*

*The present state of manufactures, commerce, interior and exterior trade?*
We never had an interior trade of any importance. Our exterior commerce has suffered very much from the beginning of the present contest. During this time we have manufactured within our families the most necessary articles of cloathing. Those of cotton will bear some comparison with the same kinds of manufacture in Europe; but those of wool, flax and hemp are very coarse, unsightly, and unpleasant: and such is our attachment to agriculture, and such our preference for foreign manufactures, that be it wise or unwise, our people will certainly return as soon as they can, to the raising raw materials, and exchanging them for finer manufactures than they are able to execute themselves.

The political œconomists of Europe have established it as a principle that every state should endeavour to manufacture for itself: and this principle, like many others, we transfer to America, without calculating the difference of circumstance which should often produce a difference of result. In Europe the lands are either cultivated, or locked up against the cultivator. Manufacture must therefore be resorted to of necessity not of choice, to support the surplus of their people. But we have an immensity of land courting the industry of the husbandman. Is it best then that all our citizens should be employed in its improvement, or that one half should be called off from that to exercise manufactures and handicraft arts for the other? Those who labour in the earth are the chosen people of God, if ever he had a chosen people, whose breasts he has made his peculiar deposit for substantial and genuine virtue. It is the focus in which he keeps alive that sacred fire, which otherwise might escape from the face of the earth. Corruption of morals in the mass of cultivators is a phænomenon of which no age nor nation has furnished an example. It is the mark set on those, who not looking up to heaven, to their own soil and industry, as does the husbandman, for their subsistance, depend for it on the casualties and caprice of customers. Dependance begets subservience and venality, suffocates the germ of virtue, and prepares

---

*Thomas Jefferson. 1787. "Query XIX, Manufactures," in *Notes on the State of Virginia*. London: John Stockdale, pp. 164–165.

fit tools for the designs of ambition. This, the natural progress and consequence of the arts, has sometimes perhaps been retarded by accidental circumstances: but, generally speaking, the proportion which the aggregate of the other classes of citizens bears in any state to that of its husbandmen, is the proportion of its unsound to its healthy parts, and is a good-enough barometer whereby to measure its degree of corruption. While we have land to labour then, let us never wish to see our citizens occupied at a work-bench, or twirling a distaff. Carpenters, masons, smiths, are wanting in husbandry: but, for the general operations of manufacture, let our work-shops remain in Europe. It is better to carry provisions and materials to workmen there, than bring them to the provisions and materials, and with them their manners and principles. The loss by the transportation of commodities across the Atlantic will be made up in happiness and permanence of government. The mobs of great cities add just so much to the support of pure government, as sores do to the strength of the human body. It is the manners and spirit of a people which preserve a republic in vigour. A degeneracy in these is a canker which soon eats to the heart of its laws and constitution.

---

# "A RISING NATION"[*]

Friends and Fellow-Citizens:

Called upon to undertake the duties of the first executive office of our country, I avail myself of the presence of that portion of my fellow-citizens which is here assembled to express my grateful thanks for the favor with which they have been pleased to look toward me, to declare a sincere consciousness that the task is above my talents, and that I approach it with those anxious and awful presentiments which the greatness of the charge and the weakness of my powers so justly inspire. A rising nation, spread over a wide and fruitful land, traversing all the seas with the rich productions of their industry, engaged in commerce with nations who feel power and forget right, advancing rapidly to destinies beyond the reach of mortal eye—when I contemplate these transcendent objects, and see the honor, the happiness, and the hopes of this beloved country committed to the issue and the auspices of this day, I shrink from the contemplation, and humble myself before the magnitude of the undertaking. Utterly, indeed, should I despair did not the presence of many whom I here see remind me that in the other high authorities provided by our Constitution I shall find resources of wisdom, of virtue, and of zeal on which to rely under all difficulties. To you, then, gentlemen, who are charged with the sovereign functions of legislation, and to those associated with you, I look with encouragement for that guidance and

---

*Thomas Jefferson. 1896. First Inaugural Address, March 4, 1801, in *A Compilation of the Messages and Papers of the Presidents, 1789-1897.* James D. Richardson, ed. Washington, DC: Government Printing Office, Vol. I, pp. 321–324.

support which may enable us to steer with safety the vessel in which we are all embarked amidst the conflicting elements of a troubled world.

During the contest of opinion through which we have passed the animation of discussions and of exertions has sometimes worn an aspect which might impose on strangers unused to think freely and to speak and to write what they think; but this being now decided by the voice of the nation, announced according to the rules of the Constitution, all will, of course, arrange themselves under the will of the law, and unite in common efforts for the common good. All, too, will bear in mind this sacred principle, that though the will of the majority is in all cases to prevail, that will to be rightful must be reasonable; that the minority possess their equal rights, which equal law must protect, and to violate would be oppression. Let us, then, fellow-citizens, unite with one heart and one mind. Let us restore to social intercourse that harmony and affection without which liberty and even life itself are but dreary things. And let us reflect that, having banished from our land that religious intolerance under which mankind so long bled and suffered, we have yet gained little if we countenance a political intolerance as despotic, as wicked, and capable of as bitter and bloody persecutions. During the throes and convulsions of the ancient world, during the agonizing spasms of infuriated man, seeking through blood and slaughter his long-lost liberty, it was not wonderful that the agitation of the billows should reach even this distant and peaceful shore; that this should be more felt and feared by some and less by others, and should divide opinions as to measures of safety. But every difference of opinion is not a difference of principle. We have called by different names brethren of the same principle. We are all Republicans, we are all Federalists. If there be any among us who would wish to dissolve this Union or to change its republican form, let them stand undisturbed as monuments of the safety with which error of opinion may be tolerated where reason is left free to combat it. I know, indeed, that some honest men fear that a republican government can not be strong, that this Government is not strong enough; but would the honest patriot, in the full tide of successful experiment, abandon a government which has so far kept us free and firm on the theoretic and visionary fear that this Government, the world's best hope, may by possibility want energy to preserve itself? I trust not. I believe this, on the contrary, the strongest Government on earth. I believe it the only one where every man, at the call of the law, would fly to the standard of the law, and would meet invasions of the public order as his own personal concern. Sometimes it is said that man can not be trusted with the government of himself. Can he, then, be trusted with the government of others? Or have we found angels in the forms of kings to govern him? Let history answer this question.

Let us, then, with courage and confidence pursue our own Federal and Republican principles, our attachment to union and representative government. Kindly separated by nature and a wide ocean from the exterminating havoc of one quarter of the globe; too high-minded to endure the degradations of the others; possessing a chosen country, with room enough for our descendants to the hundredth and thousandth generation; entertaining a due sense of our equal right to the use of our own faculties, to the acquisitions of our own industry, to honor and confidence from our fellow-citizens, resulting not from birth, but from our actions and their sense of them; enlightened by a benign religion, professed, indeed, and practiced in various forms, yet all of them inculcating honesty, truth, temperance, gratitude, and the love of man; acknowledging and adoring an overruling Providence, which by all its dispensations proves that it delights in the happiness of man here and his greater happiness hereafter—with all these blessings, what more is necessary to make us a happy and a prosperous people? Still one thing more, fellow-citizens—a wise and frugal Government, which shall restrain men from injuring one another, shall leave them otherwise free to regulate their own pursuits of industry and improvement, and shall not take from the mouth of labor the bread it has earned. This is the sum of good government, and this is necessary to close the circle of our felicities.

About to enter, fellow-citizens, on the exercise of duties which comprehend everything dear and valuable to you, it is proper you should understand what I deem the essential principles of our Government, and consequently those which ought to shape its Administration. I will compress them within the narrowest compass they will bear, stating the general principle, but not all its limitations. Equal and exact justice to all men, of whatever state or persuasion, religious or political; peace, commerce, and honest friendship with all nations, entangling alliances with none; the support of the State governments in all their rights, as the most competent administrations for our domestic concerns and the surest bulwarks against antirepublican tendencies; the preservation of the General Government in its whole constitutional vigor, as the sheet anchor of our peace at home and safety abroad; a jealous care of the right of election by the people—a mild and safe corrective of abuses which are lopped by the sword of revolution where peaceable remedies are unprovided; absolute acquiescence in the decisions of the majority, the vital principle of republics, from which is no appeal but to force, the vital principle and immediate parent of despotism; a well-disciplined militia, our best reliance in peace and for the first moments of war, till regulars may relieve them; the supremacy of the civil over the military authority; economy in the public expense, that labor may be lightly burthened; the honest payment of our debts and sacred preservation of the public faith; encouragement of agriculture, and of commerce as its handmaid; the diffusion of information and arraignment of all abuses at the bar of the public reason; freedom of religion; freedom of the press; and freedom of person under the protection of the *habeas corpus*; and trial by juries impartially selected. These principles form the bright constellation which has gone before us and guided our steps through an age of revolution and reformation. The wisdom of our sages and blood of our heroes have been devoted to their attainment. They should be the creed of our political faith, the text of civic instruction, the touchstone by which to try the services of those we trust; and should we wander from them in moments of error or of alarm, let us hasten to retrace our steps and to regain the road which alone leads to peace, liberty, and safety.

I repair, then, fellow-citizens, to the post you have assigned me. With experience enough in subordinate offices to have seen the difficulties of this the greatest of all, I have learnt to expect that it will rarely fall to the lot of imperfect man to retire from this station with the reputation and the favor which bring him into it. Without pretensions to that high confidence you reposed in our first and greatest revolutionary character, whose preeminent services had entitled him to the first place in his country's love and destined for him the fairest page in the volume of faithful history, I ask so much confidence only as may give firmness and effect to the legal administration of your affairs. I shall often go wrong through defect of judgment. When right, I shall often be thought wrong by those whose positions will not command a view of the whole ground. I ask your indulgence for my own errors, which will never be intentional, and your support against the errors of others, who may condemn what they would not if seen in all its parts. The approbation implied by your suffrage is a great consolation to me for the past, and my future solicitude will be to retain the good opinion of those who have bestowed it in advance, to conciliate that of others by doing them all the good in my power, and to be instrumental to the happiness and freedom of all.

Relying, then, on the patronage of your good will, I advance with obedience to the work, ready to retire from it whenever you become sensible how much better choice it is in your power to make. And may that Infinite Power which rules the destinies of the universe lead our councils to what is best, and give them a favorable issue for your peace and prosperity.

# 3
# Andrew Jackson (1767–1845)

In 1788 Andrew Jackson moved to what was then the frontier of America. He settled in Nashville, Tennessee, bought some property (part of which included lands recently taken from the Cherokees), drew some clients to his law practice, and prospered. Jackson easily fitted into the rough society of the Cumberland Valley, and gradually his reputation grew: He was a direct-speaking man who loved horse racing and gambling, who was a master of profanity, who had a fierce temper, and yet who had an innate dignity about him. As was frequently said of him, Jackson was loved for the enemies he made.

Jackson's political career began when he was twenty-nine years old. He was sent to Philadelphia as the first congressman from the State of Tennessee. He then spent a brief period in the Senate, but left after a single session because he heartedly disliked the "aristocratic Neebobs" with whom he had to work. It was during the otherwise grim War of 1812, however, that the legend of Andrew Jackson was born. Old Hickory, as he became known in the war, emerged renowned as an Indian fighter and as the nation's one great military hero of that conflict with England.

"Robbed" of the presidency in the 1824 election, Jackson was poised to enter office in 1828 with a mass of new voters supporting him and clamoring for dramatic change in the nation's politics. He did not disappoint his constituency—what "gentlemen" of the period called the "rabble." The first president to break the Eastern Establishment's monopoly on the office, he instituted a number of economic, political, and social reforms that were wildly popular with the common man.

The presidency of Andrew Jackson is best remembered for three major actions and policies: his 1832 veto of the Bank of the United States recharter bill; his forceful stand against South Carolina's threat of secession; and his policy of Indian removal. While he upheld the supremacy of federal law in the case of South Carolina and its nullification of the "tariff of abominations," Jackson did just the reverse in the controversy between the State of Georgia and the Cherokee Nation. After Chief Justice John Marshall's 1832 decision in *Worcester v. Georgia*, which declared unconstitutional Georgia's assertion of jurisdiction over tribal lands recognized by federal treaties, the President is rumored to have said, "John Marshall has made his decision; now let him enforce it."

Fully recognizing that the Court had no enforcement power, Jackson had no intention of forcing Georgia to comply. By a mixture of coercion and negotiation he and his successor, President Martin Van Buren, subsequently got the Cherokees and other southern tribes to cede their lands and move westward. The horrendous 1,000 mile journey of the Cherokees to Indian Territory—now Oklahoma—became known as the Trail of Tears, and a symbol of the harshness of Indian removal. By 1840 the vast majority of Indians, from the North as well as the South, were located west of the Mississippi River. But they were not to be left in peace even there for very long.

# "THE POLICY OF THE GENERAL GOVERNMENT TOWARD THE RED MAN IS NOT ONLY LIBERAL, BUT GENEROUS"*

It gives me pleasure to announce to Congress that the benevolent policy of the Government, steadily pursued for nearly thirty years, in relation to the removal of the Indians beyond the white settlements is approaching to a happy consummation. Two important tribes have accepted the provision made for their removal at the last session of Congress [the Indian Removal Act], and it is believed that their example will induce the remaining tribes also to seek the same obvious advantages.

The consequences of a speedy removal will be important to the United States, to individual States, and to the Indians themselves. The pecuniary advantages which it promises to the Government are the least of its recommendations. It puts an end to all possible danger of collision between the authorities of the General and State Governments on account of the Indians. It will place a dense and civilized population in large tracts of country now occupied by a few savage hunters. By opening the whole territory between Tennessee on the north and Louisiana on the south to the settlement of the whites it will incalculably strengthen the southwestern frontier and render the adjacent States strong enough to repel future invasions without remote aid. It will relieve the whole State of Mississippi and the western part of Alabama of Indian occupancy, and enable those States to advance rapidly in population, wealth, and power. It will separate the Indians from immediate contact with settlements of whites; free them from the power of the States; enable them to pursue happiness in their own way and under their own rude institutions; will retard the progress of decay, which is lessening their numbers, and perhaps cause them gradually, under the protection of the Government and through the influence of good counsels, to cast off their savage habits and become an interesting, civilized, and Christian community. These consequences, some of them so certain and the rest so probable, make the complete execution of the plan sanctioned by Congress at their last session an object of much solicitude.

Toward the aborigines of the country no one can indulge a more friendly feeling than myself, or would go further in attempting to reclaim them from their wandering habits and make them a happy, prosperous people. I have endeavored to impress upon them my own solemn convictions of the duties and powers of the General Government in relation to the State authorities. For the justice of the laws passed by the States within the scope of their reserved powers they are not responsible to this Government. As

---

*Andrew Jackson. 1897. Excerpt from Second Annual Message, December 6, 1830, in *A Compilation of the Messages and Papers of the Presidents*. James D. Richardson, ed. Washington, DC: Bureau of National Literature, Vol. III, pp. 1082–1086.

individuals we may entertain and express our opinions of their acts, but as a Government we have as little right to control them as we have to prescribe laws for other nations.

With a full understanding of the subject, the Choctaw and the Chickasaw tribes have with great unanimity determined to avail themselves of the liberal offers presented by the act of Congress, and have agreed to remove beyond the Mississippi River. Treaties have been made with them, which in due season will be submitted for consideration. In negotiating these treaties they were made to understand their true condition, and they have preferred maintaining their independence in the Western forests to submitting to the laws of the States in which they now reside. These treaties, being probably the last which will ever be made with them, are characterized by great liberality on the part of the Government. They give the Indians a liberal sum in consideration of their removal, and comfortable subsistence on their arrival at their new homes. If it be their real interest to maintain a separate existence, they will there be at liberty to do so without the inconveniences and vexations to which they would unavoidably have been subject in Alabama and Mississippi.

Humanity has often wept over the fate of the aborigines of this country, and Philanthropy has been long busily employed in devising means to avert it, but its progress has never for a moment been arrested, and one by one have many powerful tribes disappeared from the earth. To follow to the tomb the last of his race and to tread on the graves of extinct nations excite melancholy reflections. But true philanthropy reconciles the mind to these vicissitudes as it does to the extinction of one generation to make room for another. In the monuments and fortresses of an unknown people, spread over the extensive regions of the West, we behold the memorials of a once powerful race, which was exterminated or has disappeared to make room for the existing savage tribes. Nor is there anything in this which, upon a comprehensive view of the general interests of the human race, is to be regretted. Philanthropy could not wish to see this continent restored to the condition in which it was found by our forefathers. What good man would prefer a country covered with forests and ranged by a few thousand savages to our extensive Republic, studded with cities, towns, and prosperous farms, embellished with all the improvements which art can devise or industry execute, occupied by more than 12,000,000 happy people, and filled with all the blessings of liberty, civilization, and religion?

The present policy of the Government is but a continuation of the same progressive change by a milder process. The tribes which occupied the countries now constituting the Eastern States were annihilated or have melted away to make room for the whites. The waves of population and civilization are rolling to the westward, and we now propose to acquire the countries occupied by the red men of the South and West by a fair exchange, and, at the expense of the United States, to send them to a land where their existence may be prolonged and perhaps made perpetual. Doubtless it will be painful to leave the graves of their fathers; but what do they more than our ancestors did or than our children are now doing? To better their condition in an unknown land our forefathers left all that was dear in earthly objects. Our children by thousands yearly leave the land of their birth to seek new homes in distant regions. Does Humanity weep at these painful separations from everything, animate and inanimate, with which the young heart has become entwined? Far from it. It is rather a source of joy that our country affords scope where our young population may range unconstrained in body or in mind, developing the power and faculties of man in their highest perfection. These remove hundreds and almost thousands of miles at their own expense, purchase the lands they occupy, and support themselves at their new homes from the moment of their arrival. Can it be cruel in this Government when, by events which it can not control, the Indian is made discontented in his ancient home to purchase his lands, to give him a new and extensive territory, to pay the expense of his removal, and support him a year in his new abode? How many thousands of our own people would gladly embrace the opportunity of removing to the West on such conditions! If the offers made to the Indians were extended to them, they would be hailed with gratitude and joy.

And is it supposed that the wandering savage has a stronger attachment to his home than the settled, civilized Christian? Is it more afflicting to him to leave the graves of his fathers than it is to our brothers and children? Rightly considered, the policy of the General Government toward the red man is not only liberal, but generous. He is unwilling to submit to the laws of the States and mingle with their population. To save him from this alternative, or perhaps utter annihilation, the General Government kindly offers him a new home, and proposes to pay the whole expense of his removal and settlement.

In the consummation of a policy originating at an early period, and steadily pursued by every Administration within the present century—so just to the States and so generous to the Indians—the Executive feels it has a right to expect the cooperation of Congress and of all good and disinterested men. The States, moreover, have a right to demand it. It was substantially a part of the compact which made them members of our Confederacy. With Georgia there is an express contract; with the new States an implied one of equal obligation. Why, in authorizing Ohio, Indiana, Illinois, Missouri, Mississippi, and Alabama to form constitutions and become separate States, did Congress include within their limits extensive tracts of Indian lands, and, in some instances, powerful Indian tribes? Was it not understood by both parties that the power of the States was to be coextensive with their limits, and that with all convenient dispatch the General Government should extinguish the Indian title and remove every obstruction to the complete jurisdiction of the State governments over the soil? Probably not one of those States would have accepted a separate existence—certainly it would never have been granted by Congress—had it been understood that they were to be confined forever to those small portions of their nominal territory the Indian title to which had at the time been extinguished.

It is, therefore, a duty which this Government owes to the new States to extinguish as soon as possible the Indian title to all lands which Congress themselves have included within their limits. When this is done the duties of the General Government in relation to the States and the Indians within their limits are at an end. The Indians may leave the State or not, as they choose. The purchase of their lands does not alter in the least their personal relations with the State government. No act of the General Government has ever been deemed necessary to give the States jurisdiction over the persons of the Indians. That they possess by virtue of their sovereign power within their own limits in as full a manner before as after the purchase of the Indian lands; nor can this Government add to or diminish it.

May we not hope, therefore, that all good citizens, and none more zealously than those who think the Indians oppressed by subjection to the laws of the States, will unite in attempting to open the eyes of those children of the forest to their true condition, and by a speedy removal to relieve them from all the evils, real or imaginary, present or prospective, with which they may be supposed to be threatened.

# 4
# George Catlin (1796–1872)

After two years as a practicing attorney, George Catlin decided the law was not for him; so he took up the paintbrush and moved to New York City, where he became a portrait painter. Like a number of his contemporaries in the arts, Catlin became fascinated with "the West." The few accounts of the Indian way of life that trickled back to the East Coast in the early years of westward migration caught his imagination as nothing else had done. So in 1832 Catlin went West to see and experience first-hand whether those wondrous accounts of the land and its peoples were accurate.

Catlin spent eight years traveling throughout the West, and nearly everywhere he went he discovered something new and often something quite amazing. He painted, sketched, and wrote at a furious pace. The Yellowstone country, for example, with its geysers, hot springs, snow-capped mountains, its herds of bison and elk, and its Indian inhabitants living in harmony with their surroundings, was an experience that forever changed his life. Catlin also succeeded in changing other people's minds about the West: In 1872 (the year of his death), Congress passed an act establishing America's first national park, the Yellowstone.

Catlin's seminal work, *Letters and Notes on the Manners, Customs, and Condition of the North American Indians*, was published in 1841. In it he describes his task as one of providing "a literal and graphic description of the living manners, customs, and character of an interesting race of people, who are rapidly passing away from the face of the earth." Catlin characterized the Indian in his uncorrupted, natural state as an "honest, hospitable, faithful, brave, warlike, cruel, revengeful, relentless,—yet honourable, contemplative, and religious being." Contact with whites corrupted the Indians; they absorbed white vices, such as abuse of alcohol and prolific waste of the buffalo upon which they depended for survival. If the virtues of Indian culture were to be sustained, Catlin believed, they would need to be isolated from the corrupting influences of white civilization, and their main source of subsistence not wasted. Why not, then, preserve both the wonders of nature *and* the aboriginal way of life by setting aside a great public space to remain as it was in 1832?

George Catlin is not only credited with having first conceived of the idea of a "national park," but his portraits and sketches of Native Americans and their culture continue to be primary sources of information on a way of life that has virtually vanished in this country. He was one of the first Americans to think holistically about the land and its inhabitants, even though some readers today might find objectionable his suggestion that the Native American way of life should not evolve from what it was in the early 1800s.

# "A NATION'S PARK!"*

It is truly a melancholy contemplation for the traveller in this country, to anticipate the period which is not far distant, when the last of these noble animals [the buffalo], at the hands of white and red men, will fall victims to their cruel and improvident rapacity; leaving these beautiful green fields, a vast and idle waste, unstocked and unpeopled for ages to come, until the bones of the one and the traditions of the other will have vanished, and left scarce an intelligible trace behind.

That the reader should not think me visionary in these contemplations, or romancing in making such assertions, I will hand him the following item of the extravagancies which are practiced in these regions, and rapidly leading to the results which I have just named.

When I first arrived at this place, on my way up the river, which was in the month of May, in 1832, and had taken up my lodgings in the Fur Company's Fort, Mr. Laidlaw, of whom I have before spoken, and also his chief clerk, Mr. Halsey, and many of their men, as well as the chiefs of the Sioux, told me, that only a few days before I arrived, (when an immense herd of buffaloes had showed themselves on the opposite side of the river, almost blackening the plains for a great distance,) a party of five or six hundred Sioux Indians on horseback, forded the river about mid-day, and spending a few hours amongst them, recrossed the river at sun-down and came into the Fort with *fourteen hundred fresh buffalo tongues*, which were thrown down in a mass, and for which they required but a few gallons of whiskey, which was soon demolished, indulging them in a little, and harmless carouse.

This profligate waste of the lives of these noble and useful animals, when, from all that I could learn, not a skin or a pound of the meat (except the tongues), was brought in, fully supports me in the seemingly extravagant predictions that I have made as to their extinction, which I am certain is near at hand. In the above extravagant instance, at a season when their skins were without fur and not worth taking off, and their camp was so well stocked with fresh and dried meat, that they had no occasion for using the flesh, there is a fair exhibition of the improvident character of the savage, and also of his recklessness in catering for his appetite, so long as the present inducements are held out to him in his country, for its gratification.

In this singular country, where the poor Indians have no laws or regulations of society, making it a vice or an impropriety to drink to excess, they think it no harm to indulge in the delicious beverage, as long as they are able to buy whiskey to drink. They look to white men as wiser than themselves, and able to set them examples—they see none of these in their country but sellers of whiskey, who are constantly tendering it to them, and most of them setting the example by using it themselves; and they easily acquire a taste,

*George Catlin. 1841 *Letters and Notes on the Manners, Customs, and Condition of the North American Indians: Written During Eight Years' Travel Amongst the Wildest Tribes of Indians in North America in 1832, 33, 34, 35, 36, 37, 38, and 39*. London: George Catlin, Vol I., pp. 256-263.

that to be catered for, where whiskey is sold at sixteen dollars per gallon, soon impoverishes them, and must soon strip the skin from the last buffalo's back that lives in their country, to "be dressed by their squaws" and vended to the Traders for a pint of diluted alcohol.

From the above remarks it will be seen, that not only the red men, but red men and white, have aimed destruction at the race of these animals; and with them, *beasts* have turned hunters of buffaloes in this country, slaying them, however, in less numbers, and for far more laudable purpose than that of selling their skins. The white wolves, of which I have spoken in a former epistle, follow the herds of buffaloes as I have said, from one season to another, glutting themselves on the carcasses of those that fall by the deadly shafts of their enemies, or linger with disease or old age to be dispatched by these sneaking cormorants, who are ready at all times kindly to relieve them from the pangs of a lingering death....

Thus much I wrote of the buffaloes, and of the accidents that befall them, as well as of the fate that awaits them; and before I closed my book, I strolled out one day to the shade of a plum-tree, where I laid in the grass on a favourite bluff, and wrote thus:—

"It is generally supposed, and familiarly said, that a man *'falls'* into a reverie; but I seated myself in the shade a few minutes since, resolved to *force* myself into one; and for this purpose I laid open a small pocket-map of North America, and excluding my thoughts from every other object in the world, I soon succeeded in producing the desired illusion This little chart, over which I bent, was seen in all its parts, as nothing but the green and vivid reality. I was lifted up upon an imaginary pair of wings, which easily raised and held me floating in the open air, from whence I could behold beneath me the Pacific and the Atlantic Oceans—the great cities of the East, and the mighty rivers. I could see the blue chain of the great lakes at the North—the Rocky Mountains, and beneath them and near their base, the vast, and almost boundless plains of grass, which were speckled with the bands of grazing buffaloes!

"The world turned gently around, and I examined its surface; continent after continent passed under my eye, and yet amidst them all, I saw not the vast and vivid green, that is spread like a carpet over the Western wilds of my own country. I saw not elsewhere in the world, the myriad herds of buffaloes—my eyes scanned in vain, for they were not. And when I turned again to the wilds of my native land, I beheld them all in motion! For the distance of several hundreds of miles from North to South, they were wheeling about in vast columns and herds—some were scattered, and ran with furious wildness—some lay dead, and others were pawing the earth for a hiding-place—some were sinking down and dying, gushing out their life's blood in deep-drawn sighs—and others were contending in furious battle for the life they possessed, and the ground that they stood upon. They had long since assembled from the thickets, and secret haunts of the deep forest, into the midst of the treeless and bushless plains, as the place for their safety. I could see in an hundred places, amid the wheeling bands, and on their skirts and flanks, the leaping wild horse darting among them. I saw not the arrows, nor heard the twang of the sinewy bows that sent them; but I saw their victims fall!—on other steeds that rushed along their sides, I saw the glistening lances, which seemed to lay across them; their blades were blazing in the sun, till dipped in blood, and then I lost them! In other parts (and there were many), the vivid flash of *fire-arms* was seen—*their* victims fell too, and over their dead bodies hung suspended in air, little clouds of whitened smoke, from under which the flying horsemen had darted forward to mingle again with, and deal death to, the trampling throng.

"So strange were men mixed (both red and white) with the countless herds that wheeled and eddyed about, that all below seemed one vast extended field of battle—whole armies, in some places, seemed to blacken the earth's surface;—in other parts, regiments, battalions, wings, platoons, rank and file, and *"Indian-file"*—all were in motion; and death and destruction seemed to be the watch-word amongst them. In their turmoil, they sent up great clouds of dust, and with them came the mingled din of groans and trampling hoofs, that seemed like the rumbling of a dreadful cataract, or the roaring of distant thunder.... Hundreds and thousands were strewed upon the plains—they were flayed, and their reddened carcasses left; and about them bands of wolves, and dogs, and buzzards were seen devouring them. Contiguous, and in sight, were the distant and feeble smokes of wigwams and villages, where the skins were dragged, and dressed for white man's luxury! where they were all sold for *whiskey*, and the poor Indians laid drunk, and were crying. I cast my eyes into the towns and cities of the East, and there I beheld buffalo robes hanging at almost every door for traffic; and I saw also the curling smokes of a thousand *Stills*—and I said, 'Oh insatiable man, is thy avarice such! wouldst thou tear the skin from the back of the last animal of this noble race, *and rob thy fellow-man of his meat, and for it give him poison!'"*

Many are the rudenesses and wilds in Nature's works, which are destined to fall before the deadly axe and desolating hands of cultivating man; and so amongst her ranks of *living*, of beast and human, we often find noble stamps, or beautiful colours, to which our admiration clings; and even in the overwhelming march of civilized improvements and refinements do we love to cherish their existence, and lend our efforts to preserve them in their primitive rudeness. Such of Nature's works are always worthy of our preservation and protection; and the further we become separated (and the face of the country) from that pristine wildness and beauty, the more pleasure does the mind of enlightened man feel in recurring to those scenes, when he can have them preserved for his eyes and his mind to dwell upon.

Of such "rudenesses and wilds," Nature has no where presented more beautiful and lovely scenes, than those of the vast prairies of the West; and of *man* and *beast*, no nobler specimens than those who inhabit them—the Indian and the *buffalo*—joint and original tenants of the soil, and fugitives together from the approach of civilized man; they have fled to the great plains of the West, and there, under an equal doom, they have taken up their *last abode*, where their race will expire, and their bones will bleach together.

It may be that *power* is *right*, and *voracity* a *virtue*; and that these people, and these noble animals, are *righteously* doomed to an issue that *will* not be averted. It can be easily proved—we have a civilized science that can easily do it, or anything else that may be required to cover the iniquities of civilized man in catering for his unholy appetites. It can be proved that the weak and ignorant have no *rights*—that there can be no virtue in darkness—that God's gifts have no meaning or merit until they are appropriated by civilized man—by him brought into the light, and converted to his use and luxury. We have a mode of reasoning (I forget what it is called) by which all this can be proved, and even more. The *word* and the *system* are entirely of *civilized* origin; and latitude is admirably given to them in proportion to the increase of civilized wants, which often require a *judge* to overrule the laws of nature. I say that *we* can prove such things; but an *Indian* cannot. It is a mode of reasoning unknown to him in his nature's simplicity, but admirably adapted to subserve the interests of the enlightened world, who are always their own judges, when dealing with the savage: and who, in the present refined age, have many appetites that can only be lawfully indulged, by proving God's laws defective.

It is not enough in this polished and extravagant age, that we get from the Indian his lands, and the very clothes from his back, but the food from their mouths must be stopped, to add a new and useless article to the fashionable world's luxuries. The ranks must be thinned, and the race exterminated, of this noble animal, and the Indians of the great plains left without the means of supporting life, that white men may figure a few years longer, enveloped in buffalo robes—that they may spread them, for their pleasure and elegance, over the backs of their sleighs, and trail them ostentatiously amidst the busy throng, as a thing of beauty and elegance that had been made for them!

Reader! listen to the following calculations, and forget them not. The buffaloes (the quadrupeds from whose backs your beautiful robes were taken, and whose myriads were once spread over the whole country, from the Rocky Mountains to the Atlantic Ocean) have recently fled before the appalling appearance of civilized man, and taken up their abode and pasturage amid the almost boundless prairies of the West. An instinctive dread of their deadly foes, who made an easy prey of them whilst grazing in the forest, has led them to seek the midst of the vast and treeless plains of grass, as the spot where they would be least exposed to the assaults of their enemies; and it is exclusively in those desolate fields of silence (yet of beauty) that they are to be found—and over these vast steppes, or prairies, have they fled, like the Indian, towards the "setting sun;" until their bands have been crowded together, and their limits confined to a narrow strip of country on this side of the Rocky Mountains.

This strip of country, which extends from the province of Mexico to lake Winnepeg on the North, is almost one entire plain of grass, which is, and ever must be, useless to cultivating man. It is here, and here chiefly, that the buffaloes dwell; and with, and hovering about them, live and flourish the tribes of Indians, whom God made for the enjoyment of that fair land and its luxuries.

It is a melancholy contemplation for one who has travelled as I have, through these realms, and seen this noble animal in all its pride and glory, to contemplate it so rapidly wasting from the world, drawing the irresistible conclusion too, which one must do, that its species is soon to be extinguished, and with it the peace and happiness (if not the actual existence) of the tribes of Indians who are joint tenants with them, in the occupancy of these vast and idle plains.

And what a splendid contemplation too, when one (who has travelled these realms, and can duly appreciate them) imagines them as they *might* in future be seen, (by some great protecting policy of government) preserved in their pristine beauty and wildness, in a *magnificent park*, where the world could see for ages to come, the native Indian in his classic attire, galloping his wild horse, with sinewy bow, and shield and lance, amid the fleeting herds of elks and buffaloes. What a beautiful and thrilling specimen for America to preserve and hold up to the view of her refined citizens and the world, in future ages! A *nation's Park*, containing man and beast, in all the wild and freshness of their nature's beauty!

I would ask no other monument to my memory, nor any other enrolment of my name amongst the famous dead, than the reputation of having been the founder of such an institution.

Such scenes might easily have been preserved, and still could be cherished on the great plains of the West, without detriment to the country or its borders; for the tracts of country on which the buffaloes have assembled, are uniformly sterile, and of no available use to cultivating man.

It is on these plains, which are stocked with buffaloes, that the finest specimens of the Indian race are to be seen. It is here, that the savage is decorated in the richest costume. It is here, and here only, that his wants are all satisfied, and even the *luxuries* of life are afforded him in abundance. And here also is he the proud and honourable man (before he has had teachers or laws), above the imported wants, which beget meanness and vice; stimulated by ideas of honour and virtue, in which the God of Nature has certainly not curtailed him....

Yet, this interesting community, with its sports, its wildnesses, its languages, and all its manners and customs, could be perpetuated, and also the buffaloes, whose numbers would increase and supply them with food for ages and centuries to come, if a system of non-intercourse could be established and preserved. But such is not to be the case—the buffalo's doom is sealed, and with their extinction must assuredly sink into real despair and starvation, the inhabitants of these vast plains, which afford for the Indians, no other possible means of subsistence; and they must at last fall a prey to wolves and buzzards, who will have no other bones to pick.

# 5
# Alexis de Tocqueville (1805–1859)

Alexis de Tocqueville is the only non-American writer represented in this anthology, but no study of the American state would be complete without calling attention to one of the most astute observers of American democracy, and his masterpiece, *Democracy in America*.

De Tocqueville's formative years were deeply influenced by the effects that the French Revolution of 1789 and its Reign of Terror had upon his aristocratic family. Moreover, he personally witnessed the 1830 Revolution, after which he became convinced of the inevitable advance of democracy and the concept of equality in the Old World. He became determined to witness first-hand the New World's experiment with democracy, which was still in its early phases, in order to discern its fundamental principles and character. So he contrived a research expedition to study the American penitentiary system (regarded in Europe as the most effective and modern system available). Traveling in America for nine months (between May 1831 and February 1832) with his friend and colleague Gustave de Beaumont, de Tocqueville visited 17 of the existing 24 states, seeking to understand not just the penitentiary system but all aspects of American society.

The outcome of the trip to America not only generated a government report on the penitentiary system but also de Tocqueville's seminal 1835 work, *Democracy in America*. (de Beaumont produced *Marie*, a novel about slavery.) While *Democracy in America* drew intense American interest and won immediate acclaim as a masterpiece, de Tocqueville claimed that he wrote the book for French, not American, readers. It was a vehicle through which he tried to answer questions about the formation and applicability of democracy to his native country.

De Tocqueville saw politics in spatial terms; he looked at the interactions between geography (space), history (time), and culture as determining the particular characteristics of a society. In addition to looking at political concepts and political units, e.g., federalism, equality, political parties, and the courts, *Democracy in America* explored the role of education, religion, the press, and race relations in shaping civil society in America. A particular feature of American culture that interested de Tocqueville was the American impulse to form voluntary associations. Such organizations, he observed, enabled Americans to counter the destructive aspects of self-centered individualism (which he called egoism) found in his own country.

As he and de Beaumont traveled throughout America, de Tocqueville kept detailed notebooks of his observations and conversations, from which he extracted his classic work. The notebooks, published in the early 1860s, illustrate how his visits to the wilds of the American frontier influenced his understanding of the nation's physical circumstances and the role of the frontier in shaping American democracy. These travels also revealed to him the centrality of racism as the nation expanded into lands occupied by other cultures. The prescient de Tocqueville regarded the new nation's refusal to free its Negro slaves and to co-exist with Indians as the biggest threats to the success of the American experiment in democratic government. The publication of his notebooks coincided with the Civil War.

---

# "THE PRINCIPLE OF ASSOCIATION"*

I do not propose to speak of those political associations—by the aid of which men endeavor to defend themselves against the despotic influence of a majority—or against the aggressions of regal power. That subject I have already treated. If each citizen did not learn, in proportion as he individually becomes more feeble, and consequently more incapable of preserving his freedom single-handed, to combine with his fellow-citizens for the purpose of defending it, it is clear that tyranny would unavoidably increase together with equality.

Those associations only which are formed in civil life, without reference to political objects, are here adverted to. The political associations which exist in the United States are only a single feature in the midst of the immense assemblage of associations in that country. Americans of all ages, all conditions, and all dispositions, constantly form associations. They have not only commercial and manufacturing companies, in which all take part, but associations of a thousand other kinds—religious, moral, serious, futile, extensive, or restricted, enormous or diminutive. The Americans make associations to give entertainments, to found establishments for education, to build inns, to construct churches, to diffuse books, to send missionaries to the antipodes; and in this manner they found hospitals, prisons, and schools. If it be proposed to advance some truth, or to foster some feeling by the encouragement of a great example, they form a society. Wherever, at the head of some new undertaking, you see the government in France, or a man of rank in England, in the United States you will be sure to find an association. I met with several kinds of associations in America, of which I confess I had no previous notion; and I have often admired the extreme skill with which the inhabitants of the United States succeed in proposing a common object to the exertions of a great many men, and in getting them voluntarily to pursue it. I have since travelled over England, whence the Americans have taken some of their laws and many of their customs; and it seemed to me that the principle of association was by no means so constantly or so adroitly used in that country. The English often perform great things singly; whereas the Americans form associations for the smallest undertakings. It is evident that the former people consider association as a powerful means of action, but the latter seem to regard it as the only means they have of acting.

Thus the most democratic country on the face of the earth is that in

---

*Alexis de Tocqueville. 1900 (originally published 1835). "Of the Use Which the Americans Make of Public Associations in Civil Life," in *Democracy in America*, revised ed. Henry Reeve, trans. New York: Colonial Press, Vol. II, pp. 114–118.

which men have in our time carried to the highest perfection the art of pursuing in common the object of their common desires, and have applied this new science to the greatest number of purposes. Is this the result of accident? or is there in reality any necessary connection between the principle of association and that of equality? Aristocratic communities always contain, amongst a multitude of persons who by themselves are powerless, a small number of powerful and wealthy citizens, each of whom can achieve great undertakings single-handed. In aristocratic societies men do not need to combine in order to act, because they are strongly held together. Every wealthy and powerful citizen constitutes the head of a permanent and compulsory association, composed of all those who are dependent upon him, or whom he makes subservient to the execution of his designs. Amongst democratic nations, on the contrary, all the citizens are independent and feeble; they can do hardly anything by themselves, and none of them can oblige his fellow-men to lend him their assistance. They all, therefore, fall into a state of incapacity, if they do not learn voluntarily to help each other. If men living in democratic countries had no right and no inclination to associate for political purposes, their independence would be in great jeopardy; but they might long preserve their wealth and their cultivation: whereas if they never acquired the habit of forming associations in ordinary life, civilization itself would be endangered. A people amongst which individuals should lose the power of achieving great things single-handed, without acquiring the means of producing them by united exertions, would soon relapse into barbarism.

Unhappily, the same social condition which renders associations so necessary to democratic nations, renders their formation more difficult amongst those nations than amongst all others. When several members of an aristocracy agree to combine, they easily succeed in doing so; as each of them brings great strength to the partnership, the number of its members may be very limited; and when the members of an association are limited in number, they may easily become mutually acquainted, understand each other, and establish fixed regulations. The same opportunities do not occur amongst democratic nations, where the associated members must always be very numerous for their association to have any power.

I am aware that many of my countrymen are not in the least embarrassed by this difficulty. They contend that the more enfeebled and incompetent the citizens become, the more able and active the government ought to be rendered, in order that society at large may execute what individuals can no longer accomplish. They believe this answers the whole difficulty, but I think they are mistaken. A government might perform the part of some of the largest American companies; and several States, members of the Union, have already attempted it; but what political power could ever carry on the vast multitude of lesser undertakings which the American citizens perform every day, with the assistance of the principle of association? It is easy to foresee that the time is drawing near when man will be less and less able to produce, of himself alone, the commonest necessaries of life. The task of the governing power will therefore perpetually increase, and its very efforts will extend it every day. The more it stands in the place of associations, the more will individuals, losing the notion of combining together, require its assistance: these are causes and effects which unceasingly engender each other. Will the administration of the country ultimately assume the management of all the manufactures, which no single citizen is able to carry on? And if a time at length arrives, when, in consequence of the extreme subdivision of landed property, the soil is split into an infinite number of parcels, so that it can only be cultivated by companies of husbandmen, will it be necessary that the head of the government should leave the helm of state to follow the plough? The morals and the intelligence of a democratic people would be as much endangered as its business and manufactures, if the government ever wholly usurped the place of private companies.

Feelings and opinions are recruited, the heart is enlarged, and the human mind is developed by no other means than by the reciprocal influence of men upon each other. I have shown that these influences are almost null in democratic countries; they must therefore be artificially created, and this can only be accomplished by associations.

When the members of an aristocratic community adopt a new opinion, or conceive a new sentiment, they give it a station, as it were, beside themselves, upon the lofty platform where they stand; and opinions or sentiments so conspicuous to the eyes of the multitude are easily introduced into the minds or hearts of all around. In democratic countries the governing power alone is naturally in a condition to act in this manner; but it is easy to see that its action is always inadequate, and often dangerous. A government can no more be competent to keep alive and to renew the circulation of opinions and feelings amongst a great people, than to manage all the speculations of productive industry. No sooner does a government attempt to go beyond its political sphere and to enter upon this new track, than it exercises, even unintentionally, an insupportable tyranny; for a government can only dictate strict rules, the opinions which it favors are rigidly enforced, and it is never easy to discriminate between its advice and its commands. Worse still will be the case if the government really believes itself interested in preventing all circulation of ideas; it will then stand motionless, and oppressed by the heaviness of voluntary torpor. Governments therefore should not be the only active powers: associations ought, in democratic nations, to stand in lieu of those powerful private individuals whom the equality of conditions has swept away.

As soon as several of the inhabitants of the United States have taken up an opinion or a feeling which they wish to promote in the world, they look out for mutual assistance; and as soon as they have found each other out, they combine. From that moment they are no longer isolated men, but a power seen from afar, whose actions serve for an example, and whose language is listened to. The first time I heard in the United States that 100,000 men had bound themselves publicly to abstain from spirituous liquors, it appeared to me more like a joke than a serious engagement; and I did not at once perceive why these temperate citizens could not content themselves with drinking water by their own firesides. I at last understood that 300,000 Americans, alarmed by the progress of drunkenness around them, had made up their minds to patronize temperance. They acted just in the same way as a man of high rank who should dress very plainly, in order to inspire the humbler orders with a contempt of luxury. It is probable that if these 100,000 men had lived in France, each of them would singly have memorialized the government to watch the public-houses all over the kingdom.

Nothing, in my opinion, is more deserving of our attention than the intellectual and moral associations of America. The political and industrial associations of that country strike us forcibly; but the others elude our observation, or if we discover them, we understand them imperfectly, because we have hardly ever seen anything of the kind. It must, however, be acknowledged that they are as necessary to the American people as the former, and perhaps more so. In democratic countries the science of association is the mother of science; the progress of all the rest depends upon the progress it has made. Amongst the laws which rule human societies there is one which seems to be more precise and clear than all others. If men are to remain civilized, or to become so, the art of associating together must grow and improve in the same ratio in which the equality of conditions is increased.

# 6
# Frederick Douglass (c.1818–1895)

For Frederick Douglass, born a slave on the eastern shore of Maryland around the year 1818 (he could not be sure of the exact date), nature and the agrarian way of life never could have meant the harmonious order that Jefferson and others described. In fact it meant quite the opposite: a cruel, terrifying, nightmarish existence from which one constantly yearned to escape.

Douglass got his first taste of freedom not in the country but in the city. When he was about ten years old he was lent to a family living in Baltimore, and there Douglass experienced a new way of life. His determination to escape from servitude dates from that brief period of his life, when he found that he was treated relatively better among city folk than by plantation owners. Baltimore, with its larger, more heterogeneous population, its less tradition-bound ways, and its constant movement—all this contrasted sharply with rural life. Resolving to escape to the North someday, Douglass surreptitiously learned to read and write while in Baltimore. This became his first step toward eventual freedom.

Douglass made his escape, alone, on the third of September, 1838. His first stop was New York City, where he learned that no runaway slave was safe; there were kidnappers at every turn seeking rewards for returning slaves to the South. Finding the underground railroad, he was sent to Massachusetts, where he was astonished at the amount of wealth amassed without the aid of slaves. He met the abolitionist William Lloyd Garrison and became a lecturer for the Massachusetts Anti-Slavery Society, attacking both southern slavery and northern prejudice. He eventually traveled to England and Ireland, where friends raised funds to buy his freedom so he might return to the United States without fear. They also gave him money to start the first black-owned publishing business in the United States.

Slavery persisted in the South until the end of the Civil War in 1865—about thirty years after Douglass escaped to Boston. But even after Emancipation, most rural black people living in the South were held in place by a system of debt peonage, which was hardly better than slavery. The continued exploitation of blacks, especially in southern rural areas, left them with no illusions about the agrarian way of life for those who did not own land. It is little wonder, then, that most African Americans never held a very romantic view of nature or of agrarianism. Theirs was a radically different experience with the American landscape than that enjoyed by most whites.

# "GONE, GONE, SOLD AND GONE TO THE RICE SWAMP DANK AND LONE"*

The slaves selected to go to the Great House Farm, for the monthly allowance for themselves and their fellow-slaves, were peculiarly enthusiastic. While on their way, they would make the dense old woods, for miles around, reverberate with their wild songs, revealing at once the highest joy and the deepest sadness. They would compose and sing as they went along, consulting neither time nor tune. The thought that came up, came out—if not in the word, in the sound;—and as frequently in the one as in the other. They would sometimes sing the most pathetic sentiment in the most rapturous tone, and the most rapturous sentiment in the most pathetic tone. Into all of their songs they would manage to weave something of the Great House Farm. Especially would they do this, when leaving home. They would then sing most exultingly the following words:—

"I am going away to the Great House Farm!
0, yea! 0, yea! 0!"

This they would sing, as a chorus, to words which to many would seem unmeaning jargon, but which, nevertheless, were full of meaning to themselves. I have sometimes thought that the mere hearing of those songs would do more to impress some minds with the horrible character of slavery, than the reading of whole volumes of philosophy on the subject could do.

I did not, when a slave, understand the deep meaning of those rude and apparently incoherent songs. I was myself within the circle; so that I neither saw nor heard as those without might see and hear. They told a tale of woe which was then altogether beyond my feeble comprehension; they were tones loud, long, and deep; they breathed the prayer and complaint of souls boiling over with the bitterest anguish. Every tone was a testimony against slavery, and a prayer to God for deliverance from chains. The hearing of those wild notes always depressed my spirit, and filled me with ineffable sadness. I have frequently found myself in tears while hearing them. The mere recurrence to those songs, even now, afflicts me; and while I am writing these lines, an expression of feeling has already found its way down my cheek. To those songs I trace my first glimmering conception of the dehumanizing character of slavery. I can never get rid of that conception. Those songs still follow me, to deepen my hatred of slavery, and quicken my sympathies for my brethren in bonds. If any one wishes to be impressed with the soul-killing effects of slavery, let him go to Colonel Lloyd's plantation, and, on allowance-day, place himself in the deep pine woods, and there let him, in silence, analyze the sounds that shall pass through the chambers of his

---

*Frederick Douglass. 1845. *Narrative of the Life of Frederick Douglass, An American Slave: Written by Himself*. Boston: Anti Slavery Office, pp. 57–58, 72–75, 79, 91–93.

soul,—and if he is not thus impressed, it will only be because "there is no flesh in his obdurate heart."

I have often been utterly astonished, since I came to the north, to find persons who could speak of the singing, among slaves, as evidence of their contentment and happiness. It is impossible to conceive of a greater mistake. Slaves sing most when they are most unhappy. The songs of the slave represent the sorrows of his heart; and he is relieved by them, only as an aching heart is relieved by its tears. At least, such is my experience. I have often sung to drown my sorrow, but seldom to express my happiness. Crying for joy, and singing for joy, were alike uncommon to me while in the jaws of slavery. The singing of a man cast away upon a desolate island might be as appropriately considered as evidence of contentment and happiness, as the singing of a slave; the songs of the one and of the other are prompted by the same emotion....

I was probably between seven and eight years old when I left Colonel Lloyd's plantation. I left it with joy. I shall never forget the ecstasy with which I received the intelligence that my old master (Anthony) had determined to let me go to Baltimore, to live with Mr. Hugh Auld, brother to my old master's son-in-law, Captain Thomas Auld. I received this information about three days before my departure. They were three of the happiest days I ever enjoyed. I spent the most part of all these three days in the creek, washing off the plantation scurf, and preparing myself for my departure.

The pride of appearance which this would indicate was not my own. I spent the time in washing, not so much because I wished to, but because Mrs. Lucretia had told me I must get all the dead skin off my feet and knees before I could go to Baltimore, for the people in Baltimore were very cleanly, and would laugh at me if I looked dirty. Besides, she was going to give me a pair of trousers, which I should not put on unless I got all the dirt off me. The thought of owning a pair of trousers was great indeed! It was almost a sufficient motive, not only to make me take off what would be called by pig-drovers the mange, but the skin itself. I went at it in good earnest, working for the first time with the hope of reward.

The ties that ordinarily bind children to their homes were all suspended in my case. I found no severe trial in my departure. My home was charmless; it was not home to me; on parting from it, I could not feel that I was leaving any thing which I could have enjoyed by staying. My mother was dead, my grandmother lived far off, so that I seldom saw her. I had two sisters and one brother, that lived in the same house with me; but the early separation of us from our mother had well nigh blotted the fact of our relationship from our memories. I looked for home elsewhere, and was confident of finding none which I should relish less than the one which I was leaving. If, however, I found in my new home hardship, hunger, whipping, and nakedness, I had the consolation that I should not have escaped any one of them by staying. Having already had more than a taste of them in the house of my old master, and having endured them there, I very naturally inferred my ability to endure them elsewhere, and especially at Baltimore; for I had something of the feeling about Baltimore that is expressed in the proverb, that "being hanged in England is preferable to dying a natural death in Ireland." I had the strongest desire to see Baltimore. Cousin Tom, though not fluent in speech, had inspired me with that desire by his eloquent description of the place. I could never point out any thing at the Great House, no matter how beautiful or powerful, but that he had seen something at Baltimore far exceeding, both in beauty and strength, the object which I pointed out to him. Even the Great House itself, with all its pictures, was far inferior to many buildings in Baltimore. So strong was my desire, that I thought a gratification of it would fully compensate for whatever loss of comforts I should sustain by the exchange. I left without a regret, and with the highest hopes of future happiness.

We sailed out of Miles River for Baltimore on a Saturday morning. I remember only the day of the week, for at that time I had no knowledge of the days of the month, nor the months of the year. On setting sail, I walked aft, and gave to Colonel Lloyd's plantation what I hoped would be the last look. I then placed myself in the bows of the sloop, and there spent the remainder of the day in looking ahead, interesting myself in what was in the distance rather than in things near by or behind.

In the afternoon of that day, we reached Annapolis, the capital of the State. We stopped but a few moments, so that I had no time to go on shore. It was the first large town that I had ever seen, and though it would look small compared with some of our New England factory villages, I thought it a wonderful place for its size—more imposing even than the Great House Farm!

We arrived at Baltimore early on Sunday morning, landing at Smith's Wharf, not far from Bowley's Wharf. We had on board the sloop a large flock of sheep; and after aiding in driving them to the slaughterhouse of Mr. Curtis on Louden Slater's Hill, I was conducted by Rich, one of the hands belonging on board of the sloop, to my new home in Alliciana Street, near Mr. Gardner's ship-yard, on Fells Point.

Mr. and Mrs. Auld were both at home, and met me at the door with their little son Thomas, to take care of whom I had been given. And here I saw what I had never seen before; it was a white face beaming with the most kindly emotions; it was the face of my new mistress, Sophia Auld. I wish I could describe the rapture that flashed through my soul as I beheld it. It was a new and strange sight to me, brightening up my pathway with the light of happiness. Little Thomas was told, there was his Freddy,—and I was told to take care of little Thomas; and thus I entered upon the duties of my new home with the most cheering prospect ahead.

I look upon my departure from Colonel Lloyd's plantation as one of the most interesting events of my life. It is possible, and even quite probable, that but for the mere circumstance of being removed from that plantation to Baltimore, I should have to-day, instead of being here seated by my own table, in the enjoyment of freedom and the happiness of home, writing this Narrative, been confined in the galling chains of slavery. Going to live at Baltimore laid the foundation, and opened the gateway, to all my subsequent prosperity. I have ever regarded it as the first plain manifestation of that kind providence which has ever since attended me, and marked my life with so many favors. I regarded the selection of myself as being somewhat remarkable. There were a number of slave children that might have been sent from the plantation to Baltimore. There were those younger, those older, and those of the same age. I was chosen from among them all, and was the first, last, and only choice.

I may be deemed superstitious, and even egotistical, in regarding this event as a special interposition of divine Providence in my favor. But I should be false to the earliest sentiments of my soul, if I suppressed the opinion. I prefer to be true to myself, even at the hazard of incurring the ridicule of others, rather than to be false, and incur my own abhorrence. From my earliest recollection, I date the entertainment of a deep conviction that slavery would not always be able to hold me within its foul embrace; and in the darkest hours of my career in slavery, this living word of faith and spirit of hope departed not from me, but remained like ministering angels to cheer me through the gloom. This good spirit was from God, and to him I offer thanksgiving and praise....

I had resided but a short time in Baltimore before I observed a marked difference, in the treatment of slaves, from that which I had witnessed in the country. A city slave is almost a freeman, compared with a slave on the plantation. He is much better fed and clothed, and enjoys privileges altogether unknown to the slave on the plantation. There is a vestige of decency, a sense of shame, that does much to curb and check those outbreaks of atrocious cruelty so commonly enacted upon the plantation. He is a desperate slaveholder, who will shock the humanity of his nonslaveholding neighbors with the cries of his lacerated slave. Few are willing to incur the odium attaching to the reputation of being a cruel master; and above all things, they would not be known as not giving a slave enough to eat. Every city slaveholder is anxious to have it known of him, that he feeds his slaves well; and it is due to them to say, that most of them do give their slaves enough to eat. There are, however, some painful exceptions to this rule....

If any one thing in my experience, more than another, served to deepen my conviction of the infernal character of slavery, and to fill me with unutterable loathing of slaveholders, it was their base ingratitude to my poor old grandmother. She had served my old master faithfully from youth to old age. She had been the source of all his wealth; she had peopled his plantation with slaves; she had become a great grandmother in his service. She had rocked him in infancy, attended him in childhood, served him through life, and at his death wiped from his icy brow the cold death-sweat, and closed his eyes forever. She was nevertheless left a slave—a slave for life—a slave in the hands of strangers; and in their hands she saw her children, her grandchildren, and her great-grandchildren, divided, like so many sheep, without being gratified with the small privilege of a single word, as to their or her own destiny. And, to cap the climax of their base ingratitude and fiendish barbarity, my grandmother, who was now very old, having outlived my old master and all his children, having seen the beginning and end of all of them, and her present owners finding she was of but little value, her frame already racked with the pains of old age, and complete helplessness fast stealing over her once active limbs, they took her to the woods, built her a little hut, put up a little mud-chimney, and then made her welcome to the privilege of supporting herself there in perfect loneliness; thus virtually turning her out to die! If my poor old grandmother now lives, she lives to suffer in utter loneliness; she lives to remember and mourn over the loss of children, the loss of grandchildren, and the loss of great-grandchildren. They are, in the language of the slave's poet, Whittier,—

> "Gone, gone, sold and gone
> To the rice swamp dank and lone,
> Where the slave-whip ceaseless swings,
> Where the noisome insect stings,
> Where the fever-demon strews
> Poison with the falling dews,
> Where the sickly sunbeams glare
> Through the hot and misty air:—
>    Gone, gone, sold and gone
>    To the rice swamp dank and lone,
>    From Virginia hills and waters—
>    Woe is me, my stolen daughters!"

The hearth is desolate. The children, the unconscious children, who once sang and danced in her presence, are gone. She gropes her way, in the darkness of age, for a drink of water. Instead of the voices of her children, she hears by day the moans of the dove, and by night the screams of the hideous owl. All is gloom. The grave is at the door. And now, when weighed down by the pains and aches of old age, when the head inclines to the feet, when the beginning and ending of human existence meet, and helpless infancy and painful old age combine together—at this time, this most needful time, the time for the exercise of that tenderness and affection which children only can exercise towards a declining parent—my poor old grandmother, the devoted mother of twelve children, is left all alone, in yonder little hut, before a few dim embers. She stands—she sits—she staggers—she falls—she groans—she dies—and there are none of her children or grandchildren present, to wipe from her wrinkled brow the cold sweat of death, or to place beneath the sod her fallen remains. Will not a righteous God visit for these things?

# DISCUSSION QUESTIONS

1.  Some scholars have documented a recent decline in memberships in a variety of civic associations and social groups, ranging from fraternal organizations to bowling leagues. If Alexis de Tocqueville was correct about the importance of such associations to American democracy in the 1830s, what might this mean today? What might be the causes of a decline in American participation in civic groups?

2.  The relative merits of the Madisonian and Jeffersonian models of democracy, i.e., representative versus direct democracy, continue to be debated today. Utilizing some contemporary environmental issues, discuss resolving those issues either through more effective and fair representation or by greater grass-roots democracy.

3.  George Catlin and Andrew Jackson both wrote about the "Indian problem." Compare and contrast their views as to how they thought the country should solve this problem. To what extent have Americans moved beyond the racial stereotyping of earlier eras? To what extent are contemporary environmental issues impacted by the race issue?

4.  Frederick Douglass's biography provides a powerful description of the slave's view of agrarianism. This is far different from Jefferson's ideal. How might the different political and cultural experiences of minority groups today affect their view of rural versus urban life, their support for wilderness and public lands, and their concerns about environmental quality?

# PART II

## "Go West, Young Man, Go Forth into the Country"*

### MANIFEST DESTINY AND THE INDUSTRIAL REVOLUTION, 1840–1900

The Industrial Revolution posed the greatest threat to Thomas Jefferson's vision of an America peopled primarily by yeoman farmers. Between 1840 and 1900 the stark contrasts between the machinery of industrialization and pastoral life became evident: A nation of farms at the beginning of the nineteenth century became a nation of cities one hundred years later, so that by about 1915 the number of urban residents became equal to the number of rural folk. As the forces of industrialization spread throughout the western frontier—creating new cities in their wake—many Americans began to appreciate what was being lost to this great transformation. They developed new values about preserving wild places, and a new role for the state emerged, as a guardian of the public interest in protecting and preserving nature.

A change in societal attitudes toward nature first became manifest in intellectual and literary circles, especially in the writings of those identified with what is called the Romantic Movement. Novelists and poets such as James Fenimore Cooper, Nathaniel Hawthorne, Henry Wadsworth Longfellow, Herman Melville, Edgar Allan Poe, and Walt Whitman are all associated with this movement. Romantics rejected the cold rationality of the Enlightenment, championing instead the importance of individual feelings, emotions, and the spirit of community. Nostalgic for what was passing away almost literally before their eyes, these intellectuals delighted in the simplic-

---

*Horace Greeley, circa 1837.

**49**

ity of rural life and found peace in idyllic landscapes absent the noisy intrusions of industrialized society.

Romantics such as Emerson and Thoreau also are associated with the philosophy of Transcendentalism, which was based on the principles that there existed a reality higher than the physical, and that nature and the human spirit could be linked through the intuitive self. Transcendentalists flourished in New England in the quarter century preceding the Civil War, and their writings provided an intellectual foundation for recasting Americans' view of nature. While Emerson's understanding of nature was more abstract, and largely rooted in the urban environment, Thoreau's understanding came from firsthand knowledge of the woods and fields near his home in Concord. For two years, from 1845 to 1847, Thoreau adjourned to nearby Walden Pond in order to immerse himself in nature. Afterwards, he wrote about his experience and traveled the lecture circuit, so that his two years spent in blissful solitude became well-known. There, at Walden Pond, he claimed to have found the ultimate in individual freedom. "In Wildness is the preservation of the World," he concluded. Later in the nineteenth century a new organization, the Sierra Club, would claim this phrase as its motto.

While Transcendentalists accepted some aspects of the newly emerging egalitarian state, they also were deeply libertarian. Liberty and equality, they thought, could best be achieved through individual reform rather than societal action. Thoreau carried the maxim "that government is best which governs least" a step further, when he proclaimed: "that government is best which governs not at all." In his famous 1848 essay, "Resistance to Civil Government" (also known as "On Civil Disobedience"), Thoreau argued that the individual had a moral right to disobey unjust laws—an argument not unlike that made by Thomas Jefferson in the eighteenth century. To his credit, Thoreau not only talked the talk, but he walked the walk, spending a night in jail rather than pay his poll tax to a government that allowed slavery and fought a war with Mexico over territory. Most of the time, however, Thoreau remained above politics, so that his mentor and close friend, Ralph Waldo Emerson, lamented lost opportunities when Thoreau died. Emerson said that instead "of engineering for all America, he was the captain of a huckleberry-party."

Thoreau and others of his era equated the West with the wild and with freedom: "We go westward as into the future, with a spirit of enterprise and adventure...westward I go free." Thoreau himself never traveled outside of New England, but if his wilderness sojourn actually had taken him to the Mississippi River and beyond, he would have witnessed the westward flow of wagon trains—which reached their apex during the 1840s—transporting people and goods to what they hoped would be a better life. He might have witnessed, for example, the 1,000-strong party that gathered in Independence, Missouri, in the spring of 1843 to make the journey to Oregon's Willamette Valley. It was the first party to traverse the entire Oregon Trail by wagon. In addition to industrialization and the Civil War, then, westward migration and expansion into new territories were the most significant political and social phenomena of nineteenth century America.

As noted previously, President Jefferson instigated the westward movement with his Louisiana Purchase, but it wasn't until 1845 that a magazine editor coined the term, Manifest Destiny. What started out as a campaign theme for the Democrats in the 1846 election became a rallying cry for America. Manifest Destiny had many voices: The great poet Walt Whitman gave it a lyric voice; Horace Greeley, the journalist and politician, rallied young Americans with his call to escape the social and economic vicissitudes of the East Coast by seeking free land and fortunes to be made in the West; William Gilpin, an ardent booster of the West, blithely ignored physical realities as he tried to turn the desert into an agricultural garden; and several presidents and congresses rationalized their expansionist policies by exploiting fears of foreign aggression and by repeating over and over again the unquestioned superiority of the American way.

When James W. Marshall discovered gold at Sutter's sawmill in the Sierra Nevada Mountains in 1848, the gold rush was on: No one could stand in the way of those seeking instant wealth. The gold and silver rushes of the last half of the nineteenth century created new cities, both large and small. Some of them survived, but others disappeared almost as quickly as they appeared. California's population increased from about 14,000 in 1848 to over 100,000 by the end of 1849; by 1852 it had ballooned to 250,000. In the process, California's generous natural resource base was used without regard to waste or the future. Because there were no legal precedents as to how to treat mining claims as property or to allocate rights to the water needed for processing, miners created their own systems, often borrowing ideas from other nations' practices from whence many of them came. Gradually, the mineral-rich states and the federal government institutionalized many of these practices. The 1872 Mining Law and the western water doctrine of "prior appropriation" (both of which remain virtually unchanged today), created private property rights to these resources and allocated access based on the rule of seniority: First in time, first in right. Still, for much of the nineteenth century, life in the western United States was a virtual free-for-all; it wasn't called the "Wild West" only because of its rugged landscape, extreme climate, and fierce flora and fauna.

While scholars still vigorously debate the degree to which the Civil War was fought over economic policies and nationalism rather than slavery, nonetheless that "peculiar institution," as it has been called, was inextricably bound up with the nation's deepest crisis. The issue of slavery had been a divisive question even before the formation of the republic, and as the nation grew westward the issue was exacerbated. The admission of new states became a delicate balancing act between slave states and free states. But that compromise could not settle the question. As Abraham Lincoln said in 1858, "'A house divided against itself cannot stand'... This government cannot endure, permanently half slave and half free." When seven southern states finally seceded from the Union and formed the Confederate States of America, the stage was set for the bloodiest war in American history. Between 1861 and 1865 nearly as many Americans lost their lives in the Civil War as in *all* other wars. And, like all wars, this one exacted a heavy toll not only in lives lost but resources used up. As General William Tecumseh

Sherman's 1865 march through the South demonstrated, the destruction of land and property was used—as it often is—as a tool to undermine the people's capacity to wage war. A century after war's end, the South was still the most economically backward region of America.

The Civil War resulted in a fundamental restructuring of the Constitution. Slavery became unconstitutional with the passage of the Thirteenth Amendment, black men were given the right to vote under the Fifteenth Amendment, and under the Fourteenth Amendment states were prohibited from taking any action that would "deprive any person of life, liberty, or property, without due process of law; nor deny to any person within its jurisdiction the equal protection of the laws." Nonetheless, these amendments did little to end violence either against blacks or the southern Republican politicians who controlled state governments during the Reconstruction Era. The Republicans' progressive programs, which sought to improve the conditions of former slaves, encourage rail and canal building, improve health and educational programs, and develop the region's natural resources, required raising significant amounts of revenue. Property taxes provided the revenue source, and most property owners were white. Both northern and southern whites joined in protest against "class legislation" and the resulting redistribution of wealth. By 1877 Reconstruction had collapsed.

While the nation battled against itself in the Civil War, it also continued its war upon the Indian. The gold rush and a new network of railroads brought ever more settlers to the West, and clashes with Native Americans spread. White immigrants encroached on Indian lands and destructively exploited their natural resources. They mined the gold in the Sioux's sacred Black Hills, they attempted to capture and sell Navajos as slaves, and they generally appropriated resources—land, game, timber, and water—vital to the Indians' physical and cultural survival. Despite the peaceful intentions of Indian leaders like Chief Seattle, it proved extremely difficult for the two races to coexist. The tragic story of the buffalo, or American bison, is the most instructive on this point. As George Catlin had so poignantly recorded in his visits in 1832, the buffalo was a staple of Plains Indians' culture. All parts of the buffalo were used for subsistence, as well as religious needs, e.g., hides for cloths, dung for fuel, skulls for ceremonial use, intestines for cord, bladders for storage pouches. In the 1800s it is estimated that there were more than 40 million buffalo on the plains. By the 1870s, however, commercial hunters were killing hundreds of thousands of buffalo a day; as Catlin pointed out, the slaughter often involved taking only the buffalos' tongues and hides, leaving the rest to rot. The U.S. Army, implementing a deliberate policy of killing the buffalo in order to subdue the Indians, joined in the slaughter. By 1885 there were only 20,000 buffalo left; by 1895 fewer than 1,000.

The government created reservations to segregate the Indians from the white settlers, but these were, at best, several times smaller than their traditional lands, and, at worst, prison camps. As General Philip Sheridan, who waged war on the Indians, remarked, "We took away their country and their means of support, broke up their mode of living, their habits of life, introduced disease and decay among them, and it was for this and against this that they made war. Could anyone expect less?" Upon his capture by General O.O. Howard in 1877, Chief Joseph, the great Chief of the Nez Perce, whose tribes had aided Lewis and Clark on their journey, spoke of the toll the fighting had exacted on his people.

> Tell General Howard I know his heart. What he told me before, I have it in my heart. I am tired of fighting. Our chiefs are killed. Looking Glass is dead. Toohoolhoolzote is dead. The old men are all dead. It is the young men who say, 'Yes' or 'No.' He who led the young men is dead. It is cold, and we have no blankets. The little children are freezing to death. My people, some of them, have run away to the hills, and have no blankets, no food. No one knows where they are—perhaps freezing to death. I want to have time to look for my children. Hear me, my chiefs: I am tired. My heart is sick and sad. From where the sun now stands, I will fight no more forever. (1877)

In 1871 the government declared an end to treaty making. With the General Allotment, or Dawes Act, of 1887, it adopted another approach, known as assimilation and allotment. In this policy Indian reservations were broken up and lands allotted to the heads of Indian families in 160-acre plots; of course "surplus lands" were distributed to non-Indians. The stated goal was to hasten the assimilation of Indians into white society, but it became principally a government-sanctioned mechanism by which railroad, cattle, mining, timber, and oil companies divested the Indians of title to lands and resources. Another sad chapter in the history of relations between the two peoples was written with this statute.

During most of the nineteenth century the West was an unknown quantity, yet it was in the West—both the imagined West and the real West— where the conservation movement was born. Like its tremendously variegated landscape, Americans' notions about the West encompassed many realities, some of which competed with or contradicted others. As a consequence of these "separate realities," government action took place on many fronts simultaneously. For example, government lured homesteaders with the promise of free or nearly free land, and generous rights to mineral wealth. Yet the reality for most of these early settlers was a long and arduous trek across a formidable terrain, the harshness of eking out an existence in an unforgiving environment, the squalor and debauchery of mining towns, and murderous encounters with hostile Indians.

Government also underwrote the continuing exploration and exploitation of the West at the same time as it moved to protect some of its most unique natural treasures. When the one-armed Major John Wesley Powell and his small crew ventured down the Green and Colorado Rivers in 1869— the same year, coincidentally, that saw the completion of the first transcontinental railroad—they became the first known whites to enter this region. Twelve years later, as director of the newly created U.S. Geological Survey (USGS), Powell began the first systematic mapping of the country, filling in the details of political and physical boundaries on maps where once there were only blank spaces. (Today these maps are familiar to countless numbers of users as USGS topographic maps.)

While Powell toiled over his maps, others were busy creating a commercialized version of the West. Buffalo Bill Cody's popular Wild West show romantically portrayed the cowboy as a rugged and glamorous hero. The Beadle Dime novels popularized fictional characters such as Calamity Jane and Deadwood Dick, and they gave almost mythic attributes to real people such as Buffalo Bill and Kit Carson. The invented West glorified the cowboy, demonized the Indian, exalted the rugged and independent individual, and in the process instilled in the American consciousness powerful and lasting myths about western lands and its peoples. Even today, residents of the "New West" try to disentangle what was invented and what was real. Not an easy task!

Finally, there was the reality of the West that compelled government action to conserve resources and protect landscapes. In 1864, in the midst of the Civil War and in the same year that saw the publication of George Perkins Marsh's *Man and Nature*, Congress responded to growing public interest in scenic preservation by ceding the Yosemite Valley to the State of California. Stipulating that the land be held for "public use, resort and recreation," this act set a precedent whose importance is difficult to overstate. For the first time Congress carved out a park from the public domain lands.

The public parks movement had begun. Just eight years earlier New York City had purchased land to create Central Park, the nation's first urban park. Landscape architect Frederick Law Olmsted helped establish the principles governing this new movement, both with his design of Central Park and with his report on the management of Yosemite Valley. Viewing parks as necessary respites from the excesses of civilization, Olmsted further believed that parks must be managed without sacrificing their essential values for both present and future visitors. For Olmsted, public spaces—whether in far-off wilderness areas or in the heart of large cities—helped government to fulfil an ethical obligation for *all* its citizens.

The parks movement was aided not only by nature writers, whose narratives promoted their aesthetic and social values, but also by artists and photographers whose canvasses and lenses captured the unique features of the American landscape. George Catlin was one of the first to assist the conservation movement in this way; others followed later in the century. Albert Bierstadt and Thomas Moran, along with the photographer William Henry Jackson, helped put forbidding landscapes in a different social light by emphasizing their majesty and mystery. Thomas Moran accompanied several western expeditions, including Ferdinand Hayden's, into Yellowstone in 1871, and Powell's 1873 explorations into the canyon country of Utah and Arizona. The paintings Moran produced helped influence Congress to create the nation's first *national* park, the Yellowstone, in 1872. It was a seminal act. Between 1872 and the end of the century several more national parks were established, including Yosemite, Sequoia, General Grant, and Mount Rainier. The wild western landscape was in the process of becoming a source of national pride, even as much of the West was being tamed.

Marsh's 1864 book, *Man and Nature,* documented numerous instances of human destruction of the environment, not least of which was the near-total destruction of America's virgin forests. The book helped to develop a public interest in forestry. By the 1870s private forestry organizations were forming, and both states and the federal government were taking actions to establish forest preserves. One of the first states to do so was New York, whose 1885 act declared all state lands in a fourteen-county area of the Adirondacks and Catskills be kept "forever wild." Although bills had been introduced in Congress as early as 1876, it was not until 1891 that Congress passed the Forest Reserve Act, authorizing the president to set aside timber lands in public reservations. While both Presidents Benjamin Harrison and Grover Cleveland made substantial reservations under the act, there did not exist any legislative authority for management of the reserves until Congress passed the Organic Act of 1897. That statute defined the purpose of the forest reserves—today called national forests—as "securing favorable water flows" and "furnishing timber supplies." It also authorized officials in the executive branch to make rules and regulations concerning their use.

While governments acted upon proposals to create parks and forest reserves, other ideas fell by the wayside during the formative years of the conservation movement. For example, John Wesley Powell's prescriptions to Montana's constitutional convention to design county boundaries to conform with watersheds fell on deaf ears. So did his careful determination that only about 3 percent of the arid lands of the West should be irrigated.

The need to protect the nation's remaining forests became more apparent as the century wore on, especially as the destructive consequences of cut-and-run logging became evident. Intense fires burned through the slash of what had been the white pine forests of the Midwest. One notorious firestorm, the 1871 Peshtigo fire in Wisconsin, killed approximately 1,500 people, and occurred at almost the same time as the famous Chicago fire that burned over four square miles of the city and killed approximately 250 residents. The forest fires deprived the soil of the fertility needed either for reforestation or farming for decades to come. After they had denuded the Midwest, the timber and railroad "robber barons" looked further westward for supplies. The immense, old-growth forests of the Pacific Northwest, for example, played a significant role in railroad tycoon James J. Hill's plans for his Great Northern Railroad: "From the traffic in this lumber alone...will come our largest revenue."

That industrialization sped forward after the Civil War was due in no small part to the railroads. Probably more than any other technological development in nineteenth-century America, the "iron horse" singularly changed the social, economic, and physical face of America; indeed, it impacted just about every element of American life. Railroad junctures created sites for new cities, and the railroads connected those urban areas to the hinterlands, enabling the transport of resources from the far edges of the continent to the industrial areas of the Midwest and East. The railroads provided market access to convey the cultivated grain that replaced the prairie tall grasses and the domestic cattle that replaced the wild bison. Because of the large land grants the states and the federal government gave the railroads as inducements for their expansion, railroad corporations maintained their own land departments, which developed promotional programs encouraging settlement and providing assistance to farmers. They became extremely powerful entities in their own right. In fact, as Nathaniel

Hawthorne and other writers noted, by transforming our very notions of space and time, the railroad became *the* symbol for change in nineteenth-century America.

The last decade or so of the nineteenth century is labeled "The Gilded Age." The great fortunes made by using the natural wealth of the country—by such entrepreneurs as James J. Hill, the Vanderbilts, John D. Rockefeller, and Andrew Carnegie—undeniably aided the building of a stronger America. But it came at a heavy environmental price tag and with little regard for laborers or the public interest. "The public be damned," exclaimed William Vanderbilt, who might have been speaking for any number of the era's robber barons. It was an era—not unlike our own—where, according to a prominent historian, "great waste [was] permitted for great accomplishment, where many temptations are offered and few restraints imposed." Corruption could be found virtually everywhere.

During its heyday, the ruling elite seized upon the theory of Social Darwinism as scientific proof of their natural superiority. As advanced by the British philosopher Herbert Spencer and Yale University's Charles Sumner, Social Darwinism borrowed liberally from Charles Darwin's famous 1859 scientific treatise, *The Origin of Species*. In particular, the Social Darwinists argued that the survival of the fittest applied equally to society as it did to nature. The railroad tycoon, J.J. Hill, wrote that he saw no reason why "the Darwinian theory does not apply to railways." Explaining to one New York financier why some regional grouping of the railroads might take place "with excellent results," he continued: "If something of this kind is not done the natural theory of the survival of the fittest will be the result through the bankruptcy of the weaker lines and their final absorption by the stronger ones." Social Darwinists also argued that political and economic reforms to help the poor, i.e., the inferior and "unfit," were not only futile and misguided but actually retarded social progress. In many respects, Social Darwinism laid the foundation for the arguments advanced in the 1960s by Garrett Hardin and others of the "lifeboat ethics" school of environmental thought.

The last census of the nineteenth century, taken in 1890, became a major event in America because of a historian named Frederick Jackson Turner. After the U.S. Superintendent of the Census declared that it was no longer possible to delineate a clear line between settled and nonsettled America, Turner picked up on this casual observation and presented one of the most influential academic papers in American history. At the 1893 meeting of the American Historical Association in Chicago, which also featured the World's Columbian Exposition, the historian delivered his paper, "The Significance of the Frontier in American History." In it he discussed the powerful influence that free land had on shaping the American character and its democratic institutions. Now, as the frontier drew to a close, Turner argued that this democratizing force was being lost. A number of political leaders took Turner's thesis and used it in turn-of-the-century political debates about restricting immigration (since no frontier existed to Americanize the new arrivals), about expanding overseas (to create new frontiers), and about creating more national parks, wildlife refuges, and forests (to preserve vestiges of America's past). While forty years later Turner's arguments would be critiqued on a number of points, nevertheless it is a fact that by the end of the century Americans were not only pondering the closing of the great American frontier but many also were thinking differently about natural resources and their use. Enter the great conservationist president, Theodore Roosevelt, in 1901, to lead the way.

# 7

# Nathaniel Hawthorne (1804–1864)

A nineteenth-century writer of novels, short stories, and children's books, Nathaniel Hawthorne is best known for two great novels, *The Scarlet Letter* (1850) and *The House of the Seven Gables* (1851). Both books are invaluable studies of New England's Puritan heritage. Hawthorne's fiction typically focused on the isolation of the individual, the unpardonable sin (in which one violates the sanctity of the human heart by persecution or the subjection of one person by another), and the influence of the past. His writing reflected what fellow novelist and friend Herman Melville termed "the great power of blackness." Hawthorne was transfixed by the darker side of human nature.

Hawthorne was not the famous nature writer that his neighbors, Thoreau and Emerson, were, although memories of the wilderness and village life from his early days in Maine are revealed in his fiction. In his stories, however, these memories generally reflected the Puritan sense of wilderness as a dark and evil place. Also unlike Thoreau and Emerson, Hawthorne had a mixed response to Transcendentalism. Although he joined the utopian community Brook Farm, he left after six months, skeptical of the optimism and idealism of the Transcendentalists and the idea of intellectuals living together harmoniously.

*The American Notebooks* are a compilation of the notes Hawthorne kept between 1837 and 1853. He frequently culled his notebooks for ideas, characters, and background for his fiction. In the selection reproduced here, Hawthorne wrote about Sleepy Hollow, an idyllic place near his home in Concord, Massachusetts. Reflecting upon the "little" events he observed there, he succeeds brilliantly in capturing the meaning of a truly big event—the industrial revolution—and its impacts on society and nature. It is the sound of the locomotive that, above all else, disturbs the tranquility of Sleepy Hollow. Nathaniel Hawthorne died in 1864 deeply pessimistic over the future of an industrializing America that he saw manifested in clouds of gunsmoke and the din of Civil War cannons.

---

## "BUT, HARK! THERE IS THE WHISTLE OF THE LOCOMOTIVE"*

To sit down in a solitary place (or a busy and bustling one, if you please) and await such little events as may happen, or observe such noticeable points as the eyes fall upon around you. For instance, I sat down today—July 27th, 1844, at about ten o'clock in the forenoon—in Sleepy Hollow, a shallow space

---

*Nathaniel Hawthorne. 1972. Notebook entry of Saturday, July 27, 1844 in *The American Notebooks*. Claude M. Simpson, ed. Columbus, OH: Ohio State University Press, pp. 245–250. Reprinted with permissions from The Pierpont Morgan Library, New York (MA 577), and Ohio State University Press.

scooped out among the woods, which surround it on all sides, it being pretty nearly circular, or oval, and two or three hundred yards—perhaps four or five hundred—in diameter. The present season, a thriving field of Indian corn, now in its most perfect growth, and tasselled out, occupies nearly half of the hollow; and it is like the lap of bounteous Nature, filled with bread stuff. On one verge of this hollow, skirting it, is a terraced pathway, broad enough for a wheel-track, overshadowed with oaks, stretching their long, knotted, rude, rough arms between earth and sky; the gray skeletons, as you look upward, are strikingly prominent amid the green foliage; likewise, there are chesnuts, growing up in a more regular and pyramidal shape; white pines, also; and a shrubbery composed of the shoots of all these trees, overspreading and softening the bank on which the parent stems are growing;—these latter being intermingled with coarse grass. Observe the pathway; it is strewn over with little bits of dry twigs and decayed branches, and the sear and brown oak-leaves of last year, that have been moistened by snow and rain, and whirled about by harsh and gentle winds, since their departed verdure; the needle-like leaves of the pine, that are never noticed in falling—that fall, yet never leave the tree bare—are likewise on the paths; and with these are pebbles, the remains of what was once a gravelled surface, but which the soil accumulating from the decay of leaves, and washing down from the bank, has now almost covered. The sunshine comes down on the pathway with the bright glow of noon, at certain points; in other places, there is a shadow as deep as the glow; but along the greater portion, sunshine glimmers through shadow, and shadow effaces sunshine, imaging that pleasant mood of mind where gaiety and pensiveness intermingle. A bird is chirping overhead, among the branches, but exactly whereabout, you seek in vain to determine; indeed you hear the rustle of the leaves, as he continually changes his position. A little sparrow, indeed, hops into view, alighting on the slenderest twigs, and seemingly delighting in the swinging and heaving motion which his slight substance communicates to them; but he is not the loquacious bird, whose voice still comes, eager and busy, from his hidden whereabout. Insects are fluttering about. The cheerful, sunny hum of the flies is altogether summer-like, and so gladsome that you pardon them their intrusiveness and impertinence, which continually impels them to fly against your face, to alight upon your hands, and to buzz in your very ear, as if they wished to get into your head among your most secret thoughts. In truth, a fly is the most impertinent and indelicate thing in creation, the very type and moral of human spirits whom one occasionally meets with, and who perhaps, after an existence troublesome and vexatious to all with whom they come in contact, have been doomed to reappear in this congenial shape. Here is one intent upon alighting on my nose. In a room, now—in a human habitation—I could find in my conscience to put him to death; but here we have intruded upon his own domain, which he holds in common with all other children of earth and air— and we have no right to slay him on his own ground. Now we look about us more minutely, and observe that the acorn-cups of last year are strewn plentifully on the bank, and on the path; there is always pleasure in examining an acorn-cup, perhaps associated with fairy banquets, where they were said to compose the table-service. Here, too, are those balls which grow as excrescences on the leaves of the oak, and which young kittens love so well to play with, rolling them on the carpet. We see mosses, likewise, growing on the banks, in as great variety as the trees of the wood. And how strange is the gradual process with which we detect objects that are right before the eyes; here now are whortleberries, ripe and black, growing actually within reach of my hand, yet unseen till this moment. Were we to sit here all day, a week, a month, and doubtless a lifetime, objects would thus still be presenting themselves as new, though there would seem to be no reason why we should not have detected them all at the first moment.

Now a cat-bird is mewing at no great distance. Then the shadow of a bird flitted across a sunny spot; there is a peculiar impressiveness in this mode of being made acquainted with the flight of a bird; it affects the mind more than if the eye had actually seen it. As we look round to catch a glimpse of the winged creature, we behold the living blue of the sky, and the brilliant disk of the sun, broken and made tolerable to the eye by the intervening foliage. Now, when you are not thinking of it, the fragrance of the white pines is suddenly wafted to you by a slight, almost imperceptible breeze, which has begun to stir. Now the breeze is the gentlest sigh imaginable, yet with a spiritual potency, insomuch that it seems to penetrate, with its mild, ethereal coolness, through the outward clay, and breathe upon the spirit itself, which shivers with gentle delight; now the breeze strengthens so much as to shake all the leaves, making them rustle sharply, but has lost its most ethereal power. And now, again, the shadows of the boughs lie as motionless as if they were painted on the pathway. Now, in this stillness, is heard the long, melancholy note of a bird, complaining alone, of some wrong or sorrow, that worm, or her own kind, or the immitigable doom of human affairs has inflicted upon her. A complaining, but unresisting sufferer. And now, all of a sudden, we hear the sharp, shrill chirrup of a red squirrel, angry, it seems, with somebody, perhaps with ourselves for having intruded into what he is pleased to consider as his own domain. And hark, terrible to the ear, here is the minute but intense hum of a mosquito. Instinct prevails over all the nonsense of sentiment; we crush him at once, and there is his grim and grisly corpse, the ugliest object in nature. This incident has disturbed our tranquillity. In truth, the whole insect tribe, so far as we can judge, are made more for themselves, and less for man, than any other portion of creation. With such reflections, we look at a swarm of them, peopling, indeed, the whole air, but only visible when they flash into the sunshine; and annihilated out of visible existence, when they dart into a region of shadow, to be again re-produced as suddenly. Now we hear the striking of the village-clock, distant, but yet so near that each stroke is distinctly impressed upon the air. This is a sound that does not disturb the repose of the scene; it does not break our Sabbath; for like a Sabbath seems this place, and the more so on account of the cornfield rustling at our feet. It tells of human labor, but being so solitary now, it seems as if it were on account of the sacredness of the Sabbath. Yet it is not so, for we hear at a distance, mowers whetting their scythes; but these sounds of labor, when at a proper remoteness, do but increase the quiet of one who lies at his ease, all in a mist of his own musings. There is the tinkling of a cow-bell—a noise how peevishly dissonant, were it close at hand, but even musical now. But, hark! There is the whistle of the locomotive—the long shriek, harsh, above all other harshness, for the space of a mile cannot mollify it into harmony. It tells a story of busy men, citizens, from the hot street, who have come to spend a day in a country village; men of business; in short of all unquietness; and no wonder that it gives such a startling shriek, since it brings the noisy world into the midst of our slumbrous peace. As our thoughts repose again, after this interruption, we find ourselves gazing up at the leaves, and comparing their different aspect, the beautiful diversity of green, as the sunlight is diffused through them as a medium, or reflected from their glossy surface. You see, too, here and there, dead, leafless branches, which you had no more been aware of before, than if they had assumed this old and dry decay since you sat down upon the bank. Look at our feet; and here likewise are objects as good as new. There are two little round white fungi, which probably sprung from the ground in the course of last night, curious productions of the mushroom tribe, and which by and by will be those little things, with smoke in them, which children call puff-balls. Is there nothing else? Yes; here is a whole colony of little ant-hills, a real village of them; they are small, round hillocks, formed of minute particles of gravel, with an entrance in the centre; and through some of them blades of grass or small shrubs have sprouted up, producing an effect not unlike that of trees overshadowing a homestead. Here is a type of domestic industry—perhaps, too, something of municipal institutions—perhaps, likewise (who knows) the very model of a community, which Fourierites and others are stumbling in pursuit of. Possibly, the student of such philosophies should go to the ant, and find that nature has given him his lesson there. Meantime, like a malevolent genius, I drop a few grains of sand into the entrance of one of these dwellings, and thus quite obliterate it. And, behold, here comes one of the inhabitants, who has been abroad upon some public or private business, or perhaps to enjoy a fantastic walk—and cannot any longer find his own door. What surprise, what hurry, what confusion of mind, are expressed in all his movements! How inexplicable to him must be the agency that has effected this mischief. The incident will probably be long remembered in the annals of the ant-colony, and be talked of in the winter days, when they are making merry over their hoarded provisions. But come, it is time to move. The sun has shifted his position, and has found a vacant space through the branches, by means of which he levels his rays full upon my head. Yet now, as I arise, a cloud has come across him, and makes everything gently sombre in an instant. Many clouds, voluminous and heavy, are scattered about the sky, like the shattered ruins of a dreamer's Utopia; but we will not send our thoughts thitherward now, nor take one of them into our present observations. The clouds of any one day, are material enough, alone, for the observation either of an idle man or a philosopher.

And now how narrow, scanty, and meagre, is this record of observation, compared with the immensity that was to be observed, within the bounds which I prescribed to myself. How shallow and scanty a stream of thought, too,—of distinct and expressed thought—compared with the broad tide of dim emotions, ideas, associations, which were flowing through the haunted regions of imagination, intellect, and sentiment, sometimes excited by what was around me, sometimes with no perceptible connection with them. When we see how little we can express, it is a wonder that any man ever takes up a pen a second time.

# 8
# Frederick Law Olmsted (1822–1903)

Frederick Law Olmsted is generally considered the father of the landscape architecture profession. He had been a farmer, but a walking tour of the British Isles in 1851 convinced him of the need for landscape planning and urban design in America. Near Liverpool, in the English town of Birkenhead, a local baker encouraged him to visit the town's park. Olmsted came away from his visit greatly impressed with England's public parks, as well as with design lessons that he would later incorporate into his major projects. The journal, *The Horticulturalist*, published Olmsted's account of his visit as part of a campaign to create a large, public park in New York City. Olmsted included a slightly longer version in his *Walks and Talks of an American Farmer in England* (1852). *Walks and Talks* brought Olmsted to the attention of the *New York Daily Times*, which commissioned him to report on social conditions in the southern states. His accounts revealed to a wide audience the harsh realities of the slaveholding culture; they won him high praise and sold well, both in the United States and Europe.

By 1857, having abandoned both farming and the idea of a literary career, Olmstead found a new opportunity to work in Central Park, the public park that New York had eventually established. A year later, when Olmsted and his partner Calvert Vaux won the competition for the park's design, the profession of landscape architecture was officially born. Over the next thirty years, Olmsted helped design more than twenty great city parks, as well as a number of college campuses, cemeteries, private estates, institutional grounds, and special projects. These included Chicago's 1893 World's Columbian Exposition and the grounds of the Capitol in Washington, D.C.

In addition to his pathbreaking record of accomplishment in urban parks and community design, Olmsted left an important legacy in the area of wildland parks and scenic preservation. In 1864, the governor of California appointed Olmsted to the commission established to oversee management of Yosemite Valley and Mariposa Big Tree Grove, which Congress had just ceded to the state. Olmsted authored the commission's 1865 report, which laid out the philosophical basis for preservation; it stands as one of the great documents in park history. While this report discussed various topics such as concessionaire operations, scientific inquiry, and visitor accommodations, its most important contribution was to argue in favor of keeping parks public—and not privatizing them.

In his papers, speeches, and letters, Olmsted constantly articulated the purposes of having parks, emphasizing their spiritual, ethical, and democratic objectives. He promoted the idea that public parks could engender a better society, making individuals and communities healthier and more vigorous. He saw parks as part of a larger urban design of green and open spaces, as bastions of the democratic ideals of community and equality, and as oases where ordinary working folks, who could not afford expensive trips to the country, could be replenished by nature. Not only did Olmsted link urban planning to nature, he linked nature to the design of democratic states.

---

# "THE PEOPLE'S PARK AT BIRKENHEAD"*

Birkenhead is the most important suburb of Liverpool, having the same relation to it that Brooklyn has to New-York, or Charlestown to Boston. When the first line of Liverpool packets was established, there were not half a dozen houses here; it now has a population of many thousands, and is increasing with a rapidity hardly paralleled in the New World. This is much owing to the very liberal and enterprizing management of the land-owners, which affords an example worthy of consideration in the vicinity of many of our own large towns. There are several public squares, and the streets and places are broad, and well paved and lighted. A considerable part of the town has been built with uniformity, and a reference to general effect, from the plans, and under the direction of a talented architect, Gillespie Graham, Esq., of Edinburgh.

We received this information while crossing the Mersey in a ferry-boat, from a fellow passenger, who, though a stranger, entered into conversation, and answered our inquiries, with frankness and courtesy. Near the landing we found, by his direction, a square of eight or ten acres, enclosed by an iron fence, and laid out with tasteful masses of shrubbery, (not trees,) and gravel walks. The houses about were detached, and though of the same general style, were sufficiently varied in details not to appear monotonous. These were all of stone.

We had left this, and were walking up a long, broad street, when the gentleman who had crossed the ferry with us, joined us again, and said that as we were strangers, we might like to look at the ruins of an abbey which were in the vicinity, and he had come after us; that if we pleased he might conduct us to it. What an odd way these Englishmen have of being "gruff and reserved to strangers," thought I.

Did you ever hear of Birkenhead Abbey? I never had before. It has no celebrity, but coming upon it so fresh from the land of Youth as we did, so unexpecting of anything of the kind—though I have since seen far older ruins, and more renowned, I have never found anything so impressively aged.

At the Market place we went into a baker's shop, and while eating some buns, learned that the poorest flour in the market was American, and the best, French. French and English flour is sold in sacks, American in barrels. The baker asked us if American flour was *kiln dried*, and thought it must be greatly injured, if it was not, on that account. When we left, he obligingly

---

*Frederick Law Olmsted. 1851. "The People's Park at Birkenhead, near Liverpool." *The Horticulturist and Journal of Rural Art and Rural Taste*. VI:(April 1): pp. 224–227. Footnotes are omitted.

directed us to several objects of interest in the vicinity, and showed us through the market. The building is very large, convenient, and fine. The roof, which is mostly of glass, is high and airy, and is supported by two rows of slender iron columns, giving to the interior the appearance of three light and elegant arcades. The contrivances to effect ventilation and cleanliness, are very complete. It was built by the town, upon land given to it for the purpose, and cost $175,000.

The baker had begged of us not to leave Birkenhead without seeing their new Park, and at his suggestion we left our knapsacks with him, and proceeded to it. As we approached the entrance, we were met by women and girls, who, holding out a cup of milk, asked us—"Will you take a cup of milk, sirs! Good, cool, sweet, cow's milk, gentlemen, or right warm from the ass." And at the gate were a herd of donkies, some with cans of milk strapped to them, others saddled and bridled, to be let for ladies and children to ride.

The gateway, which is about a mile and a half from the ferry, and quite back of the town, is a great massive block of handsome Ionic architecture, standing alone, and unsupported by anything else in the vicinity, and looking, as I think, heavy and awkward. There is a sort of grandeur about it that the English are fond of, but which, when it is entirely separate from all other architectural constructions, always strikes me unpleasantly. It seems intended as an impressive preface to a great display of art within. But here, as well as at Eaton Park, and other places I have since seen, it is not followed up with great things—the grounds immediately within the grand entrance being very simple, and apparently rather overlooked by the gardener. There is a large archway for carriages, and two smaller ones for those on foot; on either side, and over these, are rooms, which probably serve as inconvenient lodges for the laborers. No porter appears, and the gates are freely open to the public.

Walking a short distance up an avenue, we passed through another light iron gate into a thick, luxuriant, and diversified garden. Five minutes of admiration, and a few more spent in studying the manner in which art had been employed to obtain from nature so much beauty, and I was ready to admit that in democratic America, there was nothing to be thought of as comparable with this People's Garden. Indeed, I was satisfied that gardening had here reached a perfection that I had never before dreamed of. I cannot attempt to describe the effect of so much taste and skill as had evidently been employed; I will only tell you, that we passed through winding paths, over acres and acres, with a constant varying surface, where on all sides were growing every variety of shrubs and flowers, with more than natural grace, all set in borders of greenest, closest turf, and all kept with most consummate neatness. At a distance of a quarter of a mile from the gate, we came to an open field of clean, bright, green-sward, closely mown, on which a large tent was pitched, and a party of boys in one part, and a party of gentlemen in another, were playing cricket. Beyond this was a large meadow with rich groups of trees, under which a flock of sheep were reposing, and girls and women with children, were playing. While watching the cricketers, we were threatened with a shower, and hastened back to look for shelter, which we found in a pagoda, on an island approached by a Chinese bridge. It was soon filled, as were the other ornamental buildings, by a crowd of those who, like ourselves, had been overtaken in the grounds by the rain; and I was glad to observe that the privileges of the garden were enjoyed about equally by all classes. There were some who even were attended by servants, and sent at once for their carriages, but a large proportion were of the common ranks, and a few women with children, or suffering from ill health, were evidently the wives of very humble laborers. There were a number of strangers, and some we observed with note-books, that seemed to have come from a distance to study from the garden. The summer-houses, lodges, bridges, &c., were all well constructed, and of undecaying materials. One of the bridges which we crossed was of our countryman, Remington's patent, an extremely light and graceful erection.

I obtained most of the following information from the head working gardener.

The site of the Park and Garden was ten years ago, a flat, sterile, clay farm. It was placed in the hands of Mr. Paxton in June, 1844, by whom it was laid out in its present form by June of the following year. Carriage roads, thirty-four feet wide, with borders of ten feet, and walks varying in width, were first drawn and made. The excavation for a pond was also made, and the earth obtained from these sources used for making mounds and to vary the surface, which has been done with much *naturalness* and taste. The whole ground was thoroughly under-drained, the minor drains of stone, the main, of tile. By these sufficient water is obtained to fully supply the pond, or lake, as they call it, which is from twenty to forty feet wide, and about three feet deep, and meanders for a long distance through the garden. It is stocked with aquatic plants, gold fish and swans.

The roads are McAdamised. On each side of the carriage way, and of all the walks, pipes for drainage are laid, which communicate with deep main drains that run under the edge of all the mounds or flower beds. The walks are laid first with six inches of fine broken stone, then three inches cinders, and the surface with six inches of fine rolled gravel. All the stones on the ground which were not used for these purposes, were laid in masses of rock-work, and mosses and rock-plants attached to them. The mounds were then planted with shrubs, and Heaths, and Ferns, and the beds with flowering plants. Between these, and the walks and drives, is everywhere a belt of turf, which, by the way, is kept close cut with short, broad scythes and shears, and swept with house-brooms, as we saw. Then the rural lodges, temple, pavilion, bridges, orchestra for a band of instrumental music, &c., were built. And so, in one year, the skeleton of this delightful garden was complete.

But this is but a small part. Besides the cricket and an archery ground, large valleys were made verdant, extensive drives arranged—plantations, clumps, and avenues of trees formed, and a large park laid out. And all this magnificent pleasure-ground is entirely, unreservedly, and forever the People's own. The poorest British peasant is as free to enjoy it in all its parts, as the British Queen. More than that, the Baker of Birkenhead had the pride of an Owner in it.

Is it not a grand good thing? But you are inquiring who *paid* for it. The honest owners—the most wise and worthy town's people of Birkenhead—in the same way that the New-Yorkers pay for the Tombs, and the Hospital, and the *cleaning*, (as they amusingly say,) of their streets.

Of the farm which was purchased, one hundred and twenty acres have been disposed of in the way I have described. The remaining sixty acres, encircling the Park and Garden, were reserved to be sold or rented, after being well graded, streeted and planted, for private building lots. Several fine mansions are already built on these, (having private entrances to the park,) and the rest now sell at $1.25 a square yard. The whole concern cost the town between five and six hundred thousand dollars. It gives employment at present, to ten gardeners and laborers in summer, and to five in winter.

The generous spirit and fearless enterprise, that has accomplished this, has not been otherwise forgetful of the health and comfort of the poor. Among other things, I remember, a public wash and bathing house for the town is provided. I should have mentioned also, in connection with the market, that in the outskirts of the town there is a range of stone slaughter-houses with stables, yards, pens, supplies of hot and cold water, and other arrangements and conveniences, that enlightened regard for health and decency would suggest.

The consequence of all these sorts of things is, that all about, the town lands, which a few years ago were almost worthless wastes, have become of priceless value; where no sound was heard but the bleating of goats and braying of asses, complaining of their pasturage, there is now the hasty click and clatter of many hundred busy trowels and hammers. You may drive through wide and thronged streets of stately edifices, where were only a few scattered huts, surrounded by quagmires. Docks of unequalled size and grandeur are building, and a forest of masts grows along the shore; and there is no doubt that this young town is to be not only remarkable as a most agreeable and healthy place of residence, but that it will soon be distinguished for extensive and profitable commerce. It seems to me to be the only town I ever saw that has been really built at all in accordance with the advanced science, taste, and enterprising spirit that are supposed to distinguish the nineteenth century. I do not doubt it might be found to have plenty of exceptions to its general character, but I did not inquire for these, nor did I happen to observe them. Certainly, in what I have noticed, it is a model town, and may be held up as an example, not only to philanthropists and men of taste, but to speculators and men of business.

# 9
# Chief Seattle (1788–1866)

As a five-year-old child, Chief Seattle witnessed the British explorer George Vancouver and his ship, *Discovery*, sail into Puget Sound, bringing the first white people into the Pacific Northwest. It was a fateful sight, an event he would recall over and over again throughout his life. At first a warrior chief, by the 1830s Christian missionaries had converted him, so that he decided to pursue a path of peace and friendship. In 1851 the Chief warmly welcomed the first permanent white settlement to the area that now bears his name. Seattle befriended the new settlers, sharing his food and resources, and assisting them in their explorations of the area. In appreciation, the new residents decided to rename their settlement after the Chief. Seattle protested because his culture believed that frequent mention of a dead person's name would disturb his or her eternal rest. Proceeding anyway, the settlers agreed to prepay the Chief a small tribute for the trouble his spirit would later encounter.

While Seattle continued to pursue a policy of peace, relations between the incoming flood of whites and other Indian tribes became strained. In January, 1855, Washington's first territorial governor and also U.S. Superintendent of Indian Affairs, Isaac I. Stevens, assembled the territory's tribes and informed them of a treaty that would put them on reservations. Chief Seattle's poetic, prophetic and deeply melancholic reply to the governor reflected a keen intellect and great wisdom. (The poet Dr. Henry Smith subsequently reproduced the speech in the *Seattle Sunday Star* on October 29, 1887.)

Afterwards, Chief Seattle signed the Port Elliott Treaty and moved his people to their new reservation. He spent his remaining years there. Other tribes, however, whose new reservations placed them far from their hunting and fishing grounds, rebelled, and more conflict with the white settlers ensued.

Over the years, Seattle's moving speech to Governor Stevens has been subject to revisions and embellishments. For example, the screenplay for the 1972 ecology movie *Home* inserted words that Seattle had not spoken. He did not say, "the earth is our mother." Neither did he describe having witnessed white men's shooting of the buffalo from passing trains: He lived in the Northwest and had never seen a buffalo. This "revised" version of his speech was widely quoted, however. Debate over various versions of the speech even led some scholars to question the 1887 version (which is reproduced below) and to ask whether Smith, not the Chief, is responsible for its ecological and spiritual eloquence.

Today, Chief Seattle's people, the Duwamish, are not recognized by the U.S. government. In 1962, the tribe received $1.32 per acre for the land taken from them. It is now industrial land south of Seattle's city center. But if Chief Seattle was correct, his people's spirits remain there.

# "MY PEOPLE ARE EBBING AWAY LIKE A FAST-RECEDING TIDE"*

Yonder sky that has wept tears of compassion on our fathers for centuries untold, and which, to us, looks eternal, may change. To-day it is fair, to-morrow it may be overcast with clouds. My words are like the stars that never set. Whatever Seattle says the great chief, Washington, can rely upon, with as much certainty as our pale-face brothers can rely upon the return of the seasons. The son of the white chief says his father sends us greetings of friendship and good-will. This is kind, for we know he has little need of our friendship in return, because his people are many. They are like the grass that covers the vast prairies, while my people are few, and resemble the scattering trees of a storm-swept plain.

The great, and I presume also good, white chief sends us word that he wants to buy our lands but is willing to allow us to reserve enough to live on comfortably. This indeed appears generous; for the red man no longer has rights that he need respect, and the offer may be wise, also, for we are no longer in need of a great country. There was a time when our people covered the whole land as the waves of a wind-ruffled sea cover its shell-paved floor. But that time has long since passed away with the greatness of tribes almost forgotten. I will not mourn over our untimely decay, nor reproach my pale-face brothers with hastening it, for we, too, may have been somewhat to blame.

When our young men grow angry at some real or imaginary wrong and disfigure their faces with black paint, their hearts, also, are disfigured and turn black, and then their cruelty is relentless and knows no bounds, and our old men are not able to restrain them.

But let us hope that hostilities between the red man and his pale-face brothers may never return. We would have everything to lose and nothing to gain.

True it is, that revenge, with our young braves, is considered gain, even at the cost of their own lives, but old men who stay at home in times of war, and old women, who have sons to lose, know better.

Our great father Washington, for I presume he is now our father as well as yours, since [King] George has moved his boundaries to the north; our great and good father, I say, sends us word by his son, who, no doubt, is a great chief among his people, that if we do as he desires, he will protect us. His brave armies will be to us a bristling wall of strength, and his great ships of war will fill our harbors so that our ancient enemies far to the northward, the Simsiams and Hydas, will no longer frighten our women and old men. Then he will be our father and we will be his children. But can this ever be? Your God loves your people and hates mine; he folds his strong arms lov-

---

*Chief Seattle. 1855. Speech to Governor Isaac Stevens of the Washington Territory. Reprinted in *Seattle Sunday Star*, October 29, 1887.

ingly around the white man and leads him as a father leads his infant son, but he has forsaken his red children; he makes your people wax strong every day, and soon they will fill the land; while my people are ebbing away like a fast-receding tide, that will never flow again. The white man's God cannot love his red children or he would protect them. They seem to be orphans and can look nowhere for help. How then can we become brothers? How can your father become our father and bring us prosperity and awaken in us dreams of returning greatness?

Your God seems to us to be partial. He came to the white man. We never saw Him; never even heard His voice; He gave the white man laws but He had no word for His red children whose teeming millions filled this vast continent as the stars fill the firmament. No, we are two distinct races and must ever remain so. There is little in common between us. The ashes of our ancestors are sacred and their final resting place is hallowed ground, while you wander away from the tombs of your fathers seemingly without regret.

Your religion was written on tables of stone by the iron finger of an angry God, lest you might forget it. The red man could never remember nor comprehend it.

Our religion is the traditions of our ancestors, the dreams of our old men, given them by the great Spirit, the visions of our sachems, and is written in the hearts of our peple.

Your dead cease to love you and the homes of their nativity as soon as they pass the portals of the tomb. They wander far off beyond the stars, are soon forgotten, and never return. Our dead never forget the beautiful world that gave them being. They still love its winding rivers, its great mountains and its sequestered vales, and they ever yearn in tenderest affection over the lonely hearted living and often return to visit and comfort them.

Day and night cannot dwell together. The red man has ever fled the approach of the white man, as the changing mists on the mountain side flee before the blazing morning sun.

However, your proposition seems a just one, and I think my folks will accept it and will retire to the reservation you offer them, and we will dwell apart and in peace, for the words of the great white chief seem to be the voice of nature speaking to my people out of the thick darkness that is fast gathering around them like a dense fog floating inward from a midnight sea.

It matters but little where we pass the remainder of our days. They are not many. The Indian's night promises to be dark. No bright star hovers about the horizon. Sad-voiced winds moan in the distance. Some grim Nemesis of our race is on the red man's trail, and wherever he goes he will still hear the sure approaching footsteps of the fell destroyer and prepare to meet his doom, as does the wounded doe that hears the approaching footsteps of the hunter. A few more moons, a few more winters, and not one of all the mighty hosts that once filled this broad land or that now roam in fragmentary bands through these vast solitudes will remain to weep over the tombs of a people once as powerful and hopeful as your own.

But why should we repine? Why should I murmur at the fate of my people? Tribes are made up of individuals and are no better than they. Men come and go like the waves of the sea. A tear, a tamanamus, a dirge, and they are gone from our longing eyes forever. Even the white man, whose God walked and talked with him, as friend to friend, is not exempt from the common destiny. We *may* be brothers after all. We shall see.

We will ponder your proposition, and when we have decided we will tell you. But should we accept it, I here and now make this the first condition: That we will not be denied the privilege, without molestation, of visiting at will the graves of our ancestors and friends. Every part of this country is sacred to my people. Every hillside, every valley, every plain and grove has been hallowed by some fond memory or some sad experience of my tribe. Even the rocks that seem to lie dumb as they swelter in the sun along the silent seashore in solemn grandeur thrill with memories of past events connected with the fate of my people, and the very dust under your feet responds more lovingly to our footsteps than to yours, because it is the ashes of our ancestors, and our bare feet are conscious of the sympathetic touch, for the soil is rich with the life of our kindred.

The sable braves, and fond mothers, and glad-hearted maidens, and the little children who lived and rejoiced here, and those whose very names are now forgotten, still love these solitudes, and their deep fastnesses at eventide grow shadowy with the presence of dusky spirits. And when the last red man shall have perished from the earth and his memory among white men shall have become a myth, these shores shall swarm with the invisible dead of my tribe, and when your children's children shall think themselves alone in the field, the store, the shop, upon the highway or in the silence of the woods they will not be alone. In all the earth there is no place dedicated to solitude. At night, when the streets of your cities and villages shall be silent, and you think them deserted, they will throng with the returning hosts that once filled and still love this beautiful land. The white man will never be alone. Let him be just and deal kindly with my people, for the dead are not altogether powerless.

# 10
# George Perkins Marsh (1801–1882)

By the time he was seven, George Perkins Marsh was reading encyclopedias and studying Greek and Latin; by the time he was thirty he had mastered twenty languages. During his youth in Vermont he spent considerable time outdoors studying nature, and observing the effects of erosion, flooding, and forest degradation. In his many failed business attempts—sheep grower, lumber dealer, and farmer—he also observed the damage done by people's misuse of the land.

Partly for financial reasons, Marsh campaigned for, and won, a seat in Congress where he fought for tariffs on behalf of northern manufacturers, for abolition, and against the annexation of Texas. All of these efforts failed. Virtually the only accomplishment of Marsh's two terms in Congress was helping to found the Smithsonian Institution.

After his congressional career, Marsh held diplomatic positions abroad, which allowed him to travel extensively throughout Europe and the Near East. There he again observed the adverse effects of human practices on nature, except that in Europe and Asia the effects were multiplied by millennia of human impacts.

Drawing upon his experiences in Vermont as well as his travels abroad, Marsh's conservation classic, *Man and Nature,* documented the harmful, often catastrophic, effects of human destructiveness on "nature's harmonies." In the book he proposed corrective measures. His was the first scientific, comprehensive, and extensively documented statement in support of forest and watershed protection in America. Writing at the same time as were the immensely influential English naturalist, Charles Darwin, and the German ecologist, Ernst Haeckel (who coined the term ecology), Marsh also explored the interrelationship between organisms and the physical environment. He wrote that "all nature is linked together by invisible bonds, and every organic creature, however low, however feeble, however dependent, is necessary to the well-being of some other among the myriad forms of life with which the Creator has peopled the earth." While human activity had produced some devastating effects even before the Industrial Revolution, Marsh argued that each great scientific and technological advancement magnified the disturbing agency of humans. He devoted over half of his book to damage being done to the nation's forests, and as a remedy he advocated a two-fold program of forest preservation plus the creation of new woodlands. Thus his voice was added to the emerging scientific forestry movement in America.

Marsh tempered his argument about the destructive influence of humans with the belief that human control of nature also could yield good results. By properly managing the environment, "higher-order" humans could ensure their survival as a species at the same time as ensuring the survival of other species. While Marsh based many of his arguments on practical, economic considerations, he also believed that an educated public would, through "enlightened self-interest," find an ethical basis for a new relationship between humans and the land. Echoes of Marsh's ideas can be found today in the work of the influential scientist and author Edward O. Wilson, whose writings we shall encounter later.

---

# "MAN IS EVERYWHERE A DISTURBING AGENT"*

The object of the present volume is: to indicate the character and, approximately, the extent of the changes produced by human action in the physical conditions of the globe we inhabit; to point out the dangers of imprudence and the necessity of caution in all operations which, on a large scale, interfere with the spontaneous arrangements of the organic or the inorganic world; to suggest the possibility and the importance of the restoration of disturbed harmonies and the material improvement of waste and exhausted regions; and incidentally, to illustrate the doctrine, that man is, in both kind and degree, a power of a higher order than any of the other forms of animated life, which, like him, are nourished at the table of bounteous nature....

Man has too long forgotten that the earth was given to him for usufruct alone, not for consumption, still less for profligate waste. Nature has provided against the absolute destruction of any of her elementary matter, the raw material of her works; the thunderbolt and the tornado, the most convulsive throes of even the volcano and the earthquake, being only phenomena of decomposition and recomposition. But she has left it within the power of man irreparably to derange the combinations of inorganic matter and of organic life, which through the night of æons she had been proportioning and balancing, to prepare the earth for his habitation, when, in the fulness of time, his Creator should call him forth to enter into its possession.

Apart from the hostile influence of man, the organic and the inorganic world are, as I have remarked, bound together by such mutual relations and adaptations as secure, if not the absolute permanence and equilibrium of both, a long continuance of the established conditions of each at any given time and place, or at least, a very slow and gradual succession of changes in those conditions. But man is everywhere a disturbing agent. Wherever he plants his foot, the harmonies of nature are turned to discords. The proportions and accommodations which insured the stability of existing arrangements are overthrown. Indigenous vegetable and animal species are extirpated, and supplanted by others of foreign origin, spontaneous production is forbidden or restricted, and the face of the earth is either laid bare or covered with a new and reluctant growth of vegetable forms, and with alien tribes of animal life. These intentional changes and substitutions constitute, indeed, great revolutions; but vast as is their magnitude and importance,

---

*George P. Marsh. 1864. *Man and Nature; or Physical Geography as Modified by Human Action*. London: Sampson Low, Son and Marston, pp. iii, 35–48. Footnotes are omitted.

they are, as we shall see, insignificant in comparison with the contingent and unsought results which have flowed from them.

The fact that, of all organic beings, man alone is to be regarded as essentially a destructive power, and that he wields energies to resist which, nature—that nature whom all material life and all inorganic substance obey—is wholly impotent, tends to prove that, though living in physical nature, he is not of her, that he is of more exalted parentage, and belongs to a higher order of existences than those born of her womb and submissive to her dictates.

There are, indeed, brute destroyers, beasts and birds and insects of prey—all animal life feeds upon, and, of course, destroys other life,—but this destruction is balanced by compensations. It is, in fact, the very means by which the existence of one tribe of animals or of vegetables is secured against being smothered by the encroachments of another; and the reproductive powers of species, which serve as the food of others, are always proportioned to the demand they are destined to supply. Man pursues his victims with reckless destructiveness; and, while the sacrifice of life by the lower animals is limited by the cravings of appetite, he unsparingly persecutes, even to extirpation, thousands of organic forms which he cannot consume.

The earth was not, in its natural condition, completely adapted to the use of man, but only to the sustenance of wild animals and wild vegetation. These live, multiply their kind in just proportion, and attain their perfect measure of strength and beauty, without producing or requiring any change in the natural arrangements of surface, or in each other's spontaneous tendencies, except such mutual repression of excessive increase as may prevent the extirpation of one species by the encroachments of another. In short, without man, lower animal and spontaneous vegetable life would have been constant in type, distribution, and proportion, and the physical geography of the earth would have remained undisturbed for indefinite periods, and been subject to revolution only from possible, unknown cosmical causes, or from geological action.

But man, the domestic animals that serve him, the field and garden plants the products of which supply him with food and clothing, cannot subsist and rise to the full development of their higher properties, unless brute and unconscious nature be effectually combated, and, in a great degree, vanquished by human art. Hence, a certain measure of transformation of terrestrial surface, of suppression of natural, and stimulation of artificially modified productivity becomes necessary. This measure man has unfortunately exceeded. He has felled the forests whose network of fibrous roots bound the mould to the rocky skeleton of the earth; but had he allowed here and there a belt of woodland to reproduce itself by spontaneous propagation, most of the mischiefs which his reckless destruction of the natural protection of the soil has occasioned would have been averted. He has broken up the mountain reservoirs, the percolation of whose waters through unseen channels supplied the fountains that refreshed his cattle and fertilized his fields; but he has neglected to maintain the cisterns and the canals of irrigation which a wise antiquity had constructed to neutralize the consequences of its own imprudence. While he has torn the thin glebe which confined the light earth of extensive plains, and has destroyed the fringe of semi-aquatic plants which skirted the coast and checked the drifting of the sea sand, he has failed to prevent the spreading of the dunes by clothing them with artificially propagated vegetation. He has ruthlessly warred on all the tribes of animated nature whose spoil he could convert to his own uses, and he has not protected the birds which prey on the insects most destructive to his own harvests.

Purely untutored humanity, it is true, interferes comparatively little with the arrangements of nature, and the destructive agency of man becomes more and more energetic and unsparing as he advances in civilization, until the impoverishment, with which his exhaustion of the natural resources of the soil is threatening him, at last awakens him to the necessity of preserving what is left, if not of restoring what has been wantonly wasted. The wandering savage grows no cultivated vegetable, fells no forest, and extirpates no useful plant, no noxious weed. If his skill in the chase enables him to entrap numbers of the animals on which he feeds, he compensates this loss by destroying also the lion, the tiger, the wolf, the otter, the seal, and the eagle, thus indirectly protecting the feebler quadrupeds and fish and fowls, which would otherwise become the booty of beasts and birds of prey. But with stationary life, or rather with the pastoral state, man at once commences an almost indiscriminate warfare upon all the forms of animal and vegetable existence around him, and as he advances in civilization, he gradually eradicates or transforms every spontaneous product of the soil he occupies....

It has been maintained by authorities as high as any known to modern science, that the action of man upon nature, though greater in *degree*, does not differ in *kind*, from that of wild animals. It appears to me to differ in essential character, because, though it is often followed by unforeseen and undesired results, yet it is nevertheless guided by a self-conscious and intelligent will aiming as often at secondary and remote as at immediate objects. The wild animal, on the other hand, acts instinctively, and, so far as we are able to perceive, always with a view to single and direct purposes. The backwoodsman and the beaver alike fell trees; the man that he may convert the forest into an olive grove that will mature its fruit only for a succeeding generation, the beaver that he may feed upon their bark or use them in the construction of his habitation. Human differs from brute action, too, in its influence upon the material world, because it is not controlled by natural compensations and balances. Natural arrangements, once disturbed by man, are not restored until he retires from the field, and leaves free scope to spontaneous recuperative energies; the wounds he inflicts upon the material creation are not healed until he withdraws the arm that gave the blow. On the other hand, I am not aware of any evidence that wild animals have ever destroyed the smallest forest, extirpated any organic species, or modified its natural character, occasioned any permanent change of terrestrial surface, or produced any disturbance of physical conditions which nature has not, of herself, repaired without the expulsion of the animal that had caused it.

The form of geographical surface, and very probably the climate of a given country, depend much on the character of the vegetable life belonging to it. Man has, by domestication, greatly changed the habits and properties of the plants he rears; he has, by voluntary selection, immensely modified the forms and qualities of the animated creatures that serve him; and he has, at the same time, completely rooted out many forms of both vegetable and animal being. What is there, in the influence of brute life, that corresponds to this? We have no reason to believe that in that portion of the American continent which, though peopled by many tribes of quadruped and fowl, remained uninhabited by man, or only thinly occupied by purely savage tribes, any sensible geographical change had occurred within twenty centuries before the epoch of discovery and colonization, while, during the same period, man had changed millions of square miles, in the fairest and most fertile regions of the Old World, into the barrenest deserts.

The ravages committed by man subvert the relations and destroy the balance which nature had established between her organized and her inorganic creations; and she avenges herself upon the intruder, by letting loose upon her defaced provinces destructive energies hitherto kept in check by organic forces destined to be his best auxiliaries, but which he has unwisely dispersed and driven from the field of action. When the forest is gone, the great reservoir of moisture stored up in its vegetable mould is evaporated, and returns only in deluges of rain to wash away the parched dust into which that mould has been converted. The well-wooded and humid hills are turned to ridges of dry rock, which encumbers the low grounds and chokes the watercourses with its debris, and—except in countries favored with an equable distribution of rain through the seasons, and a moderate and regular inclination of surface—the whole earth, unless rescued by human art from the physical degradation to which it tends, becomes an assemblage of bald mountains, of barren, turfless hills, and of swampy and malarious plains. There are parts of Asia Minor, of Northern Africa, of Greece, and even of Alpine Europe, where the operation of causes set in action by man has brought the face of the earth to a desolation almost as complete as that of the moon; and though, within that brief space of time which we call "the historical period," they are known to have been covered with luxuriant woods, verdant pastures, and fertile meadows, they are now too far deteriorated to be reclaimable by man, nor can they become again fitted for human use, except through great geological changes, or other mysterious influences or agencies of which we have no present knowledge, and over which we have no prospective control. The earth is fast becoming an unfit home for its noblest inhabitant, and another era of equal human crime and human improvidence, and of like duration with that through which traces of that crime and that improvidence extend, would reduce it to such a condition of impoverished productiveness, of shattered surface, of climatic excess, as to threaten the depravation, barbarism, and perhaps even extinction of the species....

True, there is a partial reverse to this picture. On narrow theatres, new forests have been planted; inundations of flowing streams restrained by heavy walls of masonry and other constructions; torrents compelled to aid, by depositing the slime with which they are charged, in filling up lowlands, and raising the level of morasses which their own overflows had created;

ground submerged by the encroachments of the ocean, or exposed to be covered by its tides, has been rescued from its dominion by diking; swamps and even lakes have been drained, and their beds brought within the domain of agricultural industry; drifting coast dunes have been checked and made productive by plantation; seas and inland waters have been repeopled with fish, and even the sands of the Sahara have been fertilized by artesian fountains. These achievements are more glorious than the proudest triumphs of war, but, thus far, they give but faint hope that we shall yet make full atonement for our spendthrift waste of the bounties of nature.

# 11
# William Graham Sumner (1840–1910)

Yale University Professor William Graham Sumner is often identified with Social Darwinism, that complex of economic, political, and social ideas that sought to parallel Charles Darwin's theory of evolution. Sumner, who began his career as a theologian, was heavily influenced by English philosopher Herbert Spencer and his *Study of Sociology*. In the tradition of Thomas Hobbes, Spencer's theories about the functioning of human societies stressed the negative: that there is a need for a strong state to maintain law and order, that society can be likened to a jungle where only the fittest survive, and that life outside civil society and in the state of nature is even worse than life in it.

While some scholars have argued that Professor Sumner himself was not attempting to formulate a Darwinian social theory, nevertheless his sociological writings reflect a deep appreciation for Darwin and Spencer. He spoke of the struggle for existence, defended selfish individualism, and justified unfettered laissez-faire, monopolies, and the concentration of wealth. Contrary to Enlightenment principles, Sumner argued that humans did not begin life endowed with natural rights or with equal access to the plentiful material goods of the earth. Only by eliminating competitors and succeeding in the struggle to conquer nature did civilized beings evolve. The various social classes owed nothing to one another.

Sumner's work was a reaction to several social developments and intellectual ideas extant in the United States at the time. These included labor turmoil and the organizing efforts of the nation's first unions, socialist and populist critiques of the gross inequities in wealth and power between rich and poor, and especially the writings of Henry George, whose *Progress and Poverty* (1879) proposed the "single tax" as a way of alleviating land monopoly and poverty. (The single tax advocated smashing concentrated wealth by heavily taxing the increase in the value of bare land—the unearned increment—as communities grew up around it; all other taxes on buildings and improvements, which benefitted the general community, would be abolished.)

Sumner's conservative responses to the labor and land reform movements of the late nineteenth century clearly earned him the approval of many of the era's industrial and corporate titans. But he also was a popular professor at Yale, whose students appreciated his outspoken and iconoclastic manner.

Toward the end of the century Social Darwinism became linked to ideas that justified racism, militarism, and imperialism, in addition to economic laissez-faire. Its influence diminished as public dissatisfaction with the excesses of the Gilded Age grew, and as the Progressive movement gained influence. By the time of World War I (1914), efforts to ground social theory in a Darwinian context largely had become passé.

# "NATURE [IS] A HARD-FISTED STEP-MOTHER"*

In former times, when the efforts of man to lift himself by his boot-straps were expended, not upon social enterprises, but upon enterprises in physics and the art of medicine, the reigning idols of desire were the philosopher's stone, the panacea, the fountain of youth, etc. The distinctive mark of this boastful century of ours is likely to be in history that it was the one in which the old delusions and self-deceptions of humanity, driven at last from the domain of physics by the advance of science, retreated to the domain of social phenomena and there entrenched themselves for another attempt to re-attain dominion. Accordingly we hear now about the "Banquet of Life," the "Boon of Nature," the "Patrimony of the Disinherited," and other fine phrases of the same class, all of which take for granted the question of most serious import in the whole range of interest to which they apply, viz., whether there really are any such things?

The question whether man comes into this world provided by Nature with an outfit of some kind; whether he finds any endowment awaiting him; whether he is started on the struggle for existence with some chances predetermined in his favor by Nature; whether he enters into a natural estate; whether Nature fits him out with any natural rights; whether he comes into the world as man goes to a banquet, which somebody has prepared for him, and to which he goes not by invitation, but of right; whether Nature's attitude to him is at all that of boon-giver; whether he is born to happiness and has a right to complain, if he does not have a good time, without regard to his behavior—or whether man has never found in Nature anything but a hard-fisted step-mother, who would yield only what was extorted from her; whether he has not had to conquer every good thing which he possesses; whether all rights and liberty are not a product of civilization—are questions which must be answered by an appeal to history. With the means now at our disposal there can be no doubt as to the answer. We can find no sentiment whatever in Nature; that all comes from man. We can find no disposition at all in Nature to conform her operations to man's standards, so as to do what is pleasant or advantageous to man rather than anything else. Before the tribunal of Nature a man has no more right to life than a rattle-snake; he has no more right to liberty than any wild beast; his right to the pursuit of happiness is nothing but a license to maintain the struggle for existence, if he can find within himself the powers with which to do it. In civilized society the right to live turns into the guarantee that he shall not be murdered by his fellow-men, a right which is a creation of law, order and civilization, and is guaranteed by nothing less than the stability of the social order as it has been inherited and now is. Liberty is an enlargement of earthly chances for the

---

*William Graham Sumner. 1887. "The Boon of Nature," *The Independent*. 39 (October 27): pp. 1380–1381.

individual against Nature, which has been won by generations of toil and suffering, and which depends upon civilization, as it is the product of it; the right to the pursuit of happiness is nothing but the right to live one's life out in one's own way. Instead of lying back at the origin of society it lies yet a great way in the future, when the present disposition of every one to tell his neighbors how they ought to live shall have been overcome. Probably the primitive savage was happy according to his standards. If even it were true that primitive men had and enjoyed some boon of Nature, how can it be imagined that a civilized society could get happiness for its members according to the standards of civilized society, while re-establishing any of the facts and conditions of primitive savage life? If we had to go back to the origin of civilization to get the boon, how much would the boon be worth?

In truth there is no boon, and never was. Nothing could well be more contradictory to the facts as they appear than the notion of such a thing.

It is said, of course, that the earth is the boon, that is to say, the "land." The notion which has been caught up is that the land is a gift of Nature to all and that some have monopolized it. How many were the "all" to whom it was given? How many are the "some" who have monopolized it? Plainly what is meant and ought to be said is, that the land was given to many and has been monopolized by a few. This is the very opposite of the truth. The earth was given to a few, and civilization has made it available to a large number. Monopoly is in Nature, and liberty, or relaxation of monopoly, is one of the triumphs of civilization. The "land" in this connection is a very delusive expression. Every man who stands on the earth's surface excludes every one else from so much of it as he covers. Every one who eats a loaf of bread appropriates to himself for the time-being the exclusive use and enjoyment of so many square feet of the earth's surface as were required to raise the wheat. Every one who burns wood to warm himself, or uses the fiber of cotton or wool to clothe himself, appropriates in monopoly a part of the land so far as the land is of utility or interest to man. Perhaps the most fundamental fact which makes this world a world of toil and self-denial is that two men cannot eat the same loaf of bread. This pitiless and hopeless monopoly is, in the last analysis, the reason for capital and rent, for property and rights, for law and the state, for poverty and inequality.

There are many reasons why it would appear more correct to say that Nature gave man to the earth than that she gave the earth to man. If we try to form a notion of the condition of the man who first received the boon in its fresh originality, before any body had stolen or appropriated it, we find that it was given to him in just the same sense in which it was given to the other animals, only that they had priority and were already in full possession. Man was far superior to them in organization, and he displaced them; but the nearer we get back to the pure boon, the more we find man like the other animals in his mode of existence, his grade of comfort, his standard of happiness, his relation to the "land," and his subjection to Nature. If now, we build houses several stories high, so that several men can, in effect, stand on the same square feet of the earth's surface, or if we make the same number of square feet bear two loaves of bread instead of one, we break the monopoly of Nature, but we do it by capital and the arts of civilization. Whatever we have, therefore, which is worth having is not a boon of Nature, but a conquest of civilization from Nature.

If we look at any part of the earth's surface in a state of Nature as it is when given to man, instead of finding that it fills any notion of gift or boon, we find that it offers a task of appalling magnitude. It is covered with trees, or stones, or swamps; or hostile animals of various kinds occupy it; or malaria stands guard over it. Between the "boon" and any use by man stands a series of obstacles to be overcome, dangerous and toilsome work to be done. It is a chance for the man to maintain the struggle for existence if he is strong enough to conquer obstacles. If not, then he may lie down and die of despair on the face of the boon and not a breeze, or a leaflet, or a sunbeam will vary its due course to help or pity him. This is the only attitude in which we find Nature when we come face to face with her in her original attitude toward mankind. It is only when we come to meet her, armed with knowledge, science, and capital that we force back her limitations and win some wider and easier chances of existence for ourselves.

Robinson Crusoe enjoyed the boon of Nature. He climbed to the top of his island and looked about, "monarch of all he surveyed," not a human soul to divide or dispute it with him. He sank down in despair, thinking himself the most miserable of living creatures, just because he had the boon all to himself and because the maintenance of his existence was such a crushing task. How many men in the United States to-day could maintain their existence each on a square mile of land, in its natural condition, in the temperate zone, if they were cut off from society and civilization?

Only the rudest and strongest men are now capable of breaking up land in a state of nature, and beginning the reduction of it to human use, even when they have the resources of the arts and capital, and are supported and reinforced all the time by a strong civilized society behind them. There are millions of acres of the "boon" now open to any one who will go to them, and none go but those who are at the same time physically the strongest and socially the worst off of living men. The existing land-owners of the United States are represented to be holding, unjustly, exclusive possession of what Nature had given to us all. In the sixteenth century the whole territory now in this Union stood free and open, entirely unappropriated by white men. Every one of the numerous attempts that were made to establish settlements of white men here failed. Instead of finding Nature holding out a boon which they had only to take, they found her waiting for them with famine, cold and disease. The settlement at Jamestown barely maintained itself against the hardships and toil of its situation. The Plymouth settlement would not have survived its first winter if the Indians, instead of being hostile, had not given aid. No settlement was established until it was supported by capital and maintained through a period of struggles and first conquest over Nature, by reinforcements from a secured and established civilization in the old world.

There is no boon in Nature. All the blessings we enjoy are the fruits of labor, toil, self-denial and study.

# 12
# John Wesley Powell (1834–1902)

Explorer, geologist, anthropologist, and Civil War hero, John Wesley Powell explored the Colorado and Green Rivers on what has been called the last great exploration within the continental United States. He detailed the three-month, 1,000 mile, 1869 journey in his *Exploration of the Colorado River of the West and its Tributaries* (1875). Powell's adventures made him a national hero, and he used his fame to successfully lobby Congress to fund more surveys, including a second expedition down the Colorado in 1871.

While in the West Powell developed an active interest in Native Americans and their cultures. He helped found the Smithsonian Institution's Bureau of Ethnology. As the second director of the U.S. Geological Survey, which had been established as a scientific agency in 1879, Powell began his topographic mapping project, a project that was not completed until 1991.

Powell recognized—if the clamorous voices promoting western development did not—that in the arid West "mere land is of no value, what is really valuable is the water privilege." In an 1878 report to the Secretary of the Interior, *Report on the Lands of the Arid Region of the United States*, Powell addressed the issue of development in water-scarce areas. Careful planning, he believed, would be needed to identify potential irrigable areas, and cooperative efforts would be required for development: Individual farmers simply did not have sufficient capital or labor to go it alone. Invited to address an 1893 meeting of the International Irrigation Congress, he found the delegates confidently talking as if all the remaining public domain lands could be irrigated. In response he flatly told them that this was not so, and prophetically warned that "you are piling up a heritage of conflict and litigation over water rights, for there is not sufficient water to supply these lands." The delegates booed and shouted him down.

Powell also believed that the physical realities of the West required institutions different from those that had taken root in the East. In his speech before the Montana Constitutional Convention in 1889 he urged the delegates to take a novel approach in drawing their political boundaries. While this proposal of Powell's also went unheeded, his logic is still cogent today as we increasingly recognize the complexities of managing resources across arbitrary political jurisdictions and as we seek innovative ways to govern at the landscape and watershed scale.

John Wesley Powell died in 1902, the same year that Congress passed the Newlands Act, popularly known as the Reclamation Act. This statute established the Bureau of Reclamation and created a federal program for construction and financing of western water development projects. The reclamation program incorporated many—but, significantly, not all—of Powell's ideas about careful and orderly development in the arid lands of the West, as well as the Jeffersonian ideal of promoting small family farms. The federal reclamation program would remake the face of the West in the twentieth century, but as Powell, ever the realist, might have predicted, not in the manner its early proponents envisioned.

---

# "A SYSTEM OF COUNTIES BY DRAINAGE BASINS"*

Mr. President, and Gentlemen, it is with some degree of embarrassment that I speak to you after the distinguished gentlemen who have spoken today, and who have discussed national affairs so eloquently and so ably to you. In such discussion I have taken no part. I came to this country rather as a pioneer. I am older in this country than most of you. I feel as though most of you were new comers here and were tenderfeet. I came at an early time, and I want to talk now as one of the old pioneers, if you please, and not in the capacity of a statesman. It has fallen under my observation from time to time and been a source—a theme of study for many years, the general question what would ultimately become of this country what would be the form of the industries in this country and the form of government in this country? For you are under peculiar conditions. In the eastern half of the United States we have settled governments, that is we have state and local governments adapted to the physical conditions of their country; but in the western half of America, the local, the state, the territorial, county governments and the regulations and the national government are in no sense adapted to the physical conditions of the country. And these are the problems which have been interesting me for many years, and I will illustrate it by simply stating somewhat of the physical conditions of this state now forming, and explain to you what seems to me as an old pioneer, not as a statesman, if you please—what seems to me to be the form of local government and the adaptation of institutions of these physical conditions, which are necessary for your prosperity, and which you will, as I believe, ultimately have. Montana has an area of about, if my memory serves me, ninety millions of acres. Of that ninety millions thirty-five millions of acres are mountainous—thirty-five millions of acres of land are dedicated to special industries thereby. In those mountains you will find silver and gold, copper, lead, and in the mountains more or less iron, in the flanks iron and coal. But the mountain region has something more in it of value, as you will see. The mountain region is the timber region of the country. On the plains and in the valleys no timber grows. The regions below are in part agricultural and in part pastural. And the remaining portion, leaving out the mountain area, about thirty-five million acres of land, can be redeemed by irrigation, according to the latest estimates and careful study of the matter, which we have made for

---

*John Wesley Powell. 1921. Address to the Montana Constitutional Convention, Friday, August 9, 1889, in *Proceedings and Debates of the Constitutional Convention held in the City of Helena, Montana, July 4, 1889, August 17, 1889*. Helena, MT: State Publishing Company, pp. 820–823.

the last two years. It must be understood that if thirty-five million acres of land were redeemed by irrigation in this country, it means the utilization of all its waters—it means that no drop of water, which is the blood of agriculture, if you please, the life blood of agriculture—that no drop of water falling within the area of the state shall flow beyond the boundaries of the state. It means that all the waters falling within the state will be utilized upon its lands for agriculture. That is made under some careful estimate and partial estimate of the volumes of water running in your streams, a study of the rainfall of a district, and upon a further computation that it will take one acre of water to irrigate one acre of land. Now, understand what I mean by one acre of water, for as engineers we do not reckon water in inches of flow, but in acre feet. An acre of water one foot in depth we call an acre foot, and on an average in Montana for years, irrigation of an acre of land requires an acre foot of water. It is a very simple ratio as you see. If all of the water flowing in the streams of Montana be used—not all the water flowing during the season of irrigation, but all of the water is used in irrigation, it will irrigate about thirty-five million acres; but in order to utilize all of this water and to redeem all of this land it becomes necessary to store the waters which are usually run to waste; that is the season of irrigation in Montana will vary from six weeks to nine weeks; in some few cases it will be longer than that, but in the main we may say that the time of irrigation, the season of irrigation will be about two months. With that understanding, ten months of the flow runs to waste, and in order that the thirty-five million acres of land be redeemed for agriculture within this state, it is necessary to use all that water running to waste to the sea—to store it. Then there remains twenty million acres of land which cannot be used for agriculture, which are yet in the mountains and not covered by timber, but which yet have more or less value for pasturage purposes. That is the condition, and, gentlemen, it is a magnificent heritage—ninety million acres of land: thirty-five million acres of mountains covered with forests, and with mountains filled with ores—thirty-five million acres of land as rich as any other that lies under the sun, to be made fertile, to be made to yield in vast abundance by the utilization of these waters. It is no misfortune as at first it may appear—it is no ultimate misfortune to the people that their land is arid. The thirty-five million acres of land which you have to redeem by irrigation will be to you much more valuable than if that water was distributed evenly over the country so that there was sufficient rainfall and irrigation was unnecessary. To those who have not studied the subject with care, the proposition seems perhaps somewhat quixotic, and yet there is a long line of history to prove what I have said. I will not stop to enter upon this line of the subject, but I wish to call the attention of you gentlemen to some of the conditions which you must meet in order to secure the prosperity of these people. The question of irrigation then is undoubtedly bound up with some other questions of almost equal importance, as you will see as I proceed. The timber of this country grows on the mountains; it is therefore not distributed throughout the country where it is needed. The agricultural people will have their timber lands five, ten, twenty, fifty and one hundred miles away from home, but the people who want to use that timber and who live down in the valleys and spread abroad over the plains, they are the people primarily interested in the forests, and the people who own the irrigable lands must own and must control the forest lands, for a part of their prosperity depends upon the utilization and preservation of those forests. There is still another reason. In the mountainous region like those in the arid country, a large part of the rain falls upon the mountains. Usually throughout Montana you have say from twelve to fifteen inches of rainfall in the low country and from twenty to twenty-five, forty, fifty and even sixty inches of rainfall on the mountains. The water necessary to fertilize the agricultural lands falls somewhere else—falls upon these mountains. And the men who are engaged in agriculture in the valleys and on the plains are interested in the mountains for another reason than that they must derive their source of timber from them. Every iota of value there is to the lands to be redeemed for agriculture depends upon the water with which they are supplied. The intrinsic value exists in the water. And the water falls not on their own land—the water falls elsewhere in the mountains, and hence the people who live by agriculture below have a double reason for being interested in the forests and mountains above, and ultimately they must control those mountain acres—the agriculturists must own and control not only the lands which they occupy themselves, but also the lands where the timbers grow, and also the lands where the waters fall which make their lands valuable. Now, having made this brief statement of the conditions and the facts at large, let me apply them. The state is in the formative condition. You are met here to adopt a constitution, and there are questions that ultimately will be of vast interest to these people—and I beg pardon almost for mentioning them, but I have mentioned them from the standard not of a statesman but only of a pioneer—a man in the country earlier than occupants usually and you must take them only for what they are worth from an observer, and not a statesman. But this is the point. The whole area of Montana may be easily divided into drainage basin districts of country which constitute a geographical—a physical unity; a region like the Gallatin Valley, for example, with a river flowing down through the valley with its tributaries on either side, heading out from the mountains to the very rim of the Gallatin basin on either side. Every man who settles within the valley of Gallatin comes ultimately to be interested in every part of that valley, because it is the entire Gallatin valley, the whole drainage basin, gathers the water for his farm. Only a portion of these valleys can be redeemed for agriculture; another portion will be utilized ultimately for pasturage. High up in the valleys we have the timber lands, and higher up the valleys we have the mountains where the waters are condensed. The people below must necessarily be interested in the whole drainage basin around about where these waters are gathered. Now, agricultural industry carried on under conditions where irrigation is absolutely necessary, are carried on under very peculiar conditions as compared with those of humid lands. You have not in this territory reached a condition of affairs where the matters which I now wish to present to you yet press upon you. They may in some few localities only; but very speedily the question of water rights—who owns this water, is to be the important question in this country, remember the question of land rights is comparatively a minor one as compared with water rights, and water cannot be measured out to you by meets and bounds; you cannot lay out lines and drive stakes in the clouds of the heavens from whence the waters come. They pour down today in storms and tomorrow in storms, and the year in storms, and flow down to the rivers and creeks, and you have to measure them out by gallons or by acres from day to day, from month to month and from year to year. All the great values of this Territory have ultimately to be measured to you in acre feet, and in the preparation of a constitution for this great State this great fact should be held in view. Now, without entering too largely into the question of pointing out the necessities for regulating the use of waters and the measurement of waters etc., I want to present to you what I believe to be ultimately the political system which you have got to adopt in this country, and which the United States will be compelled sooner or later ultimately to recognize. I think that each drainage basin in the arid land must ultimately become the practical unity of organization, and it would be wise if you could immediately adopt a county system which would be coincident with drainage basins, for in every such drainage basin you have got to have first the water courts. Disputes will arise from day to day about the waters, and in every district there must be ultimately a water court. There must be a corps of officers, water master or supervisors who measure out this water for the people. The general government cannot, the State government will not measure the water for you, neither can they measure it for themselves, and you have got to have local self government to manage that matter. Then the people who are interested in these waters are also interested in the timber, and the people who are interested in the waters and agricultural lands are interested in the pasturage of those lands. And now I come briefly to state what I believe should be done. First, I believe that the primary unity of organization in the arid lands should be the drainage basin which would practically have a county organization, if you please, with county courts, etc.—I need not enter into the details—then that the government of the United States should cede all of the lands of that drainage basin to the people who live in that basin. I do not believe that the government of the United States can ever keep up a police force or a system of agents to manage the timber of this country. I believe that the people of the drainage basin themselves are more interested than any other people can be in that particular drainage basin—that they are the only people who can properly administer that trust, and I believe that the people who live along every valley in this country should be the people who control three things besides the land on which they live; they should have the control of the water; they should have the control of the common or pasturage lands, and they should have the control of the timber lands; and I have no doubt but that could be secured through general legislation ultimately in this country, for the interests of this western country are being rapidly understood in the east, and the people are filling up the country so rapidly that they are very soon to be able to make the eastern people respect their wants, their needs, their rights and their wishes. The simple question which I have then to present to you, which I think would be worthy of your consideration, and which early in the history of the State or even in the adoption of your State constitution you should consider, is, what should be the primary unit of your government?

And I think that the careful study of the matter will show you that the drainage basin is the natural unit and should be a county of this State. If then you will provide a system of counties by drainage basins you have the fundamental organizations, and can in time acquire all the other rights and assume all the other duties which that organization demands. For thirty odd years I have been studying this western country when no irrigation was practical except in a few places in Utah and New Mexico and so I have been traveling about the country from year to year surveying now this portion and now that, and studying from many standpoints, and I have seen gradually agricultural industries growing up, and today within the arid region not less than seven million acres of land are cultivated by artificial irrigation, but the time will soon come when this will be multiplied tenfold and one hundredfold, for everywhere throughout the whole region west of the one hundredth meridian the people are wide awake to this problem. The mountains may be filled with gold and silver; the hills may be filled with coal and iron, but all these have little value unless there is a basis of agriculture for a prosperous people, and that you can have in all of this country. But in order that you may not have vast conflicts, in order that irrigation may be developed, that agriculture may be developed, with the least friction, with the least cost of the people, the system which I have mentioned will be of untold value. Let me call your attention to two more points just here. The first is, that litigation is a prolific source of expense and evil, and you should endeavor to provide for a proper system at the very beginning of your State for adjusting rights by your fellow citizens among yourselves. It will save you—you hardly know how much—unless you have studied irrigation in other lands you will hardly know how much, but it will save you a vast cloud, a vast amount of litigation, let me repeat once more to you and close with this, that you have three interests, all tied together, and they ought to be tied together in the organization of your body politic as they are tied together by physical conditions. The agricultural lands are dependent upon the mountains above, and the farmers below ought to know the mountains above—own the control of those mountains so far as they are the source of the timber which they must use, and own and control them so far as they are pasturage is concerned, for pasturage on a large scale, the range pasturage which has grown up in all of this western country must necessarily decay as such and must become tied up with the agriculture of the land; not that there will be less, but more stock raising in the country then, but it will be distributed instead of in the hands of the few people—it will be distributed ultimately among all those who cultivate the soil.

I thank you gentlemen for your attention.

# DISCUSSION QUESTIONS

1. In terms of having a revolutionary impact upon virtually all facets of American life, the invention of the computer in the twentieth century may be analogous to the nineteenth-century invention of the steam engine and the railroad. Discuss how the "information superhighway" will impact environmental and natural resources policies in ways that we might not have anticipated.

2. Discuss John Wesley Powell's concept of shaping political institutions and policies in concert with geographic constraints or natural features. How, for example, would the American West look today if political leaders had followed his recommendations regarding the watershed as the unit for political decision making? Do we need new political boundaries to reflect the ecosystems/watershed management approaches that are now emerging? If so, what would they look like?

3. Frederick Law Olmsted's experience with the people's park at Birkenhead, England, heavily influenced his involvement with the nascent parks movement in the United States. What lessons today might the United States borrow from other countries that might improve our approaches to environmental policy? How are Olmsted's moral and ethical arguments still enjoined in support of public places, such as city parks, national parks and forests? What might a Social Darwinist like William Graham Sumner say about setting aside public places like parks and forests?

4. The authenticity of Chief Seattle's speech has been questioned, and modern embellishments to it criticized, as efforts to romanticize Native Americans' relationship to the environment. Discuss what is known about Native Americans' use of their land and resources, and debate whether Anglos, even today, romanticize Indian culture.

5. The views on "man and nature" by George Perkins Marsh and William Graham Sumner are about as diametrically opposed as imaginable. Summarize each author's arguments. Who has the stronger argument, and why? Are these views in evidence in contemporary debates over environmental policy? If so, how?

# PART III

## "Conservation Is a Great Moral Issue"*
### FROM THE PROGRESSIVE ERA
### TO THE GREAT DEPRESSION, 1900–1932

A s Americans witnessed the growing concentration of economic power in the hands of a select few, and widespread corruption of the political process, the turn-of-the-century Progressive Movement gained momentum. Topping the Progressive agenda was an effort to curb the power of the huge firms that had gained tremendous political and economic advantage in the late nineteenth century by exploiting resources and corrupting legislatures. In President Theodore Roosevelt, the New York Republican who earned a reputation as a crusading reformer from the moment he entered politics, Progressives found the perfect voice to speak out loudly and frequently about the evils of monopoly capitalism. The Roosevelt Administration (1901–1909) began its trust-busting with the powerful railroads; it then challenged mining, power, oil, sugar, and water interests. In all, more than forty antitrust suits were brought during Roosevelt's years in the White House; and some ninety more were brought by the Democratic reformer, Woodrow Wilson, during his eight years in office (1913–1921).

Progressives in both political parties not only challenged corporate power during the first two decades of the twentieth century, they also introduced numerous political and social reforms, including the primary election, the initiative, referendum, and recall. These reforms sought to weaken the power of party bosses by giving citizens a more direct voice in governance.

---

*Theodore Roosevelt. 1910. Speech at Osawatomie, Kansas, August 31.

Progressives also broadened the electoral base by supporting the popular election of United States Senators (the Seventeenth Amendment), and by giving women the vote (the Nineteenth Amendment). They imposed a progressive income tax (Sixteenth Amendment), and instituted prohibition (Eighteenth Amendment).

Like Presidents Jefferson, Jackson, and Lincoln, Theodore Roosevelt enlarged the powers of the presidency. He used the office as a "bully pulpit" to pursue a thoroughly progressive agenda which included trust-busting, consumer protection, public health, clean government, and conservation of natural resources. He was most proud of his accomplishments in the conservation area, for he was a genuine lover of nature. As a child he became a self-taught naturalist; as a college student he devoted himself to "the strenuous life"; and as a young man mourning the death of his wife he went to the Badlands of South Dakota to find solace in a landscape that mirrored his dark feelings. During the years he spent out West, he became well versed in the problems of range management and wildlife husbandry, so that when he ascended to the presidency at the young age of forty-one, he was as educated as was Thomas Jefferson in the natural sciences.

For Roosevelt, the proper management of nature's resources could not be separated from other problems encountered in governing the nation. With his friend and confidant, Gifford Pinchot, he shared a utilitarian philosophy that stressed efficiency, expertise, wise use, sustained yield, and minimal waste. Thus, the purpose of a governmental program of conservation was to curb the excesses of the extractive industries and not completely eliminate those uses. Roosevelt, Pinchot, and others of the Progressive Era believed in a strong federal presence that would act as a countervailing power to the private sector—whatever the policy arena. Consequently, Roosevelt's eight years in the presidency mark a radical revision not only in the nation's policies toward natural resources but in other domestic and foreign policy sectors as well. An economically powerful America needed, Roosevelt believed, an equally powerful government.

His most significant acts included the creation of an Inland Waterways Commission and his enthusiastic support of the Reclamation Act of 1902, establishing the Bureau of Reclamation. The act created a fund from the sale of public lands to finance western irrigation projects. He used the Antiquities Act of 1906 (which gave the president exclusive power to preserve features of historic, prehistoric, and scientific interest by proclamation) to set aside twenty-three national monuments in eleven states and the territory of Alaska. Using his authority under the Antiquities Act and the 1891 Forest Reserve Act, Roosevelt began what evolved into a national system of game refuges. He transferred the forest reserves from the Department of the Interior to the Department of Agriculture, established the U.S. Forest Service (1905), and appointed Gifford Pinchot its first chief. When Congress passed legislation in 1907 sharply curtailing the president's power to create additional forest reserves, Roosevelt huddled with Pinchot to identify the most valuable parcels still needing federal protection: Literally overnight, before the legislation took effect, Roosevelt added another 16 million acres to the national forests. He established a National Conservation Commission, and in 1908 convened a White House governors' conference on conservation. When he left the White House a year later he was working on plans for a global conservation conference, an event that never took place because conservation was not high on the agenda of his hand-picked successor, William Howard Taft.

"Efficiency" was a core concept to those who led the Progressive Movement. Inspired, in part, by the writings of mechanical engineer and business consultant Frederick W. Taylor, Progressive conservationists allied themselves with the "scientific management" movement, which promoted efficiency in industrial operations and the professionalization of corporate management. Taylor's prescriptions for centralization of power, for a greater degree of expertise in problem-solving, for separation of planners from doers, and for increased specialization of functions extended well beyond the corporate sphere; it became an integral part of the Progressive conservationists' approach to resource management. Indeed, the movement's belief in rationality and science became reflected in all sectors of society, whether it was the corporate world, government, or academia. The scholar, Arthur Bentley, for example, argued that the investigation of group activity in American politics would eventually lead to a "political science," i.e., a scientific understanding of the governmental process. It was an era in which new scientific disciplines sprouted up almost overnight, including several social sciences. So complete was the Progressives' faith in science and progress that a leading historian described their world view as promoting "the gospel of efficiency."

But there was another vision of nature prevalent during the environmental movement's formative period. The famous naturalist and founder of the Sierra Club, John Muir, embodied the preservationist vision. In the tradition of Thoreau, Emerson, Hawthorne and other nineteenth-century Romantics, Muir experienced nature far less instrumentally: He and other preservationists valued wildness for wildness' sake, and they pushed as hard as they could for the enlargement of natural areas "free from the works of man." Wilderness, Muir firmly believed, was the only antidote available to an increasingly urbanized and industrialized population: "Thousands of tired, nerve-shaken, over-civilized people are beginning to find out that going to the mountains is going home; that wildness is necessity; and that mountain parks are useful not only as fountains of timber and irrigating rivers, but as fountains of life."

These differing approaches to conservation—best exemplified by the split between the once close friends, Muir and Pinchot—came to a head in the proposal to build a dam in the Hetch Hetchy Valley of Yosemite National Park. The dam was intended to meet San Francisco's growing need for an assured water supply, the inadequacy of which had been in evidence during the city's devastating 1906 earthquake and accompanying fires. John Muir, of course, championed the preservation of Hetch Hetchy, while the dam's supporters included the influential chief forester, Gifford Pinchot. Muir appealed to President Roosevelt, but in 1908 Roosevelt sided with the dam's supporters and the utilitarian side of the conservation movement. When the President granted the permit to build the dam, Muir was devastated.

In 1913, Congress approved, and President Woodrow Wilson signed, the final Hetch Hetchy bill. John Muir lamented: "some sort of compensation must surely come out of this dark damn-dam-damnation." It did. While the preservationists lost the battle over the dam (and the utilitarian focus of the Roosevelt-Pinchot conservationists continued as the dominant approach to resource management), the celebrated dispute had garnered national attention. Perhaps, as one historian noted, the most significant thing about the controversy is that it happened at all, for up until that time no proposal to dam a wild river had created such a public protest. But by the early teens, there clearly existed a broader constituency prepared to work for the preservation of wilderness and for a separate national park service to protect in perpetuity the nation's most wild and scenic treasures.

In 1916, the preservationists won a major victory when Congress passed legislation establishing a National Park Service and mandated it to "conserve the scenery and the natural and historic objects and the wildlife therein and to provide for the enjoyment of same in such manner and by such means as will leave them unimpaired for the enjoyment of future generations." The agency's first director, Stephen Mather, responded to this dual-faceted mission by moving to protect the parks' resources while simultaneously cultivating tourist enjoyment through enhanced automobile access. From its inception, the Park Service has been charged with finding the proper balance between resource preservation and public use, a balance that naturally has shifted with America's changing values and demographics.

A prominent Progressive Era organization lending its support to the proposal for a national park service was the General Federation of Women's Clubs. This group brought together under a national umbrella the numerous state and local women's associations existing at the turn of the century. The Federation is credited with helping secure passage of the 1902 Reclamation Act and the 1911 Weeks Act, the latter authorizing federal purchase of privately owned forest lands to protect watersheds. (Over time much valuable eastern forest land was brought into the national forest system under this act.) While the Federation supported Pinchot's forestry efforts and the creation of forest reserves, it opposed him on Hetch Hetchy and on whether a separate parks agency was needed. The Federation also went on record opposing billboards along scenic highways and supported bird and wildflower protection. It examined urban environmental issues such as sanitation and public health. Because of an emphasis on home and family, the Federation and its associated clubs stressed the link between resource conservation and the well-being of children and future generations. Viewing the local community as an extension of the home, women of the era focused on issues of civic reform as well. In the work of the philosopher John Dewey, they found support for their view of the importance of "community" in the life of the nation.

The increasing activism of women during the Progressive Era also was seen in the settlement house movement, a movement led by two prominent social workers, Jane Addams of Chicago's Hull House and Lillian Wald of the Henry Street Settlement in New York. The houses provided a setting for educated women to pursue careers in social reform throughout much of the teens and '20s. Jane Addams's associates, for example, were a "who's who" of social reformers working to improve the living environments of the poor, immigrants, minorities, and children: Florence Kelley of the National Consumer's League, who spearheaded the sweatshop investigations; Julia Lathrop of the Children's Bureau, who battled against child labor; the wealthy Chicagoans Anna and Harold Ickes, who assisted the Native Americans' demands for self-determination and equal treatment; and Dr. Alice Hamilton, who pioneered in the field of industrial toxicology. Another prominent woman coming out of the Progressive Era, Margaret Sanger, coined the term "birth control" and led the fight to provide women with reproductive information and clinical services. In focusing public attention on issues that defined nature and the environment in terms of everyday life—including better sanitation, public health, occupational hazards, and city beautification initiatives—women's groups did much to make the conservation movement a broadly based one.

While the Pinchot-Muir falling out over Hetch Hetchy reflected a fundamental division in the conservation movement—between preservationists and utilitarians—another split became evident during the period. This one was between professional foresters such as Pinchot and urban planners like J. Horace McFarland. McFarland founded the American Civic Association in 1904, which sponsored city and neighborhood improvement, landscape preservation, and "city beautiful" campaigns designed to transform the ugly leftovers of development. McFarland argued that the conservation movement had restricted its potential influence by failing to include urban areas within its domain. Pinchot, however, saw things quite differently: Forestry was a component of agriculture, with forests defined as a slow-growing crop and forestry as tree farming. As for "scenery," he said it was "altogether outside its province." These one-time good friends, Pinchot and McFarland, eventually ceased to correspond after protracted wrangling over Hetch Hetchy and whether a separate national parks agency was needed. Pinchot felt strongly that it was not.

The City Beautiful Movement, which McFarland helped to lead, promoted attractive urban environments for all people, for, he said, "there can be no exclusiveness in civic art." A major impetus for the movement was the World's Columbian Exposition, held in Chicago in 1893; one of its designers, Frederick Law Olmsted, had created such a beautiful plan that it attracted national and even international attention. The interest in urban design culminated in the country's first comprehensive zoning plan, that for New York City in 1916. Ten years later, in 1926, the Supreme Court upheld the validity of zoning in *Euclid v. Ambler Realty*. By the end of the 1920s, three-fifths of the nation's population lived under some form of zoning control.

That new voices were added to the nation's environmental dialogue during the Progressive Era is clearly evident. Women's views, for example, were given credence for the first time in formulating conservation, environmental, and public-health policies. It is hardly surprising that the political scientist Arthur Bentley was deeply impressed with the vibrance of group activity going on around him: It led him to make his classic formulation about American politics: "When the group is stated, everything is stated."

But also in evidence was an emerging fragmentation of the environmental movement. Some of the basic tenets of Progressivism, specialization of function and division of labor, began to characterize the movement. While Progressive conservationists were capable of pulling together on some issues, they also were capable of fierce intramural fighting and bickering. From the very outset, then, it has proved difficult to orchestrate the several voices of the environmental movement into a unified chorus. As new voices were added throughout the century, it became even more of an impossibility.

Another divisive issue during the era was whether the United States should participate in the war in Europe (later labeled World War I). While the nation's war effort from 1917 to 1919 reflected the Progressives' emphasis on efficient, rational, and centralized planning, it deeply divided isolationist Progressives from interventionists. Interventionists like Theodore Roosevelt and John Dewey supported U.S. entry into the war, often arguing that it would serve as a catalyst for reform. Dewey believed that participating in the war would temper America's "destructive individualism" and provide a basis for the reconstruction of public policy. President Woodrow Wilson, who as a child had witnessed the ravages of the Civil War, was at heart a pacifist, but felt compelled to call for a congressional declaration of war in 1917. It would be, he said, the "war to end all wars," fought because the "world must be made safe for democracy." Nonetheless, Wilson keenly recognized the difficulty of fighting a world war and maintaining the ideals of democratic government at home. He feared that not only intolerance and zenophobia would infect national life but that the nation's industries, put into service in the war effort, would again spin out of control. Indeed, he was right.

Suppression of free speech was one of the results of World War I. After the war the nation went through a period of general cultural intolerance, the repression of civil liberties, and race riots. The antiblack, anti-Catholic, and antiimmigrant Ku Klux Klan was reactivated during the teens and twenties; in 1925 its membership peaked at about five million. Congress passed laws that restricted immigration. Conditions for Black Americans continued to deteriorate as a result of rigid racial segregation—a policy, incidentally, supported by the Virginia-born President, Woodrow Wilson, along with his Republican successors in the White House. A revived religious fundamentalism pitted the literal interpretation of the Bible against many scientific developments, particularly Darwin's theory of evolution. That issue came to a head in the infamous "Scopes Monkey trial" in Dayton, Tennessee, where a high school biology teacher was prosecuted for breaking the state's prohibition against teaching any theory that conflicted with the biblical story of creation.

The election of 1920 indicated a backlash to the policies of the Progressives. The election of the decidedly non-Progressive Warren G. Harding as President—in a landslide victory—marked the end of an era of reform. Harding promised a "return to normalcy." For the next twelve years of Republican-controlled government, through the presidencies of Harding, Coolidge, and Hoover, the executive branch rejected the antimonopoly policies of the Progressives as destructive of economic prosperity. The "business of America is business,"declared Coolidge. These politically conservative administrations specifically rejected the Progressive thrust of a strong public presence in resource development in favor of private enterprise.

One of Harding's first actions was to cancel all work on the nearly completed Wilson Dam on the Tennessee River, a dam authorized by the wartime Congress to supply hydroelectric power for a government explosives plant at Muscle Shoals. Harding believed that the Muscle Shoals development could be run more effectively by private enterprise, a position directly counter to Theodore Roosevelt's, who as early as 1903 vetoed a bill that would have turned Muscle Shoals over to private enterprise. While the government continued to promote national planning of public works and waterway improvements (as, for example, in Section 308 of the Rivers and Harbors Act of 1927, authorizing the Corps of Engineers to develop comprehensive multiple-purpose river basin plans), the issue of private versus public power remained controversial for years—well into the Eisenhower Administration of the 1950s. Indeed, it has become an issue again in 2001, especially in California.

Harding presided over an administration tainted by corruption and scandal. The most infamous involved Teapot Dome, one of two large naval oil reserves. Harding's Secretary of the Interior, Albert B. Fall, persuaded the Secretary of the Navy to turn over administration of the reserves to his department. Only later, after Harding died in 1923 from a stroke and Vice President Calvin Coolidge became President, was it learned that Fall secretly had leased the sites to private oil companies in exchange for interest-free loans, cash, and government bonds. After being convicted of bribery, Secretary Fall spent a year in prison.

Nonetheless, the "Roaring Twenties" generally were years of economic prosperity. Firms expanded their production capacity. The Gross National Product grew, per capita income and wages increased, and consumers bought goods on credit for the first time in history. Many Americans could afford to buy a host of new consumer conveniences—refrigerators, radios, washing machines, telephones—and entertain themselves at the new moving picture theater. Henry Ford's introduction of mass-produced automobiles made them affordable—and buyers, the story goes, could have a new Ford in any color so long as it was black. By 1929 one in five American families owned a car.

Although there were some voices calling attention to the nation's forgotten Americans during these heady years, and other voices, like John Dewey's, wondering where the country's spirit of community had fled, most voices were complacent and self-congratulatory. Republicans captured the spirit of the decade when they campaigned in the 1928 elections on the slogan, "A chicken in every pot, and a car in every garage." Automobiles, combined with improved working conditions (thanks to the Progressive Era reforms), gave Americans more time to travel; visitation to parks, forests, and other scenic attractions increased dramatically. It seemed to be a time of unprecedented technical and economic progress. Indeed, in his inaugural address President Herbert Hoover triumphantly declared, "We in America today are nearer to the final triumph over poverty than ever before in the history of any land." The culture was exuberant and freewheeling. Then, in October of 1929, the stock market on Wall Street crashed.

# 13
# Theodore Roosevelt (1858–1919)

A historian described Theodore Roosevelt as believing that nothing was worth saying unless it was said at the top of one's lungs. Indeed, Roosevelt was the kind of individual from which legends are made. He was larger than life: Iconoclastic, brilliant, moralistic, energetic in the extreme, and craving both popularity and political power, he left an indelible stamp upon the state and the environment. A sickly child who almost died of asthma, the young Roosevelt became devoted to the outdoors and to physical prowess. In the mid-1880s he spent considerable time in the West, learning as much as he could about ranching, farming, hunting, and the forbidding landscape of the Dakotas. Convinced of the need to preserve game species from destruction, he helped start the Boone & Crockett Club, a sportsman's group devoted to the conservation of large game animals and their habitats.

His experience as a cowboy and hunter helped him convince the War Department to allow him to command a regiment during the Spanish-American War, where he gained notoriety and credentials as a war hero by charging up San Juan Hill with his band of Rough Riders. He returned from the war one of the most celebrated Americans of his generation. He ran successfully for Governor of New York, but his evolving progressive policies angered the corporate community and especially Tom Platt, the Republican party boss. Platt worked diligently to remove the troublesome, but popular, governor by getting him nominated as President William McKinley's running mate in the 1900 election. The only nay vote at the convention nominating Roosevelt as vice president was his own.

Later in the century, FDR's Vice President John Nance Garner would declare that the vice presidency is worth less than a bucket of warm spit. Generally true—and a fact that Tom Platt counted on—unless fate propelled one into the presidency. In September 1901, less than six months into his second term, McKinley was assassinated, and Theodore Roosevelt became the nation's twenty-sixth president. During his administration, through words and action, Roosevelt placed conservation at the top of the nation's political agenda.

Declining to run for a third term (a decision he later deeply regretted), Roosevelt left office in 1909 and took up writing for newspapers and magazines, such as the *Outlook*, where he wrote about conservation as well as politics. He also traveled and added to his reputation as a big-game hunter. His 1915 book review from the *Outlook*, excerpted here, reflects his abiding interest in, and knowledge of, the subject of wildlife conservation.

Roosevelt re-entered politics in 1912, having become disgusted with the conservative program of his hand-picked successor, William Howard Taft. Unable to wrest the Republican nomination from Taft ("naked theft," he thundered), he formed a third party and ran on the Progressive, or "Bull Moose," ticket. Roosevelt succeeded in coming in second, but it was not enough to get him back in the White House: The little-known Democratic candidate, Woodrow Wilson, succeeded Taft and continued the Progressive tradition during his eight years in office.

Though in failing health, the "bull moose" planned another run for the presidency in 1920. However, he died suddenly of a coronary embolism in 1919. Some say the death of his youngest son, Quentin, during the world war—a battle Roosevelt himself wanted to take part in—had broken his great heart.

---

# "THERE MUST BE THE LOOK AHEAD"*

The conservation of our natural resources and their proper use constitute the fundamental problem which underlies almost every other problem of our National life.... As a nation we not only enjoy a wonderful measure of present prosperity, but if this prosperity is used aright it is an earnest of future success such as no other nation will have. The reward of foresight for this Nation is great and easily foretold. But there must be the look ahead, there must be a realization of the fact that to waste, to destroy, our natural resources, to skin and exhaust the land instead of using it so as to increase its usefulness, will result in undermining in the days of our children the very prosperity which we ought by right to hand down to them amplified and developed. For the last few years, through several agencies, the Government has been endeavoring to get our people to look ahead and to substitute a planned and orderly development of our resources in place of a haphazard striving for immediate profit. Our great river systems should be developed as National water highways; the Mississippi, with its tributaries, standing first in importance, and the Columbia second, although there are many others of importance on the Pacific, the Atlantic, and the Gulf slopes. The National Government should undertake this work, and I hope a beginning will be made in the present Congress, and the greatest of all our rivers, the Mississippi, should receive especial attention. From the Great Lakes to the mouth of the Mississippi there should be a deep waterway, with deep waterways leading from it to the East and West. Such a waterway would practically mean the extension of our coast-line into the very heart of our country. It would be of incalculable benefit to our people. If begun at once it can be carried through in time appreciably to relieve the congestion of our great freight-carrying lines of railroads. The work should be systematically and continuously carried forward in accordance with some well-conceived plan. The main streams should be improved to the highest point of efficiency before the improvement of the branches is attempted; and the work should be kept free from every taint of recklessness or jobbery. The inland water-

---

*Theodore Roosevelt. Excerpt from Seventh Annual Message to Congress, December 3, 1907, in Theodore Roosevelt, *The Works of Theodore Roosevelt: Presidential Addresses and State Papers*. Part VI. n.d.. New York: P. F. Collier & Son, Publishers, pp. 1534–1545.

ways which lie just back of the whole eastern and southern coasts should likewise be developed. Moreover, the development of our waterways involves many other important water problems, all of which should be considered as part of the same general scheme. The Government dams should be used to produce hundreds of thousands of horse-power as an incident to improving navigation; for the annual value of the unused water-power of the United States perhaps exceeds the annual value of the products of all our mines. As an incident to creating the deep waterways down the Mississippi, the Government should build along its whole lower length levees which, taken together with the control of the headwaters, will at once and forever put a complete stop to all threat of floods in the immensely fertile Delta region. The territory lying adjacent to the Mississippi along its lower course will thereby become one of the most prosperous and populous, as it already is one of the most fertile, farming regions in all the world. I have appointed an Inland Waterways Commission to study and outline a comprehensive scheme of development along all the lines indicated. Later I shall lay its report before the Congress.

Irrigation should be far more extensively developed than at present, not only in the States of the Great Plains and the Rocky Mountains, but in many others, as, for instance, in large portions of the South Atlantic and Gulf States, where it should go hand in hand with the reclamation of swampland. The Federal Government should seriously devote itself to this task, realizing that utilization of waterways and water-power, forestry, irrigation, and the reclamation of lands threatened with overflow, are all interdependent parts of the same problem. The work of the Reclamation Service in developing the larger opportunities of the western half of our country for irrigation is more important than almost any other movement. The constant purpose of the Government in connection with the Reclamation Service has been to use the water resources of the public lands for the ultimate greatest good of the greatest number; in other words, to put upon the land permanent home-makers, to use and develop it for themselves and for their children and children's children. There has been, of course, opposition to this work; opposition from some interested men who desire to exhaust the land for their own immediate profit without regard to the welfare of the next generation, and opposition from honest and well-meaning men who did not fully understand the subject or who did not look far enough ahead. This opposition is, I think, dying away, and our people are understanding that it would be utterly wrong to allow a few individuals to exhaust for their own temporary personal profit the resources which ought to be developed through use so as to be conserved for the permanent common advantage of the people as a whole.

The effort of the Government to deal with the public land has been based upon the same principle as that of the Reclamation Service. The land law system which was designed to meet the needs of the fertile and well-watered regions of the Middle West has largely broken down when applied to the drier regions of the Great Plains, the mountains, and much of the Pacific slope, where a farm of 160 acres is inadequate for self-support. In these regions the system lent itself to fraud, and much land passed out of the hands of the Government without passing into the hands of the home-maker.... Three years ago a public lands commission was appointed to scrutinize the law, and defects, and recommend a remedy. Their examination specifically showed the existence of great fraud upon the public domain, and their recommendations for changes in the law were made with the design of conserving the natural resources of every part of the public lands by putting it to its best use. Especial attention was called to the prevention of settlement by the passage of great areas of public lands into the hands of a few men, and to the enormous waste caused by unrestricted grazing upon the open range. The recommendations of the Public Lands Commission are sound, for they are especially in the interest of the actual home-maker; and where the small home-maker can not at present utilize the land they provide that the Government shall keep control of it so that it may not be monopolized by a few men. The Congress has not yet acted upon these recommendations; but they are so just and proper, so essential to our National welfare, that I feel confident, if the Congress will take time to consider them, that they will ultimately be adopted.

Some such legislation as that proposed is essential in order to preserve the great stretches of public grazing land which are unfit for cultivation under present methods and are valuable only for the forage which they supply. These stretches amount in all to some 300,000,000 acres, and are open to the free grazing of cattle, sheep, horses, and goats, without restriction. Such a system, or rather lack of system, means that the range is not so much used as wasted by abuse. As the West settles the range becomes more and more over-grazed. Much of it can not be used to advantage unless it is fenced, for fencing is the only way by which to keep in check the owners of nomad flocks which roam hither and thither, utterly destroying the pastures and leaving a waste behind so that their presence is incompatible with the presence of home-makers. The existing fences are all illegal.... All these fences, those that are hurtful and those that are beneficial, are alike illegal and must come down. But it is an outrage that the law should necessitate such action on the part of the Administration. The unlawful fencing of public lands for private grazing must be stopped, but the necessity which occasioned it must be provided for. The Federal Government should have control of the range, whether by permit or lease, as local necessities may determine. Such control could secure the great benefit of legitimate fencing, while at the same time securing and promoting the settlement of the country.... The Government should part with its title only to the actual home-maker, not to the profit-maker who does not care to make a home. Our prime object is to secure the rights and guard the interests of the small ranchman, the man who ploughs and pitches hay for himself....

Optimism is a good characteristic, but if carried to an excess it becomes foolishness. We are prone to speak of the resources of this country as inexhaustible; this is not so. The mineral wealth of the country, the coal, iron, oil, gas, and the like, does not reproduce itself, and therefore is certain to be exhausted ultimately; and wastefulness in dealing with it to-day means that our descendants will feel the exhaustion a generation or two before they otherwise would. But there are certain other forms of waste which could be entirely stopped—the waste of soil by washing, for instance, which is among the most dangerous of all wastes now in progress in the United States, is easily preventable, so that this present enormous loss of fertility is entirely unnecessary. The preservation or replacement of the forests is one of the most important means of preventing this loss. We have made a beginning in forest preservation, but...so rapid has been the rate of exhaustion of timber in the United States in the past, and so rapidly is the remainder being exhausted, that the country is unquestionably on the verge of a timber famine which will be felt in every household in the land.... The present annual consumption of lumber is certainly three times as great as the annual growth; and if the consumption and growth continue unchanged, practically all our lumber will be exhausted in another generation, while long before the limit to complete exhaustion is reached the growing scarcity will make itself felt in many blighting ways upon our national welfare. About 20 per cent of our forested territory is now reserved in national forests; but these do not include the most valuable timber lands, and in any event the proportion is too small to expect that the reserves can accomplish more than a mitigation of the trouble which is ahead for the Nation. Far more drastic action is needed.... But forests, if used as all our forests have been used in the past and as most of them are still used, will be either wholly destroyed, or so damaged that many decades have to pass before effective use can be made of them again.... Surely, when these facts are so obvious, there should be no delay in taking preventive measures. Yet we seem as a Nation to be willing to proceed in this matter with happy-go-lucky indifference even to the immediate future. It is this attitude which permits the self-interest of a very few persons to weigh for more than the ultimate interest of all our people.... Of course to check the waste of timber means that there must be on the part of the public the acceptance of a temporary restriction in the lavish use of the timber, in order to prevent the total loss of this use in the future. There are plenty of men in public and private life who actually advocate the continuance of the present system of unchecked and wasteful extravagance, using as an argument the fact that to check it will of course mean interference with the ease and comfort of certain people who now get lumber at less cost than they ought to pay, at the expense of future generations.... But only a savage would, in his private affairs, show such reckless disregard of the future; yet it is precisely this reckless disregard of the future which the opponents of the forest system are now endeavoring to get the people of the United States to show. The only trouble with the movement for the preservation of our forests is that it has not gone nearly far enough, and was not begun soon enough. It is a most fortunate thing, however, that we began it when we did. We should acquire in the Appalachian and White Mountain regions all the forest lands that it is possible to acquire for the use of the Nation. These lands, because they form a National asset, are as emphatically National as the rivers which they feed, and which flow through so many States before they reach the ocean.

# "THE PROPERTY OF THE UNBORN GENERATIONS"*

...It is deeply discreditable to the people of any country calling itself civilized that as regards many of the grandest or most beautiful or most interesting forms of wild life once to be found in the land we should now be limited to describing, usually in the dryest of dry books, the physical characteristics which when living they possessed, and the melancholy date at which they ceased to live.

Ever since man in recognizably human shape made his appearance on this planet he has been an appreciable factor in the destruction of other forms of animal life, and he has been a potent factor ever since he developed the weapons known to the savages of the last few tens of thousands of years. But modern weapons have given a tremendous impetus to this destruction. Never before were such enormous quantities of big beasts and large birds slain as in the nineteenth century. Never before was there such extensive and wasteful slaughter of strange and beautiful forms of wild life as in the century which saw the greatest advance in material civilization and the most rapid spread of the civilized peoples throughout all the world.

Toward the end of that century a few civilized nations wakened to a sense of shame at what was going on. Enlightened men and women here and there began to take efficient action to restrain this senseless destruction of that which, once destroyed, could never be replaced. Gradually they roused a more general sentiment, and now there is a considerable body of public opinion in favor of keeping for our children's children, as a priceless heritage, all the delicate beauty of the lesser and all the burly majesty of the mightier forms of wild life. We are fast learning that trees must not be cut down more rapidly than they are replaced; we have taken forward steps in learning that wild beasts and birds are by right not the property merely of the people alive to-day, but the property of the unborn generations, whose belongings we have no right to squander; and there are even faint signs of our growing to understand that wild flowers should be enjoyed unplucked where they grow, and that it is barbarism to ravage the woods and fields, rooting out the mayflower and breaking branches of dogwood as ornaments for automobiles filled with jovial but ignorant picnickers from cities.

In the present century the new movement gathered head. Men began to appreciate the need of preserving wild life, not only because it was useful, but also because it was beautiful. Song-birds, shore-birds, water-fowl, birds of all kinds, add by voice and action to the joy of living of most men and women to whom the phrase "joy of living" has any real meaning. Such stately or lovely wild creatures as moose, wapiti, deer, hartbeest, zebra,

---

*Theodore Roosevelt. 1915. Book review of *Wild Life Conservation*, by William T. Hornaday; *Alaskan Bird Life* edited by Ernest Ingersoll; and *Menschen und Tiere in Deutsh-Südwest* by Adolph Fischer, in *The Outlook*, January 20.

gazelle, when protected give ample commercial returns, and, moreover, add to the landscape just as waterfalls and lofty pine-trees and towering crags add to the landscape. Fertile plains, every foot of them tilled, are of the first necessity; but great natural playgrounds of mountain, forest, cliff-walled lake, and brawling brook are also necessary to the full and many-sided development of a fine race. In just the same way the homely birds of farm and lawn and the wild creatures of the waste should all be kept. It is utterly untrue to say, as demagogues and selfish materialists sometimes unite in saying, that "the game belongs to the people"—meaning the loafers and market gunners who wish to kill it, and the wealthy and lazy gourmands who wish to eat it, without regard to the future. It is true that the game belongs to the people; but this rightly means the people who are to be born a hundred years hence just as much as the people who are alive to-day. In the same way, persons who own land, and, above all, persons who merely visit or pass through land, have no more right wantonly or carelessly to destroy birds or deface scenery than they have to pollute waters or burn down forests or let floods through levees. The sooner we appreciate these facts, the sooner we shall become a really civilized people.

Laws to protect small and harmless wild life, especially birds, are indispensable. Such laws cannot be enacted or enforced until public opinion is back of them; and associations like the Audubon Societies do work of incalculable good in stirring, rousing, and giving effect to this opinion; and men like Mr. Hornaday render all of us their debtors by the way they efficiently labor for this end, as well as for what comes only next in importance, the creation of sanctuaries for the complete protection of the larger, shyer, and more persecuted forms of wild life. This country led the way in establishing the Yellowstone Park as such a sanctuary; the British and German Empires followed, and in many ways have surpassed us. There are now many such sanctuaries and refuges in North America, middle and South Africa, and even Asia, and the results have been astounding. Many of the finer forms of animal life, which seemed on the point of vanishing, are now far more numerous than fifteen years ago, having by their rapid increase given proof of the abounding vigor of nature's fertility where nature is unmarred by man. But very much remains to be done, and there is need of the most active warfare against the forces of greed, carelessness, and sheer brutality, which, if left unchecked, would speedily undo all that has been accomplished, and would inflict literally irreparable damage.

The books before me are powerful weapons in this warfare for light against darkness. Mr. Hornaday's volume…is really a full technical treatise which should be owned and constantly used by every man and woman who is alive to our needs in this matter. He shows how much has been accomplished in creating the right type of popular opinion. He is able to tell what we have accomplished in the creation of great National playgrounds, the National parks, which are National game-preserves. The Yellowstone, Glacier, Mount Olympus, Grand Canyon, Sequoia, and other parks represent one of the best bits of National achievement which our people have to their credit of recent years. The National forests should also be made game reserves. No sale of game or market hunting should be allowed anywhere;

fortunately, the infamous traffic in millinery feathers has now been forbidden. The Federal migratory bird law is a capital piece of legislation. Mr. Hornaday shows the imperative need of protecting our shore-birds; he shows the economic value of birds to the farmer; he deals with what must, alas! be called just severity with the attitude of the average "sportsman" toward wild life.

One of the most interesting and pleasant phases of the movement of which Mr. Hornaday is one of the leaders is that which deals with the rapidity with which animals accustom themselves to protection and multiply when given the chance to do so. In New York and New England whitetail deer have enormously increased in numbers during the last thirty years. In Vermont the deer were absolutely exterminated forty years ago. Then a dozen were introduced from the Adirondacks. These have thriven and multiplied literally over a thousandfold. In forty years the original twelve individuals have increased to such an extraordinary degree that at present hunting under proper restriction is permitted, and five or six thousand deer are killed annually, without diminution of the stock. Mr. Hornaday is an entirely sane and rational man; he heartily approves of hunting, of sport carried on in legitimate fashion, as it can be, without any diminution of the amount of game. He shows that in the case of the Yellowstone elk it is urgently desirable that there should be a great increase in the killing, especially of cows; for in the absence of a sufficient number of natural foes they have increased until they now die by thousands each winter of starvation. (By the way, I venture to point out that when the cougars in the Yellowstone dwell away from the deer, antelope, and sheep, and prey only on elk, they do no damage.) Our prime duty, at present, as regards the immense majority of large or beautiful or useful mammals and the birds, is to protect them from excessive killing, or, indeed, from all killing. But when genuinely protected, birds and mammals increase so rapidly that it becomes imperative to kill them. If, under such circumstances, their numbers are not kept down by legitimate hunting—and some foolish creatures protest even against legitimate hunting—it would be necessary to have them completely exterminated by paid butchers. But the foolish sentimentalists who do not see this are not as yet the really efficient foes of wild life and of sensible movements for its preservation. The game-hog, the man who commercializes the destruction of game, and the wealthy epicure—all of these, backed by the selfish ignorance which declines to learn, are the real foes with whom we must contend. The true lovers of the chase, true sportsmen, true believers in hunting as a manly and vigorous pastime, recognize these men as their worst foes; and the great array of men and women who do not hunt, but who love wild creatures, who love all nature, must discriminate sharply between the two classes.

The Audubon Societies, which have done so much good work, have rarely done a better piece of work than in publishing the charming little book *Alaskan Bird Life*.... It has been prepared for free distribution among the people of Alaska. Surely, societies that do such work are entitled to the heartiest support from all good citizens. Let school-teachers have it free by all means; give it as a prize to exceptional pupils; but let the average man or woman pay something for such a first-class little volume. It is a book of really exceptional merit; no bird-lover in the United States or Canada—not to speak of Alaska—can afford not to have it in his or her library. It is all excellent; but best of all are the portions contributed by Mr. E. W. Nelson. Mr. Nelson is one of our best field-ornithologists, and also, one of our best closet scientific systematists; and to extraordinary powers of observation, and intense love of the wilderness of wild creatures, he adds the ability to write with singular power and charm. Nothing better of its kind has ever been done than his account in this little volume of the bird life, at all seasons of the year, in the Yukon Valley and on the islands and along the seacoast. His ear is as good as his eye. He is the first writer to do justice to the musical notes, especially the love notes, of the "sou-sou-southerly" duck, which in winter we know so well on Long Island Sound. He tells of the Lapland longspur, singing on the wing like a bobolink; and of the noisy cock ptarmigan crowing his challenge as he springs a few yards in the air when he is still the dominant figure on the snowy spring plains, before the hosts of waterfowl arrive. Mr. Nelson is the first observer graphically and fully to portray the life history of the strange emperor-goose. He is almost the first observer to describe the songs—for they are songs—of the shore-birds; and particularly attractive is his description of the aerial love-dance and love-song of the tiny and gentle semi-palmated sandpiper....

# 14
# Gifford Pinchot (1865–1946)

Forestry was an occupation largely unknown in the United States when Gifford Pinchot began his career. He went to France and Germany as a student to learn about silviculture, and he returned to America convinced that scientific forestry would not only stem the destructive waste of forest resources but also prove profitable. One of his first positions was managing George W. Vanderbilt's forest at his North Carolina Biltmore estate. Successful there, Pinchot in 1898 became director of the small and largely insignificant Division of Forestry, housed in the Department of Agriculture. The division had no control over any forest resources, since at that time nearly all federal lands were administered by the Department of the Interior. The politically astute and well-connected Pinchot worked diligently, and successfully, to get the forest reserves transferred and placed under his charge.

Few people were closer to Theodore Roosevelt than Gifford Pinchot, who credited himself with naming the new movement "conservation." In the selection here, Pinchot set forth the principles of conservation, emphasizing its "development without waste" principle and its general utilitarian thrust. Countering a criticism that conservation unnecessarily locked up resources, Pinchot addressed the question of intergenerational obligations, claiming that the policy never was to save resources from use, but rather to use them wisely and with some consideration of the future.

During his tenure as first Chief of the Forest Service, Pinchot molded the agency into a highly professional and powerful organization that reflected the ideological foundations of Progressive conservation; he deeply imprinted upon that agency the principles of scientific management, efficiency, and technocratic specialization. He served as Chief until 1910, when President Taft removed him for insubordination. Unhappy with Taft's reticent use of his executive powers in support of Roosevelt-Pinchot conservation programs, Pinchot, from his position within the Agriculture Department, had repeatedly clashed with the President's Secretary of the Interior, Richard Ballinger. When Pinchot publicly labeled Ballinger's processing of some Alaska coal claims as illegal, Taft, a judicious adherent to bureaucratic protocol and tired of Pinchot's constant harangues, fired him.

Pinchot's public life did not end after his dismissal as Forest Service Chief. He continued to promote the conservation principles he had helped develop. He served two terms as governor of Pennsylvania, and in that office supported such Progressive positions as equal pay for women, the elimination of child labor, and workers' rights. Throughout the 1930s he counseled FDR's administration on matters relating to the national forests.

Pinchot's assets were his persuasive abilities, political astuteness, and tireless promotion of the principles of Progressive conservation. He saw only two material things on earth—people and natural resources. For Pinchot, conservation of natural resources was key to the safety and prosperity of the

American people and to worldwide peace. "That is why" he proclaimed, "conservation is the greatest material question of all."

---

# "PRINCIPLES OF CONSERVATION"*

The principles which the word Conservation has come to embody are not many, and they are exceedingly simple. I have had occasion to say a good many times that no other great movement has ever achieved such progress in so short a time, or made itself felt in so many directions with such vigor and effectiveness, as the movement for the conservation of natural resources.

Forestry made good its position in the United States before the conservation movement was born. As a forester I am glad to believe that conservation began with forestry, and that the principles which govern the Forest Service in particular and forestry in general are also the ideas that control conservation.

The first idea of real foresight in connection with natural resources arose in connection with the forest. From it sprang the movement which gathered impetus until it culminated in the great Convention of Governors at Washington in May, 1908. Then came the second official meeting of the National Conservation movement, December, 1908, in Washington. Afterward came the various gatherings of citizens in convention, come together to express their judgment on what ought to be done, and to contribute, as only such meetings can, to the formation of effective public opinion.

The movement so begun and so prosecuted has gathered immense swing and impetus. In 1907 few knew what Conservation meant. Now it has become a household word. While at first Conservation was supposed to apply only to forests, we see now that its sweep extends even beyond the natural resources.

The principles which govern the conservation movement, like all great and effective things, are simple and easily understood. Yet it is often hard to make the simple, easy, and direct facts about a movement of this kind known to the people generally.

The first great fact about conservation is that it stands for development. There has been a fundamental misconception that conservation means nothing but the husbanding of resources for future generations. There could be no more serious mistake. Conservation does mean provision for the future, but it means also and first of all the recognition of the right of the present generation to the fullest necessary use of all the resources with which this country is so abundantly blessed. Conservation demands the welfare of this generation first, and afterward the welfare of the generations to follow.

The first principle of conservation is development, the use of the natural resources now existing on this continent for the benefit of the people

---

*Gifford Pinchot. 1910. *The Fight for Conservation.* Seattle: University of Washington Press, pp. 40–52.

who live here now. There may be just as much waste in neglecting the development and use of certain natural resources as there is in their destruction. We have a limited supply of coal, and only a limited supply. Whether it is to last for a hundred or a hundred and fifty or a thousand years, the coal is limited in amount, unless through geological changes which we shall not live to see, there will never be any more of it than there is now. But coal is in a sense the vital essence of our civilization. If it can be preserved, if the life of the mines can be extended, if by preventing waste there can be more coal left in this country after we of this generation have made every needed use of this source of power, then we shall have deserved well of our descendants.

Conservation stands emphatically for the development and use of water-power now, without delay. It stands for the immediate construction of navigable waterways under a broad and comprehensive plan as assistants to the railroads. More coal and more iron are required to move a ton of freight by rail than by water, three to one. In every case and in every direction the conservation movement has development for its first principle, and at the very beginning of its work. The development of our natural resources and the fullest use of them for the present generation is the first duty of this generation. So much for development.

In the second place conservation stands for the prevention of waste. There has come gradually in this country an understanding that waste is not a good thing and that the attack on waste is an industrial necessity. I recall very well indeed how, in the early days of forest fires, they were considered simply and solely as acts of God, against which any opposition was hopeless and any attempt to control them not merely hopeless but childish. It was assumed that they came in the natural order of things, as inevitably as the seasons or the rising and setting of the sun. To-day we understand that forest fires are wholly within the control of men. So we are coming in like manner to understand that the prevention of waste in all other directions is a simple matter of good business. The first duty of the human race is to control the earth it lives upon.

We are in a position more and more completely to say how far the waste and destruction of natural resources are to be allowed to go on and where they are to stop. It is curious that the effort to stop waste, like the effort to stop forest fires, has often been considered as a matter controlled wholly by economic law. I think there could be no greater mistake. Forest fires were allowed to burn long after the people had means to stop them. The idea that men were helpless in the face of them held long after the time had passed when the means of control were fully within our reach. It was the old story that "as a man thinketh, so is he"; we came to see that we could stop forest fires, and we found that the means had long been at hand. When at length we came to see that the control of logging in certain directions was profitable, we found it had long been possible. In all these matters of waste of natural resources, the education of the people to understand that they can stop the leakage comes before the actual stopping and after the means of stopping it have long been ready at our hands.

In addition to the principles of development and preservation of our resources there is a third principle. It is this: The natural resources must be developed and preserved for the benefit of the many, and not merely for the profit of a few. We are coming to understand in this country that public action for public benefit has a very much wider field to cover and a much larger part to play than was the case when there were resources enough for every one, and before certain constitutional provisions had given so tremendously strong a position to vested rights and property in general.

A few years ago President Hadley, of Yale, wrote an article which has not attracted the attention it should. The point of it was that by reason of the XIVth amendment to the Constitution, property rights in the United States occupy a stronger position than in any other country in the civilized world. It becomes then a matter of multiplied importance, since property rights once granted are so strongly entrenched, to see that they shall be so granted that the people shall get their fair share of the benefit which comes from the development of the resources which belong to us all. The time to do that is now. By so doing we shall avoid the difficulties and conflicts which will surely arise if we allow vested rights to accrue outside the possibility of governmental and popular control.

The conservation idea covers a wider range than the field of natural resources alone. Conservation means the greatest good to the greatest number for the longest time. One of its great contributions is just this, that it has added to the worn and well-known phrase, "the greatest good to the greatest number," the additional words "for the longest time," thus recognizing that this nation of ours must be made to endure as the best possible home for all its people.

Conservation advocates the use of foresight, prudence, thrift, and intelligence in dealing with public matters, for the same reasons and in the same way that we each use foresight, prudence, thrift, and intelligence in dealing with our own private affairs. It proclaims the right and duty of the people to act for the benefit of the people. Conservation demands the application of common-sense to the common problems for the common good.

The principles of conservation thus described—development, preservation, the common good—have a general application which is growing rapidly wider. The development of resources and the prevention of waste and loss, the protection of the public interests, by foresight, prudence, and the ordinary business and home-making virtues, all these apply to other things as well as to the natural resources. There is, in fact, no interest of the people to which the principles of conservation do not apply.

The conservation point of view is valuable in the education of our people as well as in forestry; it applies to the body politic as well as to the earth and its minerals. A municipal franchise is as properly within its sphere as a franchise for water-power. The same point of view governs in both. It applies as much to the subject of good roads as to waterways, and the training of our people in citizenship is as germane to it as the productiveness of the earth. The application of common-sense to any problem for the Nation's good will lead directly to national efficiency wherever applied. In other words, and that is the burden of the message, we are coming to see the logical and inevitable outcome that these principles, which arose in forestry and have their bloom in the conservation of natural resources, will have their fruit in the increase and promotion of national efficiency along other lines of national life.

The outgrowth of conservation, the inevitable result, is national efficiency. In the great commercial struggle between nations which is eventually to determine the welfare of all, national efficiency will be the deciding factor. So from every point of view conservation is a good thing for the American people.

The National Forest Service, one of the chief agencies of the conservation movement, is trying to be useful to the people of this nation. The Service recognizes, and recognizes it more and more strongly all the time, that whatever it has done or is doing has just one object, and that object is the welfare of the plain American citizen. Unless the Forest Service has served the people, and is able to contribute to their welfare it has failed in its work and should be abolished. But just so far as by coöperation, by intelligence, by attention to the work laid upon it, it contributes to the welfare of our citizens, it is a good thing and should be allowed to go on with its work.

The Natural Forests are in the West. Headquarters of the Service have been established throughout the Western country, because its work cannot be done effectively and properly without the closest contact and the most hearty coöperation with the Western people. It is the duty of the Forest Service to see to it that the timber, water-powers, mines, and every other resource of the forests is used for the benefit of the people who live in the neighborhood or who may have a share in the welfare of each locality. It is equally its duty to coöperate with all our people in every section of our land to conserve a fundamental resource, without which this Nation cannot prosper.

# 15
# John Muir (1849–1914)

John Muir once climbed to the top of a 100-foot Douglas fir in the middle of a storm just to see how trees behaved in a wild gale. Another time, he ascended—without coat or blanket—to the top of the peak that today bears his name. He had an adventurous spirit, and relished contact with the raw forces of nature, even though some of his exploits bordered on the foolhardy.

Raised in a strict Calvinist family, Muir had a talent for invention, especially for automatic, labor-saving machines. Before him lay a promising career in business, until an accident nearly blinded him. He decided instead "to devote the rest of my life to the study of the inventions of God." By 1869 he found his way to California's Sierra Nevada mountains. There Muir studied geology and plants, traveled widely, and wrote extensively about his scientific findings and adventures. He became the most eloquent advocate for wilderness of his time, and his early articles built support for establishing Yosemite, Sequoia and General Grant National Parks.

Muir's writings combined vivid descriptions of the inherent beauty of wild places with prognostications of the dangers associated with their exploitation. He drew upon the biblical schooling he received as a boy to describe nature in religious and ethical terms. Through nature one came into direct communion with the divine, and those who sought to despoil it earned his greatest scorn. As Muir's impassioned plea to save Hetch Hetchy demonstrates, the debate often became cast in terms of good versus evil, God versus Satan. Muir helped publicize and popularize preservation by outlining a spiritually based ecology, not unlike that of the Native Americans.

In 1892 Muir helped found the Sierra Club. One of its first activities was to beat back a congressional attempt supported by ranchers and timber interests to cut the size of Yosemite National Park by one-half.

Muir broke with his friend Gifford Pinchot in 1897 over the issue of sheep, which Muir described as "hoofed locusts." Hearing that the politically pragmatic Pinchot supported grazing in the forest reserves so as not to antagonize user groups, Muir announced that he would have nothing further to do with him. The break between these two conservation giants became even more manifest in the ensuing years as the controversy over Hetch Hetchy came to the fore. The decade-long battle over the valley was Muir's last; he died in 1914, one year after President Wilson signed the bill giving final approval to construct the dam.

# "DAM HETCH HETCHY! AS WELL
# DAM...THE PEOPLE'S CATHEDRALS"*

Yosemite is so wonderful that we are apt to regard it as an exceptional creation, the only valley of its kind in the world; but Nature is not so poor as to have only one of anything. Several other yosemites have been discovered in the Sierra that occupy the same relative positions on the Range and were formed by the same forces in the same kind of granite. One of these, the Hetch Hetchy Valley, is in the Yosemite National Park about twenty miles from Yosemite and is easily accessible to all sorts of travelers by a road and trail that leaves the Big Oak Flat road at Bronson Meadows a few miles below Crane Flat, and to mountaineers by way of Yosemite Creek basin and the head of the middle fork of the Tuolumne.

It is said to have been discovered by Joseph Screech, a hunter, in 1850, a year before the discovery of the great Yosemite. After my first visit to it in the autumn of 1871, I have always called it the "Tuolumne Yosemite," for it is a wonderfully exact counterpart of the Merced Yosemite, not only in its sublime rocks and waterfalls but in the gardens, groves and meadows of its flowery park-like floor. The floor of Yosemite is about 4000 feet above the sea; the Hetch Hetchy floor about 3700 foot. And as the Merced River flows through Yosemite, so does the Tuolumne through Hetch Hetchy. The walls of both are of gray granite, rise abruptly from the floor, are sculptured in the same style and in both every rock is a glacier monument.

Standing boldly out from the south wall is a strikingly picturesque rock called by the Indians, Kolana, the outermost of a group 2300 feet high, corresponding with the Cathedral Rocks of Yosemite both in relative position and form. On the opposite side of the Valley, facing Kolana, there is a counterpart of the El Capitan that rises sheer and plain to a height of 1800 feet, and over its massive brow flows a stream which makes the most graceful fall I have ever seen. From the edge of the cliff to the top of an earthquake talus it is perfectly free in the air for a thousand feet before it is broken into cascades among talus boulders. It is in all its glory in June, when the snow is melting fast, but fades and vanishes toward the end of summer. The only fall I know with which it may fairly be compared is the Yosemite Bridal Veil; but it excels even that favorite fall both in height and airy-fairy beauty and behavior. Lowlanders are apt to suppose that mountain streams in their wild career over cliffs lose control of themselves and tumble in a noisy chaos of mist and spray. On the contrary, on no part of their travels are they more harmonious and self-controlled. Imagine yourself in Hetch Hetchy on a sunny day in June, standing waist-deep in grass and flowers (as I have often stood), while the great pines sway dreamily with scarcely perceptible motion. Looking northward across the Valley you see a plain, gray granite cliff rising abruptly out of the gardens and groves to a height of 1800 feet, and in front

---

*John Muir. 1912. *The Yosemite*. New York: The Century Company, pp. 249–262.

of it Tueeulala's silvery scarf burning with irised sun-fire. In the first white outburst at the head there is abundance of visible energy, but it is speedily hushed and concealed in divine repose, and its tranquil progress to the base of the cliff is like that of a downy feather in a still room. Now observe the fineness and marvelous distinctness of the various sun-illumined fabrics into which the water is woven; they sift and float from form to form down the face of that grand gray rock in so leisurely and unconfused a manner that you can examine their texture, and patterns and tones of color as you would a piece of embroidery held in the hand. Toward the top of the fall you see groups of booming, comet-like masses, their solid, white heads separate, their tails like combed silk interlacing among delicate gray and purple shadows, ever forming and dissolving, worn out by friction in their rush through the air. Most of these vanish a few hundred feet below the summit, changing to varied forms of cloud-like drapery. Near the bottom the width of the fall has increased from about twenty-five feet to a hundred feet. Here it is composed of yet finer tissues, and is still without a trace of disorder—air, water and sunlight woven into stuff that spirits might wear.

So fine a fall might well seem sufficient to glorify any valley; but here, as in Yosemite, Nature seems in nowise moderate, for a short distance to the eastward of Tueeulala booms and thunders the great Hetch Hetchy Fall, Wapama, so near that you have both of them in full view from the same standpoint. It is the counterpart of the Yosemite Fall, but has a much greater volume of water, is about 1700 feet in height, and appears to be nearly vertical, though considerably inclined, and is dashed into huge outbounding bosses of foam on projecting shelves and knobs. No two falls could be more unlike—Tueeulala out in the open sunshine descending like thistledown; Wapama in a jagged, shadowy gorge roaring and thundering, pounding its way like an earthquake avalanche.

Besides this glorious pair there is a broad, massive fall on the main river a short distance above the head of the Valley. Its position is something like that of the Vernal in Yosemite, and its roar as it plunges into a surging trout-pool may be heard a long way, though it is only about twenty feet high. On Rancheria Creek, a large stream, corresponding in position with the Yosemite Tenaya Creek, there is a chain of cascades joined here and there with swift flashing plumes like the one between the Vernal and Nevada Falls, making magnificent shows as they go their glacier-sculptured way, sliding, leaping, hurrahing, covered with crisp clashing spray made glorious with sifting sunshine. And besides all these a few small streams come over the walls at wide intervals, leaping from ledge to ledge with birdlike song and watering many a hidden cliff-garden and fernery, but they are too unshowy to be noticed in so grand a place.

The correspondence between the Hetch Hetchy walls in their trends, sculpture, physical structure, and general arrangement of the main rock-masses and those of the Yosemite Valley has excited the wondering admiration of every observer. We have seen that the El Capitan and Cathedral rocks occupy the same relative positions in both valleys; so also do their Yosemite points and North Domes. Again, that part of the Yosemite north wall immediately to the east of the Yosemite Fall has two horizontal benches, about 500 and 1500 feet above the floor, timbered with golden-cup oak. Two benches similarly situated and timbered occur on the same relative portion of the Hetch Hetchy north wall, to the east of Wapama Fall, and on no other. The Yosemite is bounded at the head by the great Half Dome. Hetch Hetchy is bounded in the same way, though its head rock is incomparably less wonderful and sublime in form.

The floor of the Valley is about three and a half miles long, and from a fourth to half a mile wide. The lower portion is mostly a level meadow about a mile long, with the trees restricted to the sides and the river banks, and partially separated from the main, upper, forested portion by a low bar of glacier-polished granite across which the river breaks in rapids.

The principal trees are the yellow and sugar pines, digger pine, incense cedar, Douglas spruce, silver fir, the California and golden-cup oaks, balsam cottonwood, Nuttall's flowering dogwood, alder, maple, laurel, tumion, etc. The most abundant and influential are the great yellow or silver pines like those of Yosemite, the tallest over two hundred feet in height, and the oaks assembled in magnificent groves with massive rugged trunks four to six feet in diameter, and broad, shady, wide-spreading heads. The shrubs forming conspicuous flowery clumps and tangles are manzanita, azalea, spiroea, brier-rose, several species of ceanothus, calycanthus, philadelphus, wild cherry, etc.; with abundance of showy and fragrant herbaceous plants growing about them or out in the open in beds by themselves—lilies, Mariposa tulips, brodiaeas, orchids, iris, spraguea, draperia, collomia, collinsia, castilleja, nemophila, larkspur, columbine, goldenrods, sunflowers, mints of many species, honeysuckle, etc. Many fine ferns dwell here also, especially the beautiful and interesting rockferns—pellaea, and cheilanthes of several species—fringing and rosetting dry rock-piles and ledges; woodwardia and asplenium on damp spots with fronds six or seven feet high; the delicate maidenhair in mossy nooks by the falls, and the sturdy, broad-shouldered pteris covering nearly all the dry ground beneath the oaks and pines.

It appears, therefore, that Hetch Hetchy Valley, far from being a plain, common, rock-bound meadow, as many who have not seen it seem to suppose, is a grand landscape garden, one of Nature's rarest and most precious mountain temples. As in Yosemite, the sublime rocks of its walls seem to glow with life, whether leaning back in repose or standing erect in thoughtful attitudes, giving welcome to storms and calms alike, their brows in the sky, their feet set in the groves and gay flowery meadows, while birds, bees, and butterflies help the river and waterfalls to stir all the air into music—things frail and fleeting and types of permanence meeting here and blending, just as they do in Yosemite, to draw her lovers into close and confiding communion with her.

Sad to say, this most precious and sublime feature of the Yosemite National Park, one of the greatest of all our natural resources for the uplifting joy and peace and health of the people, is in danger of being dammed and made into a reservoir to help supply San Francisco with water and light, thus flooding it from wall to wall and burying its gardens and groves one or two hundred feet deep. This grossly destructive commercial scheme has long been planned and urged (though water as pure and abundant can be got from sources outside of the people's park, in a dozen different places), because of the comparative cheapness of the dam and of the territory which it is sought to divert from the great uses to which it was dedicated in the Act of 1890 establishing the Yosemite National Park.

The making of gardens and parks goes on with civilization all over the world, and they increase both in size and number as their value is recognized. Everybody needs beauty as well as bread, places to play in and pray in, where Nature may heal and cheer and give strength to body and soul alike. This natural beauty-hunger is made manifest in the little window-sill gardens of the poor, though perhaps only a geranium slip in a broken cup, as well as in the carefully tended rose and lily gardens of the rich, the thousands of spacious city parks and botanical gardens, and in our magnificent National parks—the Yellowstone, Yosemite, Sequoia, etc.—Nature's sublime wonderlands, the admiration and joy of the world. Nevertheless like anything else worth while, from the very beginning, however well guarded, they have always been subject to attack by despoiling gain-seekers and mischief-makers of every degree from Satan to Senators, eagerly trying to make everything immediately and selfishly commercial, with schemes disguised in smug-smiling philanthropy, industriously, shampiously crying, "Conservation, conservation, panutilization," that man and beast may be fed and the dear Nation made great. Thus long ago a few enterprising merchants utilized the Jerusalem temple as a place of business instead of a place of prayer, changing money, buying and selling cattle and sheep and doves; and earlier still, the first forest reservation, including only one tree, was likewise despoiled. Ever since the establishment of the Yosemite National Park, strife has been going on around its borders and I suppose this will go on as part of the universal battle between right and wrong, however much its boundaries may be shorn, or its wild beauty destroyed.

The first application to the Government by the San Francisco Supervisors for the commercial use of Lake Eleanor and the Hetch Hetchy Valley was made in 1903, and on December 22nd of that year it was denied by the Secretary of the Interior, Mr. Hitchcock, who truthfully said:

> Presumably the Yosemite National Park was created such by law because of the natural objects of varying degrees of scenic importance located within its boundaries, inclusive alike of its beautiful small lakes, like Eleanor, and its majestic wonders, like Hetch Hetchy and Yosemite Valley. It is the aggregation of such natural scenic features that makes the Yosemite Park a wonderland which the Congress of the United States sought by law to reserve for all coming time as nearly as practicable in the condition fashioned by the hand of the Creator—a worthy object of National pride and a source of healthful pleasure and rest for the thousands of people who may annually sojourn there during the heated months.

In 1907 when Mr. Garfield became Secretary of the Interior the application was renewed and granted; but under his successor, Mr. Fisher, the matter has been referred to a Commission, which as this volume goes to press still has it under consideration.

The most delightful and wonderful camp grounds in the Park are its three great valleys—Yosemite, Hetch Hetchy, and Upper Tuolumne; and they are also the most important places with reference to their positions relative to the other great features—the Merced and Tuolumne Cañons, and the High Sierra peaks and glaciers, etc., at the head of the rivers. The main part of the Tuolumne Valley is a spacious flowery lawn four or five miles long, surrounded by magnificent snowy mountains, slightly separated from other beautiful meadows, which together make a series about twelve miles in length, the highest reaching to the feet of Mount Dana, Mount Gibbs, Mount Lyell and Mount McClure. It is about 8500 feet above the sea, and forms the grand central High Sierra camp ground from which excursions are made to the noble mountains, domes, glaciers, etc.; across the Range to the Mono Lake and volcanoes and down the Tuolumne Cañon to Hetch Hetchy. Should Hetch Hetchy be submerged for a reservoir, as proposed, not only would it be utterly destroyed, but the sublime cañon way to the heart of the High Sierra would be hopelessly blocked and the great camping ground, as the watershed of a city drinking system, virtually would be closed to the public. So far as I have learned, few of all the thousands who have seen the park and seek rest and peace in it are in favor of this outrageous scheme.

One of my later visits to the Valley was made in the autumn of 1907 with the late William Keith, the artist. The leaf-colors were then ripe, and the great godlike rocks in repose seemed to glow with life. The artist, under their spell, wandered day after day along the river and through the groves and garden, studying the wonderful scenery; and, after making about forty sketches, declared with enthusiasm that although its walls were less sublime in height, in picturesque beauty and charm Hetch Hetchy surpassed even Yosemite.

That any one would try to destroy such a place seems incredible; but sad experience shows that there are people good enough and bad enough for anything. The proponents of the dam scheme bring forward a lot of bad arguments to prove that the only righteous thing to do with the people's parks is to destroy them bit by bit as they are able. Their arguments are curiously like those of the devil, devised for the destruction of the first garden—so much of the very best Eden fruit going to waste; so much of the best Tuolumne water and Tuolumne scenery going to waste. Few of their statements are even partly true, and all are misleading.

Thus, Hetch Hetchy, they say, is a "low-lying meadow." On the contrary, it is a high-lying natural landscape garden....

"It is a common minor feature, like thousands of others." On the contrary it is a very uncommon feature; after Yosemite, the rarest and in many ways the most important in the National Park.

"Damming and submerging it 175 feet deep would enhance its beauty by forming a crystal-clear lake." Landscape gardens, places of recreation and worship, are never made beautiful by destroying and burying them. The beautiful sham lake, forsooth, would be only an eyesore, a dismal blot on the landscape, like many others to be seen in the Sierra. For, instead of keeping it at the same level all the year, allowing Nature centuries of time to make new shores, it would, of course, be full only a month or two in the spring, when the snow is melting fast; then it would be gradually drained, exposing the slimy sides of the basin and shallower parts of the bottom, with the gathered drift and waste, death and decay of the upper basins, caught here instead of being swept on to decent natural burial along the banks of the river or in the sea. Thus the Hetch Hetchy dam-lake would be only a rough imitation of a natural lake for a few of the spring months, an open sepulcher for the others.

"Hetch Hetchy water is the purest of all to be found in the Sierra, unpolluted, and forever unpollutable." On the contrary, excepting that of the Merced below Yosemite, it is less pure than that of most of the other Sierra streams, because of the sewerage of camp grounds draining into it, especially of the Big Tuolumne Meadows camp ground, occupied by hundreds of tourists and mountaineers, with their animals, for months every summer, soon to be followed by thousands from all the world.

These temple destroyers, devotees of ravaging commercialism, seem to have a perfect contempt for Nature, and, instead of lifting their eyes to the God of the mountains, lift them to the Almighty Dollar.

Dam Hetch Hetchy! As well dam for water-tanks the people's cathedrals and churches, for no holier temple has ever been consecrated by the heart of man.

# 16
# Arthur Bentley (1870–1957)

Arthur Bentley believed that universal principles of politics could be found through sustained and detached scientific inquiry, and that the study of politics would eventually become just as quantitative and predictive as the natural sciences. He argued for rigorous standards of objectivity, and for separating values, ideas, and emotions from analysis. Although written during the time Bentley was still pursuing his chosen career as a journalist, *The Process of Government* is a seminal work in political science. Methodologically, it sought "to fashion a tool" for scientifically investigating the societal changes associated with the Progressive movement. Substantively, it offered "the group" as the fundamental unit of analysis.

Bentley's work extended de Tocqueville's observations about the propensity of Americans to form and use group associations, and it laid the basis for a group theory of politics. The utility of group theory—or pluralism, as it is often called—as a model for how politics really works, or should work, is still debated within the political science profession.

The discipline of political science was in its infancy in the early 1900s; its growing professionalism reflected the Progressives' emphasis on the elevation of experts in all forms of public life. While Bentley sought to gather knowledge objectively, he did so based on the belief that unmasking the facts about American political life would stimulate the public to take political action. As a Progressive scholar, Bentley thus combined professionalism with an agenda of radical political reform. Bentley's work, however, was largely ignored by his contemporaries, and didn't resurface until a half century later when David Truman restated and further developed the group theory of politics in another political science classic, *The Governmental Process*.

---

## "WHEN THE GROUPS ARE ADEQUATELY STATED, EVERYTHING IS STATED"*

It is impossible to attain scientific treatment of material that will not submit itself to measurement in some form. Measure conquers chaos. Even in biology notable advances by the use of statistical methods are being made. And what is of most importance, the material the biologist handles is of a kind that is susceptible of measurement and quantitative comparison all the way through. The occasional recrudescence of vitalism in biology is not irreconcilable with this statement. It simply indicates that from time to time some investigator directs his attention to phases of life, ever lessening in extent,

---

*Arthur F. Bentley. 1908. *The Process of Government: A Study of Social Pressures*. Chicago: University of Chicago Press, pp. 200–202, 208–209, 211–212, 214–217, 222.

which, he holds, are not measurable by present processes, and which, it pleases him to feel, will remain unmeasurable.

In the political world, the dictum, "the greatest good of the greatest number," stands for an effort to make measurements. Sometimes, of course, it is simply the rallying-cry of particular causes. If we take it, however, where it pretends to be a general rule of measurement, we shall find that it applies itself not to what actually happens in legislation, but merely to what a thinker in some particular atmosphere believes ought to be the law; and this, no matter what systematic content of "goods" is pumped into it. I hope to make it clear later that even such a generalized social theory as this is nothing but a reflection, or an index, or a label, of some particular set of demands made by some particular section of society. It is not a measure of social facts which we can use for scientific purposes, and it would not be thus useful even if logically it could be regarded as a standard of measurement, which, of course, it cannot be without further specification.

Statistics of social facts as we ordinarily get them are, of course, measurements. But even after they have been elaborately interpreted by the most expert statisticians, they must still undergo much further interpretation by the people who use them with reference to their immediate purposes of use. As they stand on the printed page, they are commonly regarded as "dead," and they receive much undeserved disparagement. But by this very token it is clear that they do not adequately state the social facts. People who are in close connection with all that rich life-activity indicated by the "feelings" and the "ideas" feel that the heart of the matter is lacking in them.

But, now, the idea and feeling elements, stated for themselves, are unmeasureable as they appear in studies of government. This is a fatal defect in them. Any pretense of measuring them, no matter with what elaborate algebra, will prove to be merely an attribution to them of powers inferred from their results. Usually they appear in social discussions with wholly fictitious values, in support of which not even a pretense of actual measurement is presented. The measurements of experimental psychology are not such measurements as we need. They are measurements of activity looked upon as within the physical individual. The social content is incidental to them and is not measured.

If a statement of social facts which lends itself better to measurement is offered, that characteristic entitles it to attention. Providing the statement does not otherwise distort the social facts, the capability of measurement will be decisive in its favor. The statement that takes us farthest along the road toward quantitative estimates will inevitably be the best statement.

In practical politics a large amount of rough measuring is done. There is measurement with the sword when one nation defeats another in war. South American revolutions, which answer to North American elections, also use the sword as their standard of measure.... In an election at its best in the United States, the measurement goes by the counting of heads. In a legislative body, likewise, the counting of heads appears. A referendum vote is political measurement.

This measuring process appears in various degrees of differentiation. In a battle the social quantities, and the measuring of those quantities which is taking place on the spot, are fused together, so that one has to make an effort to consider them separately. But in a vote in the federal House of Representatives differentiation appears. Here a much more complicated measuring process is carried through, which appears finally in a simplified form in the announcement of the vote for and against the project by the tellers. The student of political life has some hint of the measurements in the figures of the vote; but it is necessary for him to measure the measure, to go far back and examine the quantities that have been in play to produce the given results. The best of these practical political measures are indeed exceedingly crude. The practical politician himself is estimating quantities all the time; indeed his success is in direct proportion to his ability to make good estimates. He may show a preternatural skill. But his skill is of little or no direct use for the scientific student. The practical politician will never under any circumstances consent to make a plain statement of his estimates; indeed it is rare that he knows how to tell, even if he should wish to.

The quantities are present in every bit of political life. There is no political process that is not a balancing of quantity against quantity. There is not a law that is passed that is not the expression of force and force in tension. There is not a court decision or an executive act that is not the result of the same process. Understanding any of these phenomena means measuring the elements that have gone into them.

If we can get our social life stated in terms of activity, and of nothing else, we have not indeed succeeded in measuring it, but we have at least reached a foundation upon which a coherent system of measurements can be built up. Our technique may be very poor at the start, and the amount of labor we must employ to get scanty results will be huge. But we shall cease to be blocked by the intervention of unmeasurable elements, which claim to be themselves the real causes of all that is happening, and which by their spook-like arbitrariness make impossible any progress toward dependable knowledge....

The great task in the study of any form of social life is the analysis of... groups. It is much more than classification, as that term is ordinarily used. When the groups are adequately stated, everything is stated. When I say everything I mean everything. The complete description will mean the complete science, in the study of social phenomena, as in any other field. There will be no more room for animistic "causes" here than there.

But it is not our task in this work to make an analysis of the groups that operate in the whole social life. We are to confine our attention to the process of politics, and the political groups are the only ones with which we shall be directly concerned. And indeed, our task even here concerns the method of analysis, not the exact statement of the groups that are operating at any particular time or place....

It is now necessary to take another step in the analysis of the group. There is no group without its interest. An interest, as the term will be used in this work, is the equivalent of a group. We may speak also of an interest group or of a group interest, again merely for the sake of clearness in expression. The group and the interest are not separate. There exists only the one thing, that is, so many men bound together in or along the path of a certain activity. Sometimes we may be emphasizing the interest phase, sometimes the group phase, but if ever we push them too far apart we soon land in the barren wilderness. There may be a beyond-scientific question as to whether the interest is responsible for the existence of the group, or the group responsible for the existence of the interest. I do not know or care. What we actually find in this world, what we can observe and study, is interested men, nothing more and nothing less. That is our raw material and it is our business to keep our eyes fastened to it....

The interest I put forward is a specific group interest in some definite course of conduct or activity. It is first, last, and all the time strictly empirical. There is no way to find it except by observation. There is no way to get hold of one group interest except in terms of others. A group of slaves for example, is not a group of physical beings who are "slaves by nature," but a social relationship, a specified activity and interest in society. From the interest as a thing by itself no conclusion can be drawn. No fine logic, no calculus of interests will take us a single step forward in the interpreting of society. When we succeed in isolating an interest group the only way to find out what it is going to do, indeed the only way to be sure we have isolated an interest group, is to watch its progress. When we have made sure of one such interest, or group, we shall become more skillful and can make sure of another similar one with less painstaking. When we have compared many sets of groups we shall know better what to expect. But we shall always hold fast to the practical reality, and accept the interests that it offers us as the only interests we can use, studying them as impassively as we would the habits or the organic functions of birds, bees, or fishes.

Such interest groups are of no different material than the "individuals" of a society. They are activity; so are the individuals. It is solely a question of the standpoint from which we look at the activity to define it. The individual stated for himself, and invested with an extra-social unity of his own, is a fiction. But every bit of the activity, which is all we actually know of him, can be stated either on the one side as individual, or on the other side as social group activity....

When we have a group fairly well defined in terms of its interests, we next find it necessary to consider the factors that enter into its relative power of dominating other groups and of carrying its tendencies to action through their full course with relatively little check or hindrance. As the interest is merely a manner of stating the value of the group activity, so these factors of dominance are likewise just phases of the statement of the group, not separate from it, nor capable of scientific use as separate things.

First of all, the number of men who belong to the group attracts attention. Number alone may secure dominance. Such is the case in the ordinary American election, assuming corruption and intimidation to be present in such small proportions that they do not affect the result. But numbers notoriously do not decide elections in the former slave states of the South. There is a concentration of interest on political lines which often, and indeed one may say usually, enables a minority to rule a majority. I cannot stop here to discuss the extent to which majorities are represented by minorities under such circumstances, but only to note the fact. Intensity is a word that will serve as well as any other to denote the concentration of interest which gives a group effectiveness in its activity in the face of the opposition of other groups.

This intensity, like interest, is only to be discovered by observation. There is no royal road for scientific workers to take to it. Catchwords like race, ability, education, moral vigor, may serve as tags to indicate its presence, but they are of little or no help to us, and indeed they are more apt to do us positive harm by making us think we have our solutions in advance, and by blinding us to the facts that we should study. Mere vociferation must not be confused with intensity. It is one form of intensity, but very often the intensity of the talk does not correctly reflect the true intensity of the group. This must be allowed for.

Besides number and intensity, there is a technique of group activities which must be taken into account. Blows, bribes, allurements of one kind and another, and arguments also, are characteristic, and to these must be added organization. A group will differentiate under fitting circumstances a special set of activities for carrying on its work. We must learn how these specialized activities vary under different forms of group oppositions, how the technique changes and evolves. We shall find that the change in methods is produced by the appearance of new group interests, directed against the use of the method that is suppressed. If violence gives way to bribery, or bribery to some form of demagogy, or that perhaps to a method called reasoning, it will be possible, if we pursue the study carefully enough, to find the group interest that has worked the change. That group will have its own technique, no more scrupulous probably than the technique it suppresses, but vigorously exerted through the governing institutions of the society, or possibly outside those institutions.

Technique will of course vary with the intensity of interest, as for instance when assassination is adopted by revolutionists who can find no other method to make themselves felt against their opponents. Number also has intimate relations with both technique and intensity. In general it is to be said that there is no rule of thumb which will point out to us any particular lines of activity in which the most powerful groups can inevitably be found. We may sometimes find the greatest intensity over matters that still seem to us trifles, even after we think we have interpreted them in terms of underlying groups, and again we may find slight intensity where we think there ought to be the most determined effort. It is solely a matter for observation. And observation shows, here as before, that no group can be defined or understood save in terms of the other groups of the given time and place. One opposition appears and adjusts itself and another takes its place; and each opposition gets its meaning only in terms of the other oppositions and of the adjustments that have taken place between them....

As for political questions under any society in which we are called upon to study them, we shall never find a group interest of the society as a whole. We shall always find that the political interests and activities of any given group—and there are no political phenomena except group phenomena—are directed against other activities of men, who appear in other groups, political or other. The phenomena of political life which we study will always divide the society in which they occur, along lines which are very real, though of varying degrees of definiteness. The society itself is nothing other than the complex of the groups that compose it.

# 17
# Alice Hamilton (1869–1970)

Students today may still be using an updated version of Hamilton and Hardy's *Industrial Toxicology* text (1934), a fine testament to Alice Hamilton, who has been called the nation's "first great urban/industrial environmentalist." Hamilton chose to become a doctor, one of three professional occupations—the others being teacher and nurse—open to women in the late nineteenth century. (Indeed, around 1900, as many as one in five doctors was a woman, a percentage that was not reached again until the 1970s.)

She also was a resident of Hull House, Jane Addams's Chicago settlement house, which was both a home and a base for women interested in social work, public health, and improving city life. Hamilton's association with Hull House led to her interest in industrial and urban diseases, and during the first part of the twentieth century she became a leading authority on the environmental consequences of industrial activity.

Hamilton's pioneering research in the newly developing field of industrial toxicology led directly to changes in factory conditions and worker compensation laws. Her work stressing the physician's role in preventing industrial poisoning prompted changes in the medical profession itself, which began to realize that company doctors should be advocates of the workers they treated rather than simply defenders of management policy. She questioned the environmental health impacts of new industrial technologies such as solvents and petrochemicals and was deeply concerned when such technologies were introduced into the workplace before their dangers had been fully explored.

Three months after Hamilton's death in 1970 at age 101, Congress passed the Occupational Safety and Health Act. The legislation and the agency established to administer the act, the Occupational Safety and Health Administration, directed national attention to the relationship between workplace and the environment and to the work begun by Dr. Hamilton.

---

## "THE PREVENTION
## OF INDUSTRIAL POISONING"*

It is not my intention to describe in detail the practical measure by which a factory or workshop may be rendered safe from toxic dust and vapors. That is the task of the engineer, not of the physician. All that the latter can do is to make clear the principles on which methods of protection must be based and

---

*Alice Hamilton. 1925. *Industrial Poisons in the United States*. New York: Macmillan and Company, pp. 538–542.

then leave their actual execution to the experts in the mechanical trades. These principles depend on the character of the poisonous compound in question, above all on its special mode of entrance into the human body. If this is by way of the inspired air, the prevention of fumes and dust becomes the matter of first importance. Whatever money is available for factory hygiene must be expended first on mechanisms to prevent poisoning the air, even if this means a scanty equipment for the washrooms and lunchrooms.

The physician will sometimes be told that certain processes cannot be carried on without contamination of the air, that the workman must be protected in some other way, by some sort of respirator or mask. This brings him into a field of controversy in which difficulties await him. The experiments now being carried on by the United States Bureau of Mines will doubtless throw much light on the question of the efficacy of such devices against different sorts of dusts and vapors, but at present it does not seem safe to say more than this: no apparatus, respirator or army mask, through which a man can breathe with entire ease and comfort while doing heavy work, will serve to hold back all the poisonous dust or vapor in the air. If such a mask is really efficient it will cause some discomfort and difficulty to the wearer. This means that it is a device for emergency use, not for use during eight or ten hours continuously, day in and day out, for the best shop discipline would break down under a strain like that, and the foreman would have to pretend not to see the masks worn on the forehead or around the neck, if he did not wish to lose most of his men.

A mask, carefully selected for the particular poison against which protection is needed, should be provided for emergency use, during short periods only, in all places where there is danger of fumes or dust, but to place one's trust in masks for the continual protection of men is simply to close one's eyes to unpleasant facts.

If the poison belongs to those that gain entrance primarily through the skin, cleanliness of the premises, of work-benches and apparatus, is essential and in addition it is necessary to furnish clean working clothes and facilities for bathing, as well as for the usual washing of hands and face. This is already accepted as a necessity in connection with the compounds which produce trade eruptions but it is quite as essential for those which produce systemic symptoms without local irritation. If direct contact with the poison cannot be avoided, then every means must be adopted to protect the skin. As much of it as possible should be covered with clean underwear, overalls, socks, and caps, and the surface which is necessarily exposed may be covered with a bland ointment or dusted with powder or washed frequently. It must be remembered, however, that there is a risk in too much washing of the human skin and that care must be taken in such cases to use the least irritating cleansers, to avoid scrubbing, and to restore the lost oils of the skin by inunction with some animal fat.

The consensus of opinion among men experienced in such industries as the production of coal-tar intermediates, where skin absorption is of prime importance, seems to be against gloves as a protection. Gloves make the hands sweat and the skin soft and hot and in excellent condition for the absorption of poisons, and if there is even a small rip or tear in the glove letting the dust or liquid in, it will form what is practically a poultice of poison around the hand.

...[T]here are poisonous dusts which not only contaminate the air but also produce poisoning through the intestinal tract if the worker has his hands and face covered with such dust when he handles his food or his plug of tobacco. The protective measures indicated in such cases, provision of a separate lunchroom, only to be entered after thorough ablutions, are too well known to need anything more than a mention.

The factors that favor absorption of industrial poisons, or that heighten their effect...also come within the field of the physician. Heat from furnaces, steam from tubs and tanks, may seem to be outside his province: long hours and low wages, the employment of young lads and girls, may seem to him questions for the management alone, but the incidence of sickness among his charges is profoundly affected by such factors as these. He should not fail to assume some responsibility for the feeding of the employees at least so far as the noon-day meal is concerned, for if a warm, wholesome lunch is furnished them it will go far to protect them against poisoning.

The industrial physician is entrusted with the ungrateful task of selecting by physical examination, men and women whom he considers fit to face the risks of work in poisonous occupations. The textbooks warn him to reject the tuberculous, the anemic, the individual with lesions of the kidneys or heart, and this is doubtless wise, but he is an innocent optimist who believes that after all this is done he has guarded himself against distressing accidents. The management may believe that such a weeding out has rid the force of the over-susceptibilities; the wise physician knows that this is not true and that the most vigorous and blooming men and women may be the ones to develop lead encephalopathy...or benzene purpura hemorrhagica ...and that the only way to guard against this is to keep constantly on the watch for the warning signs and then to remove the victim before serious harm has been done.

To do this, it is best to make a careful classification of the different jobs in the plant, according to the degree of danger in each, and to devote special attention to the employees in the class that heads the list. New hands who are given jobs in this class should be examined at frequent intervals till the physician is able to say whether they have a normal degree of resistance to the poison in question, for if not, it is only good economy to shift them at once to other work. It will always, however, be necessary to subject all the employees in the dangerous class to routine examination, for at any time some disturbance of metabolism may break down the defenses of one who was apparently immune.

The physician should be the one to whom the education of the employers in personal prophylaxis should be entrusted, or at least he should plan and supervise it, though it may be he will not have enough of factory vernacular to "get it across." But he should insist on the necessity of such instruction. The idea is often held by employers who are using unfamiliar poisons that it is best to say nothing about them for fear of frightening the men away. This attitude on the part of the men in charge of munition works during the war was a distressing obstacle in the way of all who tried to introduce into American plants the safeguards successfully worked out in the British, which could not be done if the fiction were maintained that trinitrotoluene might indeed explode, but was otherwise quite harmless. As a matter of fact we all knew the workmen were not hoodwinked, they were only muddled. They knew perfectly well that something was there that made men ill but just what it was and how it affected them they did not know, so they ended by suspecting everything and promptly quitting the job if they fell ill, regardless of whether the illness were caused by the poison or not. The plants which were under intelligent management, with careful instruction of the men and prompt resort to the dispensary even for slight ailments, had a much lower labor turnover than those which followed the policy of secrecy.

The task of education is not easy—it is exhaustive of time and temper alike, but it is a duty which cannot be shirked, especially in unorganized industries. Trade Unionists are to a varying extent responsible for the conditions under which they work, but the great majority of the poisonous industries are unorganized. Much of the dangerous work is done by foreign-born men and women and toward these workers the responsibility of the management of the physician is far greater. Such people are like children in their readiness to accept the conditions of life, they will work long hours, in heat and filth and poisonous dust, they make no demands for security or comforts, they are quite free from the irritating interference of trade union officials. These are great advantages to the employer but if he accepts them he must accept the accompanying disadvantages. With child-like docility goes childish ignorance, recklessness and obstinacy. The management cannot throw upon such men and women the responsibility for their own health and safety. They are not capable of assuming it. For them the protection must be especially elaborate, it must be "fool-proof," the vigilance of the physician must be unrelaxed.

It may happen that the physician will be asked what to do in a department where all known mechanical devices for the prevention of poisonous dusts and vapors have been applied, and yet, because of the very nature of the process, there is still contamination of the air. In such cases there seem to be but two courses open. The dose of poison may be reduced by shortening the exposure, cutting it down perhaps to only a couple of hours in the day's shift or even less than that. Or the work may be allowed to go on under the watchful eye of the physician who knows that a certain warning symptom will appear in time for him to order a change of work before real harm has been done.... With newer poisons, it may be that the physician will have to study for himself the physiological effects in order to discover what sign or symptom can be depended on to give the needed warning of danger.

In closing, let me beg the industrial physician not to let the atmosphere of the factory befog his view of his special problem. His duty is to the producer, not to the product. If measures which he knows to be necessary are declared impossible, because they interfere with production, he may have to yield, but let it be understood that such yielding is against his judgment. A sanitary engineer may be told by a city council that it cannot afford a pure water supply and he may have no choice but to accept the verdict. But he would be greatly at fault if he allowed the city fathers to believe that the half-way measures they plan will safeguard the community against typhoid fever. In the same way the industrial physician may be obliged to abandon his plans for protecting his charges against poisoning because the expense is greater than the management will allow or because a change in the method might make the product less perfect. But in so yielding let him be careful never to sacrifice his own intellectual integrity nor adopt the standards of the non-medical man to whom the proper working of the plant is of first importance. His task is to safeguard the health of the patients who are entrusted to him, often without any volition of their own. The successful production of goods is outside his field. To the physician, always, life is more than meat and the body more than raiment.

# 18
# John Dewey (1859–1952)

Just as de Tocqueville's astute observations about American culture and institutions have framed discussions about American democracy, so have John Dewey's. The scholarly Progressive set the agenda for debate about modern issues of philosophy, education, and civic life.

Dewey is associated with the pragmatic school of philosophy, which developed an epistemology combining theory and practice. Viewing ideas as tools for solving problems encountered in the environment, he wedded philosophy to the practice of everyday life. Although he spent most of his career on university faculties, he also directly encountered the socioeconomic problems of urban and immigrant life by actively participating in the work of Jane Addams's Hull House.

Influenced by the disciplines of evolutionary biology, physics, and psychology, Dewey criticized schools of thought that detached humans from nature. Rejecting nature as a purely mechanical system, he took a more panoramic view: Nature consisted of psychophysical and physiochemical elements in constant and changing transactions with human experience.

In the field of education, Dewey advocated fundamental changes in instruction. He viewed the teacher not as a rigid taskmaster but as a guide and co-worker with the child, and advocated learning by doing. He saw education as an experimental science and linked his ideas about educational reforms to individual growth, community-building, and democracy.

While Arthur Bentley saw only group activity, Dewey focused on community. For Dewey, communal life constituted the real idea of democracy and an array of inchoate, disparate groups by themselves could never constitute a community. In the machine age, Dewey sought to reconcile Madison's large republic with notions of deliberative participatory democracy. He had a strong commitment to a participatory democracy in which all individuals affected by the consequences of a decision participate. In such a discursive democracy, as we call it today, communication is key. Democracy, he said, would have its "consummation when free social inquiry is indissolubly wedded to the art of full and moving communication." He wrote his famous book, *The Public and its Problems*, to counter those who believed in the inevitability of a more constricted public role in political life. While acknowledging the problems of modern politics, he nonetheless remained committed to democratic ideals, and the restoration of the local community as a public sphere for genuine discussion. Today, Dewey's principles are being applied in the community-based environmental movement, which is reenergizing local residents and communities as active participants in collaborative resource-management efforts.

# "THE ECLIPSE OF THE PUBLIC"*

...[T]he Public seems to be lost; it is certainly bewildered. The government, officials and their activities, are plainly with us. Legislatures make laws with luxurious abandon; subordinate officials engage in a losing struggle to enforce some of them; judges on the bench deal as best they can with the steadily mounting pile of disputes that come before them. But where is the public which these officials are supposed to represent? How much more is it than geographical names and official titles? The United States, the state of Ohio or New York, the county of this and the city of that? Is the public much more than what a cynical diplomat once called Italy: a geographical expression? Just as philosophers once imputed a substance to qualities and traits in order that the latter might have something in which to inhere and thereby gain a conceptual solidity and consistency which they lacked on their face, so perhaps our political "common-sense" philosophy imputes a public only to support and substantiate the behavior of officials. How can the latter be public officers, we despairingly ask, unless there is a public? If a public exists, it is surely as uncertain about its own whereabouts as philosophers since Hume have been about the residence and make-up of the self. The number of voters who take advantage of their majestic right is steadily decreasing in proportion to those who might use it. The ratio of actual to eligible voters is now about one-half. In spite of somewhat frantic appeal and organized effort, the endeavor to bring voters to a sense of their privileges and duties has so far been noted for failure. A few preach the impotence of all politics; the many nonchalantly practice abstinence and indulge in indirect action. Skepticism regarding the efficacy of voting is openly expressed, not only in the theories of intellectuals, but in the words of lowbrow masses: "What difference does it make whether I vote of not? Things go on just the same anyway. My vote never changed anything." Those somewhat more reflective add: "It is nothing but a fight between the ins and the outs. The only difference made by an election is as to who get the jobs, draw the salaries and shake down the plum tree."

...When the public is as uncertain and obscure as it is to-day, and hence as remote from government, bosses with their political machines fill the void between government and the public. Who pulls the strings which move the bosses and generates power to run the machines is a matter of surmise rather than of record, save for an occasional overt scandal.

...The significant thing is that familiarity has bred indifference if not contempt. Indifference is the evidence of current apathy, and apathy is testi-

---

*John Dewey. 1984. *The Public and Its Problems* (original publication date 1927) in *The Collected Works of John Dewey, Later Works, 1925–1953. Volume Two: 1925–1927,* Jo Ann Boydston, ed. Carbondale: Southern Illinois University Press, pp. 308–314, 317–324. Copyright © 1984 by the Board of Trustees, Southern Illinois University. Reprinted with permission from Southern Illinois University Press. Footnotes are omitted.

mony to the fact that the public is so bewildered that it cannot find itself. The remarks are not made with a view to drawing a conclusion. They are offered with a view to outlining a problem: What is the public? If there is a public, what are the obstacles in the way of its recognizing and articulating itself? Is the public a myth? Or does it come into being only in periods of marked social transition when crucial alternative issues stand out, such as that between throwing one's lot in with the conservation of established institutions or with forwarding new tendencies? In a reaction against dynastic rule which has come to be felt as despotically oppressive? In a transfer of social power from agrarian classes to industrial?...

Previous discussion has brought to light some conditions out of which the public is generated. It has also set forth some of the causes through which a "new age of human relationships" has been brought into being. These two arguments form the premises which, when they are related to each other, will provide our answer to the questions just raised. Indirect, extensive, enduring and serious consequences of conjoint and interacting behavior call a public into existence having a common interest in controlling these consequences. But the machine age has so enormously expanded, multiplied, intensified and complicated the scope of the indirect consequences, has formed such immense and consolidated unions in action, on an impersonal rather than a community basis, that the resultant public cannot identify and distinguish itself. And this discovery is obviously an antecedent condition of any effective organization on its part. Such is our thesis regarding the eclipse which the public idea and interest have undergone. There are too many publics and too much of public concern for our existing resources to cope with. The problem of a democratically organized public is primarily and essentially an intellectual problem, in a degree to which the political affairs of prior ages offer no parallel.

Our concern at this time is to state how it is that the machine age in developing the Great Society has invaded and partially disintegrated the small communities of former times without generating a Great Community. The facts are familiar enough; our especial affair is to point out their connections with the difficulties under which the organization of a democratic public is laboring. For the very familiarity with the phenomena conceals their significance and blinds us to their relation to immediate political problems....

There was a time when a man might entertain a few general political principles and apply them with some confidence. A citizen believed in states' rights or in a centralized federal government; in free trade or protection. It did not involve much mental strain to imagine that by throwing in his lot with one party or another he could so express his views that his belief would count in government. For the average voter to-day the tariff question is a complicated medley of infinite detail, schedules of rates specific and *ad valorem* on countless things, many of which he does not recognize by name, and with respect to which he can form no judgment. Probably not one voter in a thousand even reads the scores of pages in which the rates of toll are enumerated and he would not be much wiser if he did. The average man gives it up as a bad job. At election time, appeal to some time-worn slogan may galvanize him into a temporary notion that he has convictions on an important subject, but except for manufacturers and dealers who have some interest at stake in this or that schedule, belief lacks the qualities which attach to beliefs about matters of personal concern. Industry is too complex and intricate.

Again the voter may by personal predilection or inherited belief incline towards magnifying the scope of local governments and inveigh against the evils of centralization. But he is vehemently sure of social evils attending the liquor traffic. He finds that the prohibitory law of his locality, township, county or state, is largely nullified by the importation of liquor from outside, made easy by modern means of transportation. So he becomes an advocate of a national amendment giving the central government power to regulate the manufacture and sale of intoxicating drinks. This brings in its train a necessary extension of federal officials and powers. Thus to-day, the south, the traditional home of the states' rights doctrine, is the chief supporter of national prohibition and Volstead Act. It would not be possible to say how many voters have thought of the relation between their professed general principle and their special position on the liquor question: probably not many. On the other hand, life-long Hamiltonians, proclaimers of the dangers of particularistic local autonomy, are opposed to prohibition. Hence they play a tune *ad hoc* on the Jeffersonian flute. Gibes at inconsistency are, however, as irrelevant as they are easy. The social situation has been so changed by the factors of an industrial age that traditional general principles have little practical meaning. They persist as emotional cries rather than as reasoned ideas.

The same criss-crossing occurs with reference to regulation of railways. The opponent of a strong federal government finds, being a farmer or shipper, that rates are too high; he also finds that railways pay little attention to state boundaries, that lines once local are parts of vast systems and that state legislation and administration are ineffectual for his purpose. He calls for national regulation. Some partisan of the powers of the central government, on the other hand, being an investor in stocks and bonds, finds that his income is likely to be unfavorably affected by federal action and he promptly protests against the vexatious tendency to appeal to national aid, which has now become in his eyes a foolish paternalism. The developments of industry and commerce have so complicated affairs that a clear-cut, generally applicable, standard of judgment becomes practically impossible. The forest cannot be seen for the trees nor the trees for the forest....

Political apathy, which is a natural product of the discrepancies between actual practices and traditional machinery, ensues from inability to identify one's self with definite issues. These are hard to find and locate in the vast complexities of current life. When traditional war-cries have lost their import in practical policies which are consonant with them, they are readily dismissed as bunk. Only habit and tradition, rather than reasoned conviction, together with a vague faith in doing one's civic duty, send to the polls a considerable percentage of the fifty per cent who still vote. And of them it is a common remark that a large number vote against something or somebody rather than for anything or anybody, except when powerful agencies create a scare. The old principles do not fit contemporary life as it is lived, however well they may have expressed the vital interests of the times in which they arose. Thousands feel their hollowness even if they cannot make their feeling articulate. The confusion which has resulted from the size and ramifications of social activities has rendered men skeptical of the efficiency of political action. Who is sufficient unto these things? Men feel that they are caught in the sweep of forces too vast to understand or master. Thought is brought to a standstill and action paralyzed. Even the specialist finds it difficult to trace the chain of "cause and effect"; and even he operates only after the event, looking backward, while meantime social activities have moved on to effect a new state of affairs.

Similar considerations account for depreciation of the machinery of democratic political action in contrast with a rising appreciation of the need of expert administrators. For example, one of the by-products of the war was the investment of the government at Muscle Shoals for the manufacture of nitrogen, a chemical product of great importance to the farmer, as well as to armies in the field. The disposition and utilization of the plant have become matters of political dispute. The questions involved, questions of science, agriculture, industry and finance, are highly technical. How many voters are competent to measure all the factors involved in arriving at a decision? And if they were competent after studying it, how many have time to devote to it? It is true that this matter does not come before the electorate directly, but the technical difficulty of the problem is reflected in the confused paralysis of the legislators whose business it is to deal with it. The confused situation is further complicated by the invention of other and cheaper methods of producing nitrates. Again, the rapid development of hydro-electric and super-power is a matter of public concern. In the long run, few questions exceed it in importance. Aside from business corporations which have a direct interest in it and some engineers, how many citizens have the data or the ability to secure and estimate the facts involved in its settlement? One further illustration: Two things which intimately concern a local public are street-railway transportation and the marketing of food products. But the history of municipal politics shows in most cases a flare-up of intense interest followed by a period of indifference. Results come home to the masses of the people. But the very size, heterogeneity and mobility of urban populations, the vast capital required, the technical character of the engineering problems involved, soon tire the attention of the average voter. I think the three instances are fairly typical. The ramification of the issues before the public is so wide and intricate, the technical matters involved are so specialized, the details are so many and so shifting, that the public cannot for any length of time identify and hold itself. It is not that there is no public, no large body of persons having a common interest in the consequences of social transactions. There is too much public, a public too diffused and scattered and too intricate in composition. And there are too many publics, for conjoint actions which have indirect, serious and enduring consequences are multitudinous beyond comparison, and each one of them crosses the others and generates its own group of persons especially affected with little to hold these different publics together in an integrated whole....

The increase in the number, variety and cheapness of amusements represents a powerful diversion from political concern. The members of an inchoate public have too many ways of enjoyment, as well as of work, to give much thought to organization into an effective public. Man is a consuming and sportive animal as well as a political one. What is significant is that access to means of amusement has been rendered easy and cheap beyond anything known in the past. The present era of "prosperity" may not be enduring. But the movie, radio, cheap reading matter and motor car with all they stand for have come to stay. That they did not originate in deliberate desire to divert attention from political interests does not lessen their effectiveness in that direction. The political elements in the constitution of the human being, those having to do with citizenship, are crowded to one side. In most circles it is hard work to sustain conversation on a political theme; and once initiated, it is quickly dismissed with a yawn. Let there be introduced the topic of the mechanism and accomplishment of various makes of motor cars or the respective merits of actresses, and the dialogue goes on at a lively pace. The thing to be remembered is that this cheapened and multiplied access to amusement is the product of the machine age, intensified by the business tradition which causes provision of means for an enjoyable passing of time to be one of the most profitable of occupations.

One phase of the workings of a technological age, with its unprecedented command of natural energies, while it is implied in what has been said, needs explicit attention. The older publics, in being local communities, largely homogeneous with one another, were also, as the phrase goes, static. They changed, of course, but barring war, catastrophe and great migrations, the modifications were gradual. They proceeded slowly and were largely unperceived by those undergoing them. The newer forces have created mobile and fluctuating associational forms. The common complaints of the disintegration of family life may be placed in evidence. The movement from rural to urban assemblies is also the result and proof of this mobility. Nothing stays long put, not even the associations by which business and industry are carried on. The mania for motion and speed is a symptom of the restless instability of social life, and it operates to intensify the causes from which it springs. Steel replaces wood and masonry for buildings; ferro-concrete modifies steel, and some invention may work a further revolution. Muscle Shoals was acquired to produce nitrogen, and new methods have already made antiquated the supposed need of great accumulation of water power. Any selected illustration suffers because of the heterogeneous mass of cases to select from. How can a public be organized, we may ask, when literally it does not stay in place? Only deep issues or those which can be made to appear such can find a common denominator among all the shifting and unstable relationships. Attachment is a very different function of life from affection. Affections will continue as long as the heart beats. But attachment requires something more than organic causes. The very things which stimulate and intensify affections may undermine attachments. For these are bred in tranquil stability; they are nourished in constant relationships. Acceleration of mobility disturbs them at their root. And without abiding attachments associations are too shifting and shaken to permit a public readily to locate and identify itself.

The new era of human relationships in which we live is one marked by mass production for remote markets, by cable and telephone, by cheap printing, by railway and steam navigation. Only geographically did Columbus discover a new world. The actual new world has been generated in the last hundred years. Steam and electricity have done more to alter the conditions under which men associate together than all the agencies which affected human relationships before our time. There are those who lay the blame for all the evils of our lives on steam, electricity and machinery. It is always convenient to have a devil as well as a savior to bear the responsibilities of humanity. In reality, the trouble springs rather from the ideas and absence of ideas in connection with which technological factors operate. Mental and moral beliefs and ideals change more slowly than outward conditions. If the ideals associated with the higher life of our cultural past have been impaired, the fault is primarily with them. Ideals and standards formed without regard to the means by which they are to be achieved and incarnated in flesh are bound to be thin and wavering. Since the aims, desires and purposes created by a machine age do not connect with tradition, there are two sets of rival ideals, and those which have actual instrumentalities at their disposal have the advantage. Because the two are rivals and because the older ones retain their glamor and sentimental prestige in literature and religion, the newer ones are perforce harsh and narrow. For the older symbols of ideal life still engage thought and command loyalty. Conditions have changed, but every aspect of life, from religion and education to property and trade, shows that nothing approaching a transformation has taken place in ideas and ideals. Symbols control sentiment and thought, and the new age has no symbols consonant with its activities. Intellectual instrumentalities for the formation of an organized public are more inadequate than its overt means. The ties which hold men together in action are numerous, tough and subtle. But they are invisible and intangible. We have the physical tools of communication as never before. The thoughts and aspirations congruous with them are not communicated, and hence are not common. Without such communication the public will remain shadowy and formless, seeking spasmodically for itself, but seizing and holding its shadow rather than its substance. Till the Great Society is converted into a Great Community, the Public will remain in eclipse. Communication can alone create a great community. Our Babel is not one of tongues but of the signs and symbols without which shared experience is impossible.

# 19
# Margaret Sanger (1879–1966)

Margaret Sanger's early career brought her into contact with poor women who suffered physically and mentally from frequent and unwanted child-bearing, but who, under the law, were denied information about avoiding pregnancy. Sanger began to write articles on reproduction and birth control, hoping that her writing would ultimately produce a showdown with Anthony Comstock, a "crusader against vice." In 1873 Comstock had been instrumental in obtaining passage of a bill that barred distribution through the U.S. mails of "obscene, lewd, lascivious, filthy and indecent" materials. That law placed information on contraceptive devices within its scope. Sanger was successful in her challenge to Comstock. Indicted in 1914 by the federal government for sending birth control information through the mail, she jumped bail and fled to Europe, spending a year there until the charges were dropped amid a growing national movement in support of birth control. Two years later, in 1916, in another act of civil disobedience, she opened the nation's first birth-control clinic in a crowded tenement section of Brooklyn; it was subsequently raided by the police. As she relates in her autobiography, she continued to challenge the Comstock laws well into the 1930s. (Although many states did legalize birth control between the 1920s and the 1960s, it was not until the U.S. Supreme Court's 1965 decision in *Griswold v. Connecticut* that laws limiting a physician's right to prescribe birth control or prohibiting consenting adults to use contraceptive devices were declared unconstitutional.)

Sanger remains today, as she was throughout her life, a controversial figure. In the current debate over abortion, for example, pro-choice supporters regard her as a pioneer for women's reproductive rights and population control, while antiabortionists label her use of eugenic arguments (i.e., human improvement by genetic control) as racist and immoral. As in Margaret Sanger's day, arguments over birth control and population policy continue to be linked to societal divisions over race, class, religion, and immigration.

## "MY FIGHT FOR BIRTH CONTROL"*

My fight for birth control had begun, seventeen years previous, with a direct challenge to the iniquitous Section 211 of the Federal Penal Code. It will be recalled that this statute was invoked by the postmaster of New York City to suppress the *Woman Rebel*—it was declared unmailable because it tended to

---

*Margaret Sanger. 1931. *My Fight for Birth Control*. New York: Farrar & Rinehart, pp. 345–356. Reprinted with permission from Alexander C. Sanger.

violate the text, which declared it a crime "to induce or to incite a person to so use or apply any article, instrument, substance, drug, medicines or thing to be used or applied for the prevention of conception." Was the battle now finally to be won with the amendment of that act which had been incorporated into our federal laws due to the long agitation of that flamboyant and pathological zealot Anthony Comstock? For fifty-eight years it has remained there, silently shackling the lives of American women, perpetuating suffering and physical torture, spreading the blight of biological tragedy because of its diabolical taboos.

Now, our "doctors' bill" had been introduced into the Senate by Senator Frederick Gillett, the venerable Republican senator from Massachusetts, and a hearing was to be held before a sub-committee of the Senate Committee on the Judiciary. The date was set for February 13, 1931. An appropriate day, it flashed through my mind, as I set out for Washington—so near the birthday of our great Emancipator, who had freed the slaves. Could we free women from the worse slavery in which they had been kept by the barbaric taboos imposed upon a whole nation by a weak-kneed Congress?

Glancing over that Section 211, as the train sped toward Washington, and at its corollaries, enacted the same year—Sections 311 and 312 of the Criminal Code and the act of Congress passed in 1909, all the old indignation that I felt twenty years ago flamed up anew into a white heat. With what diabolical skill that act had been worded! With what Machiavellian shrewdness it had been designed to prevent the circulation of scientific knowledge and methods! Forever, it linked contraception with obscenity—throwing dust into the eyes of the righteous in order to slip in the fallacy that conscious procreation was a vile, filthy and indecent practice. I nearly became a fanatical feminist again: men had passed this law…mature men had permitted themselves to be led like sheep to the slaughter. It made me doubt for a moment whether humans are even capable of making laws for the behaviour of their fellowmen. Where was the spirit of liberty, of toleration, of human compassion?

Well, I warned myself, it was a situation demanding tact, diplomacy, sweetness and light. Victories! At that moment they seemed as nothing to me, as long as that legislation remained on the federal codes. There were those, I knew, who were all for a clean sweep; but long experience had convinced me that it was a step-by-step fight—that it was all very well to denounce, to theorize, to analyze academic and philosophical aspects of the right and wrong of the problem. My task was to help those conscript mothers, to bring relief not with fine, soothing, eloquent words, but to prevent the recurrences of hopeless pregnancies, the conception of wan little lives that were all too soon snuffed out.

Therefore the amendment of the bill which aimed to place the whole matter of contraceptive education in the hands of competent physicians and clinics seemed the inevitable next step in federal legislation.

It was arranged that the sub-committee on "S. 4582" would meet in Room 212 of the Senate Office Building on the morning of Friday, February 13, when its proponents would speak in favor of the bill. The following morning seventeen opponents would be heard….

As we gathered in the room that February morning, I began to sense intuitively, like a veteran warrior, that it was to be a battle against the same old enemies—the silent enemies of that Brooklyn courtroom in which, fifteen years ago, I had been sentenced, the unseen enemies who gave the police orders to raid the Town Hall meeting in 1921, who had directed the ill-considered raid upon the Clinical Research Bureau in 1929. The Roman Catholic hierarchy of course; but along with them all the forces of reaction, the hopeless dogmatists of the ages; the conformists; the reactionaries—call them Lutherans or Puritans or Fundamentalists or Pharisees—all those for whom morality means merely blind subservience to custom and tradition, to a code completed and rigid once and for eternity. They explain every occurrence that inflicts unhappiness upon human life as "the will of God," be it disease, famine, flood, epidemic, poverty, starvation, unemployment, illiteracy, or feeble-mindedness.

They are the classes always ready and active to protect their own prejudices, to enforce their intolerant will upon the population at large. By suppression, by propaganda, by trickery, by treachery, by arrogant legislation, they achieve their ends. Many of them with their blatant loudspeaking are merely the mouthpieces of the wily directors of the Church—those evil shepherds who in turn take their orders from higher up. They are skillful in using the weapons of misrepresentation; yet they cover their intentions under high-sounding phrases of traditional morality and theology.

On the other side stand the forces of reason, of tolerance, of science—forces that embody more truly the spirit of Christ than the Church ever did; the spirit of helpfulness and of compassion, of infinite understanding of human suffering and human frailty. I am no theologian; but I am certain that it was never the intention of the founder of the Christian religion to impose a hard and set sexual code upon the human race. He who associated with sinners and publicans, who attached so little importance to the sins of the flesh, who emphasized so vividly that envy and avarice were more deadly sins than adultery, would find today his religion of love and brotherhood, of selflessness, I am sure, expressing itself in the disinterested attitude of scientific research, in the work of the clinics rather than in richly decorated cathedrals or pompous rituals chanted in a language of the past....

Our time was limited to one morning—a bare hour and a half—and so we were forced to limit the number of our defenders. The room was crowded with friends and opponents. Introduced by Mrs. Hepburn, our legislative chairman, I could touch only briefly on the evils wrought by the Comstockian legislation, upon the revolutionary changes wrought in the technique of contraception since 1873. I emphasized the manifest injustice of classifying scientific, medical information with pornographic writing or pictures. I roughly sketched the appalling effects of this law upon women and children: "Since this law was established in 1873," I stated in conclusion, "more than one million and five hundred thousand mothers have passed out beyond from causes due to child bearing, and we know today that the subject of contraception is intimately associated with the deaths of mothers and affects our maternal mortality.

"It is also roughly estimated that, since that law was passed, more than fifteen million children have passed out of life during their first year of infancy; many of them were children born in conditions of poverty and their mothers' ill health. A great majority of them might have been living to-day had their mothers had a chance to recuperate from the ordeal of previous pregnancy instead of using up the vitality of the child before it was born.

"We, Mr. Chairman, believe that the effect of keeping these laws on the statute book is to keep alive hypocrisy, evasion, and a general increasing disregard for laws. We believe that there is nothing to be gained by keeping such laws on the statute books when they are known to be inimical to the personal health of mothers, to the family happiness, and to the general welfare and progress of the Nation."

Then I presented a long list of organizations which endorsed the proposed amendment—medical boards and societies, welfare committees and settlements, philanthropic organizations and foundations, religious alliances, representing such denominations as the Episcopal, the Congregational, the Universalist, the Unitarian, and even the Methodist Episcopal Churches in various sections of the United States, political organizations and trade unions leagues. Other defendants of the amendment spoke on the specific advantages to be gained for the nation and the individual....

When we gathered again the following morning at the Senate Office Building, there was an air of tense excitement in Room 212. I had prepared myself to hear the stock conventional arguments against contraception; but I was not prepared for the shrewd trickery which our opponents used to combat us. The claim was made that three large and influential bodies were opposed to the present amendment. They named the American Federation of Labor, the American Medical Association, and the Methodist Episcopal Board of Public Morals.

Under examination by Senator Bratton, one speaker was forced to admit that the American Federation of Labor had never taken any action one way or the other on the subject of birth control. The other statements were equally misleading. As I sat there, compelled to listen to the doughty representatives of such organizations—indeed, I must confess that I had never dreamed of the existence of some of them!—as the Patriotic Society, the Purity League, the Clean Books League, the Foresters, the I.O.O.F., the Knights of Columbus, I wondered how so much hypocrisy could be concentrated in one room, combined with so much stupidity and prejudice. It would require a Swift to describe how obtuse minds seem to exercise a natural affinity for each other and so combine and mobilize to search out any slight effort toward human advance and swoop down upon it in herds, trampling hopes and ideals into the mire. It was as though we were in some antediluvian age, some kingdom out of Gulliver's travels. Under these words, these exposures of medieval mental processes, one could only sit in amazement, enduring as best one could the flood of personal abuse, misrepresentation, deliberate prevarication and false statement. At the beginning I had waited expectantly, anxious to learn what honest objections could be presented. I came indeed with an open mind, hoping that I might learn some new and honest point of view. But after an hour of these flatulent tirades, I gave it up. These Catholic medical authorities blundered naïvely into the realm of morals. In that field some church or other had acquired a monopoly on God's laws and Nature's, which, we were assured, were identical with patriotism and competitive procreation....

Tiring of this incessant gabble, I closed the noise of the room from the inner chamber of my mind. I sat back to collect my own thoughts for the brief rebuttal that was to come. I could plainly hear the spasmodic groans of suffering womankind, cries of women in the agonies of childbirth, the frenzy of mothers as in grief they looked for the last time upon the faces of lost babies. These sounds surged and beat a strange rhythm upon my subconscious mind until...[i]t was time for the rebuttal.

I arose in a sort of daze. Ten minutes to reply to countless ages of prejudice, to accumulated centuries of taboo, to milleniums of misrepresentation, to the whole past of the powers of darkness! Here was the Church, not the Church of Christ, but the Church of Rome, with its two thousand years or more of organization, of power, of secret intrigue and machinations, the Church that my father had combatted when I was only a little girl, the Church that had obstructed every effort of human emancipation, every step toward the stars—the Church that had sent me to jail. How could I answer it in ten minutes?

...I heard myself vigorously denying the misrepresentations of the opponents. The ten minutes were speeding furiously by. Yet their deliberate, complicated falsehoods required specific denial.

Almost as though they were ten seconds, those minutes were up. Senator Gillett graciously granted me five minutes more, and I went on, merely unburdening without thought the convictions of years: "We who are advocating this bill are trying to do away with the surreptitious and harmful information that is at present being spread around the country without being authorized, or controlled by experts who have the right to give it. I believe that the only way to do away with the harmful information which has been mentioned here this morning is to put the subject in the hands of the medical profession to be properly controlled.

"When some one says that the happiest families are the largest ones, and that the world's great leaders have been of large families, I would like to call to your attention that the great leader of Christianity, Jesus Christ himself, was said to be an only child."

Some of our opponents rose in horror, and made the sign of the Cross. There were cries of "Blasphemy!" Confusion reigned for a few moments, but I went on, more determined than ever.

"I am not going to take much time, but I want to say that the controversy really concerns the question of differing methods of birth control. The method of self-control recommended by some of those who are here to-day, is open to them. They may use such methods. We are not imposing any method upon any individual. There are about 120,000,000 people in this country, and I suppose that a large part of that number, perhaps 15,000,000, we will say to be generous, or even 20,000,000 are Catholics, but there are 105,000,000 left who are non-Catholics. We are not imposing any legislation upon the Catholics. We in no way try to inflict our ideas upon them. They have a perfect right to use the method of self-control if they wish; but we do believe that we have just as much right under the Constitution to enjoy health, peace, and the right to the pursuit of happiness as we see it.

"So I want to say that this whole group this morning, who have represented perhaps certain moral organizations of the country, seem to me to be like the boy who is whistling to keep up courage. No doubt there has been a falling away from grace, we might say, in the past several years, and they who represent such moral standards must see that they have failed to a considerable extent when we consider that they have had so much power. They have had the laws with them, the wealth, the press, and yet they have come to-day to say they are afraid of the morals of their people if they have knowledge, if they do not continue to be kept in fear and ignorance. Then I say their moral teachings are not very deep....

"We have birth control clinics that are legally operating throughout the United States, and in almost every one of the birth control clinics we have the same records. Regardless of religion, women come to us, desperate women, women trying to live decently, trying to avoid the conditions that unwanted pregnancy and too frequent pregnancy bring. These women come in equal proportions—about thirty-three percent Protestant, thirty-two per cent Catholics, and thirty-one per cent Jewish women. They all come with the same cry:

"'Give us a chance to space our children; It not that we do not love children, because we do love them; but because we want to give them a better chance than we have had, and we know that another child born into this family only deprives the children that are already here of a decent living with the ideals that we have for them.'

"When you get five hundred Catholic women in one clinic, with confessions of 597 abortions, Mr. Chairman, I say that it is time for us all to consider this problem intelligently. It is time for us all to consider a fundamental need, the fundamental question that is involved here. Catholic women are no different from any other women. It is all the same. The great majority of women who come to birth control clinics are seeking some means of controlling the size of their family because heretofore they have had to resort to these harmful methods. This is what we are trying to eliminate. We are trying to save mothers from this great hardship, from this unnatural ordeal. In the past many women who desired to control the size of their families have had to resort to an interruption of pregnancy, a method of which we disapprove, and which this law is going to do away with eventually, I am quite certain.

"Mr. Chairman, we want children to be conceived in love, born of parents' conscious desire, and born into the world with healthy and sound bodies and sound minds."

That "doctor's bill," alas, died a premature death on March 4, 1931, still in the committee, with the expiration of the seventy-first Congress. But that does not mean that the work of the Committee for Federal Legislation for Birth Control is defeated. It means, on the other hand, that we must take up the work with renewed energy. It means that there is work that confronts every intelligent voter in this country. It means that we must organize the forces of intelligence to combat effectively the splendidly organized forces of reaction.

So it is that when I am congratulated now on recent victories such as the recent stand of the various Churches, representing Protestant acceptance of the moral integrity of birth control, or the statement of the New York Academy of Medicine, representing the approbation of the medical profession of the work accomplished in our clinics, I am made keenly aware that passive approval is not enough. We have, it is true, succeeded in enlightening public opinion. We have battered down the prejudice of the press. We have overcome the apathy and passive indifference of the medical profession. We have awakened the consciousness of the Protestant churches and their ethical leaders to the moral necessity of birth control. Yet this enlightenment, unless directed and applied, will be extinguished by the winds of dogmas unless it is applied like a hydro-electric power to the driving of the machinery of political and legislative action....

The problem of birth control in a national program concentrates all other political problems: the problems of taxation, of the care of defective and delinquents, of the standards of public education, of community life in general, of the demands made to support charities and community chests, of poverty and unemployment, of crime and the maintenance of prisons and penitentiaries, of child labor and unemployment. Therefore it is a problem that concerns in its intimate aspects every one of us, and in its remoter consequences the very life of the nation and the race.

# DISCUSSION QUESTIONS

1. Gifford Pinchot split with both John Muir and J. Horace McFarland over how to approach conservation and what subjects should be included within conservation policy. How might the conservation movement have developed in the absence of those differences? How are these differences still reflected in environmental law, policy, and institutions today?

2. Frederick Law Olmsted, Theodore Roosevelt, Gifford Pinchot, and William Graham Sumner all specifically addressed questions about what various social classes owe to one another and to future generations. Compare and contrast their beliefs. In a sense, Margaret Sanger and Alice Hamilton also discussed what various social classes owe one another. Find examples in today's environmental debates where questions of social and intergenerational equity are prominent. How, if at all, has the debate changed?

3. How is the National Park Service today grappling with its dual mission of preserving wild and historic resources as well as developing opportunities for Americans to enjoy those resources?

4. Arthur Bentley's work laid the basis for the development of the discipline of political science in the early years of the twentieth century and its quest to develop scientific approaches to the study of politics. To what extent can this goal be realized? What aspects might not be amenable to the application of rational science? What other theories, besides group theory or pluralism, are offered to explain political behavior?

5. To what extent is John Dewey's characterization of an "eclipsed public" applicable today? What kinds of institutional change might be needed to turn American society of the twenty-first century into Dewey's Great Community and to implement his concept of a genuinely deliberative public sphere? Do our newest forms of communication help or hinder that realization?

# PART IV

## "There Is Nothing So American as Our National Parks"*

### THE GREAT DEPRESSION, THE NEW DEAL, AND WORLD WAR II, 1932–1945

---

The Stock Market crash in October of 1929 marked the beginning of a decade of extreme hardship for most Americans. While Herbert Hoover was in the White House, the economic depression worsened yearly: More people were laid off from their jobs; soup and bread lines grew longer in the nation's cities; markets for food and other goods collapsed; panicked Wall Street speculators jumped out of windows; and a great, desperate migration from the country to the cities was underway by people who hoped that things would be better there. They weren't.

The collapse on Wall Street actually was preceded by an agricultural catastrophe. Years of drought combined with overutilization of a substantial portion of America's land made the decade one of the worst in history for the farming sector. Topsoil in the arid south-central region of the United States was lost by wind erosion, and that section of the country was one large dust bowl. The nation's High Plains presented a gloomy spectacle according to a number of historians: homesteads had been abandoned, grazing lands were in very poor condition, and, perhaps most significantly, ranchers gradually extended their influence and fences over the remaining public lands. In 1928, a Department of Agriculture researcher named Hugh Hammond Bennett published his seminal study of the condition of America's land. It was titled, "Soil Erosion, A Natural Menace."

---

*Franklin Delano Roosevelt. 1934. Speech at Two Medicine Chalet, Glacier National Park, August 5.

By November of 1932 Americans were desperate for change. President Hoover and the Congress, enmeshed in years of bickering, had failed to find a way out of the ever worsening crisis. So Americans voted overwhelmingly for a man who, during his campaign for the presidency, promised them a "new deal." The 1932 election of the Democratic Governor of New York, Franklin Delano Roosevelt, to the presidency, and also the election of a predominantly Democratic Congress anxious to support the new president's agenda, marked a watershed in the nation's history. America embarked on a great political odyssey under the leadership of FDR—so much so that the 1930s and '40s became known as the Roosevelt Era.

Roosevelt's response to the Great Depression was immediate and wide ranging. The New Deal, as it quickly came to be called, entailed a fundamental restructuring of the relationship between the public and private sectors. Using Keynesian economics as its intellectual foundation, the role of the federal government in economic activity was greatly enlarged during the 1930s. If his predecessor in the White House could not countenance putting unemployed Americans "on the dole," President Roosevelt had no such qualms. Asking Congress for an emergency appropriation of some $3 billion, the Administration wasted no time in creating agencies and programs designed to put people back to work, to stabilize the banking system, to halt the illegal overproduction of oil, and generally to restore Americans' confidence in their government and in themselves.

Social and economic legislation tumbled out of Congress in record speed during the early New Deal years. The key statutes included: The Agricultural Adjustment Act, the National Industrial Recovery Act, the Federal Deposit Insurance Corporation Act, the Soil Conservation Act, Civilian Conservation Corps statute, the Emergency Banking Act, the Connolly "Hot Oil" Act, and the Social Security Act of 1935, widely regarded as the centerpiece of the New Deal. A conservative Supreme Court wasted little time in declaring some of this legislation unconstitutional, and these decisions led to the famous court-packing fight of 1937. After FDR won a landslide victory in the 1936 election, in which a large Democratic majority voiced its approval of the New Deal, the President proposed his controversial court reform plan, which would have added six new justices to the Supreme Court. Congress objected and did not pass the bill. But the Court got the message and in 1937 some of the oldest justices decided it was time to retire. Roosevelt's first appointment to the Court was Hugo Black, a New Deal advocate from Alabama.

In retrospect, it is clear that America, always the "welfare laggard" among industrialized nations, found it necessary to create a relatively modest social safety net in the 1930s. The exigency of the Great Depression demanded it, and it fell to FDR and his administration to respond. The new president eloquently explained his role in this social transformation in his first inaugural address: "They [the people] have made me the present instrument of their wishes. In the spirit of the gift I take it."

A substantial number of New Deal programs and policies involved natural resources conservation and protection. Like his cousin, Theodore Roosevelt, FDR considered himself a conservationist. Both men were deeply attached to nature, and each spent as much time in the outdoors as possible. FDR was a self-taught forester who practiced silviculture on his Hyde Park estate, and often referred to himself as a "farmer." He also brought into his administration a number of committed conservationists such as Harold L. Ickes, the Interior Secretary, Agriculture Secretary Henry Wallace, economist Rexford Tugwell, who directed the Resettlement Administration, and wilderness advocate Robert Marshall, who worked first for Ickes and then for Wallace until his untimely death in 1939.

A young research biologist named Rachel Carson began her career in the federal government during the 1930s, too. Her 1962 book, *Silent Spring*, significantly furthered the environmental movement during that decade. The influential economist and public servant, John Kenneth Galbraith, also started his career as a New Dealer. Indeed, an entire generation of policy makers, from Lyndon Johnson to Ronald Reagan, came of age during the Roosevelt Era.

The new government in Washington wasted no time in fashioning a New Deal conservation policy. It contained both short- and long-term objectives. For example, one of the first acts passed in 1933 created the Civilian Conservation Corps (CCC). This program immediately put unemployed young men to work in the nation's parks and forests, and indeed in many other places where useful work needed to be done. A Public Works Administration, headed by Interior Secretary Ickes, and a Federal Emergency Relief Administration, directed by Harry Hopkins, embarked on a massive construction program of roads, schools, hospitals, dams, airports, public transit systems, public housing, sewer systems, and a great deal more. In retrospect, what was accomplished during the 1930s was nothing less than the building of the nation's infrastructure.

Key conservation legislation was passed during the New Deal that had long-term objectives and consequences. This included the Taylor Grazing Act of 1934, which created a Grazing Service in the Interior Department to manage the remaining public domain lands. The Grazing Service lasted until President Harry Truman effected an executive branch reorganization in 1946. It then became the Bureau of Land Management, an agency which is still in operation today. In addition, Hugh Hammond Bennett became director of the newly created Soil Conservation Service (today the Natural Resources Conservation Service). In that position he began to repair the ravages of the Dust Bowl by fostering soil erosion practices such as contour plowing, planting of erosion-resistant crops, retirement of excessively eroded land from cultivation and construction of small-scale irrigation facilities.

Under Roosevelt's personal direction, the national park and forest systems were expanded significantly during the '30s. The president saw an opportunity during the Depression for governmental purchase of lands east of the Mississippi River (where federal lands were virtually nonexistent), and so he directed his Agriculture and Interior Secretaries to aggressively search out cheap land that could be added to the park and forest systems. It was a farsighted policy that made the parks and forests genuinely *national* entities by the end of the decade.

Management of the nation's battlefields, like Gettysburg, was transferred from the War Department to the National Park Service. FDR proclaimed 1934 to be "National Parks Year," and urged Americans to visit their natural treasures. The First Family personally led the way with a summer trip to the Pacific Northwest, culminating in a visit to Montana's spectacular Glacier National Park. The next year, 1935, Congress passed the Historic Sites Act and this, too, proved to be a boon for the national park system. When it came to parks, forests, and wildlife refuges, the New Deal philosophy can be summed up in four words: The more, the better.

The nation's original environmentalists, the Native Americans, were forgotten no longer. With the appointment of a tireless advocate for their cause, John Collier, to head the Interior Department's Indian Service (as it was then called), the government embarked on a program to rehabilitate tribal lands and help Native Americans become economically self-sufficient. In 1934 the seminal Indian Reorganization Act was passed, which terminated the federal government's noxious allotment policy of 1887 and planted the seeds for tribal sovereignty.

Perhaps the clearest example of New Deal conservation policy, however, was the Tennessee Valley Authority (TVA). This key act was passed in 1933 at the urging of Senator George Norris of Nebraska, a lifelong advocate of comprehensive resource planning. David Lilienthal was appointed to the three-member board of commissioners, and in 1941 became its chair. The TVA embodied the Administration's model of long-range, integrated resource planning that fostered public-private partnerships, and which produced regional economic and social development. In fact, FDR wanted to extend the TVA concept to all of America's large watershed basins, and to that end he created a national resources planning board. There were related attempts to merge all of the resource-managing agencies into a single department called the Department of Conservation, but Congress refused to transfer the two agencies with the closest ties to the legislative branch, the Forest Service and the Army Corps of Engineers. (Subsequent efforts to create a Department of Conservation also have failed, for much the same reason.)

President Roosevelt was fascinated with the idea of regional resources planning whose benefits would extend to the least advantaged groups in society. He was at heart a Jeffersonian agrarian democrat who felt that the cities were "hopeless," and who believed that Americans ought to be encouraged to return to the land. When he read *The Grapes of Wrath* in 1939, he remarked that the poor, displaced people depicted in the novel were precisely the people he wanted to help all along. A number of federal programs created in the 1930s did just that, including the water resources development programs of the Bureau of Reclamation and the Corps. They not only created much needed jobs during the worst years of the economic crisis, but the massive structures erected on the nation's rivers during "The Golden Age of Dam Building" provided a growing number of farmers with irrigated land and cheap electricity. Although latter-day environmentalists decried this New Deal program, multipurpose water development projects were considered good conservation policy at the time. The voices of dissent were few, while accolades were heard throughout the country.

At the same time the United States struggled to extricate itself from the

Great Depression through New Deal liberalism, other nations of the world adopted more extreme measures. The 1930s have been referred to as the decade of "isms," when millions of desperate people turned to communism, socialism, fascism, totalitarianism, or nazism to solve their economic, political, and social crises. In Germany, Adolph Hitler rose to power at precisely the same time as did FDR. Italy embraced Mussolini, while Spain fought a civil war in which the dictator General Franco was victorious. Joseph Stalin was entrenched in the Soviet Union, while Japan turned to a reactionary regime. Early in the decade President Roosevelt saw trouble ahead, as evidenced by his references to Germany, Italy, and Japan as the "three bandit nations." Consequently, a substantial portion of New Deal spending went into building up America's armed forces, and in countering diplomatically these nations' aggression.

If the New Deal started the transformation of American society into a modern welfare state, surely the Second World War not only completed that transformation but also effected a fundamental restructuring of society, both in the United States and elsewhere. World War II, which erupted in 1939 and lasted until 1945, is the great watershed of the twentieth century. The detonation of the atomic bomb is its symbol.

The gradual military build-up during the New Deal years intensified after war was declared. The Roosevelt Administration immediately embarked on a pro-British neutrality policy in which the United States assisted Great Britain, as well as France until its fall in 1940, in their war against the Axis powers. In 1940 Roosevelt was reelected to an unprecedented third term, a result of the conflict raging in Europe and Americans' confidence in his leadership. After the Japanese attack on Pearl Harbor on December 7, 1941, Germany declared war on the United States and the country was officially at war.

The Second World War was marked by a horrific loss of life, both on the battlefields and among civilian populations. The mass destruction of people and property occurred on a scale never before seen in the civilized world. However, not only did this "total war" destroy millions of people, and along with them their societies, it also consumed the world's natural resources at an astounding rate. No one has yet calculated what the world used up in terms of raw materials during this period, but the total has to be enormous.

The war quickly became a war of production, with virtually every facet of the nation's economy—indeed, much of the world's economy—put into the conflict. With America's entry, FDR created a number of organizations to control and direct economic production. These included a Petroleum Administration for War, a Coal/Hard Fuels Administration, a War Production Board, and an Office of Price Administration. At critical times, gasoline, coal, foodstuffs, and other basic necessities were strictly rationed, while striking coal miners were put back to work by the federal government's takeover of the mines. Washington was so completely involved in the war effort that nonessential activities, such as the administration of the National Park Service, were moved out of the capitol to Chicago and other cities to make room for war-related resource management.

With raw materials in such great demand, Americans' inventive genius switched into high gear. The petrochemical revolution, as Barry Commoner later referred to it, actually began in the 1930s, but it took a quantum leap forward during the war. For example chlorofluorocarbons (CFCs) had been created a few years earlier, but the war encouraged the production of a host of new synthetic products such as nylon, dacron, and plastics. These substituted for silk, cotton, wool, and wood. Margarine replaced butter at the dinner table, while newly patented medicines treated the exotic diseases to which the American serviceman was exposed. Finally, the nation's newly constructed dams provided an essential energy supply for the aircraft and shipbuilding industries, which worked around-the-clock to keep up with Axis torpedoes and bombers.

While millions of young American men went to war, "Rosie the Riveter" went to work. In addition to the women who joined the workforce, minority Americans, who had been kept out of many occupations prior to the war, found greater economic opportunity during World War II. Whether they were in the military or serving at home, African Americans, Latinos, and Native Americans found a much changed atmosphere in the 1940s. After the war, no longer content to be second-class citizens, blacks and other minorities began the long march for equality known as the Civil Rights Movement. In a number of ways, the Second World War effected a profound and long-lasting change in the American workforce and in social relations.

The myriad of changes wrought during this horrendous war may be best symbolized by the invention of the atomic bomb. This top-secret government effort changed everything. In White Sands, New Mexico, the brilliant physicist J. Robert Oppenheimer was among the handful of people who first witnessed the awesome power unleashed by the splitting of the atom. It occurred just a few months after President Roosevelt's death, and death was on everyone's minds in 1945. Oppenheimer recalled the sacred Hindu text, the Bhagavad Gita, as he watched the world change: "I am become Death, the destroyer of worlds."

Death did not have the last word, however. In one of his most memorable speeches, Franklin Roosevelt said: "There is a mysterious cycle in human events. To some generations much is given. Of other generations much is expected. This generation of Americans has a rendezvous with destiny." Because of the terrible challenges met and conquered by Roosevelt's generation, we now remember those Americans as belonging to "the greatest generation." Like those Americans who fought and died in the Civil War, the sacrifices of the men and women of the Roosevelt Era are now part of our national identity. Their courage will not be forgotten.

# 20
# Franklin Delano Roosevelt (1882–1945)

When the thirty-second President of the United States, Franklin Delano Roosevelt, took office in March of 1933, the country was in the depths of the Great Depression. It was the severest economic crisis ever to have hit America, and the forecast was grim. Outgoing President Herbert Hoover told the President-elect just days before the inauguration, "We are at the end of our string. There is nothing more we can do."

The new President could not have disagreed more. In a stirring inaugural address given on March 4, he likened the economic depression to a state of war, and promised the American people that he would lead the nation to victory over its common enemy, a crippled economy. In a memorable statement, FDR told the anxious crowd of thousands, "we have nothing to fear but fear itself." Desperate for leadership, it was precisely what Americans had been waiting to hear.

So began one of the most eventful presidencies in American history. Franklin Roosevelt is considered to be one of the country's three greatest presidents, and the greatest of the twentieth century. His thirteen years in the White House, from 1933 until his death in 1945, spanned the most cataclysmic period of the century. No president in our history has dealt with worse crises; yet he led with unfailing courage, charm, intelligence, and optimism.

Immediately upon entering office, FDR and his New Deal Administration fought to resuscitate a nearly prostrate economy through a massive, complex program of public works and business-government alliances. It took years of pump-priming by the government before industrial production hit pre-Depression levels. Then in 1939, just as his second term was coming to an end, war in Europe erupted. FDR was elected to a third term, and went on to become a great wartime leader. As the press termed it, "Dr. New Deal," was transformed into "Dr. Win the War."

FDR was reelected to a fourth term in 1944, but by then he was gravely ill. Nevertheless, he was the Commander-in-Chief to the end. In the spring of 1945 he traveled to Yalta to meet with his wartime allies, Churchill and Stalin, to prepare for peace. It was a peace which Roosevelt did not live to see. He died on April 12, 1945, just a month before Germany surrendered. The poet Carl Sandburg captured the nation's grief and mourning in the last line of his poem to the fallen hero:

"Commander, sweet goodnight."

# "THE SPLENDID PUBLIC PURPOSE"*

I have been back on the soil of the continental United States for three days after most interesting visits to our fellow Americans in Puerto Rico, the Virgin Islands, the Canal Zone and the Territory of Hawaii. I return with the conviction that their problems are essentially similar to those of us who live on the mainland and, furthermore, that they are enthusiastically doing their part to improve their conditions of life and thereby the conditions of life of all Americans.

On Friday and Saturday I had the opportunity of seeing the actual construction work under way in the first two national projects for the development of the Columbia River Basin. At Bonneville, Oregon, a great dam, 140 miles inland, at the last place where the river leaps down over rapids to sea level, will provide not only a large development of cheap power but also will enable vessels to proceed another seventy or eighty miles into the interior of the country.

At Grand Coulee, in north central Washington, an even greater dam will regulate the flow of the Columbia River, developing power and, in the future, will open up a large tract of parched land for the benefit of this and future generations. Many families in the days to come, I am confident, will thank us of this generation for providing small farms on which they will at least be able to make an honest and honorable livelihood.

Today, for the first time in my life, I have seen Glacier Park. Perhaps I can best express to you my thrill and delight by saying that I wish every American, old and young, could have been with me today. The great mountains, the glaciers, the lakes and the trees make me long to stay here for all the rest of the summer.

Comparisons are generally objectionable and yet it is not unkind to say from the standpoint of scenery alone that if many and indeed most of our American national parks were to be set down anywhere on the continent of Europe thousands of Americans would journey all the way across the ocean in order to see their beauties.

There is nothing so American as our national parks. The scenery and wild life are native and the fundamental idea behind the parks is native. It is, in brief, that the country belongs to the people; that what it is and what it is in the process of making is for the enrichment of the lives of all of us. Thus the parks stand as the outward symbol of this great human principle.

It was on a famous night, sixty-four years ago, that a group of men who had been exploring the Yellowstone country gathered about a campfire to discuss what could be done with that wonderland of beauty. It is said that one of the party, a lawyer from the State of Montana, Cornelius

---

*Franklin Delano Roosevelt. 1957. Speech at Two Medicine Chalet, Glacier National Park, August 5, 1934, in *Franklin D. Roosevelt & Conservation 1911–1945*. Edgar B. Nixon, ed. Hyde Park, NY: General Services Administration, pp. 321–324.

Hedges, advanced the idea that the region might be preserved for all time as a national park for the benefit of all the people of the Nation. As a result of that suggestion, Yellowstone National Park was established in 1872 by Act of Congress as a "pleasuring ground" for the people. I like that phrase because, in the years that have followed, our great series of parks in every part of the Union have become indeed a "pleasuring ground" for millions of Americans.

My old friend, Franklin K. Lane, Secretary of the Interior in the Wilson Administration, well described the policies governing the national park administration when he said:

> The policy to which the Service will adhere is based on three broad principles: First, that the national parks must be maintained in absolutely unimpaired form for the use of future generations as well as those of our own time; second, that they are set apart for the use, observation, health and pleasure of the people; and, third, that the national interest must dictate all decisions affecting public or private enterprise in the parks.

The present National Park Service stands as an example of efficient and far-seeing governmental administration and to its former duties I added last year by transferring from other departments many other parks, battlefield sites, memorials and national monuments. This concentration of responsibility has thus made it possible to embark on a permanent park policy as a great recreational and educational project—one which no other country in the world has ever undertaken in such a broad way for protection of its natural and historic treasures and for the enjoyment of them by vast numbers of people.

Today I have seen some of the work of the Civilian Conservation Corps boys in this northwestern country. Of the three hundred thousand young men in these camps, 75,000 are at work in our national parks. Here, under trained leadership, we are helping these men to help themselves and their families and at the same time we are making the parks more available and more useful for the average citizen. Hundreds of miles of firebreaks have been built, fire hazards have been reduced on great tracts of timberland, thousands of miles of roadside have been cleared, 2,500 miles of trails have been constructed and 10,000 acres have been reforested. Other tens of thousands of acres have been treated for tree disease and soil erosion. This is but another example of our efforts to build, not for today alone but for tomorrow as well.

We should remember that the development of our national park system over a period of many years has not been a simple bed of roses. As is the case in the long fight for the preservation of national forests and water power and mineral deposits and other national possessions, it has been a long and fierce fight against many private interests which were entrenched in political and economic power. So, too, it has been a constant struggle to protect the public interest once cleared from private exploitation at the hands of the selfish few.

It took a bitter struggle to teach the country at large that our national resources are not inexhaustible and that, when public domain is stolen, a two-fold injury is done, for it is a theft of the treasure of the present and at the same time bars the road of opportunity to the future.

We have won the greater part of the fight to obtain and to retain these great public park properties for the benefit of the public. We are at the threshold of even more important a battle to save our resources of agriculture and industry against the selfishness of individuals.

The Secretary of the Interior in 1933 announced that this year of 1934 was to be emphasized as "National Parks Year." I am glad to say that there has been a magnificent response and that the number visiting our national parks has shown a splendid increase. But I decided today that every year ought to be "National Parks Year." That is why, with all the earnestness at my command, I express to you the hope that each and every one of you who can possibly find the means and opportunity for so doing will visit our national parks and use them as they are intended to be used. They are not for the rich alone. Camping is free, the sanitation is excellent. You will find them in every part of the Union. You will find glorious scenery of every character; you will find every climate; you will perform the double function of enjoying much and learning much.

We are definitely in an era of building, the best kind of building—the building of great public projects for the benefit of the public and with the definite objective of building human happiness.

I believe, too, that we are building a better comprehension of our national needs. People understand, as never before, the splendid public purpose that underlies the development of great power sites, the improving of navigation, the prevention of floods and of the erosion of our agricultural fields, the prevention of forest fires, the diversification of farming and the distribution of industry. We know, more and more, that the East has a stake in the West and the West has a stake in the East, that the Nation must and shall be considered as a whole and not as an aggregation of disjointed groups.

---

# "SUNDAY SERMON"*

MY FRIENDS: This being Sunday, the Governor, in cooperating with me in keeping politics out of it, says that he is not even going to introduce me.

I have been here before, and it is a great comfort to come on a Sunday in a campaign year, because on Sundays my life is made much more comfortable by not having to think about politics. Unfortunately, I do have to think about the war, because every day, including Sundays, dispatches come to me, on the train even, to tell me of the progress of our boys in Europe and in the Pacific and in the Philippines. I can't get rid of that.

---

*Franklin Delano Roosevelt. 1957. Speech at Clarksburg, West Virginia, October 29, 1944, in *Franklin D. Roosevelt & Conservation 1911–1945*. Edgar B. Nixon, ed. Hyde Park, NY: General Services Administration, pp. 602–605.

So coming up through the State today, I have been looking out of the window, and I think there is a subject that is a good subject for Sunday, because I remember the line in the poem, "Only God can make a tree." And one of the things that people have to realize all over the United States, and I think especially in West Virginia, I don't see the trees I ought to see. That is something that we in this country have fallen down on. We have been using up natural resources that we ought to have replaced. I know we can't replace coal—it will be a long time before all the coal is gone—but trees constitute something that we can replace.

We have to think not just of an annual crop, not just something that we can eat the next year, but we have to think of a longer crop, something that takes years to grow, but which in the long run is going to do more good for our children and for our grandchildren than if we leave the hills bare.

I remember a story, and it is taken out of Germany. There was a town there—I don't know what has happened in the last twenty years—but this is back when I used to be in grade school in Germany—and I used to bicycle. And we came to a town, and outside of it there was a great forest. And the interesting thing to me, as a boy even, was that the people in that town did-n't have to pay taxes. They were supported by their own forest.

Way back in the time of Louis something of France—some king—the French king was approaching this town with a large army. And the prince of the time asked the townspeople to come out to defend their principality, and he promised them that if they would keep the invader out of the town, out of the principality, he would give them the forest.

The burghers turned out. They repulsed the French king. And very soon the prince made good. He gave the forest to the town. And for over two hundred years that town in Germany had to pay no taxes. Everybody made money, because they had no taxes. In other words, it was a forest on an annual yield basis. They cut down perhaps 70 percent of what they could get out of that year's mature crop. And every year they planted new trees. And every year the proceeds from that forest paid the equivalent of taxes.

Now that is true more and more in this country. There are more and more municipalities that are reforesting their watersheds, putting trees on the top of their hills, preventing the erosion of soil. They are not on a self-sustaining basis because it has only been started within the last ten or fifteen years. And yet while only God can make a tree, we have to do a little bit to help ourselves.

I think that all of us sort of look at our lives in terms of ourselves, and yet your children, your grandchildren, your great-grandchildren, your great-great-grandchildren—some of them will be living around here, right around where the population is today. Perhaps the old house—perhaps a better, new house. And more and more we Christians are going to think about those grandchildren and great-grandchildren. It doesn't amount to very much, this cost of planting trees, and yet the hillsides of West Virginia of our grandparents' day were much more wonderful than they are now. It's largely a deforested State. And I believe that from the point of view of the beauties of nature, from the point of view of all that trees can be, and from the point of view of your own grandchildren's pocketbooks, the small number of cents, the small number of dollars that go into reforestation are going to come back a thousand-fold.

Up where I live, in the country on the Hudson River, my family had—when I was a boy—five or six hundred acres. It wasn't valuable land. And my own father, in the old days, would go in every year and cut the family needs in the way of timber.

When I was a small boy, I realized that there was waste going on; and when I went to the State Senate as a young man, somebody appointed me to the Conservation Commission. Some parts of upstate New York were being eroded, a lot of topsoil was running away, we were getting more floods than we had ever had in the old days.

And just as an experiment, I started planting a few acres each year on rundown land. I tried to pasture some skinny cows on it. And at the same time, I went into the old woods and cleaned out no'count trees, trees that were undergrown or would never amount to anything, crooked trees, rotten trees.

Well, the answer was this. When the last war came on, the old woods had some perfectly splendid trees, because I had cleaned them out, cleaned out the poor stuff. And during that war I made 4 thousand dollars, just by cutting out the mature trees. And I kept on every year. And in the wintertime, when the men weren't doing much, cleaning them out. And the trees grew.

And a quarter of a century later, there came this war. I think I cooperated with the Almighty, because I think trees were made to grow. Oh, yes, they are useful as mine timbers. I know that. But there are a lot of places in this State where there isn't any mine timber being cut out.

And in this war, back home, I cut last year—and this is not very Christian—over 4 thousand dollars' worth net of oak trees, to make into submarine chasers and landing craft and other implements of war. And I am doing it again this year.

And I hope that this use of wood for growing, for all kinds of modern inventions, plastics, and so forth, I hope that when I am able to cut some more trees, twenty or twenty-five years from now—it may not be me, it may be one of the boys—we will be able to use them at a profit not for building mine chasers or landing craft, but for turning them into some human use.

And I believe that in this country—not this State only, but a great many more—that we in the next few years, when peace comes, will be able to devote more thought to making our country more useful—every acre of it.

I remember eight years ago, I think it was, out in the west, we knew that there were great floods and a dry belt in there. We knew, also, that trees bring water and avoid floods. And so we started one of those "crackpot" things, for which I have been criticized, a thing called the shelter belt, to keep the high winds away, to hold the moisture in the soil. And the result is that that shelter belt—not much ran downhill—a great success has been made of it. And the farmers are getting more crops and better crops out there on the prairies in the lee of these rows of trees.

Forestry pays from the practical point of view. I have proved that. And so I hope—I hope to live long enough to see West Virginia with more trees in it. I hope to live to see the day when this generation will be thinking not just of themselves but also of the children and the grandchildren.

And so I had a happy day this morning in looking out at this wonderful scenery, but I couldn't take my eyes off those bare hilltops. I couldn't take my thoughts off the fact that this generation, and especially the previous generation, have been thinking of themselves and not of the future.

And so some day I hope to come back, and I hope to see a great forestry program for the whole of the State. Nearly all of it needs it. I hope to come back and be able to say, "I stopped, once upon a time, in Clarksburg, on a Sunday morning, and just avoided politics and talked to the people in Clarksburg, and they must have heard me all over the State, because they started planting trees."

And so I think my Sunday sermon is just about over. It has been good to see you, and I really do hope that I will come back here, one of these days soon.

# 21
# John Steinbeck (1902–1968)

Author John Steinbeck of California always knew he wanted to be a writer. From an early age he cultivated a keen appreciation for the Salinas Valley where he grew up, and for the coastal area around Monterey. These are the locales in which he set many of his great novels. Steinbeck himself worked off and on with the migrant laborers and the rural poor who people his books.

Steinbeck's themes of political alienation and economic struggle are evident in his first acclaimed novel, *Tortilla Flat* (1935). Employing a direct, naturalistic style, he followed *Tortilla Flat* with two more novels depicting the exploitation of the poor by an impersonal and mechanistic system of production. *Of Mice and Men* appeared in 1937, and his most famous work, *The Grapes of Wrath*, in 1939.

The *Grapes of Wrath* tells the story of the Joads, a family of dispossessed tenant farmers from Oklahoma—"Okies"—who migrate to California during the Great Depression. Once they arrive in the mythical land of milk and honey, the Joads continue to be exploited, this time by the owners and overseers of the crowded farm labor camps: Violence erupts when the workers make their stand. Although this novel of social protest won the 1940 Pulitzer Prize for fiction, it provoked tremendous controversy. Because it pitted the struggles of poor workers against the greed of large-scale farmers, Steinbeck was labeled by some as a communist propagandist, and by others a socialist visionary.

After writing his last work of fiction in 1961, Steinbeck concentrated on journalism and travelogues. Always fascinated with rural America, his *Travels with Charley: In Search of America* (1962) recounts a cross-country trip with his faithful canine companion. Steinbeck discovered both America's native beauty and its increasingly synthetic urban environment. Also during the 1960s, Steinbeck went to South Vietnam, at the request of President Johnson, to report on the war. His hawkish stand on that conflict disillusioned many of his followers who had greatly admired his incendiary work of the 1930s and '40s.

By the time of his death in 1968 John Steinbeck largely had fallen out of critical favor. There is no doubt, however, that he must be considered one of America's greatest novelists. Not only did he frankly address the great social questions of his generation, but his writing is also testimony to the need for a sense of "place." His is a genuinely native voice, especially a voice of the West.

# "THE GRAPES OF WRATH"*

The owners of the land came onto the land, or more often a spokesman for the owners came. They came in closed cars, and they felt the dry earth with their fingers, and sometimes they drove big earth augers into the ground for soil tests. The tenants, from their sun-beaten dooryards, watched uneasily when the closed cars drove along the fields. And at last the owner men drove into the dooryards and sat in their cars to talk out of the windows. The tenant men stood beside the cars for a while, and then squatted on their hams and found sticks with which to mark the dust.

In the open doors the women stood looking out, and behind them the children—corn-headed children, with wide eyes, one bare foot on top of the other bare foot, and the toes working. The women and the children watched their men talking to the owner men. They were silent.

Some of the owner men were kind because they hated what they had to do, and some of them were angry because they hated to be cruel, and some of them were cold because they had long ago found that one could not be an owner unless one were cold. And all of them were caught in something larger than themselves. Some of them hated the mathematics that drove them, and some were afraid, and some worshiped the mathematics because it provided a refuge from thought and from feeling. If a bank or a finance company owned the land, the owner man said, The Bank—or the Company—needs—wants—insists—must have—as though the Bank or the Company were a monster, with thought and feeling, which had ensnared them. These last would take no responsibility for the banks or the companies because they were men and slaves, while the banks were machines and masters all at the same time. Some of the owner men were a little proud to be slaves to such cold and powerful masters. The owner men sat in the cars and explained. You know the land is poor. You've scrabbled at it long enough, God knows.

The squatting tenant men nodded and wondered and drew figures in the dust, and yes, they knew, God knows. If the dust only wouldn't fly. If the top would only stay on the soil, it might not be so bad.

The owner men went on leading to their point: You know the land's getting poorer. You know what cotton does to the land; robs it, sucks all the blood out of it.

The squatters nodded—they knew, God knew. If they could only rotate the crops they might pump blood back into the land.

Well, it's too late. And the owner men explained the workings and the thinkings of the monster that was stronger than they were. A man can hold land if he can just eat and pay taxes; he can do that.

---

*John Steinbeck. 1939. *The Grapes of Wrath*. New York: Penguin Books, pp. 42–53. Copyright 1939, renewed © 1967 by John Steinbeck. Used by permission of Viking Penguin, a division of Penguin Putnam, Inc.

Yes, he can do that until his crops fail one day and he has to borrow money from the bank.

But—you see, a bank or a company can't do that, because those creatures don't breathe air, don't eat side-meat. They breathe profits; they eat the interest on money. If they don't get it, they die the way you die without air, without side-meat. It is a sad thing, but it is so. It is just so.

The squatting men raised their eyes to understand. Can't we just hang on? Maybe the next year will be a good year. God knows how much cotton next year. And with all the wars—God knows what price cotton will bring. Don't they make explosives out of cotton? And uniforms? Get enough wars and cotton'll hit the ceiling. Next year, maybe. They looked up questioningly.

We can't depend on it. The bank—the monster has to have profits all the time. It can't wait. It'll die. No, taxes go on. When the monster stops growing, it dies. It can't stay one size.

Soft fingers began to tap the sill of the car window, and hard fingers tightened on the restless drawing sticks. In the doorways of the sun-beaten tenant houses, women sighed and then shifted feet so that the one that had been down was now on top, and the toes working. Dogs came sniffing near the owner cars and wetted on all four tires one after another. And chickens lay in the sunny dust and fluffed their feathers to get the cleansing dust down to the skin. In the little sties the pigs grunted inquiringly over the muddy remnants of the slops.

The squatting men looked down again. What do you want us to do? We can't take less share of the crop—we're half starved now. The kids are hungry all the time. We got no clothes, torn an' ragged. If all the neighbors weren't the same, we'd be ashamed to go to meeting.

And at last the owner men came to the point. The tenant system won't work any more. One man on a tractor can take the place of twelve or fourteen families. Pay him a wage and take all the crop. We have to do it. We don't like to do it. But the monster's sick. Something's happened to the monster.

But you'll kill the land with cotton.

We know. We've got to take cotton quick before the land dies. Then we'll sell the land. Lots of families in the East would like to own a piece of land.

The tenant men looked up alarmed. But what'll happen to us? How'll we eat?

You'll have to get off the land. The plows'll go through the dooryard.

And now the squatting men stood up angrily. Grampa took up the land, and he had to kill the Indians and drive them away. And Pa was born here, and he killed weeds and snakes. Then a bad year came and he had to borrow a little money. An' we was born here. There in the door—our children born here. And Pa had to borrow money. The bank owned the land then, but we stayed and we got a little bit of what we raised.

We know that—all that. It's not us, it's the bank. A bank isn't like a man. Or an owner with fifty thousand acres, he isn't like a man either. That's the monster.

Sure, cried the tenant men, but it's our land. We measured it and broke it up. We were born on it, and we got killed on it, died on it. Even if it's no good, it's still ours. That's what makes it ours—being born on it, working it, dying on it. That makes ownership, not a paper with numbers on it.

We're sorry. It's not us. It's the monster. The bank isn't like a man.

Yes, but the bank is only made of men.

No, you're wrong there—quite wrong there. The bank is something else than men. It happens that every man in a bank hates what the bank does, and yet the bank does it. The bank is something more than men, I tell you. It's the monster. Men made it, but they can't control it.

The tenants cried, Grampa killed Indians, Pa killed snakes for the land. Maybe we can kill banks—they're worse than Indians and snakes. Maybe we got to fight to keep our land, like Pa and Grampa did.

And now the owner men grew angry. You'll have to go.

But it's ours, the tenant men cried. We—

No. The bank, the monster owns it. You'll have to go.

We'll get our guns, like Grampa when the Indians came. What then?

Well—first the sheriff, and then the troops. You'll be stealing if you try to stay, you'll be murderers if you kill to stay. The monster isn't men, but it can make men do what it wants.

But if we go, where'll we go? How'll we go? We got no money.

We're sorry, said the owner men. The bank, the fifty-thousand-acre owner can't be responsible. You're on land that isn't yours. Once over the line maybe you can pick cotton in the fall. Maybe you can go on relief. Why don't you go on west to California? There's work there, and it never gets cold. Why, you can reach out anywhere and pick an orange. Why, there's always some kind of crop to work in. Why don't you go there? And the owner men started their cars and rolled away.

The tenant men squatted down on their hams again to mark the dust with a stick, to figure, to wonder. Their sunburned faces were dark, and their sun-whipped eyes were light. The women moved cautiously out of the door-ways toward their men, and the children crept behind the women, cautiously, ready to run. The bigger boys squatted beside their fathers, because that made them men. After a time the women asked, What did he want?

And the men looked up for a second, and the smolder of pain was in their eyes. We got to get off. A tractor and a superintendent. Like factories.

Where'll we go? the women asked.

We don't know. We don't know.

And the women went quickly, quietly back into the houses and herded the children ahead of them. They knew that a man so hurt and so perplexed may turn in anger, even on people he loves. They left the men alone to fig-ure and to wonder in the dust.

After a time perhaps the tenant man looked about—at the pump put in ten years ago, with a goose-neck handle and iron flowers on the spout, at the chopping block where a thousand chickens had been killed, at the hand plow lying in the shed, and the patent crib hanging in the rafters over it.

The children crowded about the women in the houses. What we going to do, Ma? Where we going to go?

The women said, We don't know, yet. Go out and play. But don't go near your father. He might whale you if you go near him. And the women went on with the work, but all the time they watched the men squatting in the dust—perplexed and figuring.

The tractors came over the roads and into the fields, great crawlers moving like insects, having the incredible strength of insects. They crawled over the ground, laying the track and rolling on it and picking it up. Diesel tractors, puttering while they stood idle; they thundered when they moved, and then settled down to a droning roar. Snub-nosed monsters, raising the dust and sticking their snouts into it, straight down the country, across the country, through fences, through dooryards, in and out of gullies in straight lines. They did not run on the ground, but on their own roadbeds. They ignored hills and gulches, water courses, fences, houses.

The man sitting in the iron seat did not look like a man; gloved, goggled, rubber dust mask over nose and mouth, he was a part of the monster, a robot in the seat. The thunder of the cylinders sounded through the country, became one with the air and the earth, so that earth and air muttered in sympathetic vibration. The driver could not control it—straight across country it went, cutting through a dozen farms and straight back. A twitch at the controls could swerve the cat', but the driver's hands could not twitch because the monster that built the tractor, the monster that sent the tractor out, had somehow got into the driver's hands, into his brain and muscle, had goggled him and muzzled him—goggled his mind, muzzled his speech, goggled his perception, muzzled his protest. He could not see the land as it was, he could not smell the land as it smelled; his feet did not stamp the clods or feel the warmth and power of the earth. He sat in an iron seat and stepped on iron pedals. He could not cheer or beat or curse or encourage the extension of his power, and because of this he could not cheer or whip or curse or encourage himself. He did not know or own or trust or beseech the land. If a seed dropped did not germinate, it was nothing. If the young thrusting plant withered in drought or drowned in a flood of rain, it was no more to the driver than to the tractor.

He loved the land no more than the bank loved the land. He could admire the tractor—its machined surfaces, its surge of power, the roar of its detonating cylinders; but it was not his tractor. Behind the tractor rolled the shining disks, cutting the earth with blades—not plowing but surgery, pushing the cut earth to the right where the second row of disks cut it and pushed it to the left; slicing blades shining, polished by the cut earth. And pulled behind the disks, the harrows combing with iron teeth so that the little clods broke up and the earth lay smooth. Behind the harrows, the long seeders— twelve curved iron penes erected in the foundry, orgasms set by gears, raping methodically, raping without passion. The driver sat in his iron seat and he was proud of the straight lines he did not will, proud of the tractor he did not own or love, proud of the power he could not control. And when that crop grew, and was harvested, no man had crumbled a hot clod in his fingers and let the earth sift past his fingertips. No man had touched the seed, or lusted for the growth. Men ate what they had not raised, had no connection with the bread. The land bore under iron, and under iron gradually died; for it was not loved or hated, it had no prayers or curses.

At noon the tractor driver stopped sometimes near a tenant house and opened his lunch: sandwiches wrapped in waxed paper, white bread, pickle, cheese, Spam, a piece of pie branded like an engine part. He ate without relish. And tenants not yet moved away came out to see him, looked curiously while the goggles were taken off, and the rubber dust mask, leaving white circles around the eyes and a large white circle around nose and mouth. The exhaust of the tractor puttered on, for fuel is so cheap it is more efficient to leave the engine running than to heat the Diesel nose for a new start. Curious children crowded close, ragged children who ate their fried dough as they watched. They watched hungrily the unwrapping of the sandwiches, and their hunger-sharpened noses smelled the pickle, cheese, and Spam. They didn't speak to the driver. They watched his hand as it carried food to his mouth. They did not watch him chewing; their eyes followed the hand that held the sandwich. After a while the tenant who could not leave the place came out and squatted in the shade beside the tractor.

"Why, you're Joe Davis's boy!"

"Sure," the driver said.

"Well, what you doing this kind of work for—against your own people?"

"Three dollars a day. I got damn sick of creeping for my dinner—and not getting it. I got a wife and kids. We got to eat. Three dollars a day, and it comes every day."

"That's right," the tenant said. "But for your three dollars a day fifteen or twenty families can't eat at all. Nearly a hundred people have to go out and wander on the roads for your three dollars a day. Is that right?"

And the driver said, "Can't think of that. Got to think of my own kids. Three dollars a day, and it comes every day. Times are changing, mister, don't you know? Can't make a living on the land unless you've got two, five, ten thousand acres and a tractor. Crop land isn't for little guys like us any more. You don't kick up a howl because you can't make Fords, or because you're not the telephone company. Well, crops are like that now. Nothing to do about it. You try to get three dollars a day someplace. That's the only way."

The tenant pondered. "Funny thing how it is. If a man owns a little property, that property is him, it's part of him, and it's like him. If he owns property only so he can walk on it and handle it and be sad when it isn't doing well, and feel fine when the rain falls on it, that property is him, and some way he's bigger because he owns it. Even if he isn't successful he's big with his property. That is so."

And the tenant pondered more. "But let a man get property he doesn't see, or can't take time to get his fingers in, or can't be there to walk on it— why, then the property is the man. He can't do what he wants, he can't think what he wants. The property is the man, stronger than he is. And he is small, not big. Only his possessions are big—and he's the servant of his property. That is so, too."

The driver munched the branded pie and threw the crust away. "Times are changed, don't you know? Thinking about stuff like that don't feed the kids. Get your three dollars a day, feed your kids. You got no call to worry about anybody's kids but your own. You get a reputation for talking like that, and you'll never get three dollars a day. Big shots won't give you three dollars a day if you worry about anything but your three dollars a day."

"Nearly a hundred people on the road for your three dollars. Where will we go?"

"And that reminds me," the driver said, "you better get out soon. I'm going through the dooryard after dinner."

"You filled in the well this morning."

"I know. Had to keep the line straight. But I'm going through the dooryard after dinner. Got to keep the lines straight. And—well, you know Joe Davis, my old man, so I'll tell you this. I got orders wherever there's a family not moved out—if I have an accident—you know, get too close and cave the house in a little—well, I might get a couple of dollars. And my youngest kid never had no shoes yet."

"I built it with my hands. Straightened old nails to put the sheathing on. Rafters are wired to the stringers with baling wire. It's mine. I built it. You bump it down—I'll be in the window with a rifle. You even come too close and I'll pot you like a rabbit."

"It's not me. There's nothing I can do. I'll lose my job if I don't do it. And look—suppose you kill me? They'll just hang you, but long before you're hung there'll be another guy on the tractor, and he'll bump the house down. You're not killing the right guy."

"That's so," the tenant said. "Who gave you orders? I'll go after him. He's the one to kill."

"You're wrong. He got his orders from the bank. The bank told him, 'Clear those people out or it's your job.'"

"Well, there's a president of the bank. There's a board of directors. I'll fill up the magazine of the rifle and go into the bank."

The driver said, "Fellow was telling me the bank gets orders from the East. The orders were, 'Make the land show profit or we'll close you up.'"

"But where does it stop? Who can we shoot? I don't aim to starve to death before I kill the man that's starving me."

"I don't know. Maybe there's nobody to shoot. Maybe the thing isn't men at all. Maybe, like you said, the property's doing it. Anyway I told you my orders."

"I got to figure," the tenant said. "We all got to figure. There's some way to stop this. It's not like lightning or earthquakes. We've got a bad thing made by men, and by God that's something we can change." The tenant sat in his doorway, and the driver thundered his engine and started off, tracks falling and curving, harrows combing, and the phalli of the seeder slipping into the ground. Across the dooryard the tractor cut, and the hard, foot-beaten ground was seeded field, and the tractor cut through again; the uncut space was ten feet wide. And back he came. The iron guard bit into the house-corner, crumbled the wall, and wrenched the little house from its foundation so that it fell sideways, crushed like a bug. And the driver was goggled and a rubber mask covered his nose and mouth. The tractor cut a straight line on, and the air and the ground vibrated with its thunder. The tenant man stared after it, his rifle in his hand. His wife was beside him, and the quiet children behind. And all of them stared after the tractor.

# 22
# David Lilienthal (1899–1981)

In 1933 David Lilienthal, a Harvard Law School graduate specializing in labor and public utilities law, became one of the three directors of the newly created Tennessee Valley Authority (TVA). In 1941, President Roosevelt appointed Lilienthal chairman of the TVA. This massive program of regional rehabilitation and integrated resource management was a particular favorite of FDR's, as evidenced in his 1940 speech commemorating Chickamauga Dam. During World War II, the responsibilities of the TVA expanded to include activities supporting the war effort, including power supply to the top-secret Manhattan Project, located nearby in Oak Ridge, Tennessee.

Intimately involved with the creation of the Atomic Energy Commission (AEC), Lilienthal was named chair of the AEC in 1946 by President Truman. This followed a rocky and often vicious confirmation process that was part of the emerging anti-Communist fervor in postwar America. Congressmen attacked Lilienthal for being a Communist sympathizer, largely because of his liberal views on public utilities, but also because of his Eastern European Jewish roots. During Lilienthal's chairmanship of the AEC, the agency stepped up production of nuclear energy and encouraged the development of atomic energy in the private sector. A man known not for mincing words, his entire tenure was fraught with stiff opposition from Congress. He finally resigned from the post in 1950, shortly after the AEC decided to pursue development of a hydrogen bomb.

---

## "REGIONAL PILLARS OF DECENTRALIZATION"*

You cannot, of course, decentralize the functions of the federal government if the whole nation is the operating unit for the carrying out of national powers. Obviously some smaller area than the whole country must be used. In the case of the TVA, Congress and the President determined that in the development of resources that smaller unit should be based upon the natural region; this region is described in the language of the 1933 enactment as "the Tennessee River drainage basin and...such adjoining territory as may be related to or materially affected by the development consequent to this Act...."

The use of the region as an autonomous unit of development was a deliberate "experiment." The results of this departure in national policy were to be reported to the nation and become the object of study as to its

*David E. Lilienthal. 1944. *The TVA: Democracy on the March*. New York: HarperCollins, pp. 152–155, 156–158, 163–166. Copyright 1944 by David E. Lilienthal, renewed © 1972 by David E. Lilienthal. Reprinted by permission of HarperCollins Publishers, Inc.

effectiveness. It was anticipated at the time that if the experiment commended itself by its results the method might be followed or adapted to other regions. The idea that the Tennessee Valley region was set up as a kind of testing ground for the nation has been often expressed, and appears in the President's original message: "If we are successful here," he said, "we can march on, step by step, in a like development of other great natural territorial units within our borders."

The application of TVA's results in decentralized regional development to other parts of the country has become a question of some practical consequence, since from time to time bills providing for regional developments have been introduced in Congress. These proposals, some now pending, are often described or are promoted as measures that provide a "TVA" for this or that area of the country.

...[R]eferences to TVA in connection with such proposals are inaccurate and misleading unless they do in fact adopt the TVA idea in its essentials,

— a federal autonomous agency, with authority to make its decisions in the region
— responsibility to deal with resources, as a unified whole, clearly fixed in the regional agency, not divided among several centralized federal agencies
— a policy, fixed by law, that the federal regional agency work co-operatively with and through local and state agencies.

The entire TVA experiment, as I interpret it, makes it clear that no proposal for regional resource development may be described as a kind of "TVA" unless it embodies these fundamentals, which are clearly written into the TVA Act and have been the very heart and spirit of ten years of transforming that law into action.

My concern here is not whether in future legislation Congress decides to follow or to abandon these principles embodied in the TVA; this book has a deeper purpose than merely to serve as a polemic urging more regional authorities along TVA principles. But I have a responsibility to point out that, in the discussions of future resource policy, merely adopting the nomenclature "regional authority" or "regional administration" is not in itself an adoption of the TVA idea.

What constitutes a region? How large should it be for most effective development? I have no confidence in the elaborate rituals by which some technicians think they can determine what constitutes a region. No one can work out a formula for what is in reality a judgment that does not lend itself to such precise measurement. On this issue of what constitutes a region and upon the general philosophy of regionalism there is a substantial literature to which those who wish to pursue the subject are referred.

There is, however, one generalization which our specific experience in the TVA does support: the regions should not be so large that they are not, in a management sense, of "workable" size. The full potentialities of the unified approach to resources, and the opportunity to be close to the people and their problems, may be fatally impaired if the region itself is a vast one.

In my judgment the present TVA region ought not to be substantially enlarged. This "region"—the watershed plus the area of electric service that extends outside the drainage basin substantially as that area is now constituted—is about as large as it ever should be. The proposal now pending in Congress (once approved by the Senate) to add to the TVA's responsibility the development of the Cumberland River will probably be adopted after the war. This is sound. That river lies within the region and adjoins the drainage line, emptying into the Ohio two or three miles from the mouth of the Tennessee. The people of the Cumberland Valley are already participating in parts of the enterprise, and they understand it. But, with that exception and some extension of electricity beyond the area presently served, I feel strongly that substantial additions to the territorial scope of the TVA would impair its effectiveness and threaten the onset of the evils of remoteness we seek to remedy.

Those who come to have confidence in the TVA idea and seek to have it put into effect in their own regions should be warned that the task is one of adaptation and not of copying or imitation. Indeed, it is the strength of the regional idea that it tends to nourish regional differences in traditions, culture, and ways of living, without sacrifice of national unity on other fundamentals. National unity, but unity through diversity, is the essential meaning of the nation's motto, *E Pluribus Unum*.

I would be rendering a disservice if I left the impression that the TVA's methods offer a ready-made pattern to be copied literally, in all manner of situations, or that genuine decentralization in the administration of every and any kind of national function is feasible. Many functions of the federal government present entirely different problems from the development and improvement of land, water, forests, minerals. Resources have a fixed *situs* and can only be dealt with adequately at that *situs*. TVA's methods can be readily adapted to such problems. But whether regional decentralization in the genuine sense is feasible for many other functions is not a subject for generalization. While different devices must be invented, TVA's methods and experience may be of considerable aid in that process.

All through the public service and in business able men are concerning themselves with such inventions, often with notable results. The practices of decentralized administration have made considerable headway; the tendency, however, continues the other way. Lip service is paid to decentralization by legislators and administrators; they then proceed to draw to Washington the very elements of discretion and the power to decide which impose centralization in its worst forms. Members of Congress will inveigh against the evils of "concentrating power in Washington," and then almost in the same breath (unwittingly, without a doubt) will speed up that very process by passing legislation that sets up additional managerial controls in a central Washington bureau. An able Member of Congress, sincerely interested in the necessity of federal decentralization, recently introduced a comprehensive resolution proposing a broad study of the means of achieving decentralization in the government; but only a few months later the same Member introduced another measure to combine all federally owned power operations in a central "power administration" in Washington!...

There are some opponents of decentralization and regionalism who face the issue squarely. I shall not, of course, attempt to state or to answer any but the principal of their objections, some of which are put in the highly technical jargon of expertise. Behind the multiplicity of words there is often concealed some bureau's or department's "vested right" in centralized government. In this the public is little interested. It does not interest me either, for I fail to see the relevance of such an objection.

The objection that regionalism will "Balkanize" the country is a familiar and candid one usually sincerely raised. The argument is that regionalism is a kind of provincialism that divides rather than unites the country, underlining sectional animosities and obstructing a really national outlook. But such a position shows a lack of understanding of our history and of the nature of regionalism. It assumes first of all that regions, rather than the individual states, have not always been the units of important national policy development, as scholars such as Turner have made clear and as public men understand so well. In the Congressional Record we read of "the Gentleman from Indiana" or New York or Texas. The newspapers, however, are more realistic. They report the plans, meetings, and votes of the "Senators from the Corn Belt," or the "cotton bloc," or the "New England delegation in Congress."

For the practical purposes of federal legislation, this is a country of regions, not states.

The growth and development of our national policies is not the result of conflicts between states; it represents an attempted reconciliation between the interests of the various natural regions. Debates on such subjects as the tariff, inland waterway improvements, or measures relating to agriculture almost always foreshadowed votes cast for the most part on a sectional basis. It was not a war between separate states which settled one great economic and political conflict in this country. It was strife between sections. And, although only once in its history has this country resorted to arms to settle regional differences, our national policies have always been arrived at through compromises—often very costly ones to the nation's interest—between the points of view of different sections of the country. Each region has fought for its own interests, usually with little regard to the effect on the country as a whole. This is sectionalism. We avoid the word today, hoping perhaps that the evils of disunity and local selfishness will vanish if the syllables are forgotten. But it is not so easily exorcised.

Modern regionalism, by contrast, rests squarely upon the supremacy of the *national* interest. It admits that there are problems and resources common to areas larger than any single state—a river basin, for example. It recognizes that certain points of view develop in some portions of the country and are not shared by the nation as a whole. It affirms and insists, however, that the solution of regional problems and the development of regional resources are *matters of concern to the whole country*. It proposes to harmonize regional advancement with the national welfare. That concern for and supremacy of the national interest distinguishes "regionalism" from "sectionalism." Under the banner of sectionalism, states throughout our history have combined to support or to oppose federal action. Under the modern concept of regionalism, the federal government acts to meet regional needs to the end that the entire nation may profit.

The organization of the Tennessee Valley Authority is an example of this modern idea of regionalism. To create it seven states did not unite to demand special privileges to distinguish them from the country as a whole, regardless of the ensuing consequences to the national welfare. The federal legislature itself created an independent regional agency whose basic objective was to conserve the natural resources lying in the valley of the Tennessee and to develop those resources *in conformity with broad national objectives and policies*. This is the very opposite—indeed it is the antidote—of "Balkanization."

The idea of regionalism embodied in the TVA—a federal agency decentralized in fact—offers a rational way of harmonizing regional interests with the national interest. For the first time a federal implement is at hand for that task, to take the place of the usual method of political bargaining, so often wholly crude and without a basis in facts, policy, or principle....

*Decentralization frankly seeks to promote diversity; centralization requires uniformity and standardization.*

It follows quite simply that if your idea of "co-ordination" is *national uniformity* in *administration*, regionalism *will* create insuperable problems of "co-ordination." If you cannot conceive of a well-governed country that in every region is not standardized, identical, and uniform, then you do not want decentralization, and of course you would be opposed to regional authorities. If, on the other hand, diversity under broad national policies rather than uniformity in administration, adaptation to regional differences, and discretion and flexibility through the broad reaches of this greatly varied country are what appeal to you as sound, humane, and desirable, then the problems of co-ordination that cause the centralizers such concern become relatively simple and manageable.

It is difficult to exaggerate the lengths to which some men with administrative responsibility feel it is necessary to go in order to secure what they call co-ordination. This extends to matters of managerial detail. What such men would mean by the "co-ordination" of methods of federal land-buying—I use this only by way of a wholly hypothetical illustration—would be to erase differences as to the methods that might exist between federal land buyers dealing with small upland farms in east Tennessee and those applied in the flat sectionalized reaches of northern Indiana. To them a regulation respecting personnel management is not a good regulation if it does not apply uniformly throughout this whole country.

Now if your mind operates that way you would be opposed to regionalism. For only a centralized government can pour the country into such a single mold. If differences in how a public program is administered in the Tennessee Valley and in the Arkansas Valley, in Illinois and in New Mexico, disturb you, if those differences appear to be a "conflict," then you are right in assuming that regional decentralization will promote conflict.

This is not to say that under regionalism there will not be conflicts between regions. The major ones of these conflicts must be decided by Congress, as they have been since the very establishment of our central government. Other major conflicts involving the Executive Department would have to be decided by the President, as they always have been under centralized government administration.

So long as we harbor the administrative obsession that uniformity in administration is essential, the amount of co-ordination of this kind with which Congress and the President must deal and must continue to deal will be very great. Nor will regionalism eliminate all or most of these conflicts. But I do venture the assertion that it will considerably lessen them. This is true because the best place to co-ordinate is *close to the point where the conflict arises*, and not in the top levels and central offices. Industrial managers know this and practice it daily. The same thing proves true in government.

And so, looking at the whole picture, it can be said with confidence that in the national interest the difficulties of co-ordination are certainly not increased, and I think upon consideration it will be seen that they are actually diminished, by regionalism. Let the reader reflect upon the way in which the TVA has brought into the task of resource development a great host of local communities and state agencies. The problems of co-ordinating these efforts have not proved to be insuperable because TVA is a decentralized federal agency operating in the Tennessee Valley region with power to make its decisions in the field. The serious conflicts in administration are the ones which, unresolved in the local communities, find their way into the remote and often unreal atmosphere where men are dealing in "jurisdiction"and, as I have said, are preoccupied with their own institutions.

Co-ordination between a regional agency and other federal regional agencies or centralized departments is not, of course, automatic. The TVA has, from the outset, developed a comprehensive scheme of active co-operation with every other federal agency, either in Washington or in field offices, that has a responsibility or a function which could be helpful in the building of this region. In an earlier chapter I have alluded to the extent to which the changes in this valley have been due to these other federal activities; I wish to repeat and emphasize that here. The TVA has entered into hundreds of contracts with more than a score of other federal departments and bureaus. These inter-federal agency contracts and the relations carried on under them have from time to time developed serious differences on matters of importance. The task of reaching agreement has not always been an easy one. Yet there has never been any difference that could not be worked out, usually between the staffs of the agencies. In ten years no conflict between the TVA and these many federal departments and bureaus has made necessary a single conference with the President. In fact, the TVA Board has on only one occasion found it necessary to confer with the President on Authority problems in the three and a half years since the fall of France and the ensuing conversion of TVA to war needs.

The subject of regionalism has the widest ramifications, since it touches fundamental issues…. But our experience indicates clearly that the asserted danger of conflicts and the difficulties of co-ordination arising from regional decentralization are exaggerated and largely unreal.

# 23
# J. Robert Oppenheimer (1904–1967)

J. Robert Oppenheimer was a noted physicist at the University of California, Berkeley, before being appointed director of the government's top secret effort to build an atomic bomb. He decided to locate the project in the remote forests near Los Alamos, New Mexico, assembling there some of the greatest scientific minds of the twentieth century. The project faced enormous intellectual and practical obstacles, but in slightly more than two years the team had detonated the world's first nuclear bomb. In July of 1945, the inventors of the bomb watched in awe as they saw the world irrevocably change. Less than one month later President Truman made the momentous decision to drop two atomic bombs on the Japanese cities of Hiroshima and Nagasaki. With Japan's surrender in the face of this annihilating weapon, World War II finally ended.

The human costs involved in constructing the atomic bomb soon became evident, and in October of 1945 Oppenheimer announced his resignation as director of the project. His farewell speech to the Association of Los Alamos Scientists inspired many of those in attendance to work for arms control and peacetime uses of the atom. After having devoted years to the creation of weapons of mass destruction, Oppenheimer himself displayed grave misgivings about not only his role in their creation, but also the role of the scientist in general who serves two masters: the scientific profession and the state. He had no easy answers.

After leaving Los Alamos, Oppenheimer continued to contribute to the field of atomic energy. He taught and served as chair of the General Advisory Committee of the Atomic Energy Commission (AEC). He denounced the hydrogen bomb, supported the unrestricted sharing of nuclear technology, and urged an arms control agreement with the Soviet Union.

Like many intellectuals in the 1930s, Oppenheimer had been involved with several left-wing organizations. These early associations came back to haunt him, as they did others, during the McCarthy era. After a highly publicized AEC hearing in 1954, Oppenheimer's security clearance was revoked and his contract with the AEC cancelled. The postwar hysteria over communism effectively silenced Oppenheimer's voice on the gravest issues of the day.

# "A CHANGE IN THE NATURE OF THE WORLD"*

What has happened to us—it is really rather major, it is so major that I think in some ways one returns to the greatest developments of the twentieth century, to the discovery of relativity, and to the whole development of atomic theory, and its interpretation in terms of complementarity, for analogy. These things, as you know, forced us to re-consider the relations between science and common sense. They forced on us the recognition that the fact that we were in the habit of talking a certain language and using certain concepts did not necessarily imply that there was anything in the real world to correspond to these. They forced us to be prepared for the inadequacy of the ways in which human beings attempted to deal with reality, for that reality. In some ways I think these virtues, which scientists quite reluctantly were forced to learn by the nature of the world they were studying, may be useful even today in preparing us for somewhat more radical views of what the issues are than would be natural or easy for people who had not been through this experience.

But the real impact of the creation of the atomic bomb and atomic weapons—to understand that one has to look further back, look, I think, to the times when physical science was growing in the days of the renaissance, and when the threat that science offered was felt so deeply throughout the Christian world. The analogy is, of course, not perfect. You may even wish to think of the days in the last century when the theories of evolution seemed a threat to the values by which men lived. The analogy is not perfect because there is nothing in atomic weapons—there is certainly nothing that we have done here or in the physics or chemistry that immediately preceded our work here—in which any revolutionary ideas were involved. I don't think that the conceptions of nuclear fission have strained any man's attempts to understand them, and I don't feel that any of us have really learned in a deep sense very much from following this up. It is in a quite different way. It is not an idea—it is a development and a reality—but it has in common with the early days of physical science the fact that the very existence of science is threatened, and its value is threatened. This is the point that I would like to speak a little about.

I think that it hardly needs to be said why the impact is so strong. There are three reasons: one is the extraordinary speed with which things which were right on the frontier of science were translated into terms where they affected many living people, and potentially all people. Another is the fact, quite accidental in many ways, and connected with the speed, that scientists themselves played such a large part, not merely in providing the foundation for atomic weapons, but in actually making them. In this we are certainly

*J. Robert Oppenheimer. 1945. Speech to the Association of Los Alamos Scientists, Los Alamos, New Mexico, November 2. U.S. Library of Congress Manuscript Collection, 1945 file, Box 262.

closer to it than any other group. The third is that the thing we made—partly because of the technical nature of the problem, partly because we worked hard, partly because we had good breaks—really arrived in the world with such a shattering reality and suddenness that there was no opportunity for the edges to be worn off.

In considering what the situation of science is, it may be helpful to think a little of what people said and felt of their motives in coming into this job. One always has to worry that what people say of their motives is not adequate. Many people said different things, and most of them, I think, had some validity. There was in the first place the great concern that our enemy might develop these weapons before we did, and the feeling—at least, in the early days, the very strong feeling—that without atomic weapons it might be very difficult, it might be an impossible, it might be an incredibly long thing to win the war. These things wore off a little as it became clear that the war would be won in any case. Some people, I think, were motivated by curiosity, and rightly so; and some by a sense of adventure, and rightly so. Others had more political arguments and said, "Well, we know that atomic weapons are in principle possible, and it is not right that the threat of their unrealized possibility should hang over the world. It is right that the world should know what can be done in their field and deal with it." And the people added to that that it was a time when all over the world men would be particularly ripe and open for dealing with this problem because of the immediacy of the evils of war, because of the universal cry from everyone that one could not go through this thing again, even a war without atomic bombs. And there was finally, and I think rightly, the feeling that there was probably no place in the world where the development of atomic weapons would have a better chance of leading to a reasonable solution, and a smaller chance of leading to disaster, than within the United States. I believe all these things that people said are true, and I think I said them all myself at one time or another.

But when you come right down to it the reason that we did this job is because it was an organic necessity. If you are a scientist you cannot stop such a thing. If you are a scientist you believe that it is good to find out how the world works; that it is good to find out what the realities are; that it is good to turn over to mankind at large the greatest possible power to control the world and to deal with it according to its lights and its values.

There has been a lot of talk about the evil of secrecy, of concealment, of control, of security. Some of that talk has been on a rather low plane, limited really to saying that it is difficult or inconvenient to work in a world where you are not free to do what you want. I think that the talk has been justified, and that the almost unanimous resistance of scientists to the imposition of control and secrecy is a justified position, but I think that the reason for it may lie a little deeper. I think that it comes from the fact that secrecy strikes at the very root of what science is, and what it is for. It is not possible to be a scientist unless you believe that it is good to learn. It is not good to be a scientist, and it is not possible, unless you think that it is of the highest value to share your knowledge, to share it with anyone who is interested. It is not possible to be a scientist unless you believe that the knowledge of the world, and the power which this gives, is a thing which is of intrinsic value to humanity, and that you are using it to help in the spread of knowledge, and are willing to take the consequences. And, therefore, I think that this resistance which we feel and see all around us to anything which is an attempt to treat science of the future as though it were rather a dangerous thing, a thing that must be watched and managed, is resisted not because of its inconvenience—I think we are in a position where we must be willing to take any inconvenience—but resisted because it is based on a philosophy incompatible with that by which we live, and have learned to live in the past.

There are many people who try to wiggle out of this. They say the real importance of atomic energy does not lie in the weapons that have been made; the real importance lies in all the great benefits which atomic energy, which the various radiations, will bring to mankind. There may be some truth in this. I am sure that there is truth in it, because there has never in the past been a new field opened up where the real fruits of it have not been invisible at the beginning. I have a very high confidence that the fruits—the so-called peacetime applications—of atomic energy will have in them all that we think, and more. There are others who try to escape the immediacy of this situation by saying that, after all, war has always been very terrible; after all, weapons have always gotten worse and worse; that this is just another weapon and it doesn't create a great change; that they are not so bad; bombings have been bad in this war and this is not a change in that—it just adds a little to the effectiveness of bombing; that some sort of protection will be found. I think that these efforts to diffuse and weaken the nature of the crisis make it only more dangerous. I think it is for us to accept it as a very grave crisis, to realize that these atomic weapons which we have started to make are very terrible, that they involve a change, that they are not just a slight modification: to accept this, and to accept with it the necessity for those transformations in the world which will make it possible to integrate these developments into human life.

As scientists I think we have perhaps a little greater ability to accept change, and accept radical change, because of our experiences in the pursuit of science. And that may help us—that, and the fact that we have lived with it—to be of some use in understanding these problems.

It is clear to me that wars have changed. It is clear to me that if these first bombs—the bomb that was dropped on Nagasaki—that if these can destroy ten square miles, then that is really quite something. It is clear to me that they are going to be very cheap if anyone wants to make them; it is clear to me that this is a situation where a quantitative change, and a change in which the advantage of aggression compared to defense—of attack compared to defense—is shifted, where this quantitative change has all the character of a change in quality, of a change in the nature of the world. I know that whereas wars have become intolerable, and the question would have been raised and would have been pursued after this war, more ardently than after the last, of whether there was not some method by which they could be averted. But I think the advent of the atomic bomb and the facts which will get around that they are not too hard to make, that they will be universal if people wish to make them universal, that they will not constitute a real drain on the economy of any strong nation, and that their power of destruction will grow and is already incomparably greater than that of any other weapon—I think these things create a new situation, so new that there is some danger, even some danger in believing, that what we have is a new argument for arrangements, for hopes, that existed before this development took place. By that I mean that much as I like to hear advocates of a world federation, or advocates of a United Nations organization, who have been talking of these things for years—much as I like to hear them say that here is a new argument, I think that they are in part missing the point, because the point is not that atomic weapons constitute a new argument. There have always been good arguments. The point is that atomic weapons constitute also a field, a new field, and a new opportunity for realizing preconditions. I think when people talk of the fact that this is not only a great peril, but a great hope, this is what they should mean. I do not think they should mean the unknown, though sure, value of industrial and scientific virtues of atomic energy, but rather the simple fact that in this field, because it is a threat, because it is a peril, and because it has certain special characteristics, to which I will return, there exists a possibility of realizing, of beginning to realize, those changes which are needed if there is to be any peace.

Those are very far-reaching changes. They are changes in the relations between nations, not only in spirit, not only in law, but also in conception and feeling. I don't know which of these is prior; they must all work together, and only the gradual interaction of one on the other can make a reality. I don't agree with those who say the first step is to have a structure of international law. I don't agree with those who say the only thing is to have friendly feelings. All of these things will be involved. I think it is true to say that atomic weapons are a peril which affect everyone in the world, and in that sense a completely common problem, as common a problem as it was for the Allies to defeat the Nazis. I think that in order to handle this common problem there must be a complete sense of community responsibility. I do not think that one may expect that people will contribute to the solution of the problem until they are aware of their ability to take part in the solution. I think that it is a field in which the implementation of such a common responsibility has certain decisive advantages. It is a new field, in which the position of vested interests in various parts of the world is very much less serious than in others. It is serious in this country, and that is one of our problems. It is a new field, in which the role of science has been so great that it is to my mind hardly thinkable that the international traditions of science, and the fraternity of scientists, should not play a constructive part. It is a new field, in which just the novelty and the special characteristics of the technical operations should enable one to establish a community of interest which might almost be regarded as a pilot plant for a new type of international collaboration. I speak of it as a pilot plant because it is quite clear that the control of atomic weapons cannot be in itself the unique end of such operation. The only unique end can be a world that is united, and a world in which war will not occur. But those things don't happen overnight, and in this field it would seem that one could get started, and get started without meeting those insuperable obstacles which history has so often placed in the way of any effort of cooperation. Now, this is not an easy thing, and the point I want to make, the one point I want to hammer home, is what an enormous change in spirit is involved. There are things which we hold very dear, and I think rightly hold very dear; I would say that the word democracy perhaps stood for some of them as well as any other word. There are many parts of the world in which there is no democracy. There are other things which we hold dear, and which we rightly should. And when I speak of a new spirit in international affairs I mean that even to these deepest of things which we cherish, and for which Americans have been willing to die—and certainly most of us would be willing to die—even in these deepest things, we realize that there is something more profound than that; namely, the common bond with other men everywhere. It is only if you do that that this makes sense; because if you approach the problem and say, "We know what is right and we would like to use the atomic bomb to persuade you to agree with us," then you are in a very weak position and you will not succeed, because under those conditions you will not succeed in delegating responsibility for the survival of men. It is a purely unilateral statement; you will find yourselves attempting by force of arms to prevent a disaster.

I want to express the utmost sympathy with the people who have to grapple with this problem and in the strongest terms to urge you not to underestimate its difficulty. I can think of an analogy, and I hope it is not a completely good analogy: in the days in the first half of the nineteenth century there were many people, mostly in the North, but some in the South, who thought that there was no evil on earth more degrading than human slavery, and nothing that they would more willingly devote their lives to than its eradication. Always when I was young I wondered why it was that when Lincoln was President he did not declare that the war against the South, when it broke out, was a war that slavery should be abolished, that this was the central point, the rallying point, of that war. Lincoln was severely criticized by many of the Abolitionists as you know, by many then called radicals, because he seemed to be waging a war which did not hit the thing that was most important. But Lincoln realized, and I have only in the last months come to appreciate the depth and wisdom of it, that beyond the issue of slavery was the issue of the community of the people of the country, and the issue of the Union. I hope that today this will not be an issue calling for war; but I wanted to remind you that in order to preserve the Union Lincoln had to subordinate the immediate problem of the eradication of slavery, and trust—and I think if he had had his way it would have gone so—to the conflict of these ideas in a united people to eradicate it.

These are somewhat general remarks and it may be appropriate to say one or two things that are a little more programmatic, that are not quite so hard to get one's hands on. That is, what sort of agreement between nations would be a reasonable start. I don't know the answer to this, and I am very sure that no a priori answer should be given, that it is something that is going to take constant working out. But I think it is a thing where it will not hurt to have some reasonably concrete proposal. And I would go a step further and say of even such questions as the great question of secrecy—which perplexes scientists and other people—that even this was not a suitable subject for unilateral action. If atomic energy is to be treated as an international problem, as I think it must be, if it is to be treated on the basis of an international responsibility and an international common concern, the problems of secrecy are also international problems. I don't mean by that that our present classifications and our present, in many cases inevitably ridiculous, procedures should be maintained. I mean that the fundamental problem of how to treat this peril ought not to be treated unilaterally by the United States, or by the United States in conjunction with Great Britain.

The first thing I would say about any proposals is that they ought to be regarded as interim proposals, and that whenever they are made it be understood and agreed that within a year or two years—whatever seems a reasonable time—they will be reconsidered and the problems which have arisen, and the new developments which have occurred, will cause a rewriting. I think the only point is that there should be a few things in these proposals which will work in the right direction, and that the things should be accepted without forcing all of the changes, which we know must ultimately occur, upon people who will not be ready for them. This is anyone's guess, but it would seem to me that if you took these four points, it might work: first, that we are dealing with an interim solution, so recognized. Second, that the nations participating in the arrangement would have a joint atomic energy commission, operating under the most broad directives from the different states, but with a power which only they had, and which was not subject to review by the heads of State, to go ahead with those constructive applications of atomic energy which we would all like to see developed— energy sources, and the innumerable research tools which are immediate possibilities. Third, that there would be not merely the possibility of exchange of scientists and students; that very, very concrete machinery more or less forcing such exchange should be established, so that we would be quite sure that the fraternity of scientists would be strengthened and that the bonds on which so much of the future depends would have some reinforcement and some scope. And fourth, I would say that no bombs be made. I don't know whether these proposals are good ones, and I think that anyone in this group would have his own proposals. But I mention them as very simple things, which I don't believe solve the problem, and which I want to make clear are not the ultimate or even a touch of the ultimate, but which I think ought to be started right away; which I believe—though I know very little of this—may very well be acceptable to any of the nations that wish to become partners with us in this great undertaking.

One of the questions which you will want to hear more about—and which I can only partly hope to succeed in answering—is to what extent such views, essentially the view that the life of science is threatened, the life of the world is threatened, and that only by a profound revision of what it is that constitutes a thing worth fighting for and a thing worth living for can this crisis be met—to what extent these views are held by other men. They are certainly not held universally by scientists; but I think they are in agreement with all of the expressed opinions of this group, and I know that many of my friends here see pretty much eye to eye....

I would say that among scientists there are certain centrifugal tendencies which seem to me a little dangerous, but not very. One of them is the attempt to try, in this imperilled world, in which the very function of science is threatened, to make convenient arrangements for the continuance of science, and to pay very little attention to the preconditions which give sense to it. Another is the tendency to say we must have a free science and a strong science, because this will make us a strong nation and enable us to fight better wars. It seems to me that this is a profound mistake, and I don't like to hear it. The third is even odder, and it is to say, "Oh give the bombs to the United Nations for police purposes, and let us get back to physics and chemistry." I think none of these are really held very widely, but they show that there are people who are desperately trying to avoid what I think is the most difficult problem. One must expect these false solutions, and overeasy solutions, and these are three which pop up from time to time.

As far as I can tell in the world outside there are many people just as quick to see the gravity of the situation, and to understand it in terms not so different from those I have tried to outline. It is not only among scientists that there are wise people and foolish people. I have had occasion in the last few months to meet people who had to do with the Government—the legislative branches, the administrative branches, and even the judicial branches, and I have found many in whom an understanding of what this problem is, and of the general lines along which it can be solved, is very clear. I would especially mention the former Secretary of War, Mr. Stimson, who, perhaps as much as any man, seemed to appreciate how hopeless and how impractical it was to attack this problem on a superficial level, and whose devotion to the development of atomic weapons was in large measure governed by his understanding of the hope that lay in it that there would be a new world. I know this is a surprise, because most people think that the War Department has as its unique function the making of war. The Secretary of War has other functions.

I think this is another question of importance: that is, what views will be held on these matters in other countries. I think it is important to realize that even those who are well informed in this country have been slow to understand, slow to believe that the bombs would work, and then slow to understand that their working would present such profound problems. We have certain interests in playing up the bomb, not only we here locally, but all over the country, because we made them, and our pride is involved. I think that in other lands it may be even more difficult for an appreciation of the magnitude of the thing to take hold. For this reason, I'm not sure that the greatest opportunities for progress do not lie somewhat further in the future than I had for a long time thought.

There have been two or three official statements by the President which defined, as nearly as their in some measure inevitable contradictions made possible, the official policy of the Government. And I think that one must not be entirely discouraged by the fact that there are contradictions, because the contradictions show that the problem is being understood as a difficult one, is temporarily being regarded as an insoluble one. Certainly you will notice, especially in the message to Congress, many indications of a sympathy with, and an understanding of, the views which this group holds, and which I have discussed briefly tonight. I think all of us were encouraged at the phrase "too revolutionary to consider in the framework of old ideas." That's about what we all think. I think all of us were encouraged by the sense of urgency that was frequently and emphatically stressed. I think all of us must be encouraged by the recognition, the official recognition by the Government of the importance—of the overriding importance—of the free exchange of scientific ideas and scientific information between all countries of the world. It would certainly be ridiculous to regard this as a final end, but I think that it would also be a very dangerous thing not to realize that it is a precondition. I am myself somewhat discouraged by the limitation of the objective to the elimination of atomic weapons, and I have seen many articles—probably you have, too—in which this is interpreted as follows: "Let us get international agreement to outlaw atomic weapons and then let us go back to having a good, clean war." This is certainly not a very good way of looking at it. I think, to say it again, that if one solves the problems presented by the atomic bomb, one will have made a pilot plant for solution of the problem of ending war.

But what is surely the thing which must have troubled you, and which troubled me, in the official statements was the insistent note of unilateral responsibility for the handling of atomic weapons. However good the motives of this country are—I am not going to argue with the President's description of what the motives and the aims are—we are 140 million people, and there are two billion people living on earth. We must understand that whatever our commitments to our own views and ideas, and however confident we are that in the course of time they will tend to prevail, our absolute— our completely absolute—commitment to them, in denial of the views and ideas of other people, cannot be the basis of any kind of agreement.

As I have said, I had for a long time the feeling of the most extreme urgency, and I think maybe there was something right about that. There was a period immediately after the first use of the bomb when it seemed most natural that a clear statement of policy, and the initial steps of implementing it, should have been made; and it would be wrong for me not to admit that something may have been lost, and that there may be tragedy in that loss. But I think the plain fact is that in the actual world, and with the actual people in it, it has taken time, and it may take longer, to understand what this is all about. And I am not sure, as I have said before, that in other lands it won't take longer than it does in this country. As it is now, our only course is to see what we can do to bring about an understanding on a level deep enough to make a solution practicable, and to do that without undue delay....

I don't have very much more to say. There are a few things which scientists perhaps should remember, that I don't think I need to remind us of; but I will, anyway. One is that they are very often called upon to give technical information in one way or another, and I think one cannot be too careful to be honest. And it is very difficult, not because one tells lies, but because so often questions are put in a form which makes it very hard to give an answer which is not misleading. I think we will be in a very weak position unless we maintain at its highest the scrupulousness which is traditional for us in sticking to the truth, and in distinguishing between what we know to be true from what we hope may be true.

The second thing I think it right to speak of is this: it is everywhere felt that the fraternity between us and scientists in other countries may be one of the most helpful things for the future; yet it is apparent that even in this country not all of us who are scientists are in agreement. There is no harm in that; such disagreement is healthy. But we must not lose the sense of fraternity because of it; we must not lose our fundamental confidence in our fellow scientists.

I think that we have no hope at all if we yield in our belief in the value of science, in the good that it can be to the world to know about reality, about nature, to attain a gradually greater and greater control of nature, to learn, to teach, to understand. I think that if we lose our faith in this we stop being scientists, we sell out our heritage, we lose what we have most of value for this time of crisis.

But there is another thing: we are not only scientists; we are men, too. We cannot forget our dependence on our fellow men. I mean not only our material dependence, without which no science would be possible, and without which we could not work; I mean also our deep moral dependence, in that the value of science must lie in the world of men, that all our roots lie there. These are the strongest bonds in the world, stronger than those even that bind us to one another, these are the deepest bonds—that bind us to our fellow men.

# DISCUSSION QUESTIONS

1.  Discuss how Franklin Delano Roosevelt's policies blended both the heritage of Gifford Pinchot and John Muir. In your own locale, identify projects and the facilities (e.g., dams, CCC-constructed facilities and trails, shelterbelts, parks, etc.) that are the legacy of the New Deal years.
2.  The Great Depression thrust hardship and devastation upon millions of people and families, the likes of which had never been seen before and hopefully will never be seen again in the United States. How might environmental policy today either prevent or recreate the conditions that led to such diverse results as the dust bowl, economic collapse, and war?
3.  Regionalism as a basis for conceiving, formulating, and implementing policy received governmental sanction in the TVA and other programs. How does David Lilienthal's vision of regionalism compare with John Wesley Powell's? How does Lilienthal's approach counter earlier notions of group interest and participatory decision making? How would the United States appear today if the TVA idea had been applied to, for example, the Columbia River Basin and the Missouri Valley?
4.  As J. Robert Oppenheimer notes, the advent of scientific and technological achievements has carried with them blessings as well as curses. Is it possible to minimize the negative effects of innovations, especially innovations that also carry with them the potential of annihilating humans and other species? What kinds of inventions today fall into that category? What are the ethical and political obligations of scientists in balancing service to the state, to their scientific professions, to themselves, and to nature?

# PART V

## "What Was Good for the Country Was Good for General Motors, and Vice Versa"*

### POSTWAR AMERICA, 1945–1961

W orld War II had a profound impact upon the country, indeed on the entire world. The transformations in the years immediately following the war became evident in almost every sector of American life, not least of which was the impact on the natural environment. The United States emerged from the war a political, military and economic superpower, rivaled only by the Soviet Union. Tragically, the two allies during the Second World War became enemies at war's end, and a fierce competition for world dominance ensued. The Cold War Era had begun.

Much of the industrial might that the nation developed to fight the war became channeled into the creation of what the Harvard University economist, John Kenneth Galbraith, called the "affluent society." It was a society of "modern want creation," one where unrestrained production and consumption became a defining feature of democracy itself. It also was an America marked increasingly by the inability to do contradictory things: to have the atom serve both war and peace; to make the nation's lands and waterways engines of industrial production as well as wilderness playgrounds for leisure-minded Americans; and to keep America a symbol of freedom and democracy while systematically denying basic political and economic rights to blacks and other minorities.

---

*Charles E. Wilson. 1953. U.S. Secretary of Defense and CEO, General Motors Corporation, in explaining why he didn't want to sell his GM stock when he became Secretary.

Postwar America boomed; so did the nation's population. Between 1946 and 1957 birthrates increased by almost twenty-five percent. This created a generation of "baby boomers," whose retirement and lifestyle needs now define many of the twenty-first century's problems. However, population growth *per se* did not become perceived as an environmental problem until well into the 1960s. During the '50s, the growth of the American family was viewed as a positive phenomenon.

This new industrial state, as Galbraith described it in a 1967 book, was characterized by the widespread availability of new consumer goods. Automatic clothes washers and dryers, air conditioning units, electric blankets, garbage disposals, televisions, disposable diapers, lightweight plastic foam, phosphate detergents, and fast-food chains appeared for the first time. Many products were conveniently packaged and disposable. To the horror of scientists like Barry Commoner and Rachel Carson, the production of man-made plastics and pesticides increased with virtually no thought given to their long-term effects. Car ownership became a necessity, and commercial jet aircraft were put into service for an increasingly mobile public. By 1952 the President's Commission on Materials Policy reported that the United States had become the biggest raw materials consumer of the non-communist world: With 10 percent of the population and 8 percent of the land base, Americans consumed nearly half of the total annual volume of raw materials including coal, copper, iron ore, zinc, natural gas, and crude oil. Galbraith put it more bluntly: In creating postwar America, the nation had developed a "gargantuan appetite" for natural resources and energy consumption.

The necessary wartime relationship between big business and big government continued to thrive in peacetime. It was not only Charles Wilson, CEO of General Motors and President Eisenhower's Secretary of Defense, who linked the viability of business with the general well-being of the country. As happened during the 1920s, the business of the state and the business of business blurred. Government invested heavily in industrial expansion, and provided a generally friendly regulatory climate. Corporate America also moved easily into the agricultural sector. The number of farms and farmers decreased while those remaining grew into larger, specialized, and capital-intensive corporate enterprises generously subsidized by government programs. Corporate executives moved back and forth between appointments in government and business: Eisenhower's first cabinet, for instance, was described as "eight millionaires and a millionairess."

Atomic power production epitomized the complexities of the government-industry nexus during the postwar period. As President Eisenhower pointed out in his 1961 Farewell Address, a new and largely secret industry tied to nuclear weapons production prospered in government-sponsored laboratories and contractor facilities throughout the '50s. Although the Atomic Energy Commission, created in 1946, initially concentrated on overseeing weapons production in the United States, by the early 1950s there were pressures to promote more peaceful uses of nuclear technology. In 1953, the President announced his "Atoms for Peace" program, and one year later the government's monopoly on nuclear technology was abandoned.

Approval was given for the development of privately owned and operated power plants. Nuclear power, its supporters famously predicted, would be "too cheap to meter." Although other technological miracles appeared during this period, this one was far off the mark. Even with government subsidies, such as the 1957 Price-Anderson Act, the nuclear industry never became the energy panacea its promoters dreamed of.

Water-resources development provided another example of the close connections that emerged between private interests and government. It also illustrated the contradictions existing within society over incompatible uses of the same resource. While President Truman (1945–1953) initially supported the continuation of FDR's integrated, long-range planning approach, the administration increasingly became preoccupied with the Cold War and the conflict in Korea. Democrats also became concerned over Republican charges of "socialism," especially as the 1952 election drew closer. As a result, political support for the creation of TVA-like institutions waned.

This meant that new initiatives in water resources increasingly fell within the purview of Congress and the federal agencies charged with their implementation. At nearly the same time as Marjory Stoneman Douglas was writing her natural history of the Florida Everglades, meant to inform the public about their uniqueness, the Harvard political scientist, Arthur Maass, was researching the political dynamics that eventually doomed the Everglades to development. What happened to America's only "river of grass," as Douglas calls it, is a classic case of interest-group politics running amok. On the one hand, the Everglades was designated a national park in 1947, the same year as Douglas's book appeared. On the other hand, the iron triangle of interests to develop Florida's economy via the massive engineering of the state's inland waterways also was at work. In his 1951 classic study, *Muddy Waters*, Maass described in detail how congressional committees, local and state business interests, and federal agencies such as the Army Corps of Engineers and the Bureau of Reclamation work in concert to promote economic development.

National park status did little to save the Everglades, so that by the 1990s—nearly fifty years later—federal and state authorities were hard at work designing a plan to preserve what is left of this unique landscape. The Everglades story happened time and again throughout the period that Marc Reisner, author of the best selling *Cadillac Desert* (1986), called "the go-go years" of water development.

Pressures on the nation's land and timber supply also intensified during the postwar period. The demographic profile of America changed dramatically during the '40s and '50s, and with it there emerged a significant housing shortage. Government programs such as the GI Bill for returning veterans, a stepped-up program of logging on the national forests, generous credit and mortgage policies, and tax breaks helped the postwar generation realize the American Dream of single-family home ownership in new "suburban" developments. One of the first to be constructed was by the entrepreneur, William Levitt, who in 1949 converted a Long Island potato field into a community of look-alike tract homes. "Levittown" became synonymous with affordable yet monotonous developments across the nation. Such developments appeared to meet the needs of white, middle-class America at mid-century: a home of one's own, located on the outskirts of the city so that one could drive the family automobile to work. As a result of this suburbanization and black migration from the South to the industrial North, the nation's inner cities increasingly became "dark ghettos."

Although many Americans were leaving the city for "the country," suburbia was hardly what the great naturalist, Aldo Leopold, had in mind when he wrote about the need to reestablish "the land ethic" in postwar America. Leopold's 1949 book, *A Sand County Almanac*, was destined to become a classic, but not for another decade or more. His ideas were too radical for the times. When he talked about "thinking like a mountain" and respecting nature and other living creatures, he didn't have in mind backyard bird feeders and carefully manicured front lawns. The land ethic, which harkens back to Jeffersonian agrarian democracy, and which also recalls the Native American world view, was hard to come by. One had to work at it. To be in touch with nature, Leopold eloquently argued, one had to be *in* nature. It was not for everybody—and certainly not for the new suburbanite.

In fact, suburbia was making the rural way of life an even rarer phenomenon in the United States, as urban sprawl consumed more and more agricultural land. (It is a trend, incidentally, that is still underway at the beginning of the twenty-first century.) The politically popular road construction programs of the '40s and '50s provided incentives for suburban growth. President Eisenhower, for example, considered the interstate highway system his most important domestic accomplishment. And in addition to roads, suburbia demanded new infrastructure—water works, sewers, sidewalks, electric service, and public schools. Because postwar government incentives generally favored suburban flight, it came at the expense of the urban core. While both the Great Depression and World War II had fostered migration from rural areas to the cities, the postwar white flight of the cities' 9-to-5 workers to suburban "bedroom communities" left the core to those who could not afford to move. Poor and minority neighborhoods in the inner city deteriorated, later to become obliterated by urban renewal programs. By 1960, it is estimated that fully one-third of the land in many cities had become parking lots.

After the war, families who hadn't had a vacation since Pearl Harbor began to take time off. Well-paying jobs, more leisure time, and increased automobile ownership generated pressure for outdoor recreation opportunities; as a result visitation to the national parks and forests soared. In order to accommodate the outdoor recreating public, both the National Park Service and the Forest Service launched ambitious programs in the 1950s: Supported by the Eisenhower Administration and generously funded by Congress, Mission 66 and Operation Outdoors greatly improved public accommodations in the nation's parks and forests. Between 1956 and 1966 the Park Service built 114 visitor centers, two staff training centers, and constructed or upgraded 2000 miles of roads. It built three times as many miles of new trails and created over 1500 parking spaces to accommodate 50,000 more cars. Between 1954 and 1966 visits to the user-friendly national parks nearly tripled.

The Forest Service's Operation Outdoors was that agency's initiative to meet the new demand for outdoor recreation. The agency wanted to show that it could provide recreational services and at the same time meet America's growing demand for wood. It also wanted to thwart efforts to transfer its recreational lands to the Park Service. In 1956, one of the Forest Service's supporters in Congress, Senator Hubert Humphrey (D-MN), introduced key legislation that finally was enacted in 1960: The Multiple Use-Sustained Yield Act (MUSY) codified for the first time the many uses to which the national forests could be put. Symbolically, outdoor recreation appeared first on the list, and it has been a federal program whose importance has increased over time. All federal resource agencies now count outdoor recreation as among their most important programs, even though the program is not always as well funded as it was during the '50s and early '60s.

Although air and water pollution did not become major national concerns until the 1960s, Congress did respond in the '50s to the embryonic problem. The first federal air pollution control act was passed in 1955; the legislation, however, deemed air pollution a state and local problem, with the role of the federal government limited to providing research and technical service. Similarly, legislation passed in 1948 and 1956 dealt with water pollution. Those acts authorized more federal research on the problem, and provided grants and loans to local governments for the planning and construction of municipal wastewater treatment plants. The first major effort to develop a comprehensive plan for water pollution began in 1957 with a cooperative venture between the Public Health Service and the Corps of Engineers in the Arkansas-Red River Basin. Policy makers would build upon these initiatives in the coming years.

Coloring everything in postwar America, however, was the Cold War. The two superpowers of the period engaged in a massive, hugely expensive arms build-up and funded covert operations around the world. Europe became divided into eastern and western blocs, with an "iron curtain," as Winston Churchill memorably put it, separating them. The United States assumed a central role in international politics: The Truman Doctrine (1947) spelled out a policy of communist containment and American aid to anticommunist governments; the Marshall Plan (1947) provided generous economic assistance for the rebuilding of Europe; and the North Atlantic Treaty (1949) promised military assistance within a new organization called NATO. In Asia, the Cold War turned hot; by 1950 American soldiers again were fighting overseas, this time in Korea.

The nuclear arms race created a "balance of terror" in which "mutual assured destruction" (MAD) represented the uneasy equilibrium. The need to counter communist aggression overrode all concerns about the economic, ethical, political, and environmental consequences of the arms race. Aboveground thermonuclear tests at the Bikini Atoll in the Pacific and in the Nevada desert clearly presented grave health and environmental risks, yet they continued for much of the decade. A few voices were raised in objection—e.g., the Democratic candidate for President in 1956, Adlai Stevenson, and one of his supporters named Barry Commoner—but they were drowned out by widespread fears of communist takeover. It took a very courageous person, like J. Robert Oppenheimer, to speak about all the costs of nuclear technology. Shortly after the end of the war he declared, "In some crude sense, which no vulgarity, no humor, no overstatement can quite extinguish, the physicists have known sin, and this is a knowledge which they cannot lose." Statements like this led the government to revoke the Father of the A-Bomb's security clearance.

All told, the magnitude of the environmental and human health consequences of the arms race did not become manifest until the 1970s and '80s, when the federal government confronted the high monetary costs of containing and cleaning up pollution at defense installations and contractor facilities, and when it acknowledged the high incidence of cancer among uranium miners and Americans living close to the testing sites. After years of foot-dragging, the government eventually compensated, as best it could, these unintended victims of the Cold War.

America's "return to normalcy" tried to turn back the clock on the economic and social advances made during the war by women, African Americans, Native Americans, and other minorities. But in the face of strong forces to recreate the America of yesterday, the movement towards racial and gender equality doggedly carried on. The civil rights movement scored a major victory in 1954 when the Supreme Court, under newly appointed Chief Justice Earl Warren, issued its landmark decision, *Brown v. Board of Education*. In overturning the Court's 1896 "separate but equal" decision (*Plessy v. Ferguson*), it planted the seeds that would burst into full bloom in the 1960s in the form of the civil rights, equal rights, and environmental rights movements. President Truman's courageous 1948 Executive Order integrating the armed forces also was of enormous importance to minorities in postwar America.

Still, it was an uphill battle for ethnic minorities and women. In fact, the gains made by Native Americans during the Roosevelt years were all but lost during the Eisenhower years. Rather than the government seeking additional protections for tribal sovereignty and Indian rights, it embarked in the '50s on a "termination policy": Federal legislation and administrative orders sought to assimilate Indians by dissolving tribes, withdrawing government services, dividing reservation land and assets among individual tribal members, and moving Indians to urban areas. As such, the government's overall objectives were not unlike those of Andrew Jackson's in the 1820s and '30s.

Why the policy of termination or assimilation? Conservatives claimed that Native American tribalism was communistic, and that tribal commons posed an internal threat to the principles of private property and individualism. Alternatively, some liberals feared that reservations might be a form of segregation that the Supreme Court declared unconstitutional in the *Brown* decision. Indeed, the assimilation policy made for strange political bedfellows.

Many tribes fought termination, fearing a loss of their cultures, their unique identities, as well as their lands. And just as the policy of allotment at the turn of the twentieth century had transferred considerable land and resources to nontribal entities, the policy of termination had the same result. Instead of assimilating Native Americans into the mainstream, they were driven further into poverty and disillusionment.

Several tribes also protested various water reclamation projects that the government had forced upon them. These included the Kinzua Dam in Pennsylvania, the Tuscarora Power Project in New York, and the Everglades Reclamation Project in Florida. Most projects proceeded in spite of the protests and resulted in the tribes receiving minimal compensation. An example was the huge Pick-Sloan Project on the Missouri River. Authorized in 1944, the five dams constructed by the Corps of Engineers after the war inundated 550 square miles of tribal lands, while almost all of the electric and irrigation benefits flowed to non-Indians.

Many of the economic gains women achieved during the war also were lost. In Detroit's automobile industry, for example, women staged a protest over losing their jobs to returning war veterans. Remarked the actress Fannie Hurst, "A sleeping sickness is spreading among the women of the land. They are retrogressing into…that thing called Home." After the war, college and university enrollment for females dropped below that of 1920. The women who continued to work were invariably paid less than men, and were channeled into "women's occupations"—secretaries, school teachers, and nurses. Popular television series such as "Father Knows Best," "Leave it to Beaver," and "Donna Reed" portrayed the idyllic American family in which there was a strict division of labor between father and mother.

By the end of the '50s eighty-six percent of the American population owned a television set, arguably the invention that has had the most significant impact on the nation's politics and culture during the second half of the twentieth century. Most Americans also owned an automobile, a product whose environmental impact is impossible to overstate.

Already by this time the American standard of living had become the envy of the rest of the world. Cold War spending provided an abundance of jobs, while fostering the development of new civilian and military technologies. When the Soviet Union launched Sputnik in 1957, the government's response was to greatly increase higher education funding (the National Defense Education Act of 1958). Defense appropriations rose significantly, from 12.9 billion in fiscal year 1950 to 40.0 billion in fiscal year 1961. Domestic appropriations also grew. There appeared to be little need to choose between "guns" and "butter" during these halcyon days.

Yet, gradually throughout the decade, scholars and writers began questioning the prevailing value structure of postwar America. William Whyte's *The Organization Man* described how corporations enforced conformity among their employees. David Riesman's *The Lonely Crowd* described an "other-directed" society in which Americans readily succumbed to peer group influences and in the process lost their core values. As noted, Galbraith's *The Affluent Society* critiqued society's preoccupation with materialism and mindless consumption, and sociologist C. Wright Mills produced a compelling political analysis titled *The Power Elite*. Unlikely as the voice was, even the genial Eisenhower sounded warnings in his 1961 farewell address. The President not only cautioned Americans that they were in danger of losing their liberties to a powerful "military-industrial complex," but also that society was "plundering…the precious resources of tomorrow" in its impulse to live only for the present.

Three days after Eisenhower's memorable address, the torch was passed to a new generation. One of the oldest individuals to have served as president was succeeded by the youngest ever to have been elected to the high office. In his stirring inaugural address, President John F. Kennedy told the nation: "Ask not what your country can do for you—ask what you can do for your country." The nation, especially its youth, listened and acted. As the decade of activism wore on, Kennedy's bold challenge became increasingly linked to environmental issues. The younger generation of Americans asked not what nature could do for the state, but what the state could do for nature.

# 24
# Marjory Stoneman Douglas (1890–1998)

Marjory Stoneman Douglas began her career as a newspaper reporter on her father's newspaper, *The Miami Herald*. After serving in the Red Cross in Europe during World War I she returned to the *Herald* as a literary columnist and editorial writer. She wrote frequently about Florida's rapid commercial development. Douglas eventually gave up reporting to spend all of her time writing. She wrote many short stories, but the work she is best known for is the nonfiction book, *The Everglades: River of Grass.*

The book started out as a study of the Miami River, a volume in the Rivers of America series. Douglas soon wondered whether the Miami was too small for profiling, so she suggested to the series editor that the history of the Miami River ought to be linked to the Everglades. When he agreed, she wrote in her autobiography: "I was hooked with an idea that would consume me for the rest of my life." The research for the book led her into the field of hydrology, and from numerous discussions with experts she formulated the description of the Everglades as a "river of grass." The phrase caught the public's attention and *The Everglades: River of Grass* (1947) became a bestseller.

The beautifully written book detailed the fragility of the Everglades ecosystem and alerted the public to the dangers of excessive development in South Florida. It also helped to transform public perceptions about the significance of wetlands, which previously were called swamps and useful only if drained. The same year that her book appeared enough land was acquired by the federal government to make the Everglades National Park a reality. Douglas had been an ardent crusader for the park ever since its congressional authorization in 1937. For her and countless others, it was a dream come true.

Douglas continued to fight for the preservation of Florida's natural areas throughout her long life. In her late seventies, she helped found the organization, Friends of the Everglades. It successfully fought the construction of a jetport in the Big Cypress wetlands. Today the organization—with close to 5,000 members—works to protect and restore the Greater Kissimmee-Okeechobee-Everglades ecosystem through legal channels as well as public education.

Douglas died in 1998 at the age of 108. While she lived long enough to see several initiatives taken to protect and restore the Everglades' fragile ecosystem, the future of the world's only Everglades is still in jeopardy. In 1996 Florida voters approved an amendment to their state constitution for its restoration, but rejected a penny-a-pound tax on the state's sugar industry to pay for it. In the immediate future, controversy is likely to continue swirling around the massive plan to "re-plumb"southern Florida. A multibillion dollar project, funded jointly by the federal government and the State of Florida, the task involves a myriad of agencies, including the Army Corps of Engineers, the EPA, the South Florida Water Management District, municipal governments, and interest groups. Saving the Everglades remains a work in progress.

# "THE TRUTH OF THE RIVER
# IS THE GRASS"*

There are no other Everglades in the world.

They are, they have always been, one of the unique regions of the earth, remote, never wholly known. Nothing anywhere else is like them: their vast glittering openness, wider than the enormous visible round of the horizon, the racing free saltness and sweetness of their massive winds, under the dazzling blue heights of space. They are unique also in the simplicity, the diversity, the related harmony of the forms of life they enclose. The miracle of the light pours over the green and brown expanse of saw grass and of water, shining and slow-moving below, the grass and water that is the meaning and the central fact of the Everglades of Florida. It is a river of grass.

The great pointed paw of the state of Florida, familiar as the map of North America itself, of which it is the most noticeable appendage, thrusts south, farther south than any other part of the mainland of the United States. Between the shining aquamarine waters of the Gulf of Mexico and the roaring deep-blue waters of the north-surging Gulf Stream, the shaped land points toward Cuba and the Caribbean. It points toward and touches within one degree of the tropics.

More than halfway down that thrusting sea-bound peninsula nearly everyone knows the lake that is like a great hole in that pawing shape, Lake Okeechobee, the second largest body of fresh water, it is always said, "within the confines of the United States." Below that lie the Everglades.

They have been called "the mysterious Everglades" so long that the phrase is a meaningless platitude. For four hundred years after the discovery they seemed more like a fantasy than a simple geographic and historic fact. Even the men who in the later years saw them more clearly could hardly make up their minds what the Everglades were or how they could be described, or what use could be made of them. They were mysterious then. They are mysterious still to everyone by whom their fundamental nature is not understood.

Off and on for those four hundred years the region now called "The Everglades" was described as a series of vast, miasmic swamps, poisonous lagoons, huge dismal marshes without outlet, a rotting, shallow, inland sea, or labyrinths of dark trees hung and looped about with snakes and dripping mosses, malignant with tropical fevers and malarias, evil to the white man.

Even the name, "The Everglades," was given them and printed on a map of Florida within the past hundred years. It is variously interpreted. There were one or two other names we know, which were given them before that, but what sounds the first men had for them, seeing first, centuries and centuries before the discovering white men, those sun-blazing solitudes, we shall never know.

The shores that surround the Everglades were the first on this continent known to white men. The interior was almost the last. They have not yet been entirely mapped.

Spanish mapmakers, who never saw them, printed over the unknown blank space where they lay on those early maps the words "El Laguno del Espiritu Santo." To the early Spanish they were truly mysterious, fabulous with a wealth they were never able to prove.

The English from the Bahamas, charting the Florida coasts in the early seventeen hundreds, had no very clear idea of them. Gerard de Brahm, the surveyor, may have gone up some of the east-coast rivers and stared out on that endless, watery bright expanse, for on his map he called them "River Glades." But on the later English maps "River" becomes "Ever," so it is hard to tell what he intended.

The present name came into general use only after the acquisition of Florida from Spain in 1819 by the United States. The Turner map of 1823 was the first to use the word "Everglades." The fine Ives map of 1856 prints the words separately, "Ever Glades." In the text of the memorial that accompanied the map they were used without capitals, as "ever glades."

The word "glade" is of the oldest English origin. It comes from the Anglo-Saxon "glaed," with the "ae" diphthong, shortened to "glad." It meant "shining" or "bright," perhaps as of water. The same word was used in the Scandinavian languages for "a clear place in the sky, a bright streak or patch of light," as *Webster's International Dictionary* gives it. It might even first have referred to the great openness of the sky over it, and not to the land at all.

In English for over a thousand years the word "glaed" or "glyde" or "glade" has meant an open green grassy place in the forest. And in America of the English colonies the use was continued to mean stretches of natural pasture, naturally grassy.

But most dictionaries nowadays end a definition of them with the qualifying phrase, "as of the Florida Everglades." So that they have thus become unique in being their own, and only, best definition.

Yet the Indians, who have known the Glades longer and better than any dictionary-making white men, gave them their perfect, and poetic name, which is also true. They called them "Pa-hay-okee," which is the Indian word for "Grassy Water." Today Everglades is one word and yet plural. They are the only Everglades in the world.

Men crossed and recrossed them leaving no trace, so that no one knew men had been there. The few books or pamphlets written about them by Spaniards or surveyors or sportsmen or botanists have not been generally read. Actually, the first accurate studies of Everglades geology, soil, archaeology, even history, are only just now being completed.

The question was at once, where do you begin? Because, when you think of it, history, the recorded time of the earth and of man, is in itself something like a river. To try to present it whole is to find oneself lost in the sense of continuing change. The source can be only the beginning in time and space, and the end is the future and the unknown. What we can know lies somewhere between. The course along which for a little way one proceeds, the changing life, the varying light, must somehow be fixed in a moment clearly, from which one may look before and after and try to comprehend wholeness.

So it is with the Everglades, which have that quality of long existence in their own nature. They were changeless. They are changed.

They were complete before man came to them, and for centuries afterward, when he was only one of those forms which shared, in a finely balanced harmony, the forces and the ancient nature of the place.

Then, when the Everglades were most truly themselves, is the time to begin with them....

The Everglades begin at Lake Okeechobee.

That is the name later Indians gave the lake, a name almost as recent as the word "Everglades." It means "Big Water." Everybody knows it.

Yet few have any idea of those pale, seemingly illimitable waters. Over the shallows, often less than a foot deep but seven hundred fifty or so square miles in actual area, the winds in one gray swift moment can shatter the reflections of sky and cloud whiteness standing still in that shining, polished, shimmering expanse. A boat can push for hours in a day of white sun through the short, crisp lake waves and there will be nothing to be seen anywhere but the brightness where the color of the water and the color of the sky become one. Men out of sight of land can stand in it up to their armpits and slowly "walk in" their long nets to the waiting boats. An everglade kite and his mate, questing in great solitary circles, rising and dipping and rising again on the wind currents, can look down all day long at the water faintly green with floating water lettuce or marked by thin standing lines of reeds, utter their sharp goat cries, and be seen and heard by no one at all.

There are great shallow islands, all brown reeds or shrubby trees thick in the water. There are masses of water weeds and hyacinths and flags rooted so long they seem solid earth, yet there is nothing but lake bottom to stand on. There the egret and the white ibis and the glossy ibis and the little blue herons in their thousands nested and circled and fed.

A long northeast wind, a "norther," can lash all that still surface to dirty vicious gray and white, over which the rain mists shut down like stained rolls of wool, so that from the eastern sand rim under dripping cypresses or the west ridge with its live oaks, no one would guess that all that waste of empty water stretched there but for the long monotonous wash of waves on unseen marshy shores.

Saw grass reaches up both sides of that lake in great enclosing arms, so that it is correct to say that the Everglades are there also. But south, southeast and southwest, where the lake water slopped and seeped and ran over and under the rock and soil, the greatest mass of the saw grass begins. It stretches as it always has stretched, in one thick enormous curving river of grass, to the very end. This is the Everglades.

It reaches one hundred miles from Lake Okeechobee to the Gulf of Mexico, fifty, sixty, even seventy miles wide. No one has ever fought his way along its full length. Few have ever crossed the northern wilderness of nothing but grass. Down that almost invisible slope the water moves. The grass stands. Where the grass and the water are there is the heart, the current, the meaning of the Everglades.

The grass and the water together make the river as simple as it is unique. There is no other river like it. Yet within that simplicity, enclosed within the river and bordering and intruding on it from each side, there is subtlety and diversity, a crowd of changing forms, of thrusting teeming life. And all that becomes the region of the Everglades.

The truth of the river is the grass. They call it saw grass. Yet in the botanical sense it is not grass at all so much as a fierce, ancient, cutting sedge. It is one of the oldest of the green growing forms in this world.

There are many places in the South where this saw grass, with its sharp central fold and edges set with fine saw teeth like points of glass, this sedge called *Cladium jamaicensis*, exists. But this is the greatest concentration of saw grass in the world. It grows fiercely in the fresh water creeping down below it. When the original saw grass thrust up its spears into the sun, the fierce sun, lord and power and the first cause over the Everglades as of all the green world, then the Everglades began. They lie wherever the saw grass extends: 3,500 square miles, hundreds and thousands and millions, of acres, water and saw grass.

The first saw grass, exactly as it grows today, sprang up and lived in the sweet water and the pouring sunlight, and died in it, and from its own dried and decaying tissues and tough fibers bright with silica sprang up more fiercely again. Year after year it grew and was fed by its own brown rotting, taller and denser in the dark soil of its own death. Year after year after year, hundreds after hundreds of years, not so long as any geologic age but long in botanic time, far longer than anyone can be sure of, the saw grass grew. Four thousand years, they say, it must at least have grown like that, six feet, ten feet, twelve feet, even fifteen in places of deepest water. The edged and folded swords bristled around the delicate straight tube of pith that burst into brown flowering. The brown seed, tight enclosed after the manner of sedges, ripened in dense brownness. The seed was dropped and worked down in the water and its own ropelike mat of roots. All that decay of leaves and seed covers and roots was packed deeper year after year by the elbowing upthrust of its own life. Year after year it laid down new layers of virgin muck under the living water.

There are places now where the depth of the muck is equal to the height of the saw grass. When it is uncovered and brought into the sunlight, its stringy and grainy dullness glitters with the myriad unrotted silica points, like glass dust.

At the edges of the Glades, and toward those southern- and southwesternmost reaches where the great estuary or delta of the Glades river takes another form entirely, the saw grass is shorter and more sparse, and the springy, porous muck deposit under it is shallower and thinner. But where the saw grass grows tallest in the deepest muck, there goes the channel of the Glades.

The water winks and flashes here and there among the saw grass roots, as the clouds are blown across the sun. To try to make one's way among these impenetrable tufts if to be cut off from all air, to be beaten down by the sun and ripped by the grassy saw-toothed edges as one sinks in mud and water over the roots. The dried yellow stuff holds no weight. There is no earthly way to get through the mud or the standing, keen-edged blades that crowd these interminable miles.

Or in the times of high water in the old days, the flood would rise until the highest tops of that sharp grass were like a thin lawn standing out of water as blue as the sky, rippling and wrinkling, linking the pools and spreading and flowing on its true course southward.

A man standing in the center of it, if he could get there, would be as lost in saw grass, as out of sight of anything but saw grass as a man drowning in the middle of Okeechobee—or the Atlantic Ocean, for that matter—would be out of sight of land.

The water moves. The saw grass, pale green to deep-brown ripeness, stands rigid. It is moved only in sluggish rollings by the vast push of the winds across it. Over its endless acres here and there the shadows of the dazzling clouds quicken and slide, purple-brown, plum-brown, mauve-brown, rust-brown, bronze. The bristling, blossoming tops do not bend easily like standing grain. They do not even in their own growth curve all one way but stand in edged clumps, curving against each other, all the massed curving blades making millions of fine arching lines that at a little distance merge to a huge expanse of brown wires or bristles or, farther beyond, to deep-piled plush. At the horizon they become velvet. The line they make is an edge of velvet against the infinite blue, the blue-and-white, the clear fine primrose yellow, the burning brass and crimson, the molten silver, the deepening hyacinth sky.

The clear burning light of the sun pours daylong into the saw grass and is lost there, soaked up, never given back. Only the water flashes and glints. The grass yields nothing.

Nothing less than the smashing power of some hurricane can beat it down. Then one can see, from high up in a plane, where the towering weight and velocity of the hurricane was the strongest and where along the edges of its whorl it turned less and less savagely and left the saw grass standing. Even so, the grass is not flattened in a continuous swath but only here and here and over there, as if the storm bounced or lifted and smashed down again in great hammering strokes or enormous cat-licks.

Only one force can conquer it completely and that is fire. Deep in the layers of muck there are layers of ashes, marks of old fires set by lightning or the early Indians. But in the early days the water always came back and there were long slow years in which the saw grass grew and died, laying down again its tough resilient decay.

This is the saw grass, then, which seems to move as the water moved, in a great thick arc south and southwestward from Okeechobee to the Gulf. There at the last imperceptible incline of the land the saw grass goes along the headwaters of many of those wide, slow, mangrove-bordered freshwater rivers, like a delta or an estuary into which the salt tides flow and draw back and flow again.

The mangrove becomes a solid barrier there, which by its strong, arched and labyrinthine roots collects the sweepage of the fresh water and the salt and holds back the parent sea. The supple branches, the oily green leaves, set up a barrier against the winds, although the hurricanes prevail easily against them. There the fresh water meets the incoming salt, and is lost.

It may be that the mystery of the Everglades is the saw grass, so simple, so enduring, so hostile. It was the saw grass and the water which divided east coast from west coast and made the central solitudes that held in them the secrets of time, which has moved here so long unmarked.

# 25
# Aldo Leopold (1887–1948)

Aldo Leopold, founder of the discipline of wildlife management, began his career as a forester with the newly created U.S. Forest Service. His life ended prematurely in 1948 while he fought a fire near his beloved Sand County, Wisconsin farm, known as "the Shack." In 1935—the same year that he helped found the Wilderness Society—he had acquired the abandoned, worked-out, 120-acre farm situated along the Wisconsin River. The Shack served as a family weekend retreat, a laboratory for ecological restoration, and as a source for Leopold's profound reflections on nature. Accepted for publication just days before his death, *A Sand County Almanac* has become a "must read" for environmental professionals as well as college students.

Leopold had one of the most perceptive intellects of the twentieth century regarding natural and political phenomena. He also had a capacity to change his views when confronted with new information. For example, as a young man working for the Forest Service in Arizona and New Mexico, he wrote and spoke about the need to eliminate predators such as wolves and mountain lions, railing against the "vermin," "varmint," and "skulking marauders" of the forest. But then he had an epiphany: After he and some others shot a female wolf and her pups, Leopold learned something he had not known as he watched the "fierce green fire" go out of the old wolf's eyes. He did not become opposed to hunting, but he did realize the necessity for, and beauty in, nature's predators.

While in the Southwest he also successfully urged the Forest Service to establish the first designated wilderness area within the Gila National Forest in New Mexico. Other areas followed in the 1930s.

After leaving the Forest Service, Leopold continued to write. He published a textbook, *Game Management*, and in 1933 the University of Wisconsin offered him the first professorship of game management in the United States. As a faculty member, he continued to define the emerging discipline of wildlife management and to refine his own thinking as an ecologist. Leopold became convinced that genuine conservation principles could be realized only with a fundamental change in the nation's attitude toward land and its resources. His work relates environmental science with social ethics, as in his Golden Rule of Ecology: "A thing is right when it tends to preserve the integrity, stability, and beauty of the biotic community. It is wrong when it tends otherwise."

Recognizing that "wilderness is the raw material out of which man has hammered the artifact called civilization," Leopold posed the enduring question of "whether a still higher 'standard of living' is worth its cost in things natural, wild, and free." In concluding that "nothing could be more salutary at this stage than a little healthy contempt for a plethora of material blessings," he provided a scientific and philosophical basis not only for "the land ethic" but for the argument made later in the 1970s that inanimate objects should be given standing to sue in their own right.

## "THINKING LIKE A MOUNTAIN"*

A deep chesty bawl echoes from rimrock to rimrock, rolls down the mountain, and fades into the far blackness of the night. It is an outburst of wild defiant sorrow, and of contempt for all the adversities of the world.

Every living thing (and perhaps many a dead one as well) pays heed to that call. To the deer it is a reminder of the way of all flesh, to the pine a forecast of midnight scuffles and of blood upon the snow, to the coyote a promise of gleanings to come, to the cowman a threat of red ink at the bank, to the hunter a challenge of fang against bullet. Yet behind these obvious and immediate hopes and fears there lies a deeper meaning, known only to the mountain itself. Only the mountain has lived long enough to listen objectively to the howl of a wolf.

Those unable to decipher the hidden meaning know nevertheless that it is there, for it is felt in all wolf country, and distinguishes that country from all other land. It tingles in the spine of all who hear wolves by night, or who scan their tracks by day. Even without sight or sound of wolf, it is implicit in a hundred small events: the midnight whinny of a pack horse, the rattle of rolling rocks, the bound of a fleeing deer, the way shadows lie under the spruces. Only the ineducable tyro can fail to sense the presence or absence of wolves, or the fact that mountains have a secret opinion about them.

My own conviction on this score dates from the day I saw a wolf die. We were eating lunch on a high rimock, at the foot of which a turbulent river elbowed its way. We saw what we thought was a doe fording the torrent, her breast awash in white water. When she climbed the bank toward us and shook out her tail, we realized our error: it was a wolf. A half-dozen others, evidently grown pups, sprang from the willows and all joined in a welcoming mêlée of wagging tails and playful maulings. What was literally a pile of wolves writhed and tumbled in the center of an open flat at the foot of our rimrock.

In those days we had never heard of passing up a chance to kill a wolf. In a second we were pumping lead into the pack, but with more excitement than accuracy: how to aim a steep downhill shot is always confusing. When our rifles were empty, the old wolf was down, and a pup was dragging a leg into impassable slide-rocks.

We reached the old wolf in time to watch a fierce green fire dying in her eyes. I realized then, and have known ever since, that there was something new to me in those eyes—something known only to her and to the mountain. I was young then, and full of trigger-itch; I thought that because fewer wolves meant more deer, that no wolves would mean hunters' paradise. But after seeing the green fire die, I sensed that neither the wolf nor the mountain agreed with such a view.

---

*Aldo Leopold. 1949. From *A Sand County Almanac: And Sketches Here and There*. New York: Oxford University Press, pp. 129–133. Copyright 1949, 1977 by Oxford University Press, Inc. Used by permission of Oxford University Press, Inc.

Since then I have lived to see state after state extirpate its wolves. I have watched the face of many a newly wolfless mountain, and seen the south-facing slopes wrinkle with a maze of new deer trails. I have seen every edible bush and seedling browsed, first to anaemic desuetude, and then to death. I have seen every edible tree defoliated to the height of a saddlehorn. Such a mountain looks as if someone had given God a new pruning shears, and forbidden Him all other exercise. In the end the starved bones of the hoped for deer herd, dead of its own too-much, bleach with the bones of the dead sage, or molder under the high-lined junipers.

I now suspect that just as a deer herd lives in mortal fear of its wolves, so does a mountain live in mortal fear of its deer. And perhaps with better cause, for while a buck pulled down by wolves can be replaced in two or three years, a range pulled down by too many deer may fail of replacement in as many decades.

So also with cows. The cowman who cleans his range of wolves does not realize that he is taking over the wolf's job of trimming the herd to fit the range. He has not learned to think like a mountain. Hence we have dust-bowls, and rivers washing the future into the sea.

We all strive for safety, prosperity, comfort, long life, and dullness. The deer strives with his supple legs, the cowman with trap and poison, the statesman with pen, the most of us with machines, votes, and dollars, but it all comes to the same thing: peace in our time. A measure of success in this is all well enough, and perhaps is a requisite to objective thinking, but too much safety seems to yield only danger in the long run. Perhaps this is behind Thoreau's dictum: In wildness is the salvation of the world. Perhaps this is the hidden meaning in the howl of the wolf, long known among mountains, but seldom perceived among men.

---

# "THE LAND ETHIC"*

When god-like Odysseus returned from the wars in Troy, he hanged all on one rope a dozen slave-girls of his household whom he suspected of misbehavior during his absence.

This hanging involved no question of propriety. The girls were property. The disposal of property was then, as now, a matter of expediency, not of right and wrong.

Concepts of right and wrong were not lacking from Odysseus' Greece: witness the fidelity of his wife through the long years before at last his black-prowed galleys clove the wine-dark seas for home. The ethical structure of that day covered wives, but had not yet been extended to human chattels. During the three thousand years which have since elapsed, ethical criteria

*Aldo Leopold. 1949. From *A Sand County Almanac: And Sketches Here and There.* New York: Oxford University Press, pp. 201–211, 214. Copyright 1949, 1977 by Oxford University Press, Inc. Used by permission of Oxford University Press, Inc.

have been extended to many fields of conduct, with corresponding shrink-ages in those judged by expediency only....

This extension of ethics, so far studied only by philosophers, is actually a process in ecological evolution. Its sequences may be described in ecological as well as in philosophical terms. An ethic, ecologically, is a limitation on freedom of action in the struggle for existence. An ethic, philosophically, is a differentiation of social from anti-social conduct. These are two definitions of one thing. The thing has its origin in the tendency of interdependent individuals or groups to evolve modes of co-operation. The ecologist calls these symbioses. Politics and economics are advanced symbioses in which the original free-for-all competition has been replaced, in part, by co-operative mechanisms with an ethical content.

The complexity of co-operative mechanisms has increased with population density, and with the efficiency of tools. It was simpler, for example, to define the anti-social uses of sticks and stones in the days of the mastodons than of bullets and billboards in the age of motors.

The first ethics dealt with the relation between individuals; the Mosaic Decalogue is an example. Later accretions dealt with the relation between the individual and society. The Golden Rule tries to integrate the individual to society; democracy to integrate social organization to the individual.

There is as yet no ethic dealing with man's relation to land and to the animals and plants which grow upon it. Land, like Odysseus' slave-girls, is still property. The land-relation is still strictly economic, entailing privileges but not obligations.

The extension of ethics to this third element in human environment is, if I read the evidence correctly, an evolutionary possibility and an ecological necessity. It is the third step in a sequence. The first two have already been taken. Individual thinkers since the days of Ezekiel and Isaiah have asserted that the despoliation of land is not only inexpedient but wrong. Society, however, has not yet affirmed their belief. I regard the present conservation movement as the embryo of such an affirmation.

An ethic may be regarded as a mode of guidance for meeting ecological situations so new or intricate, or involving such deferred reactions, that the path of social expediency is not discernible to the average individual. Animal instincts are modes of guidance for the individual in meeting such situations. Ethics are possibly a kind of community instinct in-the-making....

All ethics so far evolved rest upon a single premise: that the individual is a member of a community of interdependent parts. His instincts prompt him to compete for his place in that community, but his ethics prompt him also to co-operate (perhaps in order that there may be a place to compete for).

The land ethic simply enlarges the boundaries of the community to include soils, waters, plants, and animals, or collectively: the land.

This sounds simple: do we not already sing our love for and obligation to the land of the free and the home of the brave? Yes, but just what and whom do we love? Certainly not the soil, which we are sending helter-skelter downriver. Certainly not the waters, which we assume have no function except to turn turbines, float barges, and carry off sewage. Certainly not the plants, of which we exterminate whole communities without batting an eye. Certainly not the animals, of which we have already extirpated many of the largest and most beautiful species. A land ethic of course cannot prevent the alteration, management, and use of these 'resources,' but it does affirm their right to continued existence, and, at least in spots, their continued existence in a natural state.

In short, a land ethic changes the role of *Homo sapiens* from conqueror of the land-community to plain member and citizen of it. It implies respect for his fellow-members, and also respect for the community as such.

In human history, we have learned (I hope) that the conqueror role is eventually self-defeating. Why? Because it is implicit in such a role that the conqueror knows, *ex cathedra*, just what makes the community clock tick, and just what and who is valuable, and what and who is worthless, in community life. It always turns out that he knows neither, and this is why his conquests eventually defeat themselves.

In the biotic community, a parallel situation exists. Abraham knew exactly what the land was for: it was to drip milk and honey into Abraham's mouth. At the present moment, the assurance with which we regard this assumption is inverse to the degree of our education.

The ordinary citizen today assumes that science knows what makes the community clock tick; the scientist is equally sure that he does not. He knows that the biotic mechanism is so complex that its workings may never be fully understood.

That man is, in fact, only a member of a biotic team is shown by an ecological interpretation of history. Many historical events, hitherto explained solely in terms of human enterprise, were actually biotic interactions between people and land. The characteristics of the land determined the facts quite as potently as the characteristics of the men who lived on it.

Consider, for example, the settlement of the Mississippi valley. In the years following the Revolution, three groups were contending for its control: the native Indian, the French and English traders, and the American settlers. Historians wonder what would have happened if the English at Detroit had thrown a little more weight into the Indian side of those tipsy scales which decided the outcome of the colonial migration into the cane-lands of Kentucky. It is time now to ponder the fact that the cane-lands, when subjected to the particular mixture of forces represented by the cow, plow, fire, and axe of the pioneer, became bluegrass. What if the plant succession inherent in this dark and bloody ground had, under the impact of these forces, given us some worthless sedge, shrub, or weed? Would Boone and Kenton have held out? Would there have been any overflow into Ohio, Indiana, Illinois, and Missouri? Any Louisiana Purchase? Any transcontinental union of new states? Any Civil War?

Kentucky was one sentence in the drama of history. We are commonly told what the human actors in this drama tried to do, but we are seldom told that their success, or the lack of it, hung in large degree on the reaction of particular soils to the impact of the particular forces exerted by their occupancy. In the case of Kentucky, we do not even know where the bluegrass came from—whether it is a native species, or a stowaway from Europe.

Contrast the cane-lands with what hindsight tells us about the Southwest, where the pioneers were equally brave, resourceful, and persevering. The impact of occupancy here brought no bluegrass, or other plant fitted to withstand the bumps and buffetings of hard use. This region, when grazed by livestock, reverted through a series of more and more worthless grasses, shrubs, and weeds to a condition of unstable equilibrium. Each recession of plant types bred erosion; each increment to erosion bred a further recession of plants. The result today is a progressive and mutual deterioration, not only of plants and soils, but of the animal community subsisting thereon. The early settlers did not expect this: on the ciénegas of New Mexico some even cut ditches to hasten it. So subtle has been its progress that few residents of the region are aware of it. It is quite invisible to the tourist who finds this wrecked landscape colorful and charming (as indeed it is, but it bears scant resemblance to what it was in 1848).

This same landscape was 'developed' once before, but with quite different results. The Pueblo Indians settled the Southwest in pre-Columbian times, but they happened *not* to be equipped with range livestock. Their civilization expired, but not because their land expired.

In India, regions devoid of any sod-forming grass have been settled, apparently without wrecking the land, by the simple expedient of carrying the grass to the cow, rather than vice versa. (Was this the result of some deep wisdom, or was it just good luck? I do not know.)

In short, the plant succession steered the course of history; the pioneer simply demonstrated, for good or ill, what successions inhered in the land. Is history taught in this spirit? It will be, once the concept of land as a community really penetrates our intellectual life....

Conservation is a state of harmony between men and land. Despite nearly a century of propaganda, conservation still proceeds at a snail's pace; progress still consists largely of letterhead pieties and convention oratory. On the back forty we still slip two steps backward for each forward stride.

The usual answer to this dilemma is 'more conservation education.' No one will debate this, but is it certain that only the *volume* of education needs stepping up? Is something lacking in the *content* as well?

It is difficult to give a fair summary of its content in brief form, but, as I understand it, the content is substantially this: obey the law, vote right, join some organizations, and practice what conservation is profitable on your own land; the government will do the rest.

Is not this formula too easy to accomplish anything worth-while? It defines no right or wrong, assigns no obligation, calls for no sacrifice, implies no change in the current philosophy of values. In respect of land-use, it urges only enlightened self-interest. Just how far will such education take us? An example will perhaps yield a partial answer.

By 1930 it had become clear to all except the ecologically blind that southwestern Wisconsin's topsoil was slipping seaward. In 1933 the farmers were told that if they would adopt certain remedial practices for five years, the public would donate CCC labor to install them, plus the necessary machinery and materials. The offer was widely accepted, but the practices were widely forgotten when the five-year contract period was up. The farmers continued only those practices that yielded an immediate and visible economic gain for themselves.

This led to the idea that maybe farmers would learn more quickly if they themselves wrote the rules. Accordingly the Wisconsin Legislature in 1937 passed the Soil Conservation District Law. This said to farmers, in effect: *We, the public, will furnish you free technical service and loan you specialized machinery, if you will write your own rules for land-use. Each county may write its own rules, and these will have the force of law.* Nearly all the counties promptly organized to accept the proffered help, but after a decade of operation, *no county has yet written a single rule.* There has been visible progress in such practices as strip-cropping, pasture renovation, and soil liming, but none in fencing woodlots against grazing, and none in excluding plow and cow from steep slopes. The farmers, in short, have selected those remedial practices which were profitable anyhow, and ignored those which were profitable to the community, but not clearly profitable to themselves.

When one asks why no rules have been written, one is told that the community is not yet ready to support them; education must precede rules. But the education actually in progress makes no mention of obligations to land over and above those dictated by self-interest. The net result is that we have more education but less soil, fewer healthy woods, and as many floods as in 1937.

The puzzling aspect of such situations is that the existence of obligations over and above self-interest is taken for granted in such rural community enterprises as the betterment of roads, schools, churches, and baseball teams. Their existence is not taken for granted, nor as yet seriously discussed, in bettering the behavior of the water that falls on the land, or in the preserving of the beauty or diversity of the farm landscape. Land-use ethics are still governed wholly by economic self-interest, just as social ethics were a century ago.

To sum up: we asked the farmer to do what he conveniently could to save his soil, and he has done just that, and only that. The farmer who clears the woods off a 75 per cent slope, turns his cows into the clearing, and dumps its rainfall, rocks, and soil into the community creek, is still (if otherwise decent) a respected member of society. If he puts lime on his fields and plants his crops on contour, he is still entitled to all the privileges and emoluments of his Soil Conservation District. The District is a beautiful piece of social machinery, but it is coughing along on two cylinders because we have been too timid, and too anxious for quick success, to tell the farmer the true magnitude of his obligations. Obligations have no meaning without conscience, and the problem we face is the extension of the social conscience from people to land.

No important change in ethics was ever accomplished without an internal change in our intellectual emphasis, loyalties, affections, and convictions. The proof that conservation has not yet touched these foundations of conduct lies in the fact that philosophy and religion have not yet heard of it. In our attempt to make conservation easy, we have made it trivial....

When the logic of history hungers for bread and we hand out a stone, we are at pains to explain how much the stone resembles bread. I now describe some of the stones which serve in lieu of a land ethic.

One basic weakness in a conservation system based wholly on economic motives is that most members of the land community have no economic value. Wildflowers and songbirds are examples. Of the 22,000 higher plants and animals native to Wisconsin, it is doubtful whether more than 5 per cent can be sold, fed, eaten, or otherwise put to economic use. Yet these creatures are members of the biotic community, and if (as I believe) its stability depends on its integrity, they are entitled to continuance.

When one of these non-economic categories is threatened, and if we happen to love it, we invent subterfuges to give it economic importance. At the beginning of the century songbirds were supposed to be disappearing. Ornithologists jumped to the rescue with some distinctly shaky evidence to the effect that insects would eat us up if birds failed to control them. The evidence had to be economic in order to be valid.

It is painful to read these circumlocutions today. We have no land ethic yet, but we have at least drawn nearer the point of admitting that birds should continue as a matter of biotic right, regardless of the presence or absence of economic advantage to us....

To sum up: a system of conservation based solely on economic self-interest is hopelessly lopsided. It tends to ignore, and thus eventually to eliminate, many elements in the land community that lack commercial value, but that are (as far as we know) essential to its healthy functioning. It assumes, falsely, I think, that the economic parts of the biotic clock will function without the uneconomic parts. It tends to relegate to government many functions eventually too large, too complex, or too widely dispersed to be performed by government.

An ethical obligation on the part of the private owner is the only visible remedy for these situations.

# 26
# Arthur Maass (1917–   )
# and Harold L. Ickes (1874–1952)

Congressional spending on domestic water projects increased significantly following the Second World War, as did criticisms of the Army Corps of Engineers and its close working relationship with the legislative branch. A leading critic was Harvard University political science professor Arthur Maass, whose 1951 book, *Muddy Waters: The Army Engineers and the Nation's Rivers*, took the Corps and Congress to task. The book has become a classic study of administrative power, in which Maass addressed the fundamental issue of accountability, that is, "the extent to which an administrative agency conducts itself as a responsible instrument of government." Maass concluded that, overall, "the Corps has failed to grow to the task."

Maass argued that the Corps' unusual independence from its executive branch superiors, and its close alliance with Congress, resulted in projects benefitting primarily local interests and not the national interest. Moreover, administrative overlaps with the functions of the Bureau of Reclamation, the Federal Power Commission, and the Soil Conservation Service created excessive duplication, confusion, and competition. Maass advocated transferring the agency's civil works functions from the Department of the Army to the Interior Department, something that Interior Secretary Harold Ickes championed in the 1930s and 1940s.

In the mid-1950s Maass organized the Harvard Water Program to examine national water resources issues. This work criticized most federal water projects as being too narrowly focused. Better planning technologies, closer coordination among the various agencies involved in water development planning, and the inclusion of disciplines other than engineering and economics in the planning process would be needed to develop multipurpose projects that served national goals.

By 1970, however, Maass discerned significant changes in the Corps and he began to defend the agency he once criticized, rebutting, for example, journalist Elizabeth Drew's widely read 1969 *Atlantic Monthly* article, "Dam Outrage: the Story of the Corps of Engineers." Professor Maass continued to influence national water resources policy well into the 1990s.

A powerful introduction to *Muddy Waters* was written by Harold L. Ickes, who served as Secretary of the Interior for thirteen years, from 1933 until 1946. Ickes was instrumental in fashioning the conservation and preservation policies of the New Deal, as well as in mobilizing the nation's resources for use in World War II. In his capacity as Franklin Roosevelt's Interior Secretary, Ickes is remembered for transforming a scandal-ridden department into one that genuinely promoted conservation values. Under his firm guidance, the national park system was significantly enlarged while commercial development was kept to a minimum, a Grazing Service was established to protect the remaining public domain lands, the Indian Service was reorganized to better serve Native Americans, a soil erosion service was created (which was subsequently transferred to the Agriculture Department), and an embryonic wilderness system was established on public lands controlled by the Interior Department. During the decade of the 1930s, Ickes promoted the idea of a Department of Conservation, which would bring all the federal resource agencies under one roof. It was an idea whose time has yet to come.

One of FDR's most talented aides, Ickes also served as Public Works Administrator, Oil Administrator, Petroleum Administrator for War, and Administrator for Hard Fuels. In these capacities he distinguished himself as an honest, intelligent, irascible, and hard-working public servant. He was dedicated not only to the conservation cause but to the furtherance of civil rights and civil liberties: It is significant that one of his first acts as Interior Secretary was to desegregate the department's public facilities. In fact, Ickes believed that both conservation and racial equality were necessary manifestations of American democracy.

---

# "THAT AMAZING AMERICAN PHENOMENON, THE PORK BARREL"*
## H.L. Ickes

One way to describe the Corps of Army Engineers would be to say that it is the most powerful and most pervasive lobby in Washington. The aristocrats who constitute it are our highest ruling class. They are not only the political elite of the army, they are the perfect flower of bureaucracy. At least, this is the reflection that their mirrors disclose to them. Within the fields that they have elected to occupy, they are the law—and therefore above the law. Senator Douglas of Illinois said on the floor of the Senate on March 29, 1950, "They [the Army Engineers] become the Congress of the United States." And on page 248 of the Report to the House of Representatives of its Appropriations Committee in 1950, its chairman, Representative Clarence Cannon of Missouri, wrote, "The Chief of Engineers has committed the Government and is continuing to commit the Government to the expenditure of funds far in excess of amounts contemplated by the Congress."

Since the greatest power of government under the American system is the power to appropriate money, it would seem that Senator Douglas employed derogatory and belittling language in referring to the Army Engineers as he did. Yet the senior senator from Illinois is customarily one of the

---

*Harold L. Ickes. 1951. "Foreword" in Arthur Maass, *Muddy Waters: The Army Engineers and the Nation's Rivers*. Cambridge, MA: Harvard University Press, pp. ix–xiv. Copyright © 1951 by the President and Fellows of Harvard College. Copyright © renewed 1990 by Arthur Aaron Maass, Michael Hufschmidt, and Michael Dorfman. Reprinted by permission from Harvard University Press.

most courteous of men. According to Representative Cannon, these gentle-men make monetary commitments which the Congress must later make good and thus they arrogate to themselves powers above those of the Congress. They regard themselves as "the engineer consultants (if and when they choose to consult) and contractors" of the Congress and therefore as independent of any other executive agency of however high degree. When they demean themselves to report to anyone in the Government, it is to the Congress. Their record shows that they not only regard themselves as independent of the Secretary of the Army and the Secretary of Defense, but even of the President.

When Herbert Hoover was in the White House, the Corps of Engineers casually brushed him aside, although he himself was a member of their profession. Franklin D. Roosevelt once considered transferring the civil activities of the Corps to the Department of the Interior where they belong, but did not succeed. Specific and direct orders from President Roosevelt were disregarded with a casualness that was not pretended. In his turn, President Truman has tried to impress upon the Corps of Army Engineers that he is, by the Constitution, the Commander in Chief of the Armed Forces of the Nation. He was strong enough to fire General Douglas MacArthur but, so far, the Army Engineers have successfully defied him.

A small, powerful, and exclusive clique of about two hundred Army officers controls some fifty thousand civilian employees. They constitute the core of the Corps. But let no one make the mistake of assuming that the officers who make up this tight little army machine recognize any civilian engineer, however eminent, as an equal. The civilian engineers may include a few men who are regarded as equivalent in rank to an army sergeant or corporal but, in mass, these civilians are rated in the minds of their self-conscious superiors as little better than privates. A civilian engineer may not expect rank or recognition or decoration. These are the exclusive prerogatives of the inbred two hundred.

The Corps of Engineers has grown strong on the basis of the work of competent civilian engineers for over a century. This is not to imply that the officer engineers lack competence; it is merely to suggest that, necessarily, a few officer engineers could not hope to accomplish what has been done by more numerous and, on the average, just as able civilians. Not only have the Army Engineers long regarded themselves as above the civilian control that the top generals seem to recognize and to prefer as conforming to American concepts; to an amazing measure they are above such controls. They cannot be dismissed from office except through the drastic action of a court-martial. Their worst fate is to be transferred to a military post, and that is rarely done except as a warning to others that they should always strive to please their own army superiors in the Corps. The conviction that an Army Engineer can be disciplined only by the Corps binds all the more closely together this exclusive and ingrowing clique.

The Army Engineers are doubtless brave soldiers, when they work at their trade, but to a surprising and disproportionate degree, they have gradually accepted and adapted themselves to the safer and less rigorous field of flood control. They have taken on, over the years, always with the taxpayer standing by with open purse, such warlike and dangerous undertakings as the regulation and development of domestic and industrial water supplies, the creation and supervision of navigation facilities, the irrigation of farm lands, and the development of hydroelectric power. They have even been reaching out greedily for the function of land drainage. Every little drop of water that falls is a potential flood to the ubiquitous Army Engineers and they therefore assume it to be their duty to control its destiny from the cradle to the grave....

That amazing American phenomenon, the pork barrel, emerged in complete and functioning order from the teeming Corps of Army Engineers. The theory behind it is that the harder the people scratch to pay their taxes, the more money there will be for the Corps of Army Engineers to scratch out of the Treasury with the aid of Congress in order to maintain its control of that body by building, or promising to build, more or less justifiable or downright unjustifiable projects in the various states and districts for which senators and representatives may claim credit during the next election campaign. What matters it if many of these projects are against the wishes of, or even in defiance of orders from, the President himself? An Army Corps' "Operation Santa Claus" is a two-pronged affair—the Engineers lobbying directly for an appropriation by the Congress while inciting local constituencies to bring pressure to bear upon their senators and representatives.

The power-hungry Army Engineers will commit Federal funds without interest and without thought of repayment for projects that it has been settled National policy to build only upon an obligation to repay. For instance, they fought brazenly for the right to build Pine Flat Dam on the Kings River in California and won. Originally, this was to be a reclamation project. Under the Reclamation Law, the water users benefitted by Pine Flat Dam would repay in installments the estimated value of the water used by them for irrigation purposes. This would go into a revolving fund, out of which additional reclamation protects in future might be financed without undue drains upon the Treasury.

Under the pretext of "flood control" and despite both oral and written orders to the contrary from President Roosevelt, the Army Engineers defiantly lobbied through the Congress a bill giving it the authority to build this dam, although its real purpose was to provide irrigation water and generate power. The fact is, Kings River drains into Tulare Lake and there is no question of building a harbor or of deepening or widening a waterway since Lake Tulare has no outlet to the sea. This project is by nature a reclamation project; and it will cost from fifty million to seventy million dollars to build it in the middle of Central Valley, whose general development has already made great strides under the direction of the Bureau of Reclamation. The unjustifiable trespass by the Corps of Engineers upon this project merely means the addition of another cook when the brew was already in the hands of an expert chef.

Themselves spoilsmen in spirit, the Army Engineers never worry about land speculators. In this project, they are working hand and glove with the Kings River Water Users Association which has not done anything in return for, or in repayment of, this great public irrigation benefit. Nor are the Army Engineers interested in enforcing the 160-acre provisions of the Reclamation Act, passed during the administration of President Theodore Roosevelt for the purpose of preventing such land monopolies as that of the Kern County Land Company in California, which controls irrigated and irrigable land to the amount of 53,000 of the total of 58,000 acres in the county. The company is generously willing to allow the Federal Government to provide supplemental water to it free of cost.

It is to be doubted whether any Federal agency in the history of this country has so wantonly wasted money on worthless projects as has the Corps of Army Engineers. It is beyond human imagination. Gradually, even the Army Engineers themselves have come to learn, at the cost of hundreds of millions of dollars of the taxpayers' money, that the way to control a flood is to prevent it by containing rising spring freshets behind dams with spillways in the upper tributaries of the rivers so that the flow can be regulated. On the upper Missouri at Fort Peck, Montana, with Public Works money the Army Engineers, some years ago, built a great earth dam. It is not generally known, but as it was being filled, a serious fault developed. The Army Engineers hurried without fanfare to Washington to beg for more money in order to make good on their own bad engineering. Unofficial expert opinion was to the effect that, if this break had occurred when the dam was full, or nearly full, it would have caused one of the most disastrous floods in history....

As Dr. Maass realizes, the Corps of Engineers has not coördinated its activities with those of other agencies of the executive branch. He adds what ought to be a truism, but not so far as this introvert agency is concerned: "An administrative agency should be responsible for formulating, as well as executing, public policy. The agency has a responsibility to seek a legislative policy that is clear, consistent, feasible, and consonant with community values. The Corps of Engineers contends that it is not, and should not be, concerned with policies. The development of policies and programs is regarded as the sole duty of Congress. The Corps considers itself as no more than the executing agent of specific Congressional directives—'the engineer consultants to, and contractors for, the Congress of the United States.'"

This conception of the Corps' duty would make of it an administrative monstrosity. Some obsequious lackey of the Army Engineers ought to supply an ice bag for the nigh-bursting head of the Engineers and advise "the Engineer consultants to, and contractors for, the Congress of the United States" to read deeply enough into the Constitution to discover whether it contains even a slight intimation that the legislative branch of the government was set up by the founding fathers to pass laws, the execution of any part of which would be the exclusive duty and responsibility of a minor executive agency.

How surprised the signers of the Constitution would have been if someone had suggested that the time would come when a newly created Corps of Army Engineers would refuse to submit to the authority of the Department in which it was placed, or even to that of the President himself. The President was intended to be and, with the rare exception of the Corps of Army Engineers, generally is regarded by all branches, agencies, and individual officers of the government to be the head of the Executive Branch of the Government. Moreover, despite their disingenuous, but purposeful, protestations to the contrary, the Engineers do, when they feel like it, make policy without even consulting Congress or reporting to it.

No more lawless or irresponsible Federal group than the Corps of Army Engineers has ever attempted to operate in the United States, either outside of or within the law. If the people of the country were but half aware of the general subserviency of their representatives and senators in the Congress to this insubordinate and self-seeking clique, they would quickly demand that the Congress reassume its dignity and prestige which have been borrowed surreptitiously by the Army Engineers within which to masquerade. In order to put a stop to the reckless and wastrel behavior of the Corps of Engineers, the people should provide a Congress willing and strong enough to take back its usurped and misused power. The President cannot act without the support of the Congress. The Congress has not acted because of the torporific effect of the pork barrel. For too many years the Corps of Army Engineers has been an insubordinate secret society whose slogan has been "One for all and all for one." Nothing could be worse for the country than this wilful and expensive Corps of Army Engineers closely banded together in a self-serving clique in defiance of their superior officers and in contempt of the public welfare. The United States has had enough of "mutiny *for* the bounty."

---

# "ADJUSTMENT OF GROUP INTERESTS"*
## A. Maass

The groundwork has been laid now for an evaluation of how the Corps of Engineers meets the requirements of administrative responsibility.... How does this planning process adapt itself to an adjustment of group interests? Does the process reveal an effective responsibility of the Engineers to the public organized as interest groups?

The planning process appears to be specifically organized in response to the need for an adjustment of group interests at the several levels at which these interests may become articulate. A recapitulation of the process in these terms reveals a minimum of thirty-two stages at which group interests may be able to present their views to the Corps and Congress. Of these thirty-two stages, fifteen may involve contacts between interest groups and the Engineer Department. At three of these fifteen stages, public hearings are regularly provided for; at two additional stages, Engineer Department instructions require consultation with local interests; and at the remaining

*Arthur Maass. 1951. *Muddy Waters: The Army Engineers and the Nation's Rivers*. Cambridge, MA: Harvard University Press, pp. 37–38, 40, 45–52. Copyright © 1951 by the President and Fellows of Harvard College. Copyright © renewed 1990 by Arthur Aaron Maass, Michael Hufschmidt, and Michael Dorfman. Reprinted by permission from Harvard University Press. Footnotes are omitted.

ten, the extent of consultation varies with particular circumstances, but the necessity for a constant awareness of the current attitudes of local interests is emphasized in all Engineer publications....

The individuals and groups which take advantage of the many opportunities to present their views before the Engineers have developed interesting patterns of relations with the Corps....

Municipal, county, water district, and State officials; local industries; and local and State organized interest groups take fullest advantage of the opportunities to be heard by District Engineers and the Board of Engineers. Chambers of commerce, boards of trade, representatives of local manufacturing concerns, flood control district officials, municipal engineers—these are among the "local interests" whose desires "activate the democratic course" of the authorization process.

In addition, every large geographic region in which river and harbor developments are of importance is represented by at least one powerful regional pressure group. These groups are often quite active in the entire planning process; and a statement of the objectives of two groups, one interested in navigation and the other, flood control, is desirable....

The National Rivers and Harbors Congress is perhaps the most important and most effective of the water development interest groups. Organized originally in the year 1901, the Congress in its own words "was a pioneer in the struggle for the protection of our national resources and has taken a leading and active part in this fight for nearly four decades. The National Rivers and Harbors Congress...representing as it does the entire country affords a means for securing coordinated and united action by all the interests concerned with the various phases of water development."

This comprehensive pressure group counts in its membership the "local interests" (state and local officials, local industrial and trade organizations, contractors); the United States Congress (Representatives and Senators are honorary members); and the Corps of Engineers (Officers of the Corps engaged in rivers and harbors work are all ex officio members). The honorary members, Members of Congress, take a very active part in the Rivers Congress, though they are in a real sense the lobbied. In 1949, for example, the President was Senator John McClellan of Arkansas, a member of the Public Works Committee, of the subcommittee of the Committee on Appropriations which handles Engineer Corps funds, and chairman of the Committee on Expenditures in the Executive Departments—to which the Hoover Commission recommendations proposing reorganization of the USED had been referred. McClellan, as a member of the Hoover Commission, had dissented from those recommendations which would divest the Army of rivers and harbors functions. The national vice-presidents of the pressure group were Senator Wherry of Nebraska, Republican floor leader and a member of the Appropriations subcommittee on Engineer Corps funds; Representative Whittington of Mississippi, for a long time chairman of the House Committee on Flood Control and then chairman of the reorganized Committee on Public Works; and Representative Case of South Dakota, a member of the House subcommittee which considers appropriations for the Corps. The chairman of the board, until his recent death, was

Senator Overton of Louisiana, long a senior member of the Senate committee which handles rivers and harbor legislation. The chairman of the powerful Projects Committee of the organization was Representative Sid Simpson of Illinois, a former member of the Committee on Rivers and Harbors.

In the past the ex officio members, officers of the Corps, also have taken part in the proceedings of the pressure group, and the relations between the Rivers and Harbors Congress and the Engineers have always been cordial. In addressing the convention of the Congress in 1940, Maj. Gen. Julian Schley, Chief of Engineers, said, "I feel that I am among old friends whose interests coincide with those of the Department I represent." The feeling of coincidence of interests appears to be mutual, as evidenced by the resolutions concerning the Corps of Engineers regularly approved at conventions of the Congress....

Perhaps the most interesting and important aspect of the Rivers and Harbors Congress is the work of the Projects Committee. When the National Congress was formed in 1901, its slogan was "a policy, not a project." The purpose was not to urge any specific waterway improvements but primarily to interest the public and the Federal Congress in the development of waterways in general. In 1935, however, the Congress reversed its policy, agreed to promote certain waterway improvements actively, and for that purpose organized a Projects Committee....

The Members of Congress whose projects the Rivers and Harbors Congress endorses are grateful to the group for the support received. For example, Representative Lex Green of Florida, in speaking to the 1939 convention of the Congress about the Florida Ship Canal, said: "I can't go further into this, but I did want you to know that we appreciate the force which your organization has given to bring this matter to the favorable attention of those who are now on the Rivers and Harbors Committee of the House and the Commerce Committee of the Senate. Your continued cooperation in this, the greatest of all waterway developments in our land, will be appreciated and, with your continued cooperation, work will begin on it within the next year or year and a half."

Furthermore, officers of the Rivers and Harbors Congress receive excellent treatment before Congressional committees. In testifying in support of certain endorsed projects these officers emphasize the fact that the projects are the very ones which have been so ably justified and defended in the Projects Committee of their organization by certain Senators and Representatives.

In addition to Federal legislators, the advocates who appear before the Projects Committee include representatives of State and municipal governments, flood control and water conservation associations and districts, regional and local interest groups, and, indeed, the Corps of Engineers. At the same Projects Committee meeting in March 1940, for example: "Captain J. W. Moreland, United States Army Engineer corps and District Engineer in the St. Paul office, gave the committee further information on projects in that area. There is a drastic shortage of water in Minnesota, he declared. Among the projects on which Captain Moreland spoke were the Lac Qui Parle project, the Rousseau River project and the Red River flood control project."

As a general rule, the Projects Committee will not place in the endorsed class any project which does not have a favorable, or at best a noncommittal, report from the Army Engineers. An official publication of the Congress states that "it is generally the policy of the organization to follow the recommendations of the United States Army Engineers...in advocating projects...."

In addition to supporting endorsed projects and generally increased appropriations for water resources development, the Congress has consistently opposed valley authorities, any executive reorganization which might affect the USED, and the assumption by the United States of any jurisdiction over the tidelands. It has given a very limited approval to Federal hydroelectric installations and opposes all Federal steam plants.

It is difficult to evaluate the general effectiveness of the Rivers and Harbors Congress because it serves as a clearinghouse for uniting and coördinating the activities of many local and sectional interests. The Congress itself puts forth bold claims as to its influence:

"The influence of the National Rivers and Harbors Congress has been perhaps a more controlling force on legislation approved than that of any other organization.... Thus far there has been no adverse criticism of any of the recommendations made by the Congress in its resolutions and reports, and virtually every bill passed by the federal Congress for the improvement of harbors and waterways has been composed almost in toto of projects previously investigated and recommended by the National Rivers and Harbors Congress."

"The [Rivers and Harbors] Congress is the country's oldest and largest water organization and *occupies semi-official status* by reason of its close liaison with the governmental agencies, legislative and executive, responsible for public works...."

Though the group may be correct in making these claims, we shall be content to accredit it with being one of the most effective lobbies in Washington today....

With these additional facts concerning the group interests with which the Engineer Department coöperates and the nature of this coöperation, what conclusions may be drawn concerning the responsibility of the executive agency to the people organized as interest groups?

It has already been pointed out that the Corps of Engineers has recognized the nature of the responsibility delegated to it by Congress to adjust group interests in planning for water development projects, and has conducted its organization and operations in accordance therewith. Through a planning procedure which involves a decentralization of organization and administration, the Engineers have encouraged participation by local interests for the purposes of (1) protecting and safeguarding the respective interests; (2) obtaining information desired and necessary for the planning of projects; and (3) making possible an adjustment of diverse viewpoints and the winning of consent for proposed action based on such an adjustment.

As for the techniques of interest group adjustment, the Corps of Engineers has formalized the participation of group interests in the planning process so as to avoid the dangers of irresponsible action resulting from informal pressure on an administrative agency. For the most part, techniques of consultation, rather than those of shared participation, with interest groups have been used so that an incentive is placed upon the Engineers to win assent, and the interest groups are free to criticize. In this connection the cordial relations between the National Rivers and Harbors Congress and the Corp of Engineers should be mentioned. Many would question that the Engineers, as employees of a Government department, should be members and participate in the activities of a large pressure group. Although the USED-Rivers Congress tie-up is not a clear instance of shared participation in administration, it does involve more than executive consultation with a pressure group. Only insofar as consultation alone is involved does it meet the established criteria for administrative responsibility.

We have said that the Engineers encourage local participation for the purpose of protecting and safeguarding the respective interests. In order to really succeed in this purpose, the Corps must make certain that the groups whose interests it seeks to adjust represent all those likely to be affected by the proposed developments. Unfortunately, this is seldom the case; and it cannot be said that opportunities for interest representation are in fact equalized. This is because the Corps has traditionally emphasized the highly local aspects of water developments. The survey planning procedure is so oriented that each individual project is considered almost exclusively in the light of effects on the area immediately adjacent to the improvement; so that insufficient attention is paid to the interests of those in the wider area where the effects may be of even greater long-run significance. This local emphasis begins with the requirement that all surveys be authorized by Congress. The Members of Congress who propose survey items usually do so in response to requests of local interests in their districts. These interests often have neither the desires nor abilities to visualize the relationships of the improvements they seek to basin-wide developments. As indicated, the local emphasis is accentuated by the Corps of Engineers. It seeks to limit the scope of investigations to what was intended by the Congressmen responsible for the particular authorizations. And it has developed procedures designed to obtain the views of interest groups where they are most articulate, and this is most often at the limited local level.

# 27
# John Kenneth Galbraith (1908– )

Born in Canada, John Kenneth Galbraith emigrated to the United States in 1931 and began teaching economics at Harvard and Princeton Universities. During World War II he held a number of government positions, including deputy director of the Office of Price Administration. After the war he returned to Harvard and continued to be a close advisor to Democratic politicians. He served as Ambassador to India (1961–1963) under President John F. Kennedy.

Between 1952 and 1967 Galbraith wrote three widely read books critiquing conventional economic theory and the functioning of America's free-market economy: *American Capitalism: The Concept of Countervailing Power* (1952), *The Affluent Society* (1958), and *The New Industrial State* (1967).

A Keynesian economist, Galbraith often advocated government spending to stimulate economic growth and to provide goods and services not provided by the private sector—pollution control, for example. In *The New Industrial State* he criticized the shift in power to the technical and managerial experts within corporations who plan and control production. He also argued that in certain areas of the economy, the private sector is not as effective as the public sector. In *The Affluent Society* he noted Americans' growing obsession with consumer goods. He argued that classical economic theory, which grew out of efforts to interpret a world of mass poverty, had not adjusted its premises to a world of affluence. His call for a new economics was far ahead of its time.

An unrepentant liberal and a person of great wit, Galbraith once described himself as an "independent operator at the guerilla level of American politics." But this was hardly the case. In a 1970 interview published in the *Village Voice*, he said, "I've been fighting for a long time for a lot of different things—to end the war [in Vietnam], to curb the Pentagon and the military-industrial complex, for women's rights, for an end to racism, for environmental controls, for rights for homosexuals, and many more.... Public opinion has changed a great deal and I predict it's going to keep on changing and moving to the left. I want to keep fighting to help bring this about." In fact, John Kenneth Galbraith has influenced public policy in America for almost sixty years.

# "THE THEORY OF CONSUMER DEMAND"*

We are, to be sure, regularly told that production is not everything. We set no small store by reminders that there is a spiritual side to life; those that remind are assured a respectful hearing. But it is significant that these are always reminders; they bring to mind what is usually forgotten. No one doubts that in the general course of life one must be sensible and practical. It is an index of the prestige of production in our national attitudes that it is identified with the sensible and the practical. And no greater compliment can be paid to the forthright intelligence of any businessman than to say that he understands production. Scientists are not without prestige in our day, but to be really useful we still assume that they should be under the direction of a production man. "Any device or regulation which interferes, or can be conceived as interfering, with [the] supply of more and better things is resisted with unreasoning horror, as the religious resist blasphemy, or the warlike pacifism."

The importance of production transcends our boundaries. We are regularly told—in the conventional wisdom it is the most frequent justification of our civilization, even our existence—that the American standard of living is "the marvel of the world." To a very considerable extent, it is.

As Tawney observed, we are rarely conscious of the quality of the air we breathe. But in Los Angeles, where it is barely sufficient for its freight, we take it seriously. Similarly those who reside on a recently reclaimed desert see in the water in the canals the evidence of their unnatural triumph over nature. And the Chicagoan in Sarasota sees in his tanned belly the proof of his intelligence in escaping his dark and frozen habitat. But where sun and rain are abundant, though they are no less important, they are taken for granted. In the world of Ricardo goods were scarce. They were also closely related, if not to the survival, at least to the elemental comforts of man. They fed him, covered him when he was out of doors, and kept him warm when he was within. It is not surprising that the production by which these goods were obtained was central to men's thoughts.

Now goods are abundant. More die in the United States of too much food than of too little. Where the population was once thought to press on the food supply, now the food supply presses relentlessly on the population. No one can seriously suggest that the steel which comprises the extra four or five feet of purely decorative distance on our automobiles is of prime urgency. For many women and some men clothing has ceased to be related to protection from exposure and has become, like plumage, almost exclusively erotic. Yet production remains central to our thoughts. There is no tendency to take it, like sun and water, for granted; on the contrary, it continues to measure the quality and progress of our civilization.

*John Kenneth Galbraith. 1958. *The Affluent Society*. Boston: Houghton Mifflin Co., pp. 122–124, 139–140, 143–147, 155–158. Copyright © 1958 by John Kenneth Galbraith. Reprinted by permission from Houghton Mifflin Co. All rights reserved. Footnotes are omitted.

Our preoccupation with production is, in fact, the culminating consequence of powerful historical and psychological forces—forces which only by an act of will we can hope to escape. Productivity, as we have seen, has enabled us to avoid or finesse the tensions anciently associated with inequality and its inconvenient remedies. It has become central to our strivings to reduce insecurity. ...[I]ts importance is buttressed by a highly dubious but widely accepted psychology of want; by an equally dubious but equally accepted interpretation of national interest; and by powerful vested interest. So all embracing, indeed, is our sense of the importance of production as a goal that the first reaction to any questioning of this attitude will be, "What else is there?" So large does production bulk in our thoughts that we can only suppose that a vacuum must remain if it should be relegated to a smaller role. Happily,...there are other things. But first we must examine more closely our present preoccupation with production. For nothing better suggests the extent to which it is founded on tradition and social myth than the highly stylized attitudes with which we approach it and, in particular, the traditional and highly irrational emphasis we accord to the different methods of expanding economic product....

Both the ancient preoccupation with production and the pervasive modern search for security have culminated in our time in a concern for production. Increased real income provides us with an admirable detour around the rancor anciently associated with efforts to redistribute wealth. A high level of production has become the keystone of effective economic security. There remains, however, the task of justifying the resulting flow of goods. Production cannot be an incidental to the mitigation of inequality or the provision of jobs. It must have a *raison d'être* of its own. At this point, economists and economic theory have entered the game. So, rather more recently, have those who profess to be philosophers on problems of defense and national security. The result has been an elaborate and ingenious defense of the importance of production as such. It is a defense which makes the urgency of production largely independent of the volume of production. In this way economic theory has managed to transfer the sense of urgency in meeting consumer need that once was felt in a world where more production meant more food for the hungry, more clothing for the cold, and more houses for the homeless to a world where increased output satisfies the craving for more elegant automobiles, more exotic food, more erotic clothing, more elaborate entertainment—indeed for the entire modern range of sensuous, edifying, and lethal desires.

Although the economic theory which defends these desires and hence the production that supplies them has an impeccable (and to an astonishing degree even unchallenged) position in the conventional wisdom, it is illogical and meretricious and in degree even dangerous....

The theory of consumer demand, as it is now widely accepted, is based on two broad propositions, neither of them quite explicit but both extremely important for the present value system of economists. The first is that the urgency of wants does not diminish appreciably as more of them are satisfied or, to put the matter more precisely, to the extent that this happens it is not demonstrable and not a matter of any interest to economists or for economic policy. When man has satisfied his physical needs, then psychologically grounded desires take over. These can never be satisfied or, in any case, no progress can be proved. The concept of satiation has very little standing in economics. It is neither useful nor scientific to speculate on the comparative cravings of the stomach and the mind.

The second proposition is that wants originate in the personality of the consumer or, in any case, that they are given data for the economist. The latter's task is merely to seek their satisfaction. He has no need to inquire how these wants are formed. His function is sufficiently fulfilled by maximizing the goods that supply the wants.

The examination of these two conclusions must now be pressed. The explanation of consumer behavior has its ancestry in a much older problem, indeed the oldest problem of economics, that of price determination. Nothing originally proved more troublesome in the explanation of prices, i.e., exchange values, than the indigestible fact that some of the most useful things had the least value in exchange and some of the least useful had the most. As Adam Smith observed: "Nothing is more useful than water; but it will purchase scarce anything; scarce anything can be had in exchange for it. A diamond, on the contrary, has scarce any value in use: but a very great quantity of other goods may frequently be had in exchange for it."

In explaining value, Smith thought it well to distinguish between "value in exchange" and "value in use" and sought thus to reconcile the paradox of high utility and low exchangeability. This distinction begged questions rather than solved them and for another hundred years economists sought for a satisfactory formulation. Finally, toward the end of the last century—though it is now recognized that their work had been extensively anticipated—the three economists of marginal utility (Karl Menger, an Austrian; William Stanley Jevons, an Englishman; and John Bates Clark, an American) produced more or less simultaneously the explanation which in broad substance still serves. The urgency of desire is a function of the quantity of goods which the individual has available to satisfy that desire. The larger the stock the less the satisfactions from an increment. And the less, also, the willingness to pay. Since diamonds for most people are in comparatively meager supply, the satisfaction from an additional one is great, and the potential willingness to pay is likewise high. The case of water is just the reverse. It also follows that where the supply of a good can be readily increased at low cost, its value in exchange will reflect that ease of reproduction and the low urgency of the marginal desires it thus comes to satisfy. This will be so no matter how difficult it may be (as with water) to dispense entirely with the item in question.

The doctrine of diminishing marginal utility, as it was enshrined in the economics textbooks, seemed to put economic ideas squarely on the side of the diminishing importance of production under conditions of increasing affluence. With increasing per capita real income, men are able to satisfy additional wants. These are of a lower order of urgency. This being so, the production that provides the goods that satisfy these less urgent wants must also be of smaller (and declining) importance. In Ricardo's England, the supply of bread for many was meager. The satisfaction resulting from an increment in the bread supply—from a higher money income, bread prices being the same, or the same money income, bread prices being lower—was great. Hunger was lessened; life itself might be extended. Certainly any measure to increase the bread supply merited the deep and serious interest of the public-spirited citizen.

In the contemporary United States the supply of bread is plentiful and the supply of bread grains even redundant. The yield of satisfactions from a marginal increment in the wheat supply is small. To a Secretary of Agriculture it is indubitably negative. Measures to increase the wheat supply are not, therefore, a socially urgent preoccupation of publicly concerned citizens. These are more likely to be found spending their time devising schemes for the effective control of wheat production. And having extended their bread consumption to the point where its marginal utility is very low, people have gone on to spend their income on other things. Since these other goods entered their consumption pattern after bread, there is a presumption that they are not very urgent either—that *their* consumption has been carried, as with wheat, to the point where marginal utility is small or even negligible. So it must be assumed that the importance of marginal increments of all production is low and declining. The effect of increasing affluence is to minimize the importance of economic goals. Production and productivity become less and less important.

The concept of diminishing marginal utility was, and remains, one of the indispensable ideas of economics. Since it conceded so much to the notion of diminishing urgency of wants, and hence of production, it was remarkable indeed that the situation was retrieved. This was done—and brilliantly. The diminishing urgency of wants was not admitted. In part this was accomplished in the name of refined scientific method which, as so often at the higher levels of sophistication, proved a formidable bulwark of the conventional wisdom. Obvious but inconvenient evidence was rejected on the grounds that it could not be scientifically assimilated. But even beyond this, it has been necessary at times simply to close one's eyes to phenomena which could not be reconciled with convenience....

The even more direct link between production and wants is provided by the institutions of modern advertising and salesmanship. These cannot be reconciled with the notion of independently determined desires, for their central function is to create desires—to bring into being wants that previously did not exist. This is accomplished by the producer of the goods or at his behest. A broad empirical relationship exists between what is spent on production of consumers' goods and what is spent in synthesizing the desires for that production. A new consumer product must be introduced with a suitable advertising campaign to arouse an interest in it. The path for an expansion of output must be paved by a suitable expansion in the advertising budget. Outlays for the manufacturing of a product are not more important in the strategy of modern business enterprise than outlays for the manufacturing of demand for the product. None of this is novel. All would be regarded as elementary by the most retarded student in the nation's most primitive school of business administration. The cost of this want formation is formidable. In 1956 total advertising expenditure—though, as noted, not all of it may be assigned to the synthesis of wants—amounted to about ten billion dollars. For some years it had been increasing at a rate in excess of a billion dollars a year. Obviously, such outlays must be integrated with the theory of consumer demand. They are too big to be ignored.

But such integration means recognizing that wants are dependent on production. It accords to the producer the function both of making the goods and of making the desires for them. It recognizes that production, not only passively through emulation, but actively through advertising and related activities, creates the wants it seeks to satisfy.

The businessman and the lay reader will be puzzled over the emphasis which I give to a seemingly obvious point. The point is indeed obvious. But it is one which, to a singular degree, economists have resisted. They have sensed, as the layman does not, the damage to established ideas which lurks in these relationships. As a result, incredibly, they have closed their eyes (and ears) to the most obtrusive of all economic phenomena, namely modern want creation.

This is not to say that the evidence affirming the dependence of wants on advertising has been entirely ignored. It is one reason why advertising has so long been regarded with such uneasiness by economists. Here is something which cannot be accommodated easily to existing theory. More pervious scholars have speculated on the urgency of desires which are so obviously the fruit of such expensively contrived campaigns for popular attention. Is a new breakfast cereal or detergent so much wanted if so much must be spent to compel in the consumer the sense of want? But there has been little tendency to go on to examine the implications of this for the theory of consumer demand and even less for the importance of production and productive efficiency. These have remained sacrosanct. More often the uneasiness has been manifested in a general disapproval of advertising and advertising men, leading to the occasional suggestion that they shouldn't exist. Such suggestions have usually been ill received.

And so the notion of independently determined wants still survives. In the face of all the forces of modern salesmanship it still rules, almost undefiled, in the textbooks. And it still remains the economist's mission—and on few matters is the pedagogy so firm—to seek unquestioningly the means for filling these wants. This being so, production remains of prime urgency. We have here, perhaps, the ultimate triumph of the conventional wisdom in its resistance to the evidence of the eyes. To equal it one must imagine a humanitarian who was long ago persuaded of the grievous shortage of hospital facilities in the town. He continues to importune the passers-by for money for more beds and refuses to notice that the town doctor is deftly knocking over pedestrians with his car to keep up the occupancy.

And in unraveling the complex we should always be careful not to overlook the obvious. The fact that wants can be synthesized by advertising, catalyzed by salesmanship, and shaped by the discreet manipulations of the persuaders shows that they are not very urgent. A man who is hungry need never be told of his need for food. If he is inspired by his appetite, he is immune to the influence of Messrs. Batten, Barton, Durstine & Osborn. The latter are effective only with those who are so far removed from physical want that they do not already know what they want. In this state alone men are open to persuasion.

The general conclusion of these pages is of such importance for this essay that it had perhaps best be put with some formality. As a society becomes increasingly affluent, wants are increasingly created by the process by which they are satisfied. This may operate passively. Increases in consumption, the counterpart of increases in production, act by suggestion or emulation to create wants. Or producers may proceed actively to create wants through advertising and salesmanship. Wants thus come to depend on output. In technical terms it can no longer be assumed that welfare is greater at an all-round higher level of production than at a lower one. It may be the same. The higher level of production has, merely, a higher level of want creation necessitating a higher level of want satisfaction. There will be frequent occasion to refer to the way wants depend on the process by which they are satisfied. It will be convenient to call it the Dependence Effect....

Perhaps the thing most evident of all is how new and varied become the problems we must ponder when we break the nexus with the work of Ricardo and face the economics of affluence of the world in which we live. It is easy to see why the conventional wisdom resists so stoutly such change. It is a far, far better thing to have a firm anchor in nonsense than to put out on the troubled seas of thought.

# 28

# Dwight D. Eisenhower (1890–1969)

Before being elected President in 1952, Dwight Eisenhower (nicknamed Ike) had held no public office. He had, however, a distinguished military career, and had also served for a brief time as President of Columbia University in New York. A graduate of West Point, President Roosevelt named Eisenhower supreme commander of the Allied forces in Europe during World War II. His successful conduct of operations in that theater not only made him extremely popular in Europe, but also led many Americans to urge him to run for the office of president. Lobbied by both parties, Eisenhower finally agreed to step aside from his postwar duties as the first military commander of the North Atlantic Treaty Organization (NATO) and accept the Republican nomination in the 1952 election. Ike won by a landslide, with 55 percent of the popular vote.

As president, Eisenhower was a moderate Republican. He was conservative on economic matters, a liberal on many social issues, and supported an internationalist foreign policy. He emphasized the decentralization of bureaucracy, the pursuit of fiscal responsibility, and stressed partnerships (reducing federal expenditures and encouraging local contributions) in the development of water and power resources. Modern scholars continue to debate whether Eisenhower was a lackluster, passive president who delegated too much decision-making responsibility to his aides and cabinet officials, or whether he quietly, but effectively, maintained stability and political support during the height of the Cold War frenzy.

During his presidency, Eisenhower suffered three major illnesses, which raised serious questions about presidential succession in case of disability, and which led to passage of the Twenty-Fifth Amendment. Retaining his popularity throughout his two terms, Ike left office with the good will of the American people intact. His Farewell Address is noteworthy for its somber tone and cautionary words about the condition of American democracy and the nation's social values. A few months after leaving office Eisenhower's lifetime rank of General of the Army was restored by Congress.

## "THE MILITARY-INDUSTRIAL COMPLEX"*

My fellow Americans:

Three days from now, after half a century in the service of our country, I shall lay down the responsibilities of office as, in traditional and solemn ceremony, the authority of the Presidency is vested in my successor.

---

*Dwight D. Eisenhower. Farewell Address, January 17, 1961, in *Public Papers of the President of the United States 1961*. Washington DC: U.S. Government Printing Office, pp. 1035–1040.

This evening I come to you with a message of leave-taking and farewell, and to share a few final thoughts with you, my countrymen.

Like every other citizen, I wish the new President, and all who will labor with him, Godspeed. I pray that the coming years will be blessed with peace and prosperity for all.

Our people expect their President and the Congress to find essential agreement on issues of great moment, the wise resolution of which will better shape the future of the Nation.

My own relations with the Congress, which began on a remote and tenuous basis when, long ago, a member of the Senate appointed me to West Point, have since ranged to the intimate during the war and immediate postwar period, and finally, to the mutually interdependent during these past eight years.

In this final relationship, the Congress and the Administration have, on most vital issues, cooperated well, to serve the national good rather than mere partisanship, and so have assured that the business of the Nation should go forward. So, my official relationship with the Congress ends in a feeling, on my part, of gratitude that we have been able to do so much together.

We now stand ten years past the midpoint of a century that has witnessed four major wars among great nations. Three of these involved our own country. Despite these holocausts America is today the strongest, the most influential and most productive nation in the world. Understandably proud of this pre-eminence, we yet realize that America's leadership and prestige depend, not merely upon our unmatched material progress, riches and military strength, but on how we use our power in the interests of world peace and human betterment.

Throughout America's adventure in free government, our basic purposes have been to keep the peace; to foster progress in human achievement, and to enhance liberty, dignity and integrity among people and among nations. To strive for less would be unworthy of a free and religious people. Any failure traceable to arrogance, or our lack of comprehension or readiness to sacrifice would inflict upon us grievous hurt both at home and abroad.

Progress toward these noble goals is persistently threatened by the conflict now engulfing the world. It commands our whole attention, absorbs our very beings. We face a hostile ideology—global in scope, atheistic in character, ruthless in purpose, and insidious in method. Unhappily the danger it poses promises to be of indefinite duration. To meet it successfully, there is called for, not so much the emotional and transitory sacrifices of crisis, but rather those which enable us to carry forward steadily, surely, and without complaint the burdens of a prolonged and complex struggle—with liberty the stake. Only thus shall we remain, despite every provocation, on our charted course toward permanent peace and human betterment.

Crises there will continue to be. In meeting them, whether foreign or domestic, great or small, there is a recurring temptation to feel that some spectacular and costly action could become the miraculous solution to all current difficulties. A huge increase in newer elements of our defense;

development of unrealistic programs to cure every ill in agriculture; a dramatic expansion in basic and applied research—these and many other possibilities, each possibly promising in itself, may be suggested as the only way to the road we wish to travel.

But each proposal must be weighed in light of a broader consideration: the need to maintain balance in and among national programs—balance between the private and the public economy, balance between cost and hoped for advantage—balance between the clearly necessary and the comfortably desirable; balance between our essential requirements as a nation and the duties imposed by the nation upon the individual; balance between actions of the moment and the national welfare of the future. Good judgment seeks balance and progress; lack of it eventually finds imbalance and frustration.

The record of many decades stands as proof that our people and their government have, in the main, understood these truths and have responded to them well, in the face of stress and threat. But threats, new in kind or degree, constantly arise. I mention two only.

A vital element in keeping the peace is our military establishment. Our arms must be mighty, ready for instant action, so that no potential aggressor may be tempted to risk his own destruction.

Our military organization today bears little relation to that known by any of my predecessors in peacetime, or indeed by the fighting men of World War II or Korea.

Until the latest of our world conflicts, the United States had no armaments industry. American makers of plowshares could, with time and as required, make swords as well. But now we can no longer risk emergency improvisation of national defense; we have been compelled to create a permanent armaments industry of vast proportions. Added to this, three and a half million men and women are directly engaged in the defense establishment. We annually spend on military security more than the net income of all United States corporations.

This conjunction of an immense military establishment and a large arms industry is new in the American experience. The total influence—economic, political, even spiritual—is felt in every city, every State house, every office of the Federal government. We recognize the imperative need for this development. Yet we must not fail to comprehend its grave implications. Our toil, resources and livelihood are all involved; so is the very structure of our society.

In the councils of government, we must guard against the acquisition of unwarranted influence, whether sought or unsought, by the military-industrial complex. The potential for the disastrous rise of misplaced power exists and will persist.

We must never let the weight of this combination endanger our liberties or democratic processes. We should take nothing for granted. Only an alert and knowledgeable citizenry can compel the proper meshing of the huge industrial and military machinery of defense with our peaceful methods and goals, so that security and liberty may prosper together.

Akin to, and largely responsible for the sweeping changes in our industrial-military posture, has been the technological revolution during recent decades.

In this revolution, research has become central; it also becomes more formalized, complex, and costly. A steadily increasing share is conducted for, by, or at the direction of, the Federal government.

Today, the solitary inventor, tinkering in his shop, has been overshadowed by task forces of scientists in laboratories and testing fields. In the same fashion, the free university, historically the fountainhead of free ideas and scientific discovery, has experienced a revolution in the conduct of research. Partly because of the huge costs involved, a government contract becomes virtually a substitute for intellectual curiosity. For every old blackboard there are now hundreds of new electronic computers.

The prospect of domination of the nation's scholars by Federal employment, project allocations, and the power of money is ever present—and is gravely to be regarded.

Yet, in holding scientific research and discovery in respect, as we should, we must also be alert to the equal and opposite danger that public policy could itself become the captive of a scientific-technological elite.

It is the task of statesmanship to mold, to balance, and to integrate these and other forces, new and old, within the principles of our democratic system—ever aiming toward the supreme goals of our free society.

Another factor in maintaining balance involves the element of time. As we peer into society's future, we—you and I, and our government—must avoid the impulse to live only for today, plundering, for our own ease and convenience, the precious resources of tomorrow. We cannot mortgage the material assets of our grandchildren without risking the loss also of their political and spiritual heritage. We want democracy to survive for all generations to come, not to become the insolvent phantom of tomorrow.

Down the long lane of the history yet to be written America knows that this world of ours, ever growing smaller, must avoid becoming a community of dreadful fear and hate, and be, instead, a proud confederation of mutual trust and respect.

Such a confederation must be one of equals. The weakest must come to the conference table with the same confidence as do we, protected as we are by our moral, economic, and military strength. That table, though scarred by many past frustrations, cannot be abandoned for the certain agony of the battlefield.

Disarmament, with mutual honor and confidence, is a continuing imperative. Together we must learn how to compose differences, not with arms, but with intellect and decent purpose. Because this need is so sharp and apparent I confess that I lay down my official responsibilities in this field with a definite sense of disappointment. As one who has witnessed the horror and the lingering sadness of war—as one who knows that another war could utterly destroy this civilization which has been so slowly and painfully built over thousands of years—I wish I could say tonight that a lasting peace is in sight.

Happily, I can say that war has been avoided. Steady progress toward our ultimate goal has been made. But, so much remains to be done. As a private citizen, I shall never cease to do what little I can to help the world advance along that road.

So—in this my last good night to you as your President—I thank you for the many opportunities you have given me for public service in war and peace. I trust that in that service you find some things worthy; as for the rest of it, I know you will find ways to improve performance in the future.

You and I—my fellow citizens—need to be strong in our faith that all nations, under God, will reach the goal of peace with justice. May we be ever unswerving in devotion to principle, confident but humble with power, diligent in pursuit of the Nations' great goals.

To all the peoples of the world, I once more give expression to America's prayerful and continuing aspiration:

We pray that peoples of all faiths, all races, all nations, may have their great human needs satisfied; that those now denied opportunity shall come to enjoy it to the full; that all who yearn for freedom may experience its spiritual blessings; that those who have freedom will understand, also, its heavy responsibilities; that all who are insensitive to the needs of others will learn charity; that the scourges of poverty, disease and ignorance will be made to disappear from the earth, and that, in the goodness of time, all peoples will come to live together in a peace guaranteed by the binding force of mutual respect and love.

Thank you and goodnight.

# DISCUSSION QUESTIONS

1. The postwar economic boom had profound effects upon American society that rivaled those of the industrial revolution of the mid–1800s. Discuss some of the ways developments following WWII (e.g., television, the automobile, commercial jet travel, growth in the defense industry, the emergence of suburbia) affected environmental and social policies. What long-term effects are still evident in contemporary society?

2. Explore the rise of consumerism and mass advertising and how these developments impacted environmental concerns. How, as John Kenneth Galbraith argues, is consumer demand fueled? In what respects does his evaluation of the market economy hold true today? What arguments might be advanced to counter Galbraith's assertions?

3. As Harold L. Ickes and Arthur Maass explored, and President Eisenhower warned of, the close relationship of governmental agencies and business interests in America was a troubling phenomenon. Yet, historically, as we have seen, public opinion shifts its perspective on the question of identifying the public interest with business interests. Compare the Gilded Age, the Roaring Twenties, postwar America, and today. What balance is being struck today? What are the consequences for democracy as well as for environmental policy?

4. In addition to warning of the effects of the military-industrial complex, President Eisenhower also warned of the growing dependence of the nation's scholars on federally funded research dollars. How might the dependence of the scientific research community upon government projects and government funding affect its ability to address and solve environmental problems? Compare Eisenhower's discussion with that of J. Robert Oppenheimer's.

5. Discuss why Aldo Leopold's Golden Rule of Ecology and his Land Ethic are still appealing today as the basis for reforming current approaches to environmental policy making. What concepts and political strategies did Marjory Stoneman Douglas contribute to the environmental dialogue?

# PART VI

## "Flower Power"
## THE ENVIRONMENTAL MOVEMENT
## IN FULL BLOOM, 1961–1980

---

Between 1961 and 1980, the country witnessed the culmination of a long-term trend toward the centralization of power in Washington, D.C. Indicative of this was a growing dependence of state and local governments on federal largesse. For example, by 1976 the financial dependence of state and local governments on federal dollars was eight times what it had been in 1960. Fueling this redefinition of federalism was the passage of congressional legislation and executive orders that expanded the federal government's regulatory responsibilities in numerous areas: in civil rights, consumer protection, occupational safety, and environmental quality. During the 1960s most states were perceived as dragging their feet on the critical issues of the time, so it took "the feds" to force action in these areas. As a result, the federal bureaucracy expanded greatly during this period; both old-line and newly created agencies were given vast discretionary authority to implement the many new domestic policy initiatives. The period became known as one of centralized federalism, when federal policy makers worked—often at odds—with state, tribal, and local officials at finding a system of revenue- and responsibility-sharing acceptable to all parties. Ronald Reagan's election in 1980 signaled that much of this work was a lost cause.

But America in the '60s and '70s also was deeply enmeshed in the Cold War. Military spending continued to significantly increase alongside spending on social welfare and quality-of-life programs. In providing both guns and butter, it was often difficult to discern the difference. President Kennedy's promise to put a man on the moon before the end of the decade, for instance, was as much a part of the arms race as it was an unprecedented domestic challenge for America's scientific establishment. Such ambitious programs were costly, though; and deficit spending became the norm throughout this era, a pattern which extended through the '80s and even into the '90s.

Fighting communism in the 1960s took the United States into Vietnam. The war proved to be unpopular, divisive, and costly both in terms of lives lost and money spent. "Flower children" assembled to protest the war: Instead of war slogans they displayed the peace sign; instead of guns they carried flowers. Their motto became: "Make love, not war!" But the '60s generation also protested against other strictures of society, and worked generally toward creating a more egalitarian society. Within the social context of widespread protest and political reform, the environmental movement came into full bloom.

While Rachel Carson's *Silent Spring* certainly was not the first best-selling book to examine the environmental consequences of human impact upon the natural world (recall, for example, Marsh's *Man and Nature* and Douglas's *River of Grass*), its publication in 1962 is generally credited with reigniting the environmental movement after a decade of relative quiescence. *Silent Spring* chillingly detailed the effects of widespread, indiscriminate pesticide use not only on insects but also on the creatures who ate the insects. In fact, one of the book's major contributions was to popularize a complex, scientific concept, that of the biological food chain. Her non-polemical, but beautifully written criticism of the unquestioning embrace of these chemical technologies by both the scientists who developed them and the industries that profited from them, made *Silent Spring* a household word and its author the heroine of the growing environmental movement.

A year after the publication of *Silent Spring*, President John Kennedy's Secretary of the Interior, Stewart Udall, published *The Quiet Crisis*. Udall wanted his book to be a political action call on behalf of "the inner space that is our home." As Interior Secretary he had an ideal vantage point to pursue his goals, especially in view of the fact that both President Kennedy and his successor Lyndon B. Johnson (LBJ) wanted environmental protection to be part of their legacies.

In the Johnson administration environmentalists had another significant ally in the First Lady. Wanting to make a contribution in her own right, Lady Bird Johnson spent much of her time promoting greater educational opportunities for all Americans and protecting the natural environment. She was a leader in the beautification movement, and her efforts to visually improve the nation's capital encompassed both the monumental Washington that tourists see and its inner city where a majority of Washingtonians in fact live. Another of her legacies was the Highway Beautification Act of 1965. The law's opponents ridiculed the First Lady's "whim," and criticized her for stepping down from "the pedestal of the dutiful preoccupied wife of the President" to actively support the law's passage. (Lady Bird Johnson was neither the first nor the last First Lady to be subjected to this type of criticism.)

All told, during the Johnson administration some 278 conservation and beautification measures were enacted. They included the addition of 100 million acres to the national park system, the creation of 200 miles of national seashore, and the creation of a national system of rural and urban trails. Among the most significant acts passed during this period were the Wilderness Act (1964), the Land and Water Conservation Fund Act (1964), the National Historic Preservation Act (1966), and the Wild and Scenic Rivers Act (1968). It was a record of conservation and preservation that rivaled the New Deal's accomplishments.

In addition to traditional conservation concerns, an emerging problem in the 1960s was that of air and water pollution. As society became more complex, and new issues were added to the national agenda, the environmental movement accordingly diversified and specialized once again. One branch increasingly focused its attention on such issues as urban smog, industrial and municipal discharges into waterways and the atmosphere, and radioactive fall-out from nuclear testing. The biologist Barry Commoner became a leader of this segment of the environmental movement; throughout the '50s and '60s he called attention to radioactive milk in upstate New York, the "death" (by eutrophication) of Lake Erie, and the "burning"of the Cuyahoga River. His 1971 book, *The Closing Circle*, presented a strong indictment of the powerful nuclear and petrochemical industries—and the politicians who did their bidding—for having caused most of the pollution problems in the United States and elsewhere.

Both the Johnson and Nixon administrations responded to the growing pollution problem. The first piece of legislation to specifically target primary sources of air pollution, automobiles and trucks, was passed in 1965 (the Motor Vehicle Air Pollution Control Act). More stringent air and water pollution laws also were passed on a regular basis by an activist legislative branch urged on by activist chief executives. To deal with the new class of problems, three federal agencies were created during the Nixon administration: The Environmental Protection Agency (EPA), the National Oceanographic and Atmospheric Administration (NOAA), and the Occupational Safety and Health Administration (OSHA).

LBJ's vision of a Great Society was not confined to controlling pollution and preserving natural areas. Important as these activities were, the Great Society also meant confronting the unintended social effects of an increasingly urbanized and technology-dependent America, the paradox of poverty in the midst of plenty, and the continued existence of racial prejudice. The President launched a frontal attack on all of these problems.

Johnson was at the forefront of a virtual tidal wave of egalitarianism that flowed over the country in the '60s and '70s. It found expression in demands for desegregation of public facilities, for the promotion of civil liberties, for tribal sovereignty, for women's rights, and for a fairer system of political representation. Groups that traditionally had little voice in the political process began to be heard. These included African Americans, Latinos, Native Americans, and women. At the same time, residents of urban areas demanded greater political representation in their state legislatures through reapportionment, while young Americans secured the right to vote through passage of the Twenty-Sixth Amendment.

The long struggle for racial equality gained momentum in the early 1960s with a series of lunch counter sit-ins and freedom rides in the South. The defining moment for the civil rights movement occurred in August of 1963, when over 200,000 people rallied in Washington, D.C., to hear the Reverend Dr. Martin Luther King, Jr., deliver one of the greatest speeches ever given. Rich with allusions to nature—such as "Mississippi, a desert state sweltering with the heat of injustice and oppression"—King's "I Have a Dream" speech created a new vision of American democracy. It also aroused the nation's conscience.

After this epochal address, events moved quickly. Blacks and other minorities secured formal political equality with the passage of the Civil Rights Act of 1964, the Voting Rights Act of 1965, the ratification of the Twenty-Fourth Amendment banning the poll tax, and a number of Supreme Court cases outlawing various forms of discrimination. But each stride forward caused a growing backlash in many parts of the country, especially in the South. The nonviolent struggle espoused by King and other civil rights leaders increasingly turned violent. There were beatings, bombings, and assassinations, including Dr. King's own assassination in 1968. King's death in April touched off race riots in many of America's largest cities, including the nation's capital. Then, the Democratic candidate for President, Robert Kennedy, the former president's brother, was assassinated in June of 1968, thus making that year the *anneé terrible* of the period.

Not since the Civil War had America seen such violence. It became evident that despite the substantial gains of the 1960s, the civil rights struggle was not over. Gaining widespread social acceptance for racial equality would take much longer, and the battle would have to move from the streets into the corridors of public and private power. Out of the political chaos of the '60s came the "affirmative action" programs of the '70s.

In 1975—nine years after Chicano rights activist Rodolfo Gonzales founded the Crusade for Justice—Congress broadened the protections of the Voting Rights Act of 1965 to include Spanish-speaking Americans and other linguistic minorities. This milestone came after nearly a decade of activism and organizing by Hispanic Americans. Their leader in the struggle for economic and political equality was the California-based activist, Cesar Chavez. Chavez and his co-workers spent the 1960s and '70s organizing the United Farm Workers Union in the fields of central California.

Their concern was not only for a decent wage but also for a more healthy work environment. In his frequently quoted 1969 "Letter from Delano," addressed to the President of the California Grape and Tree Fruit League, Chavez wrote movingly about how his people had to endure the poisons of the vineyard where they worked from dawn to dusk. Based on Martin Luther King's "Letter from a Birmingham Jail," Chavez's poignant plea for decent treatment for farm workers stirred consciences and produced results: it called national attention to the appalling conditions found on many of America's farms, which were increasingly dominated by "agribusiness" interests, and was instrumental in banning DDT and other chemical agents used in the farm sector. Rachel Carson would have been pleased.

Always at the spiritual and ethical center of America's environmental movement were the American Indians. However, despite their special place in America's intellectual and emotional landscape, the political reality was that Native Americans were perhaps the most forgotten and neglected of all groups. During the 1960s and '70s tribal peoples became determined to change that unenviable status. Not surprisingly, their demands for tribal sovereignty were intertwined with issues of land ownership and resource use.

At the same time as African Americans were sitting in at southern lunch counters Native Americans were staging fish-ins in the Pacific Northwest. The fish-ins, which began in 1964, protested governmental efforts to restrict traditional tribal fishing activities. They didn't end until 1974, when a federal district court judge reaffirmed tribal rights under an existing treaty. Sport and commercial fishermen responded by hanging the judge in effigy on the courthouse steps, and the State of Washington refused to obey the judge's decree. State officials gave in only after the Supreme Court in 1979 affirmed the decision, noting that "Except for some desegregation cases...the district court has faced the most concerted official and private efforts to frustrate a decree of a federal court witnessed in this century." (The controversy, it is worth noting, has risen again; this time environmentalists are protesting tribal whale hunting off the Washington coast.)

Indian activism spread across the country. A group of Indians took control of Alcatraz Island in 1969 and occupied it for nineteen months. In 1972 Native Americans entered the Department of the Interior in Washington, D.C., and occupied the offices of the Bureau of Indian Affairs. A number of other protests occurred on federal lands elsewhere in America. The protests served to educate the American public about the government's long record of breaking treaties, of denying access to valuable land and water resources, of destroying Indian culture, and of perpetuating tribal poverty. So did several best-selling books written by the Native American scholar and activist, Vine Deloria, Jr. In his *Custer Died for Your Sins* (1969) and *God is Red* (1973), the Indian movement found a powerful voice which succeeded in capturing widespread attention on behalf of Indian rights.

As the demands for tribal self-determination grew louder, some in government began to listen. President Richard Nixon proved to be very sympathetic to Indian demands. He made several bold decisions restoring tribal lands to the Pueblo, Warm Springs, and Yakima tribes, and he successfully pressured Congress to change its termination policy of the 1950s. "Except for FDR," Deloria claims, "Nixon was the best president ever for Indians."

The status of women in American life also changed dramatically during this period. Young women increasingly went to college or into the workforce, they delayed marriage and childbirth, and they participated in the antiwar, civil rights, Native American, and environmental movements. They also formed a movement of their own: It was initially called the Women's Liberation Movement but later became known as the Feminist Movement. While certainly not all women of this generation participated in the movement's demands for equality at home and at work, nearly all were affected by the creation in the '60s of "the pill"—a revolutionary development if ever there was one. With the Supreme Court's 1965 decision in *Griswold v. Connecticut*, protecting its use from state interference, Margaret Sanger's "long fight for birth control" was over. The mass marketing of a relatively safe, inexpensive oral contraceptive probably did as much to change the status of women as did anything during this period. Coupled with the still-controversial 1973 Supreme Court decision legalizing abortion, it gave women full reproductive rights and responsibilities for the first time in history and dramatically changed relations between men and women.

Ironically, just as men and women in the United States and other industrialized societies began planning the size of their families, and as population growth in advanced industrialized nations stabilized, several environmentalists sounded alarm bells about the dangers of *over*population. The Stanford University biologist Paul Ehrlich and the University of California economist Garrett Hardin each published an environmental blockbuster in 1968. Ehrlich's *The Population Bomb* and Hardin's "The Tragedy of the Commons" declared a catastrophe in the making: With world population growing exponentially since 1950, the strain on natural resources was reaching the breaking point. Something needed to be done immediately, they argued. Societies could choose either to implement coercive birth control policies or have their people endure mass suffering, starvation, disease, and early death. There were no optimistic scenarios for this branch of the environmental movement, which went on to found Zero Population Growth (ZPG). They also succeeded in getting the attention of international organizations such as the United Nations, and the Food and Agricultural Organization. With the publication of the Club of Rome's report on population growth in 1972, family planning on a global scale commenced.

But other environmentalists, most notably Barry Commoner, were appalled by what the "population doomsayers" were saying. Determining who should live and who not, as Hardin's essay implied, was too reminiscent of Hitler's Germany and Stalin's Soviet Union. During the 1960s and '70s a lively intellectual debate ensued over the fundamental causes of the environmental crisis, with one side stressing overpopulation and the other the world's economic and political systems that inequitably distributed wealth and other resources. It is a debate that continues today, as the rich nations of the world struggle over which if any aid programs will best serve the desperately poor, most of whom live in sub-Saharan Africa.

The animating political force of the era, that of egalitarianism, even extended beyond identifiable population groups. At the same time as minority groups, women's groups, and those living in urban areas challenged the political and legal status quo, the proposal to grant legal rights to environmental objects surfaced. The legal scholar Christopher Stone published his classic essay, *Should Trees Have Standing?*, in 1972. Immediately, Justice William O. Douglas used it in the celebrated Supreme Court case, *Sierra Club v. Morton*. Douglas argued that yes, the time had come to allow trees, streams, lakes, and other environmental objects to sue on their own behalf. With human representatives, of course. The significance of the 5-4 decision against broadening the criterion of standing in this manner was not that it wasn't adopted; rather, it was that it almost was adopted. Nightmare scenarios of flooding the courts by this, that, and the other "group," all claiming that they were suing on behalf of some environmental object, came close to being realized with this landmark decision in environmental law.

While the courts refused to drastically broaden standing, as urged by Professor Stone, Justice Douglas, and others, congressional legislation passed during this period had much the same effect. Many environmentalists considered the passage of the National Environmental Policy Act (NEPA) of 1969 the crowning achievement of a decade of activism. This significant, much-studied act was the first to declare a *national* policy of environmental protection. It also led the way for an executive reorganization under the Nixon administration which created the Environmental Protection Agency. Finally, it required that all federal agencies submit an environmental impact statement (EIS) for their proposed projects and programs. Citizens began to sue the federal government arguing violation of NEPA's procedures.

But NEPA was just the beginning. With the presidency in crisis over the Watergate scandal and its aftermath, Congress in the 1970s took the lead on environmental policy and enacted dozens of important statutes. Many of them contained liberal citizen suit provisions. They included: The Federal Water Pollution Control Act Amendments of 1972 and 1977, the Marine Mammal Protection Act of 1972, the Coastal Zone Management Act of 1972, the Endangered Species Act of 1973, the Safe Drinking Water Act of 1974, the National Forest Management Act of 1976, the Toxic Substances Control Act of 1976, the Resource Conservation and Recovery Act of 1976, the Federal Land Policy and Management Act of 1976, the Surface Mining and Control Act of 1977, the Clean Air Act of 1977, and the Comprehensive Environmental Response, Compensation and Liability Act of 1980 (the "Superfund" Act).

Even a partial listing of all the environmental legislation enacted during the 1960s and '70s gives one the sense that there were political and administrative problems in the making. Could legislators *really* have considered fully the content and ramifications of so many federal statutes enacted in such a short period of time? How did all of the policies fit together? Did agencies have the necessary funds and staff to implement highly complex statutes involving very specialized scientific knowledge? How would state and local governments—not to mention business and industry—respond to this barrage of new federal policies and programs? Would the "command-and-control" and "technology-forcing" approaches, contained in several of these statutes, work?

Among the first scholars to address these questions was the political scientist Theodore Lowi. In one of the most influential books about public policy written during the past thirty years, Lowi presents a devastating critique of what he calls "interest-group liberalism." His lengthy argument is complex and intellectually challenging, but the essence is that the federal government in the '60s and '70s became "formless" and essentially hostile to the rule of law. It superimposed upon a pluralist society—which is a positive characteristic of America—a pluralist government: that is, a government that responds to every whim of every conceivable interest group. A pluralist government is a negative development because the state no longer speaks authoritatively to its citizens. Moreover, the only difference between Republicans and Democrats, Lowi argues, is the special interests each party serves. Finally, Congress during this period delegated most of its power to the executive branch of government. This is not only unconstitutional, he claims, but it is a recipe for producing endless litigation brought by organized interests challenging bureaucratic rule-making. The argument in *The End of Liberalism* (1969, 1979) was unusually prescient: Virtually all of the pathologies of national politics discussed in the next section are covered in this study.

The twenty-year period that witnessed the environmental movement in full bloom ended with an energy crisis and with an emerging trend towards political decentralization. In fact, a handful of states never needed cajoling or coercing by federal officials to protect their natural heritage. They were ahead of the curve throughout this entire period, and a number of them, including Hawaii, Maine, Oregon, Vermont, and Florida enacted comprehensive land-use policies at the same time as national land-use planning bills failed to pass. Oregon's colorful and outspoken governor, Tom McCall, instituted his "Visit Oregon, But Don't Stay" policy in 1967, and the nation's first bottle bill. For contemporary environmentalists, the State of Oregon is the role model for what is called "sustainable development," whose central goal is finding a sensible mix of environmental protection and economic growth.

Of utmost concern through the entire decade of the 1970s was the source and cost of the nation's energy supply. Presidents Nixon, Ford, and Carter all wrestled with problems that resulted from the creation of the energy cartel known as OPEC (Organization of Petroleum Exporting Countries). The Arab oil embargo in 1973 dramatically signaled the end of an era of cheap, abundant, and reliable supply. Long lines at the gas station underscored the need to reduce national dependence on imported oil. But defining a clear course of action proved more difficult as advocates for one energy strategy squared off against others. "Hard-path" solutions, such as coal, nuclear, and natural gas, were pitted against "soft-path" solutions, such as energy conservation, solar, and wind power.

The Santa Barbara oil spill in 1969, which had contributed significantly to the public's growing environmental awareness, cast doubt on the feasibility of off-shore oil and gas drilling. Only after protracted debate and litigation did the nation's oil companies get approval for the Trans-Alaska pipeline, which would bring oil from the North Slope to the port of Valdez. Further, while the Alaska National Interest and Lands Conservation Act of 1980 settled some management issues relating to federal lands in Alaska, it did not resolve the controversy—still going on—over oil drilling in the Arctic National Wildlife Refuge. Nevertheless, this historic act protecting more than 100 million acres from development assured President Jimmy Carter—and one of its primary sponsors, Arizona's Congressman Morris Udall—of permanent places in America's pantheon of great environmentalists.

Domestic coal production entailed a host of other environmental problems: from the water pollution and land degradation effects of strip mining, to the air pollutants emanating from coal-fired power plants, and finally to the hydrocarbon emissions that scientists were just beginning to investigate for their effects upon the earth's climate. Despite governmental subsidies, constructing fail-safe nuclear power plants was proving to be extremely expensive, and the 1979 nuclear accident at the Three Mile Island plant in Pennsylvania raised serious concerns about plant safety. Disposal of nuclear wastes also presented special and seemingly unresolvable problems. Finally, there were few sites left in the United States where large hydroelectric dams could be located, and evidence was accumulating over the deleterious effects dams had on in-stream ecosystems, especially native fish populations.

President Jimmy Carter (1976-1980) offered the most ambitious plan of all to solve the nation's energy crisis. Throughout his four short years in office he told Americans that the crisis was "the moral equivalent of war." He suggested they put on sweaters and turn down their thermostats in winter, he created a Department of Energy in 1977 to investigate alternative, renewable energy resources, he installed solar panels on the White House, and he delivered speech after speech on energy and the environment. But Americans weren't listening to this prophet from Georgia. In the wake of Watergate and Vietnam, and the ongoing embarrassment over the American hostages in Iran, the public had become extremely cynical about politics. It is probably impossible to calculate how many billions of dollars America wasted during the '80s and '90s on energy consumption, especially expensive imported oil to drive its fleet of RVs and SUVs, but the cost has to be enormous—especially the indirect costs to the environment. Had Americans paid heed to President Carter, we would not be witnessing at the dawn of the twenty-first century a reprise of the energy crisis of the 1970s.

# 29
# Rachel Carson (1907–1964)

In some respects Rachel Carson was not the most likely person to reignite the environmental movement of the 1960s. She was a quiet loner who grew up taking long, solitary walks in the woods surrounding her Pennsylvania home. Unlike some others in this collection, Carson never actively sought out the limelight. As an adult, she combined a childhood passion for writing with an interest in biology. While taking a master's degree in zoology at Johns Hopkins University, she obtained a summer appointment at the Marine Biological Laboratory in Woods Hole, Massachusetts. From this experience she became fascinated with the mysteries of the sea.

In 1935, at the height of the depression and desperate for a job, Carson was hired by the U.S. Bureau of Fisheries, precursor to the U.S. Fish and Wildlife Service. Her main duties were to write radio scripts and public information articles. In her off-hours she also wrote, publishing her first book, *Under the Sea-Wind*, in 1941. Unfortunately, the book came out just before the invasion at Pearl Harbor, so sales were meager. Undaunted, she began work on a second book, *The Sea Around Us* (1951). Good thing: The book spent 86 weeks on the bestseller list. Then, *Under the Sea Wind* was reissued and it too became a best seller. Now financially independent, Carson left her government job to pursue writing full time. Another popular book, *The Edge of the Sea* (1955), followed.

The impetus for *Silent Spring* came when Carson received a letter from a friend in the Boston area that detailed the death of the neighborhood songbirds immediately after municipal aerial spraying of pesticides. Long convinced of the need for a public statement about the dangers of such chemicals, Carson began a laborious process of researching pesticides and other toxic pollutants. Her research focused primarily on DDT, which had been viewed as a miracle substance since its invention in the late '30s. Prior to writing *Silent Spring* Carson had never taken a strong stand on environmental issues, but in what turned out to be her last book she argued cogently against both modern agricultural practices and the indiscriminate spraying of "pests" in urban areas. Insecticides, she wrote, more properly ought to be called "biocides."

The publication of *Silent Spring* in 1962 produced widespread praise as well as intense criticism. The book, with its images of a world bereft of the beauty of birds and their singing, became a worldwide bestseller that served as the catalyst for the environmental movement. Spokesmen for the nation's powerful chemical industry, however, vociferously rejected Carson's findings, claiming they were inaccurate and alarmist. The personal attacks were vicious. A former Secretary of Agriculture in the Eisenhower Administration labeled her a spinster and a Communist; another critic charged that the book was so well written it had to be written by a man; and yet another portrayed her as a hysterical woman unable to deal rationally with the facts. The President's Science Advisory Committee, however, confirmed Carson's findings.

In May of 1964, President Johnson signed an amendment to the Federal Insecticide, Fungicide, and Rodenticide Act (FIFRA) that strengthened existing regulations of many widely used pesticides, and in 1972 the Environmental Protection Agency banned DDT. But the quiet woman who created such a controversy did not live to see the results of her scholarship. She died of cancer in April, 1964.

# "IT WAS A SPRING WITHOUT VOICES"*

*A Fable for Tomorrow*
There was once a town in the heart of America where all life seemed to live in harmony with its surroundings. The town lay in the midst of a checkerboard of prosperous farms, with fields of grain and hillsides of orchards where, in spring, white clouds of bloom drifted above the green fields. In autumn, oak and maple and birch set up a blaze of color that flamed and flickered across a backdrop of pines. Then foxes barked in the hills and deer silently crossed the fields, half hidden in the mists of the fall mornings.

Along the roads, laurel, viburnum and alder, great ferns and wildflowers delighted the traveler's eye through much of the year. Even in winter the roadsides were places of beauty, where countless birds came to feed on the berries and on the seed heads of the dried weeds rising above the snow. The countryside was, in fact, famous for the abundance and variety of its bird life, and when the flood of migrants was pouring through in spring and fall people traveled from great distances to observe them. Others came to fish the streams, which flowed clear and cold out of the hills and contained shady pools where trout lay. So it had been from the days many years ago when the first settlers raised their houses, sank their wells, and built their barns.

Then a strange blight crept over the area and everything began to change. Some evil spell had settled on the community: mysterious maladies swept the flocks of chickens; the cattle and sheep sickened and died. Everywhere was a shadow of death. The farmers spoke of much illness among their families. In the town the doctors had become more and more puzzled by new kinds of sickness appearing among their patients. There had been several sudden and unexplained deaths, not only among adults but even among children, who would be stricken suddenly while at play and die within a few hours.

There was a strange stillness. The birds, for example—where had they gone? Many people spoke of them, puzzled and disturbed. The feeding stations in the backyards were deserted. The few birds seen anywhere were moribund; they trembled violently and could not fly. It was a spring without voices. On the mornings that had once throbbed with the dawn chorus of robins, catbirds, doves, jays, wrens, and scores of other bird voices there was now no sound; only silence lay over the fields and woods and marsh.

On the farms the hens brooded, but no chicks hatched. The farmers complained that they were unable to raise any pigs—the litters were small and the young survived only a few days. The apple trees were coming into bloom but no bees droned among the blossoms, so there was no pollination and there would be no fruit.

The roadsides, once so attractive, were now lined with browned and withered vegetation as though swept by fire. These, too, were silent, deserted by all living things. Even the streams were now lifeless. Anglers no longer visited them, for all the fish had died.

In the gutters under the eaves and between the shingles of the roofs, a white granular powder still showed a few patches; some weeks before it had fallen like snow upon the roofs and the lawns, the fields and streams.

No witchcraft, no enemy action had silenced the rebirth of new life in this stricken world. The people had done it themselves.

This town does not actually exist, but it might easily have a thousand counterparts in America or elsewhere in the world. I know of no community that has experienced all the misfortunes I describe. Yet every one of these disasters has actually happened somewhere, and many real communities have already suffered a substantial number of them. A grim specter has crept upon us almost unnoticed, and this imagined tragedy may easily become a stark reality we all shall know.

What has already silenced the voices of spring in countless towns in America? This book is an attempt to explain.

*The Obligation to Endure*
The history of life on earth has been a history of interaction between living things and their surroundings. To a large extent, the physical form and the habits of the earth's vegetation and its animal life have been molded by the environment. Considering the whole span of earthly time, the opposite effect, in which life actually modifies its surroundings, has been relatively slight. Only within the moment of time represented by the present century has one species—man—acquired significant power to alter the nature of his world.

During the past quarter century this power has not only increased to one of disturbing magnitude but it has changed in character. The most alarming of all man's assaults upon the environment is the contamination of air, earth, rivers, and sea with dangerous and even lethal materials. This pollution is for the most part irrecoverable; the chain of evil it initiates not only in the world that must support life but in living tissues is for the most part irreversible. In this now universal contamination of the environment, chemicals are the sinister and little-recognized partners of radiation in changing the very nature of the world—the very nature of its life. Strontium 90, released through nuclear explosions into the air, comes to earth in rain or drifts down as fallout, lodges in soil, enters into the grass or corn or wheat grown there, and in time takes up its abode in the bones of a human being, there to remain until his death. Similarly, chemicals sprayed on croplands or forests or gardens lie long in soil, entering into living organisms, passing from one to another in a chain of poisoning and death. Or they pass mysteriously by underground streams until they emerge and, through the alchemy of air and sunlight, combine into new forms that kill vegetation, sicken cattle, and work unknown harm on those who drink from once pure wells. As Albert Schweitzer has said, "Man can hardly even recognize the devils of his own creation."

It took hundreds of millions of years to produce the life that now inhabits the earth—eons of time in which that developing and evolving and diversifying life reached a state of adjustment and balance with its surroundings. The environment, rigorously shaping and directing the life it supported, contained elements that were hostile as well as supporting. Certain rocks gave out dangerous radiation; even within the light of the sun, from which all life draws its energy, there were short-wave radiations with power to injure. Given time—time not in years but in millennia—life adjusts, and a balance has been reached. For time is the essential ingredient; but in the modern world there is no time.

The rapidity of change and the speed with which new situations are created follow the impetuous and heedless pace of man rather than the deliberate pace of nature. Radiation is no longer merely the background radiation of rocks, the bombardment of cosmic rays, the ultraviolet of the sun that have existed before there was any life on earth; radiation is now the unnatural creation of man's tampering with the atom. The chemicals to which life is asked to make its adjustment are no longer merely the calcium and silica and copper and all the rest of the minerals washed out of the rocks and carried in rivers to the sea; they are the synthetic creations of man's inventive mind, brewed in his laboratories, and having no counterparts in nature.

To adjust to these chemicals would require time on the scale that is nature's; it would require not merely the years of a man's life but the life of generations. And even this, were it by some miracle possible, would be futile, for the new chemicals come from our laboratories in an endless stream; almost five hundred annually find their way into actual use in the United States alone. The figure is staggering and its implications are not easily grasped—500 new chemicals to which the bodies of men and animals are required somehow to adapt each year, chemicals totally outside the limits of biologic experience.

Among them are many that are used in man's war against nature. Since the mid-1940's over 200 basic chemicals have been created for use in killing insects, weeds, rodents, and other organisms described in the modern vernacular as "pests"; and they are sold under several thousand different brand names.

These sprays, dusts, and aerosols are now applied almost universally to farms, gardens, forests, and homes—nonselective chemicals that have the power to kill every insect, the "good" and the "bad," to still the song of birds and the leaping of fish in the streams, to coat the leaves with a deadly film, and to linger on in soil—all this though the intended target may be only a few weeds or insects. Can anyone believe it is possible to lay down such a barrage of poisons on the surface of the earth without making it unfit for all life? They should not be called "insecticides," but "biocides."

The whole process of spraying seems caught up in an endless spiral. Since DDT was released for civilian use, a process of escalation has been going on in which ever more toxic materials must be found. This has happened because insects, in a triumphant vindication of Darwin's principle of the survival of the fittest, have evolved super races immune to the particular insecticide used, hence a deadlier one has always to be developed—and then a deadlier one than that. It has happened also because...destructive insects often undergo a "flareback," or resurgence, after spraying, in numbers greater than before. Thus the chemical war is never won, and all life is caught in its violent crossfire.

Along with the possibility of the extinction of mankind by nuclear war, the central problem of our age has therefore become the contamination of man's total environment with such substances of incredible potential for harm—substances that accumulate in the tissues of plants and animals and even penetrate the germ cells to shatter or alter the very material of heredity upon which the shape of the future depends.

Some would-be architects of our future look toward a time when it will be possible to alter the human germ plasm by design. But we may easily be doing so now by inadvertence, for many chemicals, like radiation, bring about gene mutations. It is ironic to think that man might determine his own future by something so seemingly trivial as the choice of an insect spray.

All this has been risked—for what? Future historians may well be amazed by our distorted sense of proportion. How could intelligent beings seek to control a few unwanted species by a method that contaminated the entire environment and brought the threat of disease and death even to their own kind? Yet this is precisely what we have done. We have done it, moreover, for reasons that collapse the moment we examine them. We are told that the enormous and expanding use of pesticides is necessary to maintain farm production. Yet is our real problem not one of *overproduction*? Our farms, despite measures to remove acreages from production and to pay farmers *not* to produce, have yielded such a staggering excess of crops that the American taxpayer in 1962 is paying out more than one billion dollars a year as the total carrying cost of the surplus-food storage program. And is the situation helped when one branch of the Agriculture Department tries to reduce production while another states, as it did in 1958, "It is believed generally that reduction of crop acreages under provisions of the Soil Bank will stimulate interest in use of chemicals to obtain maximum production on the land retained in crops."

All this is not to say there is no insect problem and no need of control. I am saying, rather, that control must be geared to realities, not to mythical situations, and that the methods employed must be such that they do not destroy us along with the insects.

The problem whose attempted solution has brought such a train of disaster in its wake is an accompaniment of our modern way of life. Long before the age of man, insects inhabited the earth—a group of extraordinarily varied and adaptable beings. Over the course of time since man's advent, a small percentage of the more than half a million species of insects have come into conflict with human welfare in two principal ways: as competitors for the food supply and as carriers of human disease.

Disease-carrying insects become important where human beings are crowded together, especially under conditions where sanitation is poor, as in time of natural disaster or war or in situations of extreme poverty and deprivation. Then control of some sort becomes necessary. It is a sobering fact, however,...that the method of massive chemical control has had only limited success, and also threatens to worsen the very conditions it is intended to curb.

Under primitive agricultural conditions the farmer had few insect problems. These arose with the intensification of agriculture—the devotion of immense acreages to a single crop. Such a system set the stage for explosive increases in specific insect populations. Single-crop farming does not take advantage of the principles by which nature works; it is agriculture as an engineer might conceive it to be. Nature has introduced great variety into the landscape, but man has displayed a passion for simplifying it. Thus he undoes the built-in checks and balances by which nature holds the species within bounds. One important natural check is a limit on the amount of suitable habitat for each species. Obviously then, an insect that lives on wheat can build up its population to much higher levels on a farm devoted to wheat than on one in which wheat is intermingled with other crops to which the insect is not adapted.

The same thing happens in other situations. A generation or more ago, the towns of large areas of the United States lined their streets with the noble elm tree. Now the beauty they hopefully created is threatened with complete destruction as disease sweeps through the elms, carried by a beetle that would have only limited chance to build up large populations and to spread from tree to tree if the elms were only occasional trees in a richly diversified planting.

Another factor in the modern insect problem is one that must be viewed against a background of geologic and human history: the spreading of thousands of different kinds of organisms from their native homes to invade new territories. This worldwide migration has been studied and graphically described by British ecologist Charles Elton in his recent book *The Ecology of Invasions*. During the Cretaceous Period, some hundred million years ago, flooding seas cut many land bridges between continents and living things found themselves confined in what Elton calls "colossal separate nature reserves." There, isolated from others of their kind, they developed many new species. When some of the land masses were joined again, about 15 million years ago, these species began to move out into new territories—a movement that is not only still in progress but is now receiving considerable assistance from man.

The importation of plants is the primary agent in the modern spread of species, for animals have almost invariably gone along with the plants, quarantine being a comparatively recent and not completely effective innovation. The United States Office of Plant Introduction alone has introduced almost

200,000 species and varieties of plants from all over the world. Nearly half of the 180 or so major insect enemies of plants in the United States are accidental imports from abroad, and most of them have come as hitchhikers on plants.

In new territory, out of reach of the restraining hand of the natural enemies that kept down its numbers in its native land, an invading plant or animal is able to become enormously abundant. Thus it is no accident that our most troublesome insects are introduced species.

These invasions, both the naturally occurring and those dependent on human assistance, are likely to continue indefinitely. Quarantine and massive chemical campaigns are only extremely expensive ways of buying time. We are faced, according to Dr. Elton, "with a life-and-death need not just to find new technological means of suppressing this plant or that animal"; instead we need the basic knowledge of animal populations and their relations to their surroundings that will "promote an even balance and damp down the explosive power of outbreaks and new invasions."

Much of the necessary knowledge is now available but we do not use it. We train ecologists in our universities and even employ them in our governmental agencies but we seldom take their advice. We allow the chemical death rain to fall as though there were no alternative, whereas in fact there are many, and our ingenuity could soon discover many more if given opportunity.

Have we fallen into a mesmerized state that makes us accept as inevitable that which is inferior or detrimental, as though having lost the will or the vision to demand that which is good? Such thinking, in the words of the ecologist Paul Shepard, "idealizes life with only its head out of water, inches above the limits of toleration of the corruption of its own environment.... Why should we tolerate a diet of weak poisons, a home in insipid surroundings, a circle of acquaintances who are not quite our enemies, the noise of motors with just enough relief to prevent insanity? Who would want to live in a world which is just not quite fatal?"

Yet such a world is pressed upon us. The crusade to create a chemically sterile, insect-free world seems to have engendered a fanatic zeal on the part of many specialists and most of the so-called control agencies. On every hand there is evidence that those engaged in spraying operations exercise a ruthless power. "The regulatory entomologists...function as prosecutor, judge and jury, tax assessor and collector and sheriff to enforce the own orders," said Connecticut entomologist Neely Turner. The most flagrant abuses go unchecked in both state and federal agencies.

It is not my contention that chemical insecticides must never be used. I do contend that we have put poisonous and biologically potent chemicals indiscriminately into the hands of persons largely or wholly ignorant of their potentials for harm. We have subjected enormous numbers of people to contact with these poisons, without their consent and often without their knowledge. If the Bill of Rights contains no guarantee that a citizen shall be secure against lethal poisons distributed either by private individuals or by public officials, it is surely only because our forefathers, despite their considerable wisdom and foresight, could conceive of no such problem.

I contend, furthermore, that we have allowed these chemicals to be used with little or no advance investigation of their effect on soil, water, wildlife, and man himself. Future generations are unlikely to condone our lack of prudent concern for the integrity of the natural world that supports all life.

There is still very limited awareness of the nature of the threat. This is an era of specialists, each of whom sees his own problem and is unaware of or intolerant of the larger frame into which it fits. It is also an era dominated by industry, in which the right to make a dollar at whatever cost is seldom challenged. When the public protests, confronted with some obvious evidence of damaging results of pesticide applications, it is fed little tranquilizing pills of half truth. We urgently need an end to these false assurances, to the sugar coating of unpalatable facts. It is the public that is being asked to assume the risks that the insect controllers calculate. The public must decide whether it wishes to continue on the present road, and it can do so only when in full possession of the facts. In the words of Jean Rostand, "The obligation to endure gives us the right to know."

# 30
# Garrett Hardin (1915–    )

Garrett Hardin was a professor of biology and human ecology at the University of California at Santa Barbara for over thirty years from 1948 until his retirement in 1978. He has been both praised for addressing politically sensitive environmental issues and roundly criticized for his extreme solutions to those problems. His best known essay, "The Tragedy of the Commons," is one of the most frequently cited scientific papers in America; since its publication in 1968, it has appeared in over one hundred anthologies. In it Hardin argued that overpopulation inexorably leads to less individual freedom. This is so because population pressures result in overutilization of the earth's "commons"—its oceans, lakes, forests, wildernesses—and consequently these become polluted. To solve the pollution problem, and to avert worldwide ecological disaster, humans must make a social contract that involves "mutual coercion, mutually agreed upon." This entails new rules, particularly in the area of population control. Even before *Roe v. Wade* (1973), Hardin was a staunch advocate of legalized abortion.

In another well-known and controversial essay, "Lifeboat Ethics," published in 1974, Hardin argued against U.S. foreign assistance to poor countries. A lifeboat almost full of rich nations would only capsize by letting aboard all the world's poor. Providing assistance, he argued, only aggravates the poor nations' population problems; it is therefore rational for us to "row away." Hardin also linked current U.S. immigration policy to the metaphor of the lifeboat. Arguing that immigration is simply another way of overloading the boat, Hardin proposed strict controls on the number of immigrants allowed to enter the country.

Believing that society resists certain ideas because they are socially taboo, Hardin has labeled himself a "stalker of the wild taboos"—the title of his 1973 book. Acknowledging that many people view him as heartless and find his ideas abhorrent, Hardin defends himself by saying that he is an interdisciplinary iconoclast in search of solutions for living in a world containing an unprecedented number of people: at present, approximately 6 billion.

---

## "FREEDOM IN A COMMONS BRINGS RUIN TO ALL"*

The population problem has no technical solution; it requires a fundamental extension in morality....

---

*Garrett Hardin. 1968. "The Tragedy of the Commons." *Science* 162:1243–1248. Copyright © 1968 by the American Association for the Advancement of Science. Reprinted with permission. Footnotes are omitted.

At the end of a thoughtful article on the future of nuclear war, Wiesner and York concluded that: "Both sides in the arms race are...confronted by the dilemma of steadily increasing military power and steadily decreasing national security. *It is our considered professional judgment that this dilemma has no technical solution.* If the great powers continue to look for solutions in the area of science and technology only, the result will be to worsen the situation."

I would like to focus your attention not on the subject of the article (national security in a nuclear world) but on the kind of conclusion they reached, namely that there is no technical solution to the problem. An implicit and almost universal assumption of discussions published in professional and semipopular scientific journals is that the problem under discussion has a technical solution. A technical solution may be defined as one that requires a change only in the techniques of the natural sciences, demanding little or nothing in the way of change in human values or ideas of morality.

In our day (though not in earlier times) technical solutions are always welcome. Because of previous failures in prophecy, it takes courage to assert that a desired technical solution is not possible. Wiesner and York exhibited this courage; publishing in a science journal, they insisted that the solution to the problem was not to be found in the natural sciences. They cautiously qualified their statement with the phrase, "It is our considered professional judgment...." Whether they were right or not is not the concern of the present article. Rather, the concern here is with the important concept of a class of human problems which can be called "no technical solution problems," and, more specifically, with the identification and discussion of one of these.

It is easy to show that the class is not a null class. Recall the game of tick-tack-toe. Consider the problem, "How can I win the game of tick-tack-toe?" It is well known that I cannot, if I assume (in keeping with the conventions of game theory) that my opponent understands the game perfectly. Put another way, there is no "technical solution" to the problem. I can win only by giving a radical meaning to the word "win." I can hit my opponent over the head; or I can drug him; or I can falsify the records. Every way in which I "win" involves, in some sense, an abandonment of the game, as we intuitively understand it. (I can also, of course, openly abandon the game—refuse to play it. This is what most adults do.)

The class of "No technical solution problems" has members. My thesis is that the "population problem," as conventionally conceived, is a member of this class. How it is conventionally conceived needs some comment. It is fair to say that most people who anguish over the population problem are trying to find a way to avoid the evils of overpopulation without relinquishing any of the privileges they now enjoy. They think that farming the seas or developing new strains of wheat will solve the problem—technologically. I try to show here that the solution they seek cannot be found. The population problem cannot be solved in a technical way, any more than can the problem of winning the game of tick-tack-toe.

...We can make little progress in working toward optimum population size until we explicitly exorcize the spirit of Adam Smith in the field of practical demography. In economic affairs, *The Wealth of Nations* (1776) popularized the "invisible hand," the idea that an individual who "intends only his own gain," is, as it were, "led by an invisible hand to promote…the public interest." Adam Smith did not assert that this was invariably true, and perhaps neither did any of his followers. But he contributed to a dominant tendency of thought that has ever since interfered with positive action based on rational analysis, namely, the tendency to assume that decisions reached individually will, in fact, be the best decisions for an entire society. If this assumption is correct it justifies the continuance of our present policy of laissez-faire in reproduction. If it is correct we can assume that men will control their individual fecundity so as to produce the optimum population. If the assumption is not correct, we need to reexamine our individual freedoms to see which ones are defensible.…

The rebuttal to the invisible hand in population control is to be found in a scenario first sketched in a little-known pamphlet in 1833 by a mathematical amateur named William Forster Lloyd (1794–1852). We may well call it "the tragedy of the commons," using the word "tragedy" as the philosopher Whitehead used it: "The essence of dramatic tragedy is not unhappiness. It resides in the solemnity of the remorseless working of things." He then goes on to say, "This inevitableness of destiny can only be illustrated in terms of human life by incidents which in fact involve unhappiness. For it is only by them that the futility of escape can be made evident in the drama."

The tragedy of the commons develops in this way. Picture a pasture open to all. It is to be expected that each herdsman will try to keep as many cattle as possible on the commons. Such an arrangement may work reasonably satisfactorily for centuries because tribal wars, poaching, and disease keep the numbers of both man and beast well below the carrying capacity of the land. Finally, however, comes the day of reckoning, that is, the day when the long-desired goal of social stability becomes a reality. At this point, the inherent logic of the commons remorselessly generates tragedy.

As a rational being, each herdsman seeks to maximize his gain. Explicitly or implicitly, more or less consciously, he asks, "What is the utility *to me* of adding one more animal to my herd?" This utility has one negative and one positive component.

1) The positive component is a function of the increment of one animal. Since the herdsman receives all the proceeds from the sale of the additional animal, the positive utility is nearly +1.

2) The negative component is a function of the additional overgrazing created by one more animal. Since, however, the effects of overgrazing are shared by all the herdsmen, the negative utility for any particular decision-making herdsman is only a fraction of −1.

Adding together the component partial utilities, the rational herdsman concludes that the only sensible course for him to pursue is to add another animal to his herd. And another; and another.… But this is the conclusion reached by each and every rational herdsman sharing a commons. Therein is the tragedy. Each man is locked into a system that compels him to increase his herd without limit—in a world that is limited. Ruin is the destination toward which all men rush, each pursuing his own best interest in a society that believes in the freedom of the commons. Freedom in a commons brings ruin to all.

Some would say that this is a platitude. Would that it were! In a sense, it was learned thousands of years ago, but natural selection favors the forces of psychological denial. The individual benefits as an individual from his ability to deny the truth even though society as a whole, of which he is a part, suffers. Education can counteract the natural tendency to do the wrong thing, but the inexorable succession of generations requires that the basis for this knowledge be constantly refreshed....

In an approximate way, the logic of the commons has been understood for a long time, perhaps since the discovery of agriculture or the invention of private property in real estate. But it is understood mostly only in special cases which are not sufficiently generalized. Even at this late date, cattlemen leasing national land on the western ranges demonstrate no more than an ambivalent understanding, in constantly pressuring federal authorities to increase the head count to the point where overgrazing produces erosion and weed-dominance. Likewise, the oceans of the world continue to suffer from the survival of the philosophy of the commons. Maritime nations still respond automatically to the shibboleth of the "freedom of the seas." Professing to believe in the "inexhaustible resources of the oceans," they bring species after species of fish and whales closer to extinction.

The National Parks present another instance of the working out of the tragedy of the commons. At present, they are open to all, without limit. The parks themselves are limited in extent—there is only one Yosemite Valley— whereas population seems to grow without limit. The values that visitors seek in the parks are steadily eroded. Plainly, we must soon cease to treat the parks as commons or they will be of no value to anyone.

What shall we do? We have several options. We might sell them off as private property. We might keep them as public property, but allocate the right to enter them. The allocation might be on the basis of wealth, by the use of an auction system. It might be on the basis of merit, as defined by some agreed-upon standards. It might be by lottery. Or it might be on a first-come, first-served basis, administered to long queues. These, I think, are all the reasonable possibilities. They are all objectionable. But we must choose—or acquiesce in the destruction of the commons that we call our National Parks....

In a reverse way, the tragedy of the commons reappears in problems of pollution. Here it is not a question of taking something out of the commons, but of putting something in—sewage, or chemical, radioactive, and heat wastes into water; noxious and dangerous fumes into the air; and distracting and unpleasant advertising signs into the line of sight. The calculations of utility are much the same as before. The rational man finds that his share of the cost of the wastes he discharges into the commons is less than the cost of purifying his wastes before releasing them. Since this is true for everyone, we are locked into a system of "fouling our own nest," so long as we behave only as independent, rational, free-enterprisers.

The tragedy of the commons as a food basket is averted by private property, or something formally like it. But the air and waters surrounding us cannot readily be fenced, and so the tragedy of the commons as a cesspool must be prevented by different means, by coercive laws or taxing devices that make it cheaper for the polluter to treat his pollutants than to discharge them untreated. We have not progressed as far with the solution of this problem as we have with the first. Indeed, our particular concept of private property, which deters us from exhausting the positive resources of the earth, favors pollution. The owner of a factory on the bank of a stream—whose property extends to the middle of the stream—often has difficulty seeing why it is not his natural right to muddy the waters flowing past his door. The law, always behind the times, requires elaborate stitching and fitting to adapt it to this newly perceived aspect of the commons.

The pollution problem is a consequence of population. It did not much matter how a lonely American frontiersman disposed of his waste. "Flowing water purifies itself every 10 miles," my grandfather used to say, and the myth was near enough to the truth when he was a boy, for there were not too many people. But as population became denser, the natural chemical and biological recycling processes became overloaded, calling for a redefinition of property rights....

It is a mistake to think that we can control the breeding of mankind in the long run by an appeal to conscience....

The social arrangements that produce responsibility are arrangements that create coercion, of some sort. Consider bank-robbing. The man who takes money from a bank acts as if the bank were a commons. How do we prevent such action? Certainly not by trying to control his behavior solely by a verbal appeal to his sense of responsibility. Rather than rely on propaganda we follow Frankel's lead and insist that a bank is not a commons; we seek the definite social arrangements that will keep it from becoming a commons. That we thereby infringe on the freedom of would-be robbers we neither deny nor regret.

The morality of bank-robbing is particularly easy to understand because we accept complete prohibition of this activity. We are willing to say "Thou shalt not rob banks," without providing for exceptions. But temperance also can be created by coercion. Taxing is a good coercive device. To keep downtown shoppers temperate in their use of parking space we introduce parking meters for short periods, and traffic fines for longer ones. We need not actually forbid a citizen to park as long as he wants to; we need merely make it increasingly expensive for him to do so. Not prohibition, but carefully biased options are what we offer him. A Madison Avenue man might call this persuasion; I prefer the greater candor of the word coercion.

Coercion is a dirty word to most liberals now, but it need not forever be so. As with the four-letter words, its dirtiness can be cleansed away by exposure to the light, by saying it over and over without apology or embarrassment. To many, the word coercion implies arbitrary decisions of distant and irresponsible bureaucrats; but this is not a necessary part of its meaning. The only kind of coercion I recommend is mutual coercion, mutually agreed upon by the majority of the people affected.

To say that we mutually agree to coercion is not to say that we are required to enjoy it, or even to pretend we enjoy it. Who enjoys taxes? We all grumble about them. But we accept compulsory taxes because we recognize that voluntary taxes would favor the conscienceless. We institute and (grumblingly) support taxes and other coercive devices to escape the horror of the commons.

An alternative to the commons need not be perfectly just to be preferable. With real estate and other material goods, the alternative we have chosen is the institution of private property coupled with legal inheritance. Is this system perfectly just? As a genetically trained biologist I deny that it is. It seems to me that, if there are to be differences in individual inheritance, legal possession should be perfectly correlated with biological inheritance—that those who are biologically more fit to be the custodians of property and power should legally inherit more. But genetic recombination continually makes a mockery of the doctrine of "like father, like son" implicit in our laws of legal inheritance. An idiot can inherit millions, and a trust fund can keep his estate intact. We must admit that our legal system of private property plus inheritance is unjust—but we put up with it because we are not convinced, at the moment, that anyone has invented a better system. The alternative of the commons is too horrifying to contemplate. Injustice is preferable to total ruin.

It is one of the peculiarities of the warfare between reform and the status quo that it is thoughtlessly governed by a double standard. Whenever a reform measure is proposed it is often defeated when its opponents triumphantly discover a flaw in it. As Kingsley Davis has pointed out, worshipers of the status quo sometimes imply that no reform is possible without unanimous agreement, an implication contrary to historical fact. As nearly as I can make out, automatic rejection of proposed reforms is based on one of two unconscious assumptions: (i) that the status quo is perfect; or (ii) that the choice we face is between reform and no action; if the proposed reform is imperfect, we presumably should take no action at all, while we wait for a perfect proposal.

But we can never do nothing. That which we have done for thousands of years is also action. It also produces evils. Once we are aware that the status quo is action, we can then compare its discoverable advantages and disadvantages with the predicted advantages and disadvantages of the proposed reform, discounting as best we can for our lack of experience. On the basis of such a comparison, we can make a rational decision which will not involve the unworkable assumption that only perfect systems are tolerable....

Perhaps the simplest summary of this analysis of man's population problems is this: the commons, if justifiable at all, is justifiable only under conditions of low-population density. As the human population has increased, the commons has had to be abandoned in one aspect after another.

First we abandoned the commons in food gathering, enclosing farm land and restricting pastures and hunting and fishing areas. These restrictions are still not complete throughout the world.

Somewhat later we saw that the commons as a place for waste disposal would also have to be abandoned. Restrictions on the disposal of domestic sewage are widely accepted in the Western world; we are still struggling to close the commons to pollution by automobiles, factories, insecticide sprayers, fertilizing operations, and atomic energy installations.

In a still more embryonic state is our recognition of the evils of the commons in matters of pleasure. There is almost no restriction on the propagation of sound waves in the public medium. The shopping public is assaulted with mindless music, without its consent. Our government is paying out billions of dollars to create supersonic transport which will disturb 50,000 people for every one person who is whisked from coast to coast 3 hours faster. Advertisers muddy the airwaves of radio and television and pollute the view of travelers. We are a long way from outlawing the commons in matters of pleasure. Is this because our Puritan inheritance makes us view pleasure as something of a sin, and pain (that is, the pollution of advertising) as the sign of virtue?

Every new enclosure of the commons involves the infringement of somebody's personal liberty. Infringements made in the distant past are accepted because no contemporary complains of a loss. It is the newly proposed infringements that we vigorously oppose; cries of "rights" and "freedom" fill the air. But what does "freedom" mean? When men mutually agreed to pass laws against robbing, mankind became more free, not less so. Individuals locked into the logic of the commons are free only to bring on universal ruin; once they see the necessity of mutual coercion, they become free to pursue other goals. I believe it was Hegel who said, "Freedom is the recognition of necessity."

The most important aspect of necessity that we must now recognize, is the necessity of abandoning the commons in breeding. No technical solution can rescue us from the misery of overpopulation. Freedom to breed will bring ruin to all. At the moment, to avoid hard decisions many of us are tempted to propagandize for conscience and responsible parenthood. The temptation must be resisted, because an appeal to independently acting consciences selects for the disappearance of all conscience in the long run, and an increase in anxiety in the short.

The only way we can preserve and nurture other and more precious freedoms is by relinquishing the freedom to breed, and that very soon. "Freedom is the recognition of necessity"—and it is the role of education to reveal to all the necessity of abandoning the freedom to breed. Only so, can we put an end to this aspect of the tragedy of the commons.

# 31
# Paul Ehrlich (1932–    )

Paul Ehrlich has been at the forefront of population debates since his 1968 best-selling book, *The Population Bomb,* made the Stanford University professor a talk-show celebrity and sought-after public speaker. Many of Ehrlich's ideas constitute a revival of eighteenth-century Malthusian thought: That most people, most of the time, will suffer from hunger and want, and that the only factors checking population growth are famine, disease, and war. In *The Population Bomb* Ehrlich predicted that all these dreadful effects of the population explosion of the twentieth century were about to be realized. Ehrlich's scenarios detailed the awful future to come, including one scenario of thermonuclear war in which only cockroaches survive. Even his most optimistic forecast saw one-fifth of the planet's population starving by 1983.

Ehrlich lambasted people in positions of power for either ignoring the population problem or recommending ineffective solutions. He denounced the Catholic Church for its anti-birth control stance, and condemned the U.S. Department of Agriculture for its red ant eradication program, citing it as an example of shortsighted pest control. He recommended creation of a Department of Population and Environment to coordinate and enforce stringent population control programs, and he recommended that the United States insist that underdeveloped nations implement population control programs before receiving food aid. He also helped found Zero Population Growth (ZPG). Ehrlich's later writings softened somewhat, but he has not abandoned his original thesis.

In addition to Barry Commoner, one of Ehrlich's most vociferous critics, was University of Maryland economist Julian Simon. Simon believed that humans are infinitely innovative, and that this intelligence, coupled with technological advances and free markets, will continually make the world a better place for humans. Simon argued that more people means greater productivity, and greater productivity means more innovation— eventually leading to greater wealth and prosperity for all. In 1980 Simon challenged Ehrlich's predictions of imminent scarcity, and bet him that the price (hence scarcity) of a number of critical minerals would be less a decade hence, in 1990. Ehrlich lost the bet. For population and technology "optimists" such as Simon, Ehrlich's "doomsday" scenarios and "repressive" solutions exemplify the worst features of the modern environmental movement. Others, however, remain convinced that overpopulation is the fundamental problem.

# "POPULATION CONTROL IS THE ONLY ANSWER"*

The battle to feed all of humanity is over. In the 1970's the world will undergo famines—hundreds of millions of people are going to starve to death in spite of any crash programs embarked upon now. At this late date nothing can prevent a substantial increase in the world death rate, although many lives could be saved through dramatic programs to "stretch" the carrying capacity of the earth by increasing food production. But these programs will only provide a stay of execution unless they are accompanied by determined and successful efforts at population control. Population control is the conscious regulation of the numbers of human beings to meet the needs, not just of individual families, but of society as a whole.

Nothing could be more misleading to our children than our present affluent society. They will inherit a totally different world, a world in which the standards, politics, and economics of the 1960's are dead. As the most powerful nation in the world today, *and its largest consumer*, the United States cannot stand isolated. We are today involved in the events leading to famine; tomorrow we may be destroyed by its consequences.

Our position requires that we take immediate action at home and promote effective action worldwide. We must have population control at home, hopefully through a system of incentives and penalties, but by compulsion if voluntary methods fail. We must use our political power to push other countries into programs which combine agricultural development and population control. And while this is being done we must take action to reverse the deterioration of our environment before population pressure permanently ruins our planet. The birth rate must be brought into balance with the death rate or mankind will breed itself into oblivion. We can no longer afford merely to treat the symptoms of the cancer of population growth; the cancer itself must be cut out. Population control is the only answer.

## The Problem

I have understood the population explosion intellectually for a long time. I came to understand it emotionally one stinking hot night in Delhi a couple of years ago. My wife and daughter and I were returning to our hotel in an ancient taxi. The seats were hopping with fleas. The only functional gear was third. As we crawled through the city, we entered a crowded slum area. The temperature was well over 100, and the air was a haze of dust and smoke. The streets seemed alive with people. People eating, people washing, people sleeping. People visiting, arguing, and screaming. People thrusting their hands through the taxi window, begging. People defecating and urinating. People clinging to buses. People herding animals. People, people, people,

---

*Paul Ehrlich. 1968. *The Population Bomb*. New York: Ballantine Books, pp. xi, 15–16, 132–142, 197–198. Reprinted with permission from Paul R. Ehrlich.

people. As we moved slowly through the mob, hand horn squawking, the dust, noise, heat, and cooking fires gave the scene a hellish aspect. Would we ever get to our hotel? All three of us were, frankly, frightened. It seemed that anything could happen—but, of course, nothing did. Old India hands will laugh at our reaction. We were just some overprivileged tourists, unaccustomed to the sights and sounds of India. Perhaps, but since that night I've known the *feel* of overpopulation.

*Getting Our House in Order*
The key to the whole business, in my opinion, is held by the United States. We are the most influential superpower; we are the richest nation in the world. At the same time we are also just one country on an ever-shrinking planet. It is obvious that we cannot exist unaffected by the fate of our fellows on the other end of the good ship Earth. If their end of the ship sinks, we shall at the very least have to put up with the spectacle of their drowning and listen to their screams. Communications satellites guarantee that we will be treated to the sights and sounds of mass starvation on the evening news, just as we now can see Viet Cong corpses being disposed of in living color and listen to the groans of our own wounded. We're unlikely, however, to get off with just our appetites spoiled and our consciences disturbed. We are going to be sitting on top of the only food surpluses available for distribution, and those surpluses will not be large. In addition, it is not unreasonable to expect our level of affluence to continue to increase over the next few years as the situation in the rest of the world grows ever more desperate. Can we guess what effect this growing disparity will have on our "shipmates" in the UDCs [under-developed countries]? Will they starve gracefully, without rocking the boat? Or will they attempt to overwhelm us in order to get what they consider to be their fair share?

We, of course, cannot remain affluent and isolated. At the moment the United States uses well over half of all the raw materials consumed each year. Think of it. Less than 1/15th of the population of the world requires more than all the rest to maintain its inflated position. If present trends continue, in 20 years we will be much less than 1/15th of the population, and yet we may use some 80% of the resources consumed. Our affluence depends heavily on many different kinds of imports: ferroalloys (metals used to make various kinds of steel), tin, bauxite (aluminum ore), rubber, and so forth. Will other countries, many of them in the grip of starvation and anarchy, still happily supply these materials to a nation that cannot give them food? Even the technological optimists don't think we can free ourselves of the need for imports in the near future, so we're going to be up against it. But, then, at least our balance of payments should improve!

So, beside our own serious population problem at home, we are intimately involved in the world crisis. We are involved through our import-export situation. We are involved because of the possibilities of global ecological catastrophe, of global pestilence, and of global thermonuclear war. Also, we are involved because of the humanitarian feelings of most Americans.

We are going to face some extremely difficult but unavoidable decisions. By how much, and at what environmental risk, should we increase our food production in an attempt to feed the starving? How much should we reduce the grain-finishing of beef in order to have more food for export? How will we react when asked to balance the lives of a million Latin Americans against, say, a 30 cent per pound rise in the average price of beef? Will we be willing to slaughter our dogs and cats in order to divert pet food protein to the starving masses in Asia? If these choices are presented one at a time, out of context, I predict that our behavior will be "selfish." Men do not seem to be able to focus emotionally on distant or long-term events. Immediacy seems to be necessary to elicit "selfless" responses. Few Americans could sit in the same room with a child and watch it starve to death. But the death of several million children this year from starvation is a distant, impersonal, hard-to-grasp event. You will note that I put quotes around "selfish" and "selfless." The words describe the behavior only out of context. The "selfless" actions necessary to aid the rest of the world and stabilize the population are our only hope for survival. The "selfish" ones work only toward our destruction. Ways must be found to bring home to all the American people the reality of the threat to their way of life—indeed to their very lives.

Obviously our first step must be to immediately establish and advertise drastic policies designed to bring our own population size under control. We must define a goal of a stable optimum population size for the United States and display our determination to move rapidly toward that goal. Such a move does two things at once. It improves our chances of obtaining the kind of country and society we all want, and it sets an example for the world. The second step is very important, as we also are going to have to adopt some very tough foreign policy positions relative to population control, and we must do it from a psychologically strong position. We will want to disarm one group of opponents at the outset: those who claim that we wish others to stop breeding while we go merrily ahead. We want our propaganda based on "do as we do"—not "do as we say."

So the first task is population control at home. How do we go about it? Many of my colleagues feel that some sort of compulsory birth regulation would be necessary to achieve such control. One plan often mentioned involves the addition of temporary sterilants to water supplies or staple food. Doses of the antidote would be carefully rationed by the government to produce the desired population size. Those of you who are appalled at such a suggestion can rest easy. The option isn't even open to us, thanks to the criminal inadequacy of biomedical research in this area. If the choice now is either such additives or catastrophe, we shall have catastrophe. It might be possible to develop such population control tools although the task would not be simple. Either the additive would have to operate equally well and with minimum side effects against both sexes, or some way would have to be found to direct it only to one sex and shield the other. Feeding potent male hormones to the whole population might sterilize and defeminize the women, while the upset in the male population and society as a whole can be well imagined. In addition, care would have to be taken to see to it that the sterilizing substance did not reach livestock, either through water or garbage.

Technical problems aside, I suspect you'll agree with me that society would probably dissolve before sterilants were added to the water supply by the government. Just consider the fluoridation controversy! Some other way will have to be found. Perhaps the most workable system would be to reverse the government's present system of encouraging reproduction and replace it with a series of financial rewards and penalties designed to discourage reproduction. For instance, we could reverse our present system of tax exemptions. Since taxes in essence purchase services from the government and since large families require more services, why not make them pay for them? The present system was designed at a time when larger population size was not viewed as undesirable. But no sane society wants to promote larger population size today. The new system would be quite simple (but, of course, not retroactive!). For each of the first two children, an additional $600 would be added to the "taxable income" figure from which the taxes are calculated. For each subsequent child, $1,200 would be added. In order to prevent hardship, minimum levels would be established guaranteeing each family enough for food, clothing, and shelter. Therefore a family with three children and only $4,000 income might pay little or no taxes, but parents making $25,000 who had ten children would pay for their reproductive irresponsibility by forking over the taxes on $35,800. In short, the plush life would be difficult to attain for those with large families—which is as it should be, since they are getting their pleasure from their children, who are being supported in part by more responsible members of society.

On top of the income tax reversal, luxury taxes should be placed on layettes, cribs, diapers, diaper services, expensive toys, always with the proviso that the essentials be available without penalty to the poor (just as free food now is). There would, of course, have to be considerable experimenting on the level of financial pressure necessary to achieve the population goals. To the penalties could be added some incentives. A governmental "first marriage grant" could be awarded each couple in which the age of both partners was 25 or more. "Responsibility prizes" could be given to each couple for each five years of childless marriage, or to each man who accepted irreversible sterilization (vasectomy) before having more than two children. Or special lotteries might be held—tickets going only to the childless. Adoption could be subsidized and made a simple procedure. Considering the savings in school buildings, pollution control, unemployment compensation, and the like, these grants would be a money-making proposition. But even if they weren't, the price would be a small one to pay for saving our nation.

Obviously, such measures would need coordination by a powerful governmental agency. A federal Department of Population and Environment (DPE) should be set up with the power to take whatever steps are necessary to establish a reasonable population size in the United States and to put an end to the steady deterioration of our environment. The DPE would be given ample funds to support research in the areas of population control and environmental quality. In the first area it would promote intensive investigation of new techniques of birth control, possibly leading to the development of mass sterilizing agents such as were discussed above. This research will not only give us better methods to use at home; they are absolutely essential if we are to help the UDCs to control their populations. Many peoples lack the incentive to use the Pill. A program requiring daily attention just will not work. This is one reason why a Papal decision to accept the Pill but not other methods of birth control would be only a small step in the right direction. The DPE also would encourage more research on human sex determination, for if a simple method could be found to guarantee that first-born children were males, then population control problems in many areas would be somewhat eased. In our country and elsewhere couples with only female children "keep trying" in hope of a son.

Two other functions of the DPE would be to aid Congress in developing legislation relating to population and environment, and to inform the public of the needs for such legislation. Some of these needs are already apparent. We need a federal law guaranteeing the right of *any* woman to have an abortion if it is approved by a physician. We need federal legislation guaranteeing the right to voluntary sterilization for both sexes and protecting physicians who perform such operations from legal harassment. We need a federal law requiring sex education in schools—sex education that includes discussion of the need for regulating the birth rate and of the techniques of birth control. Such education should begin at the earliest age recommended by those with professional competence in this area—certainly before junior high school....

Fortunately, there are hopeful signs that the anti-human notions that have long kept Western society in a state of sexual repression no longer hold sway over many of our citizens. With a rational atmosphere mankind should be able to work out the problems of de-emphasizing the reproductive role of sex. These problems include finding substitutes for the sexual satisfaction which many women derive from childbearing and finding substitutes for the ego satisfaction that often accompanies excessive fatherhood. A rational atmosphere should also make it easier to deal with the problems of venereal disease and of illegitimacy. The role of marriage would become one of providing the proper environment for the rearing of wanted children. All too often today marriage either provides a "license" for sexual activity or a way of legitimizing the results of premarital sexual activity.

If we take the proper steps in education, legislation, and research, we should be able in a generation to have a population thoroughly enjoying its sexual activity, while raising smaller numbers of physically and mentally healthier children. The population should be relatively free of the horrors created today by divorce, illegal abortion, venereal disease, and the psychological pressures of a sexually repressive and repressed society. Much, of course, needs to be done, but support for action in these directions is becoming more and more common in the medical profession, the clergy, and the public at large. If present trends can be continued, we should be able to minimize and in some cases reverse social pressures against population control at home and to influence those abroad in the same direction....

*What If I'm Wrong?*
Any scientist lives constantly with the possibility that he may be wrong. If he asks important questions, it is inevitable that some of the time he will

come up with wrong answers. Many are caught before they see print; many are enshrined in the scientific literature. I've published a few myself, as some of my colleagues would gladly testify. Therefore it is important for you to consider that I, and many of the people who share my views, are just plain wrong, that we are alarmists, that technology or a miraculous change in human behavior or a totally unanticipated miracle in some other form will "save the day." Naturally, I find this highly unlikely; otherwise I would not have written this book. But the possibility must be considered.

To cover this contingency, I would like to propose an analogue to Pascal's famous wager. Pascal considered the only safe course for a man was to believe in God. If there was no God, it made no difference, but if there was, you ended up in heaven. In other words, play it safe. If I'm right, we will save the world. If I'm wrong, people will still be better fed, better housed, and happier, thanks to our efforts.

Will anything be lost if it turns out later that we can support a much larger population than seems possible today? Suppose we move to stabilize the size of the human population after the "time of famines" at two billion people, and we achieve that goal by 2050. Suppose that in 2051 someone invents a machine that will produce nutritious food or anything else man wants in limitless quantities out of nothing. Assume also that in 2051 mankind decides that the Earth is underpopulated with just two billion people. Men decide that they want more company. Fortunately, people can be produced in vast quantities by unskilled labor who enjoy their world. In about 500 years, with the proper encouragement of reproduction, the Earth could be populated to a density of about 100 individuals per square foot of surface (land and sea). That is a density that should please the loneliest person.

Remember, above all, that more than half of the world is in misery now. That alone should be enough to galvanize us into action, regardless of the exact dimensions of the future disaster now staring *Homo sapiens* in the face.

# 32
# Cesar Chavez (1927–1993)

During the Depression, when Cesar Chavez was ten, his family lost their farm in Yuma, Arizona. They became migrant workers, moving from one farm labor camp in Arizona and California to another. Cesar Chavez grew up experiencing first-hand the kind of poverty and oppression John Steinbeck wrote about in *The Grapes of Wrath*, and which the famous reporter Edward R. Murrow later depicted in his 1959 television documentary, "Harvest of Shame."

In 1952 Chavez joined the Community Service Organization, a self-help organization founded by political activist Saul Alinsky. He became a full-time organizer, helping in voter registration drives, and fighting to end discrimination against Chicanos. In 1962 Chavez moved to Delano, in California's San Joaquin Valley, where he founded the National Farm Workers Association: It was the first successful effort at organizing migrant farm workers. By 1965 Chavez's union had joined with the AFL-CIO in a strike against California's powerful grape growers. In 1966 the two unions merged to form the United Farm Workers (UFW). Within a year of the strike the wine-grape growers agreed to terms with the union.

However, the table-grape growers proved more intransigent; they circumvented the strike by importing Mexican workers. In 1968 Chavez countered by launching a successful national boycott of table grapes. By 1970 most of the table-grape growers had signed contracts with the UFW. Chavez then launched a lettuce boycott. The success of Chavez's union, however, was sapped by a jurisdictional dispute with the Teamster's Union, which was not settled until 1977 when the two agreed that the UFW would have organizing jurisdiction over the field workers.

In 1988 Chavez began a fast to protest the heavy use of pesticides on the nation's farmlands. Their use, he declared, "threatens to choke out the life of our people and also the life system that supports us all. This solution to this deadly crisis will not be found in the arrogance of the powerful, but in solidarity with the weak and helpless."

Chavez emerged in the 1960s as the most compelling voice of the Chicano people, and remained so until his death in 1993. His stature within the movement came in part because he himself had been a migrant worker, in part because of his unwavering commitment to nonviolence (like his contemporary, Martin Luther King), and in part because of his ability to mobilize clergymen, civil rights groups, and political leaders behind what many saw as a just and urgent cause.

The selection below, Chavez's 1969 Good Friday "Letter from Delano," was reprinted in the *Christian Century* and the *National Catholic Reporter*. To this day, Chavez's United Farm Workers fights on behalf of farm workers' rights, including such environmental issues as occupational health, sustainable agriculture, pesticide use, and water conservation.

# "WE ARE NOT BEASTS OF BURDEN... WE ARE MEN"*

Dear Mr. Barr [President, California Grape and Tree Fruit League]:

I am sad to hear about your accusations in the press that our union movement and table grape boycott have been successful because we have used violence and terror tactics. If what you say is true, I have been a failure and should withdraw from the struggle; but you are left with the awesome moral responsibility, before God and man, to come forward with whatever information you have so that corrective action can begin at once. If for any reason you fail to come forth to substantiate your charges, then you must be held responsible for committing violence against us, albeit violence of the tongue. I am convinced that you as a human being did not mean what you said but rather acted hastily under pressure from the public relations firm that has been hired to try to counteract the tremendous moral force of our movement. How many times we ourselves have felt the need to lash out in anger and bitterness.

Today on Good Friday 1969 we remember the life and the sacrifice of Martin Luther King, Jr., who gave himself totally to the nonviolent struggle for peace and justice. In his "Letter from Birmingham Jail" Dr. King describes better than I could our hopes for the strike and boycott: "Injustice must be exposed, with all the tension its exposure creates, to the light of human conscience and the air of national opinion before it can be cured." For our part I admit that we have seized upon every tactic and strategy consistent with the morality of our cause to expose that injustice and thus to heighten the sensitivity of the American conscience so that farm workers will have without bloodshed their own union and the dignity of bargaining with their agribusiness employers. By lying about the nature of our movement, Mr. Barr, you are working against nonviolent social change. Unwittingly perhaps, you may unleash that other force which our union by discipline and deed, censure and education has sought to avoid, that panacean short-cut: that senseless violence which honors no color, class or neighborhood.

You must understand—I must make you understand—that our membership and the hopes and aspirations of the hundreds of thousands of the poor and dispossessed that have been raised on our account are, above all, human beings, no better and no worse than any other cross-section of human society; we are not saints because we are poor, but by the same measure neither are we immoral. We are men and women who have suffered and endured much, and not only because of our abject poverty but because we have been kept poor. The colors of our skins, the languages of our cultural

*Cesar Chavez. 1969. "Letter from Delano," *Christian Century* 86 (17) pp. 539–540. Copyright © 1969 Christian Century Foundation. Reprinted with permission from the April 23, 1969, issue of the *Christian Century*.

and native origins, the lack of formal education, the exclusion from the democratic process, the numbers of our slain in recent wars—all these burdens generation after generation have sought to demoralize us, to break our human spirit. But God knows that we are not beasts of burden, agricultural implements or rented slaves; we are men. And mark this well, Mr. Barr, we are men locked in a death struggle against man's inhumanity to man in the industry that you represent. And this struggle itself gives meaning to our life and ennobles our dying.

As your industry has experienced, our strikers here in Delano and those who represent us throughout the world are well trained for this struggle. They have been under the gun, they have been kicked and beaten and herded by dogs, they have been cursed and ridiculed, they have been stripped and chained and jailed, they have been sprayed with the poisons used in the vineyards; but they have been taught not to lie down and die nor to flee in shame, but to resist with every ounce of human endurance and spirit. To resist not with retaliation in kind but to overcome with love and compassion, with ingenuity and creativity, with hard work and longer hours, with stamina and patient tenacity, with truth and public appeal, with friends and allies, with mobility and discipline, with politics and law, and with prayer and fasting. They were not trained in a month or even a year; after all, this new harvest season will mark our fourth full year of strike and even now we continue to plan and prepare for the years to come. Time accomplishes for the poor what money does for the rich.

This is not to pretend that we have everywhere been successful enough or that we have not made mistakes. And while we do not belittle or underestimate our adversaries—for they are the rich and the powerful and they possess the land—we are not afraid nor do we cringe from the confrontation. We welcome it! We have planned for it. We know that our cause is just, that history is a story of social revolution, and that the poor shall inherit the land.

Once again, I appeal to you as the representative of your industry and as a man. I ask you to recognize and bargain with our union before the economic pressure of the boycott and strike takes an irrevocable toll; but if not, I ask you to at least sit down with us to discuss the safeguards necessary to keep our historical struggle free of violence. I make this appeal because as one of the leaders of our nonviolent movement, I know and accept my responsibility for preventing, if possible, the destruction of human life and property. For these reasons and knowing of Gandhi's admonition that fasting is the last resort in place of the sword, during a most critical time in our movement last February 1968 I undertook a 25-day fast. I repeat to you the principle enunciated to the membership at the start of the fast: if to build our union required the deliberate taking of life, either the life of a grower or his child, or the life of a farm worker or his child, then I choose not to see the union built.

Mr. Barr, let me be painfully honest with you. You must understand these things. We advocate militant nonviolence as our means for social revolution and to achieve justice for our people, but we are not blind or deaf to the desperate and moody winds of human frustration, impatience and rage that blow among us. Gandhi himself admitted that if his only choice were cowardice or violence, he would choose violence. Men are not angels, and time and tide wait for no man. Precisely because of these powerful human emotions, we have tried to involve masses of people in their own struggle. Participation and self-determination remain the best experience of freedom, and free men instinctively prefer democratic change and even protect the rights guaranteed to seek it. Only the enslaved in despair have need of violent overthrow.

This letter does not express all that is in my heart, Mr. Barr. But if it says nothing else it says that we do not hate you or rejoice to see your industry destroyed; we hate the agribusiness system that seeks to keep us enslaved, and we shall overcome and change it not by retaliation or bloodshed but by a determined nonviolent struggle carried on by those masses of farm workers who intend to be free and human.

# 33
# Barry Commoner (1917–    )

In 1970 *Time* magazine called Washington University biologist Barry Commoner the "Paul Revere of Ecology." For over fifty years he has been at the forefront of the environmental movement, calling public attention to environmentally destructive governmental policies, as well as to the multinational corporations' "colonialism" in the developing world. As a scientist himself, Commoner maintains that the scientific community has a moral obligation to inform citizens of all the facts concerning new scientific and technological developments. Scientists also have a leadership role to play. Practicing what he preached, Commoner was instrumental in forming several grass-roots organizations across the country. One of the first was the St. Louis Committee for Nuclear Information (later named the Committee for Environmental Information). The work of the committee played an important part in securing Senate ratification of the Limited Nuclear Test Ban Treaty of 1963. In 1980 Commoner was the Citizens' Party candidate for president.

Commoner's best known work, *The Closing Circle: Nature, Man, and Technology*, appeared in 1971 at the height of the environmental movement. Building upon the Native American world view that all life is circular, Commoner cogently argued that industrialized societies such as America have broken the circle. The circle, or ecosphere as it has come to be called, maintains a delicate balance of life, in which all elements are connected. But the creation of nuclear weapons and synthetic products in the twentieth century, and their widespread introduction into the environment, has caused an unprecedented ecological crisis. For Commoner, it is not population growth or merely affluence which is the root cause of environmental degradation: It is to be found in the nuclear and petrochemical industries that developed so hastily over the past few decades. Nature—including humankind—has not had time to assimilate these thousands of new products and processes.

In *The Closing Circle* Commoner also described "four laws of ecology." These easily remembered axioms are, even today, widely quoted: 1) *Everything is connected to everything else.* The ecosphere, and all ecosystems which make up the ecosphere, are comprised of interconnected organisms and processes. 2) *Everything must go somewhere.* This is a restatement of a basic law of physics: Matter is indestructible. It simply changes form. In nature there is no "waste"; one organism's excretion is another's food. 3) *Nature knows best.* Human technology cannot "improve" on nature because nature has had billions of years of "R&D" with which to perfect its systems. Any purely human-directed change within a natural system is likely to be detrimental to that system. 4) *There is no such thing as a free lunch.* Where there is a gain, there is also a loss (cost). A society's material wealth (i.e., GNP) should include its costs to the natural environment and to people's quality of life.

Barry Commoner published another important book in 1992, *Making Peace With the Planet*. Well into his eighties, he remained active in what has been a lifelong passion, the reconciliation of man and nature.

---

# "TO SURVIVE, WE MUST CLOSE THE CIRCLE"*

The over-all evidence seems clear. The chief reason for the environmental crisis that has engulfed the United States in recent years is the sweeping transformation of productive technology since World War II. The economy has grown enough to give the United States population about the same amount of basic goods, per capita, as it did in 1946. However, productive technologies with intense impacts on the environment have displaced less destructive ones. The environmental crisis is the inevitable result of this counterecological pattern of growth....

An understanding of the environmental crisis illuminates the need for social changes which contain, in their broader sweep, the solution of the environmental crisis as well.

But there is a sharp contrast between the logic of ecology and the state of the real world in which environmental problems are embedded. Despite the constant reference to palpable, everyday life experiences—foul air, polluted water, and rubbish heaps—there is an air of unreality about the environmental crisis. The complex chemistry of smog and fertilizers and their even more elaborate connections to economic, social, and political problems are concepts that deal with real features of modern life, but they remain *concepts*. What is real in our lives and, in contrast to the reasonable logic of ecology, chaotic and intractable, is the apparently hopeless inertia of the economic and political system; its fantastic agility in sliding away from the basic issues which logic reveals; the selfish maneuvering of those in power, and their willingness to use, often unwittingly, and sometimes cynically, even environmental deterioration as a step toward more political power; the frustration of the individual citizen confronted by this power and evasion; the confusion that we all feel in seeking a way out of the environmental morass. To bring environmental logic into contact with the real world we need to relate it to the over-all social, political, and economic forces that govern both our daily lives and the course of history.

We live in a time that is dominated by enormous technical power and extreme human need. The power is painfully self-evident in the megawattage of power plants, and in the megatonnage of nuclear bombs. The human need is evident in the sheer numbers of people now and soon to

---

*Barry Commoner. 1971. *The Closing Circle*. New York: Alfred A. Knopf, pp. 177, 293–300. Copyright © 1971 by Barry Commoner. Reprinted by permission from Alfred A. Knopf, a Division of Random House Inc.

be living, in the deterioration of their habitat, the earth, and in the tragic world-wide epidemic of hunger and want. The gap between brute power and human need continues to grow, as the power fattens on the same faulty technology that intensifies the need.

Everywhere in the world there is evidence of a deep-seated failure in the effort to use the competence, the wealth, the power at human disposal for the maximum good of human beings. The environmental crisis is a major example of this failure. For we are in an environmental crisis because the means by which we use the ecosphere to produce wealth are destructive of the ecosphere itself. The present system of production is self-destructive; the present course of human civilization is suicidal.

The environmental crisis is somber evidence of an insidious fraud hidden in the vaunted productivity and wealth of modern, technology-based society. This wealth has been gained by rapid short-term exploitation of the environmental system, but it has blindly accumulated a debt to nature (in the form of environmental destruction in developed countries and of population pressure in developing ones)—a debt so large and so pervasive that in the next generation it may, if unpaid, wipe out most of the wealth it has gained us. In effect, the account books of modern society are drastically out of balance, so that, largely unconsciously, a huge fraud has been perpetrated on the people of the world. The rapidly worsening course of environmental pollution is a warning that the bubble is about to burst, that the demand to pay the global debt may find the world bankrupt.

This does *not* necessarily mean that to survive the environmental crisis, the people of industrialized nations will need to give up their "affluent" way of life.... [T]his "affluence," as judged by conventional measures—such as GNP, power consumption, and production of metals— is itself an illusion. To a considerable extent it reflects ecologically faulty, socially wasteful types of production rather than the actual welfare of individual human beings. Therefore, the needed productive reforms can be carried out without seriously reducing the present level of *useful* goods available to the individual; and, at the same time, by controlling pollution the quality of life can be improved significantly.

There are, however, certain luxuries which the environmental crisis, and the approaching bankruptcy that it signifies, will, I believe, force us to give up. These are the *political* luxuries which have so long been enjoyed by those who can benefit from them: the luxury of allowing the wealth of the nation to serve preferentially the interests of so few of its citizens; of failing fully to inform citizens of what they need to know in order to exercise their right of political governance; of condemning as anathema any suggestion which re-examines basic economic values; of burying the issues revealed by logic in a morass of self-serving propaganda.

To resolve the environmental crisis, we shall need to forego, at last, the luxury of tolerating poverty, racial discrimination, and war. In our unwitting march toward ecological suicide we have run out of options. Now that the bill for the environmental debt has been presented, our options have become reduced to two: either the rational, social organization of the use and distribution of the earth's resources, or a new barbarism.

This iron logic has recently been made explicit by one of the most insistent proponents of population control, Garrett Hardin. Over recent years he has expounded on the "tragedy of the commons"—the view that the world ecosystem is like a common pasture where each individual, guided by a desire for personal gain, increases his herd until the pasture is ruined for all. Until recently, Hardin drew two rather general conclusions from this analogy: first, that "freedom in a commons brings ruin to all," and second, that the freedom which must be constrained if ruin is to be avoided is not the derivation of private gain from a social good (the commons), but rather "the freedom to breed."

Hardin's logic is clear, and follows the course outlined earlier: if we accept as unchangeable the present governance of a social good (the commons, or the ecosphere) by private need, then survival requires the immediate, drastic limitation of population. Very recently, Hardin has carried this course of reasoning to its logical conclusion; in an editorial in *Science*, he asserts:

> Every day we [i.e., Americans] are a smaller minority. We are increasing at only one per cent a year; the rest of the world increases twice as fast. By the year 2000, one person in twenty-four will be an American; in one hundred years only one in forty-six.... If the world is one great commons, in which all food is shared equally, then we are lost. Those who breed faster will replace the rest.... In the absence of breeding control a policy of "one mouth one meal" ultimately produces one totally miserable world. In a less than perfect world, the allocation of rights based on territory must be defended if a ruinous breeding race is to be avoided. It is unlikely that civilization and dignity can survive everywhere; but better in a few places than in none. Fortunate minorities must act as the trustees of a civilization that is threatened by uninformed good intentions.

Here, only faintly masked, is barbarism. It denies the equal right of all the human inhabitants of the earth to a humane life. It would condemn most of the people of the world to the material level of the barbarian, and the rest, the "fortunate minorities," to the moral level of the barbarian. Neither within Hardin's tiny enclaves of "civilization," nor in the larger world around them, would anything that we seek to preserve—the dignity and the humaneness of man, the grace of civilization—survive.

In the narrow options that are possible in a world gripped by environmental crisis, there is no apparent alternative between barbarism and the acceptance of the economic consequence of the ecological imperative—that the social, global nature of the ecosphere must determine a corresponding organization of the productive enterprises that depend on it.

One of the common responses to a recitation of the world's environmental ills is a deep pessimism, which is perhaps the natural aftermath to the shock of recognizing that the vaunted "progress" of modern civilization is only a thin cloak for global catastrophe. I am convinced however, that once we pass beyond the mere awareness of impending disaster and begin to understand *why* we have come to the present predicament, and where the alternative paths ahead can lead, there is reason to find in the very depths of the environmental crisis itself a source of optimism.

There is, for example, cause for optimism in the very complexity of the issues generated by the environmental crisis; once the links between the separate parts of the problem are perceived, it becomes possible to see new means of solving the whole. Thus, confronted separately, the need of developing nations for new productive enterprises, and the need of industrialized countries to reorganize theirs along ecologically sound lines, may seem hopelessly difficult. However, when the link between the two—the ecological significance of the introduction of synthetic substitutes for natural products—is recognized, ways of solving both can be seen. In the same way, we despair over releasing the grip of the United States on so much of the world's resources until it becomes clear how much of this "affluence" stresses the environment rather than contributes to human welfare. Then the very magnitude of the present United States share of the world's resources is a source of hope—for its reduction through ecological reform can then have a large and favorable impact on the desperate needs of the developing nations.

I find another source of optimism in the very nature of the environmental crisis. It is not the product of man's *biological* capabilities, which could not change in time to save us, but of his *social* actions—which are subject to much more rapid change. Since the environmental crisis is the result of the social mismanagement of the world's resources, then it can be resolved and man can survive in a humane condition when the social organization of man is brought into harmony with the ecosphere.

Here we can learn a basic lesson from nature: that nothing can survive on the planet unless it is a cooperative part of a larger, global whole. Life itself learned that lesson on the primitive earth. For it will be recalled that the earth's first living things, like modern man, consumed their nutritive base as they grew, converting the geochemical store of organic matter into wastes which could no longer serve their needs. Life, as it first appeared on the earth, was embarked on a linear, self-destructive course.

What saved life from extinction was the invention, in the course of evolution, of a new life-form which reconverted the waste of the primitive organisms into fresh, organic matter. The first photosynthetic organisms transformed the rapacious, linear course of life into the earth's first great ecological cycle. By closing the circle, they achieved what no living organism, alone, can accomplish—survival.

Human beings have broken out of the circle of life, driven not by biological need, but by the social organization which they have devised to "conquer" nature: means of gaining wealth that are governed by requirements conflicting with those which govern nature. The end result is the environmental crisis, a crisis of survival. Once more, to survive, we must close the circle. We must learn how to restore to nature the wealth that we borrow from it.

In our progress-minded society, anyone who presumes to explain a serious problem is expected to offer to solve it as well. But none of us—singly or sitting in committee—can possibly blueprint a specific "plan" for resolving the environmental crisis. To pretend otherwise is only to evade the real meaning of the environmental crisis: that the world is being carried to the brink of ecological disaster not by a singular fault, which some clever scheme can correct, but by the phalanx of powerful economic, political, and social forces that constitute the march of history. Anyone who proposes to cure the environmental crisis undertakes thereby to change the course of history.

But this is a competence reserved to history itself, for sweeping social change can be designed only in the workshop of rational, informed, collective social action. That we must act is now clear. The question which we face is how.

# 34
# William O. Douglas (1898–1980)

Appointed to the Supreme Court by President Franklin Roosevelt, William O. Douglas was a champion of civil liberties, the rights of minorities, and environmental protection. During his thirty-six years on the bench he wrote over 1,000 opinions. He was in the majority in the Apportionment Cases, in the School Desegregation cases, in cases upholding the Civil Rights Act of 1964 and the Voting Rights Act of 1965, and in a long line of cases that applied many of the protections in the Bill of Rights to state actions via the due process clause of the Fourteenth Amendment.

Douglas's most famous opinion occurred in the 1965 case, *Griswold v. Connecticut*, which invalidated a state law prohibiting the use of contraceptive devices. In finding the law unconstitutional, Douglas's opinion declares that a right of privacy, such as in marriage, can be inferred from several of the provisions of the Bill of Rights, including the First, Third, Fourth, Fifth, and Ninth Amendments. In addition to making birth control a constitutionally protected right, the right of privacy enunciated in the *Griswold* case formed the constitutional basis upon which the Court later decided the still-controversial *Roe v. Wade* (1973).

Justice Douglas was a staunch environmentalist and an advocate for wilderness preservation. In this regard, no other Supreme Court jurist before or since can match his achievements. He traveled extensively, writing of his wilderness experiences in two books, *My Wilderness: The Pacific West* (1960), and its sequel, *My Wilderness: East to Katahdin* (1961). In 1965 he published *A Wilderness Bill of Rights*, in which he presented the case for giving specific legal protections to wilderness. Deeply influenced by Aldo Leopold's *A Sand County Almanac*, Douglas linked his bill of rights for wilderness to the creation of a national land-use ethic. His last book on the environment, *The Three Hundred Year War: A Chronicle of Ecological Disaster* (1972) is a pessimistic view of humans' ability to overcome the dangers posed by the technology and materialism running rampant in modern society.

In addition to his nature writings, Douglas also engaged in direct action on behalf of environmental causes. He participated in numerous protests, and gave speeches opposing public policies that he considered detrimental to environmental quality. One of his most successful protests related to a 1954 proposal to turn the towpath along the old Chesapeake & Ohio Canal near the nation's capital into a highway. Douglas led a highly publicized nine-day hike along the 189-mile canal to protest the proposed road. Two years later the government dropped the highway plans; it turned the towpath instead into a national historic park. Today that park is dedicated to Justice Douglas.

It is not surprising, then, that when the Sierra Club's celebrated lawsuit against developing California's isolated Mineral King Valley reached the high court, it was Douglas who argued in favor of granting standing to natural objects in their own right. His 1972 dissenting opinion in *Sierra Club v. Morton* is one of the most important in the history of environmental law.

# "THE VOICE OF THE INANIMATE OBJECT SHOULD NOT BE STILLED"*

The critical question of "standing" would be simplified and also put neatly in focus if we fashioned a federal rule that allowed environmental issues to be litigated before federal agencies or federal courts in the name of the inanimate object about to be disposed, defaced, or invaded by roads and bulldozers and where injury is the subject of public outrage. Contemporary public concern for protecting nature's ecological equilibrium should lead to the conferral of standing upon environmental objects to sue for their own preservation. See Stone, Should Trees Have Standing? Toward Legal Rights for Natural Objects, 45 S. Cal. L. Rev. 450 (1972). This suit would therefore be more properly labeled as *Mineral King* v. *Morton*.

Inanimate objects are sometimes parties in litigation. A ship has a legal personality, a fiction found useful for maritime purposes. The corporation sole—a creature of ecclesiastical law—is an acceptable adversary and large fortunes ride on its cases. The ordinary corporation is a "person" for purposes of the adjudicatory processes, whether it represents proprietary, spiritual, aesthetic, or charitable causes.

So it should be as respects valleys, alpine meadows, rivers, lakes, estuaries, beaches, ridges, groves of trees, swampland, or even air that feels the destructive pressures of modern technology and modern life. The river, for example, is the living symbol of all the life it sustains or nourishes—fish, aquatic insects, water ouzels, otter, fisher, deer, elk, bear, and all other animals, including man, who are dependent on it or who enjoy it for its sight, its sound, or its life. The river as plaintiff speaks for the ecological unit of life that is part of it. Those people who have a meaningful relation to that body of water—whether it be a fisherman, a canoeist, a zoologist, or a logger—must be able to speak for the values which the river represents and which are threatened with destruction.

I do not know Mineral King. I have never seen it nor travelled it, though I have seen articles describing its proposed "development."... The Sierra Club in its complaint alleges that "One of the principal purposes of the Sierra Club is to protect and conserve the national resources of the Sierra Nevada Mountains." The District Court held that this uncontested allegation made the Sierra Club "sufficiently aggrieved" to have "standing" to sue on behalf of Mineral King.

---

*William O. Douglas. 1972. Dissenting opinion in *Sierra Club* v. *Morton* (405 U.S. 727, 1972). Footnotes are omitted.

Mineral King is doubtless like other wonders of the Sierra Nevada such as Tuolumne Meadows and the John Muir Trail. Those who hike it, fish it, hunt it, camp in it, or frequent it, or visit it merely to sit in solitude and wonderment are legitimate spokesman for it, whether they may be a few or many. Those who have that intimate relation with the inanimate object about to be injured, polluted, or otherwise despoiled are its legitimate spokesmen....

The Solicitor General...takes a wholly different approach. He considers the problem in terms of "government by the Judiciary." With all respect, the problem is to make certain that the inanimate objects, which are the very core of America's beauty, have spokesmen before they are destroyed. It is, of course, true that most of them are under the control of a federal or state agency. The standards given those agencies are usually expressed in terms of the "public interest." Yet "public interest" has so many differing shades of meaning as to be quite meaningless on the environmental front. Congress accordingly has adopted ecological standards in the National Environmental Policy Act of 1969..., and guidelines for agency action have been provided by the Council on Environmental Quality....

Yet the pressures on agencies for favorable action one way or the other are enormous. The suggestion that Congress can stop action which is undesirable is true in theory; yet even Congress is too remote to give meaningful direction and its machinery is too ponderous to use very often. The federal agencies of which I speak are not venal or corrupt. But they are notoriously under the control of powerful interests who manipulate them through advisory committees, or friendly working relations, or who have that natural affinity with the agency which in time develops between the regulator and the regulated. As early as 1894, Attorney General Olney predicted that regulatory agencies might become "industry-minded," as illustrated by his forecast concerning the Interstate Commerce Commission:

> The Commission is or can be made of great use to the railroads. It satisfies the public clamor for supervision of the railroads, at the same time that supervision is almost entirely nominal. Moreover, the older the commission gets to be, the more likely it is to take a business and railroad view of things....

Years later a court of appeals observed, "the recurring question which has plagued public regulation of industry [is] whether the regulatory agency is unduly oriented toward the interests of the industry it is designed to regulate, rather than the public interest it is supposed to protect."...

The Forest Service—one of the federal agencies behind the scheme to despoil Mineral King—has been notorious for its alignment with lumber companies, although its mandate from Congress directs it to consider the various aspects of multiple use in its supervision of the national forests.

The voice of the inanimate object, therefore, should not be stilled. That does not mean that the judiciary takes over the managerial functions from the federal agency. It merely means that before these priceless bits of Americana (such as a valley, an alpine meadow, a river, or a lake) are forever lost or are so transformed as to be reduced to the eventual rubble of our urban environment, the voice of the existing beneficiaries of these environmental wonders should be heard.

Perhaps they will not win. Perhaps the bulldozers of "progress" will plow under all the aesthetic wonders of this beautiful land. That is not the present question. The sole question is, who has standing to be heard?

Those who hike the Appalachian Trail into Sunfish Pond, New Jersey, and camp or sleep there, or run the Allagash in Maine, or climb the Guadalupes in West Texas, or who canoe and portage the Quetico Superior in Minnesota, certainly should have standing to defend those natural wonders before courts or agencies, though they live 3,000 miles away. Those who merely are caught up in environmental news or propaganda and flock to defend these waters or areas may be treated differently. That is why these environmentalist issues should be tendered by the inanimate object itself. Then there will be assurances that all of the forms of life which it represents will stand before the court—the pileated woodpecker as well as the coyote and bear, the lemmings as well as the trout in the streams. Those inarticulate members of the ecological group cannot speak. But those people who have so frequented the place as to know its values and wonders will be able to speak for the entire ecological community.

Ecology reflects the land ethic; and Aldo Leopold wrote in *A Sand County Almanac...*, "The land ethic simply enlarges the boundaries of the community to include soils, waters, plants, and animals, or collectively, the land."

That, as I see it, is the issue of "standing" in the present case and controversy.

# 35
# Vine Deloria, Jr. (1933–    )

Professor, lawyer, writer, and tribal member of the Standing Rock Sioux, Vine Deloria, Jr., provided a strong voice for the Native American self-determination movement of the 1960s and 1970s. His first best-selling book, *Custer Died For Your Sins* (1969), described the government's long and often bloody history of mistreating the country's aboriginal peoples. It argued against the policy of termination that began in the 1950s and proposed measures needed to gain tribal self-rule. That was the beginning of a prolific scholarly and public speaking career. During the next two decades he wrote or edited numerous books (including, *We Talk, You Listen* (1971), *Of Utmost Good Faith* (1971), *God Is Red* (1973), *Behind the Trail of Broken Treaties* (1974), and *Red Earth, White Lies* (1995). He also authored countless articles that helped to dispel the stereotype of the Indian in American political culture, and to replace it with a more genuine understanding. Deloria's forceful, and at times outraged and sarcastic, assessment of Indian-Anglo relationships gave public expression to the feelings and sentiments of many Native Americans. Both his writing and his activism helped arouse the conscience of the American people to what was happening on the reservation.

Deloria's writings also exhibit an abiding interest in theology and ecology. His book, *God Is Red* (1973, 1994), for example, draws distinctions between the spiritual bases of Native American and European religions and their cultures. It is sharply critical of Christianity and its attitudes toward nature. In contrast to the religions of Native Americans, which seek harmony with the environment and find the Sacred in place and space, Christian doctrines have separated humans from the natural world, seeing in nature merely a vast cornucopia of resources to be exploited. These exploitive attitudes, he argued, have created a possibly irreversible ecological disaster. In his controversial *Red Earth, White Lies* (1995), Deloria extended his critique of European religion and culture to Western science. While Western science, he argued, is as much based on myth as it is on empirically demonstrated fact, it also has failed, until perhaps recently, to recognize Indian oral tradition as a legitimate system of knowledge. Thus science, as well as religious and political institutions, have contributed to the public's uninformed and caricatured views of the Native American.

In addition to helping found the Indian law movement and having recently published what will be *the* source book on Indian-American treaties, Vine Deloria, Jr., is also credited with helping to establish Native American Studies as a field of scholarship.

# "THE AMERICAN INDIAN MOVEMENT"*

"We are at war with the United States," Vernon Bellecourt cried. "To your stations!" In 1972 as Indian protesters rushed into the Bureau of Indian Affairs headquarters building in the nation's capitol, Washington policemen prepared for a siege, and the first dramatic confrontation between American Indians and the federal government in more than a century began.

During the fall of 1972 there were continual complaints by American Indians about a number of shootings in Indian country in which Indians had been murdered without reason. Local officials did their best to cover up the incidents, and when the Indians appealed to the federal government for redress, they met with studied delays and deaf ears. So in early October, a caravan known as the Trail of Broken Treaties had been formed.

Coming initially from Seattle and Los Angeles, automobile caravans filled with Indian protesters, winding their way toward the nation's capital, visited the different reservations along the route and picked up more protesters at each stop. Rallies were held on the larger reservations, where the grievances of a century were recited by the reservation residents. Tribal officials, fearful that their favored status as Interior Department mascots would be jeopardized, hastily began to downgrade the importance of the protest, implying that it was primarily a movement by urban Indians who had no relationship with the tribal community. Yet a considerable number of reservation people joined the caravan, so that by the time it reached Washington, D.C., more than 80 percent of the participants were reservation residents.

The trouble began when the protesters discovered that no food and lodging provisions had been made for the stay in Washington. The advance men, who were supposed to have made room and board arrangements, actually spent their time making pronouncements and speaking to groups, instead of doing the tedious and unromantic jobs of locating churches, hotels, and dormitories for the caravan participants. The Interior officials were astounded to learn that there was no lodging available to the protesters, since the advance men had assured them that everything had been taken care of.

During a conference in the Bureau of Indian Affairs building, the government officials offered to find a lodging place for the protesters as a ploy for getting them to leave the building's immediate vicinity. Participants began to gather in the auditorium of the Bureau of Indian Affairs to wait for final word on their disposition for the night, and when some government building guards began to push some of the younger protesters around, fear of violence spread through the building. People were reluctant to leave, thinking they would immediately be arrested or worse by the police waiting outside. When word came to the people quietly waiting in the auditorium

---

*Vine Deloria, Jr. 1994. *God Is Red: A Native View of Religion*. Golden, CO: Fulcrum Publishing, pp. 3–11, 15–17, 20–22. Reprinted with permission from Vine Deloria, Jr. Footnotes are omitted.

that police guards had clashed with some of the protestors near one of the doors, the tension broke: the Indians sealed off the Bureau building, taking control of every door and window that could possibly be used by the police to enter.

The building was taken over by the Trail of Broken Treaties protesters on Friday night, November 3, 1972, the weekend before the Presidential elections. Government negotiations began almost immediately and continued through the weekend; Indian leaders promised to vacate the building, but continuous threats of violence from the police surrounding the building held the invaders in a virtual state of panic. The building suffered tremendous damage each time a potential invasion by the police seemed imminent. Desks and files were randomly piled against outside doors and windows in an effort to defend the building.

During the weekend some of the Indians attempted to go to Arlington Cemetery to hold religious services for fallen Indian war dead, particularly Ira Hayes, hero of Iwo Jima, and Sgt. Ernest Rice, a Winnebago hero of the Korean War, who was buried in Arlington when the good people of Iowa refused to allow his burial in a white cemetery in Sioux City. The caravan people went to federal court hoping to have reversed the U.S. Army order that banned the protesters from the national cemetery on the basis that they constituted a partisan political group. But the tensions between the Indians and the government were so high by the time the court ruled in their favor on Monday that few caravan members bothered to go to the service. Most of them remained within the building, hoping to protect the caravan's elderly and children.

On November 9, nearly a full week after occupying the Bureau of Indian Affairs headquarters, the Trail of Broken Treaties Indians left Washington. During that time, the protesters removed numerous government records and files as "hostage" material to ensure a peaceful departure. Capital police eschewed the brutality practiced on other occasions rather than risk a retaliatory burning and destruction of government files. The protesters scattered and returned to their reservations, leaving the nation shocked and dismayed. According to stories in the *Washington Post*, the damage to the building was $2.3 million, a figure that the newspaper said was exceeded only by the 1906 San Francisco earthquake and fire and the burning of Washington by the British during the War of 1812. In the history of destruction of federal property, the Trail of Broken Treaties protest was given a respectable third place. Later testimony before the House Subcommittee on Indian Affairs placed the actual damage at something more than a couple of thousand dollars, and the figure continued to decline as more specific knowledge was gained about what had actually been destroyed.

In the wake of the destruction, even moderate and sympathetic Indians were dismayed by the activists' actions. The Bureau of Indian Affairs headquarters had contained priceless objects of Indian art, including paintings by Indians of notable stature (now deceased). The activists hardly gave a thought to preserving Indian cultural treasures. Their fear of violence was so intense that they simply chose whatever was at hand to use in the barricades. From Acee Blue Eagle's irreplaceable paintings to the urinals in the men's room, the Bureau of Indian Affairs was destroyed.

Elected tribal officials were brought to Washington, where Robert Robertson, director of the Vice-President's National Council of Indian Opportunity, orchestrated their protests and demands for the prosecution of the protest leaders. The fact that the tribal chairmen were little more than puppets in Robertson's hand negated much of their impact in Indian country. But the rage and concern of Indians across the nation was evident. At best the lofty moral stance of the American Indian community lay in ruins. Indians were no longer the silent peaceful individuals who refused to take dramatic steps to symbolize their grievances. They had become simply another protest group.

The capture of the headquarters of the Bureau of Indian Affairs by the Indians of the Trail of Broken Treaties Caravan was the climatic event of a movement that had remained, for the most part, on the back pages of the nation's newspapers. For nearly a decade, the Indian people's frustration and rage had been rising, but in most cases in which the movement was reported, it was considered a pleasant respite from the fury, confusion, and threats of the blacks and Chicanos. The message of the American Indian, a recital of broken promises and loss of sacred lands, never reached the public in a form making it possible to capitalize on the outpouring of good will that the American public held for American Indians.

This public had heard Indian complaints about broken treaties and confiscation of sacred mountains for years. But what did it matter? The public was confused at almost every turn. What could be done about a broken treaty now? Most Americans thought that the respective tribes' problems were facts of American history, not problems of the present. There was no outpouring of assistance for Indians comparable to the frenzy that gripped the North at the height of the Civil Rights movement.

Throughout the last decade, Indian activists chose, sometimes cleverly and sometimes stupidly, symbols that they believed would convey the importance of their lands and religions to the rest of America. In a nation where few people had ever questioned the superiority of Anglo-Saxon and Christian values, the Indians' emphasis on land and religion seemed an anachronistic fantasy of the American frontier. Many people applauded the Indian activists, but it is doubtful if very many understood them. Even the greatest success of the last century, the restoration of the sacred Blue Lake area to the people of Taos Pueblo in New Mexico, failed to achieve any significance in the general populace's worldview. In the Blue Lake controversy, the whole distinction between Indians and non-Indians could have been seen—if anyone had been interested.

Theodore Roosevelt, on a great conservation trip in 1906, decided that the timberlands in northern New Mexico should be placed in a national forest for their protection. Carson National Forest was created by Executive Order, and when the government surveyors had finished laying out the boundaries, the sacred Blue Lake, central to the practice of the Pueblo religion, was safely within the forest. The people of the Pueblo immediately petitioned the government for the lake's restoration. They explained that it was their major religious shrine and that the Pueblo would die without its sanctuary for the perpetuation of its religion. The Interior Department sided with the Pueblo in 1912, supporting a return of the lake to them.

The Department of Agriculture, however, had other ideas. It considered the forest the personal property of the Secretary of Agriculture and refused to allow the lands to be restored. The valuable timber that grew on the slopes of Blue Lake was an incentive to the officials in the Department of Agriculture to keep the area. They saw their task as keeping the area safely away from the rest of American society until the timber companies were ready to use it. In that way they could assure themselves of a powerful outside constituency at appropriations times, thus guaranteeing their continuance as a government agency.

The struggle continued for a period of sixty-four years without the Agriculture Department budging the slightest inch in its position. After the Second World War, it appeared as though the battle had been won by Agriculture. Clinton P. Anderson, conservative Democrat from New Mexico, served first as Secretary of Agriculture (1945–48) and then as U.S. Senator from New Mexico, on the Senate's Interior Committee (1949–70). In due time Anderson, who had come to Washington in the 1930s as a youngster and friend of Lyndon B. Johnson and the New Deal power structure, achieved a prominent place on the Interior Committee and substantial influence in Congress. Since any Indian legislation to return Blue Lake had to go through the Interior Committee, the fight was regarded as over.

In 1965 the Indian Claims Commission heard the claims of the Taos Indians against the United States. The commissioners admitted that the United States had illegally taken the Blue Lake area and offered a substantial sum as compensation. The commissioners were astounded when the Indians refused the money. They wanted the Blue Lake area returned to them. If the commission would not do that, the Indians did not want it said that they had sold their sacred shrine. They told the commission that they would refuse the compensation.

It seemed that for someone in America to turn down a dollar was unusual. When it was a little group of Indians living on the edge of starvation, it presented a more profound and difficult moral question than is usually raised in government circles. The Indian Claims Commission agreed to settle the remainder of the case without making any decision on Blue Lake, while the Pueblo went to Congress to see if they could get the lands restored.

Led by Paul Bernal, a spokesman for the Taos Indians, the movement to restore Blue Lake to the Pueblo began in 1965. Paul traveled across the nation many times, speaking to groups and urging them to contact their senators and congressmen to demand support for the bill to restore the lake to the Indians. A groundswell gradually built; one by one, senators on the Interior Committee began to break their united front. Other congressmen began to take interest in the restoration as the persistent Taos spokesmen refused to accept the series of compromises offered by Clinton Anderson in an effort to still the movement.

In November 1970 President Nixon took a hand in the matter, and the White House began to apply pressure on its friends in Congress to get Blue Lake returned to the Taos people. The extent of the national support Bernal had generated can be understood by the entrance of Richard Nixon into the controversy. If the movement was so politically strong as to entice President Nixon to take sides, it had to be a winning hand.

The Senate Interior Committee still had major anti-Indian personalities on it, however, in the Democratic lineup of Chairman Henry Jackson, Clinton Anderson, Lee Metcalf, and Alan Bible. Anderson steered his compromise bill to give what basically amounted to a continued-use permit to the Pueblo, dependent on the goodwill of the Forest Service. The Senate Interior Committee amended the House of Representatives' bill, which allowed the Pueblo to take the land in trust.

When the compromise bill hit the Senate floor, Senators Fred Harris and Robert Griffin offered a bipartisan amendment to the Anderson compromise. The surprises in voting underscored the effectiveness of the Indian lobbyists. The voting also showed that many of the senators had been hiding under liberal and conservative labels and were forced to come out into the open on the vote. Frank Church, until then regarded as an Indian enemy, voted with the Indians. Barry Goldwater, generally chastised for his dogged conservatism, also supported Taos. Lee Metcalf and Henry Jackson, regarded as liberals, bitterly opposed the Indians, Metcalf going so far as to deride the Indian religion on the Senate floor, trying to stop the amendment.

In December 1970 President Nixon signed into law the bill that restored 44,000 acres surrounding the sacred Blue Lake to the people of the Taos Pueblo. The significance of the law could not be overestimated. It was the first clear sign, as Senator Charles Percy noted in his speech on the bill, that the Indian religious practices would be given equal respect along with Christian ceremonies.

Remembering the Blue Lake fight, let us examine the approximate chronology of the recent Indian activist incidents and review the issues raised in each demonstration. Present in all of them, we shall find something of the same integrating force, the same desire for communal integrity exemplified in the Blue Lake struggle.

A great many small and sporadic events were crowded into the last decade of the Indian movement, but the year 1969 probably marks the beginning of the massive and sustained drive by American Indians to bring their message to the American public.… The major event of 1969, of course, was the occupation of Alcatraz Island in November. Shortly after the island was closed as a prison in 1964, a number of Sioux Indians then living in the San Francisco Bay Area landed on the island and claimed it under the 1868 Fort Laramie Treaty with their tribe. In 1964 there were few people around in the Indian community willing to risk a prison sentence to demonstrate a legal technicality, so the invasion sputtered and died. For the record, the first Indian invasion of Alcatraz was led by Allen Cottier, Dick MacKenzie, and Adam Nordwall.

The years passed, and the people always kept a wary eye on the island.

Adam Nordwall, in particular, figured that given sufficient manpower and favorable press, a successful invasion could be pulled off. As early as the winter of 1969, plans had been made secretly in the Bay Area to land on the island and reverse the doctrine of Discovery in favor of the Indians. But still lacking was that certain spark to bind the different Bay Area groups together as a feasible force.

As October ended a large convention of Indian groups met in San Francisco to form a national organization for Indians living in urban areas throughout the country. The night after the convention dispersed, the Indian Center caught fire and burned completely. It was a singularly tragic event for San Francisco's Indian population, which had laboriously build its center over two decades. The center formed the focus of community life for Indians living in the area. Suddenly they were without a meeting place, lacked the social services that their programs had provided, and had practically no way to begin again.

The stage was set for the invasion. On November 9, a little more than a week after the San Francisco Indian Center had burned, a small contingent of Indians landed on the island and spent several exciting hours being chased by the watchmen, who had been hired to keep people away from the abandoned prison island. Not the least discouraged when they were taken ashore the next morning, the Indian invaders, mostly college students from Berkeley and San Francisco State College, reorganized and ten days later landed some two hundred Indian people on the rocks, securing it for a period of eighteen months....

The intent of the Alcatraz Indians was to set up a total community on the former prison island that would redeem it from its tragic past. An ecological center to replace the barren and rusted prison cellblock was conceived; the sacred plants of all tribes could be grown there and used in healing ceremonies. An Indian university was also advocated. It would be a place where history would not be interpreted so as to justify a program of systematically extinguishing the country's original inhabitants, but rather a place where a true history of the inner relationships of various cultures would be created. A job training center and one for Indian artists and craftsmen was planned; the latter would help pay the overhead for the operations of the whole community. This was the broad scope of the dreaming young college students who landed on Alcatraz....

And thus it went, rocketing from coast to coast. The Indian movement covered a variety of topics in obscure and nameless places during 1970. For example, in June the big explosion was the attempt of the Pitt River Indians to reclaim their lands once again from the Pacific Gas and Electric Company. Led by Mickey Gemmill and Richard Oakes, who had commanded the Alcatraz occupation through its first crucial months, a task force of Indians occupied the lands near Big Bend, California.

Again the issue was twofold. The lands had been illegally taken from the Indians without any due process guaranteed them by the federal Constitution. The Indians had been excluded from the California claims case on the grounds that they had separate and identifiable claims to particular lands. And the religious community question was ever present. The Pitt

River Indians wanted lands to reconstitute their tribal life, including reestablishment of their tribal religion, which depended on that particular location near Mount Shasta. The Indians were arrested and tried for trespass but... were acquitted.

The summer of 1970 saw the movement overflow its channel and expand into almost every state where any significant number of Indians lived. In almost every case an immediate and identifiable injustice with respect to confiscation of Indian lands was the issue. The Indians of Chicago established an Indian village as a protest against housing discrimination in the city, pointing out that they had been forced into the cities because their lands had been taken by the government.

The American Indian Movement occupied the dormitories of Augustana College in Sioux Falls, South Dakota, as a protest against the lethargy of the churches in assisting Indians. AIM had earlier been to a meeting of the National Council of Churches with no visible effect. As AIM chapters became active, the movement spread to cities with federal surplus property. A lighthouse was seized at Sault Sainte Marie, Michigan. Federal property in Milwaukee was invaded to bring about the establishment of a school. USAF property in Minneapolis was seized by the home chapter of the American Indian Movement.

As the final hearings on the passage of the Blue Lake restoration bill were being heard in the nation's capital, in Wisconsin the DRUMS organization, fiercely anti-terminationist Menominees seeking repeal of their termination law of almost a decade ago, began a series of demonstrations to save their lake lands. The Tuscaroras, Western members of the Iroquois League, drove a group of whites from their reservation, where they had been living in a trailer park. The summer ended in spectacular fashion with the demonstration at Sheep Mountain in the Badlands of South Dakota and a capture of Mount Rushmore in the Black Hills. The protest involved restoration of Indian lands taken from the Oglala Sioux during the Second World War for target practice and never returned.

The first phase of the Indian movement spent itself as the tendency of activists to make claims on federal lands ebbed. It was apparent that the American public would not support a general policy of restoration of tribal lands. At the national political conventions in 1972, the Indian delegates pushed through amendments to both platforms advocating return of federal surplus lands to tribes, but the amendments were hardly understood by the delegates. They received approval primarily because, as David Brinkley was heard to remark, "They do love Indians."

# 36
# Tom McCall (1913–1983)

During his tenure as governor of Oregon (1966–1974), Tom McCall, a moderate Republican, gained a reputation as a socially progressive and innovative public official whose environmental policies served as a model for other states.

While working as a newspaper and television journalist in 1962, McCall produced an award-winning documentary on the 300-mile Willamette River. Titled "Pollution in Paradise," it described the Oregon river as an "open sewer clogged with effluent from pulp and paper mills." After his election as Governor in 1966—in a campaign where environmental issues figured prominently—McCall actively pursued efforts to clean up the river by appointing himself interim director of the state's Sanitary Authority. In that capacity he helped establish water quality standards for the state's rivers. Reelected in 1970 with environmental protection again a major part of his platform, he pushed more than 100 environmental protection bills through the legislature, including legislation to protect Oregon's beaches from development. The first state-level bill requiring deposits on soft drink and beer bottles also passed during his second term. With the energy crisis of 1973 capturing headlines, Governor McCall instituted several emergency energy conservation measures that set the standard for state response—including a ban on all outdoor lighting displays, and the limiting of gasoline sales based on odd-even numbered license plates.

Protecting Oregon from unchecked growth was McCall's priority. He created considerable state and national controversy with his "Visit Oregon, But Don't Stay" policy. He not only feared excessive population growth in the state, but worried about the negative impacts of increased tourism. In 1973 he helped secure passage of one of the first state-level land use planning bills. Despite several unsuccessful attempts to reverse the legislation, the legislation remains today a model of state land use planning, and Governor Tom McCall a model of what an energetic executive can accomplish. Since the '70s, the State of Oregon has been a leader in the environmental quality movement.

---

## "VISIT OREGON, BUT DON'T STAY!"*

Thousands of Jaycees were assembled from all parts of the country at Portland's Civic Auditorium on a June morning in 1971. They were listening to what seemed a whimsical welcoming message from the Governor of

---

*Tom McCall. 1977. *Tom McCall: Maverick*. Portland, OR: Binford and Mort, pp. 190–202. Reprinted with permission from Binford and Mort.

Oregon, chuckling along with the warmth of the words and the usual one-liners. "We want you to visit our State of Excitement often," I said. "Come again and again. But, for heaven's sake, don't move here to live." I got stares of disbelief and a moment of silence. Then, the delegates burst into a clap of laughter.

To ease any tensions, I added a softener: "Or, if you do have to move in to live, don't tell any of your neighbors where you are going."

It was touch and go on that speech, because, tongue-in-cheek though it seemed, it violated a cardinal ethic known as Western Hospitality. But someone had to raise the point, somehow, sometime—and within 18 months we were wondering if Oregon's flora and fauna could stand even unlimited tourist visitations. Since then, similar official mutterings have been heard in a number of states, California and Florida included, but the Oregon shot was indeed the one heard round the world.

For years, some Oregonians had said that our state was getting far too many tourists. I saw merit to their argument. And, at the same time, I was skeptical of the development-at-any-cost policy which had been pursued by the Hatfield Administration. When I came on as governor in 1967, the state had an economic development quarterly called "Growth." I had it renamed "Quality" and it was later redesignated "Progress."

I minced few words about livability. When I spoke before a group of Los Angeles businessmen in March of 1969, I said: "Oregon has not been an over-eager lap-dog to the economic master. Oregon has been wary of smoke-stacks and suspicious of rattle and bang. Oregon has not camped, cup in hand, at anyone's affluent doorstep. Oregon has wanted industry only when that industry was willing to want what Oregon is."

In my first three years as governor, I appeared in films promoting Oregon for the Highway Department's Travel Information Division. I declined to do a film in 1970. I thought it was time to evaluate how many more tourists we could handle and how many we could absorb into our population. It struck me that there was little need to advertise for more tourists.

The rest of the nation really didn't begin to notice what we were doing until January 12, 1971, when I was interviewed on the CBS Evening News by Terry Drinkwater. I said then: "Come visit us again and again. This is a state of excitement. But, for heaven's sake, don't come here to live."

This interview generated a tremendous amount of mail. Most of it was favorable. People were very perceptive about what we were trying to do.... There were, to be sure, some negative comments. M. C. McCauley of Santa Barbara, California, wrote, "The personal freedom to live where we choose remains a cherished privilege."

Senator Mark Hatfield's response was defensive. He said, "My eight years as governor gave Oregon the highest economic growth and greatest progress on recreation facilities of any West Coast state. Now, when I go around the country, people ask me, 'Is it true your governor doesn't want industry or people to come into Oregon?'"

I was not surprised by the Hatfield criticism. The Senator has enough vanity that he hates to see anyone else from Oregon get attention, and he may have recognized that his policies had helped mark Oregon for the swarm. Another factor was that I was being mentioned as a possible challenge for his senate seat in 1972.

The national Jaycee convention was, as mentioned earlier, the next forum where I enunciated this new policy. As a result of that speech, the Governor's Office began getting letters about whether it was necessary for out-of-state residents to apply for special permits to visit Oregon. I would explain that all we were trying to do was to make sure that we preserved the kind of life that they would come to Oregon as vacationists to enjoy.

My "Visit, but Don't Stay" remarks were reported in the *New York Times* shortly before I was to address a luncheon audience of New York businessmen at the St. Regis Hotel. I told them that the often-quoted remark was not intended to seal Oregon's borders.

"We are being realistic," I said. "We know we cannot, at this time, support a human tidal wave of migration. We haven't the jobs for that kind on onrush—we haven't the facilities—and we are determined to maintain our magnificent environment.... When we say 'visit often but don't come to live,' we aren't being hostile or provincial. We are being prudent. It is not our intention to lure anyone to a promised land that becomes, instead, an environmental disaster.

"It may sound presumptuous, or immodest, but the context in which I pitch to you is this: Oregon is accepting a few applications for location of branch offices by a carefully screened set of corporations with reputations for honoring the sanctity of the environment."

We were interested only in healthy, imaginative, nonpolluting industry. I could go to New York and say at the St. Regis Hotel, "If you want to become a member of our club we'd like to have you, but we don't like rattle and bang and smoke and dirt. If you abide by our rules, you can be a member of our club."

To a remarkable degree, it worked. I had great support from Oregon industry. One of my most prized possessions is an award which I received in 1970 from Associated Oregon Industries....

I was criticized by tourist associations and motel owners for suggesting that we consider amending the welcome mat for tourists. They were outraged at the inhospitable tone of it all. I pointed out that we were hosting more tourists than ever before, and if they were not getting their share then perhaps they should look somewhere other than the Governor's Office. The downtrend at run-of-the-mill lodgings began long before my well-publicized statements.

One of the most vitriolic exchanges came when I spoke before a Kiwanis Club in San Diego. An indignant San Diegan wrote to the club, erroneously, that I was the guy that invented "Don't Californicate Oregon." He suggested that they reject me on a slogan, "Don't Oregonize California."

Oddly enough, the most protective Oregonians are former Californians. They seem to resent bitterly the intrusion of another Californian. Where members of the James G. Blaine Society, a group formed by Portland author Stewart Holbrook in the 1940s, would like to have a ten-foot fence around Oregon, these transplanted Californians favor a 50-foot fence against their former neighbors.

Much of our own effort had to be couched in humor because there was no way we could legally prohibit people from coming. The greeting-card industry was particularly helpful in injecting some comic relief into a controversial issue. Frank Beeson, an artist and humorist from Eugene, came up with the "Oregon Ungreeting Card." They became a great commercial success. Most of them emphasized the rain: "In Oregon, you don't tan, you rust!"; "You can tell when summer is near in Oregon…the rain feels warmer!"; "Last year in Oregon, 677 people fell off their bikes and drowned"; and "Oregonians never water their lawns—they simply drain them."

Another card said, "Tom Lawson McCall, Governor, on behalf of the citizens of the Great State of Oregon, cordially invites you to visit Washington or California or Idaho or Nevada or Afghanistan." I laughed heartily when I received the first of these cards.

At first, my statement seemed to work in reverse. More people were coming to see what it was we were trying to hide. The tourism numbers jumped from nine million to twelve million. A Salem *Capital Journal* editorial said, "McCall stayaway speeches draw more and more attention to the state and in the end discourage no one."

After this leap in tourism, I raised the question of how many tourists we could accommodate. I began wondering about twenty-four million feet trampling the flora and scaring the fauna. Someone said, "That's terrible for you to say when we depend so much on tourism." I retorted, "How'd you like to have a billion tourists if you depend on it so much?"

There is an optimum of tourists that you can handle without destroying those renewable resources and making the state unpleasant.…

Oregon has been a major battleground for land-use planning. One of the reasons I tried to warn outsiders away was because we hadn't done enough planning to be able to know how to handle a major population increase. Oregon's population growth rate is twice that of California and three times that of Washington State. The one theme I consistently hit on was that we didn't want to be a link in the megalopolis spreading south from Seattle and north from San Francisco, because we would be committing some of the richest farmland in America to supermarkets and suburbs.

Oregon's first initiative in statewide land-use planning was Senate Bill 10, which was adopted by the 1969 Legislature. It required each city and county to begin land planning, with the provision that, if they did not, the governor would step in and do it for them. A coalition of developers, farmers and businessmen fought the law. I regarded it as a building block for the future and was a staunch defender of the concept. Opponents of land-use planning sought to force a referendum on Senate Bill 10 in 1970, although it was originally proposed by an interim committee composed mainly of farm interests. I was pelted with such bitter epithets as "King Tom" and "Hitler."

"Repeal Senate Bill 10," I intoned, "and you might as well throw me out too because I refuse to preside over the deterioration of Oregon's quality environment." The challenge was as brash as it was politically inept. Voters, when thus dared, would usually throw both the bill and the taunting official over the side. But this was a time of rising environmental consciousness and the monumental land planning and zoning legislation was kept on the statute books and I was reelected....

...Oregon hasn't always handled its lands right. Our coastal estuaries are not considerable in their acreage, but they are extremely important in maintaining biological systems. Former Council on Environmental Quality Director Russell Peterson says, "The work of an estuary amounts to about $83,000 an acre and is a producer of plant and animal life." In Oregon, this had not been understood and our estuaries had been treated cavalierly. When some cases of filling wetlands came before the Land Board, we turned them down. We also rejected some people's applications to establish marinas. In 1970 I prohibited state construction in estuaries. It would have been a double standard to ban private development, as the state was merrily filling them for bridges and highways.

The most abused land in Oregon is on the central coast. Developers carved it up with a buffalo hunter mentality. Lincoln City was a model of strip city grotesque. By the fall of 1972, the pelt skinners had moved in for the kill. Local officials had approved a subdivision of 1,400 lots with a drainfield area for only 600 houses. Thirty-nine of 60 water systems did not meet state standards. Department of Environmental Quality inspectors found 34 cases of raw sewage flowing onto the beach. I declared a moratorium on construction in Lincoln County, which brought heated protest from developers and real estate salesmen. But it sent them a message that hucksterism in land sales would not be tolerated.

Coastal planning is the area where most of the volatility is generated in Oregon, California, Texas, Alaska, or any coastal state. The closer you get to the ocean, the hotter the land-use planning issue becomes. Four and one-half percent of the people live along the Oregon Coast. This doesn't mean they should be overruled, unless their conduct of managing their resources is antisocial and against the best interests of balanced protection and development. This has often been the case. We've got some of the worst foulups on the coast, some of the ugliest coastal strips in the United States. One of the most respected federal officials in the Coastal Zone Management Program told me, "I worked in the South and was constantly frustrated by red-necked local officials. I came out to the Oregon Coast and it's just as bad."

The public is far ahead of these local officials who cater to developers and exploiters. They know how fragile the coast is.

The drawback of Senate Bill #10 was that it did not give local governments the tools and the technical help to draw up comprehensive plans. All it did was give them ten goals to go by—and no money to achieve them. So I found that it was almost futile to go in under these conditions.

I called for a new land-use planning law in what became known as my "grasping wastrels" speech, my opening address to the 1973 Legislature:

"There is a shameless threat to our environment and to the whole quality of life—unfettered despoiling of the land. Sagebrush subdivisions, coastal 'condomania,' and the ravenous rampage of suburbia in the Willamette Valley all threaten to mock Oregon's status as the environmental model for the nation. We are dismayed that we have not stopped misuse of the land, our most valuable finite natural resource.

"We are in dire need of a state land-use policy, new subdivision laws, and new standards for planning and zoning by cities and counties. The interests of Oregon for today and in the future must be protected from grasping wastrels of the land. We must respect another truism. Unlimited and unregulated growth leads inexorably to a lowered quality of life."

State Senator Ted Hallock, the chairman of the Senate Environmental and Land Use Committee, and State Senator Hector Macpherson sponsored Senate Bill 100, the most substantial land-use planning legislation ever proposed in Oregon. Opponents of the bill said the state was tampering with "private property" and would confiscate land. The Oregon Rural Landowners' Association said Senate Bill 100 was "the biggest land grab since our great-grandparents took this land away from the Indians 150 years ago."

I retorted that without a statewide law there was "a very real danger that uncontrolled development will clear-cut the state of its livability."

When the bill fell into trouble, former Department of Environmental Quality Administrator L. B. Day was asked to chair an ad hoc committee which would rewrite the bill. All points of view were represented. Several concessions were made. They deleted the "areas of critical state concern" clause, placing greater emphasis on local planning and citizen participation. Day said then, "We're talking about planning that basically comes from the bottom up, not from the top down." The Governor was no longer to be the enforcer. The Land Conservation and Development Commission was instead charged with this.

I went before a legislative committee on behalf of L. B.'s compromise. "In most respects," I told the Environmental and Land Use Committee, "it is more satisfactory than the original Senate Bill 100." After much debate and several other changes, the bill was passed by both houses of the legislature. I signed it into law on May 29, 1973.

The LCDC went into operation in February of 1974 with L. B. Day as its chairman. A conservative State Senator, Lynn Newbry, denounced L. B. as "public enemy number one" and me as "public enemy number two" for appointing him head of DEQ in 1971. L.B. was a Teamsters Union official who gave more to his state in time, agony, and hard work than just about anyone. We stood shoulder to shoulder in many a fight. In the spring of 1976, L. B. said he was tired of playing games with "two-bit elected officials who don't take responsibility." I told him that he was overestimating their worth, which couldn't be more than a nickel.

L. B. vigorously pushed local governments to prepare their comprehensive plans. Some said he was too abrasive. But he was also pragmatic. He told me that he hoped to have LCDC in place in five years. I said, "L. B., five years would be 1981. That would be twelve years after the passage of our first statewide planning act, Senate Bill 10. Why so slow?"

He said, "You can't move any faster than the people will let you move." Governor Straub accepted L. B.'s resignation in July of 1976 to appease backers of an initiative to repeal Senate Bill 100. It was unfortunate that Straub would not stick by this courageous administrator. To his credit, he did name an excellent replacement for L. B. in John Mosser. Happily, the repeal measure was defeated by an enlightened electorate. In the same election,

November 2, 1976, the voters opted to retain regional councils of government which my administration had launched nine years earlier.

But we have to continue the hard work if we are to retain the paradise that's not yet lost and recapture the paradise that was. As I was leaving office, I helped organize a group called "1,000 Friends of Oregon" to serve as a watchdog on the implementation of land-use planning. It is the only single-purpose public-law corporation that I know of. Glenn Jackson, chairman of the State Transportation Commission, and Allen Bateman from Klamath County were among those who started the "1,000 Friends." Whenever the land-use law is threatened, the "1,000 Friends" have stepped in to make certain that it isn't gutted.

# 37
# James Earl Carter (1924–    )

The Democratic Governor of Georgia, Jimmy (James Earl) Carter, capitalized on public disgust with Washington politicians to narrowly defeat President Gerald Ford in the November 1976 election.

As president he championed human rights and nuclear weapons limitations, while his domestic agenda stressed environmental issues, especially the need for a new energy policy. While both Presidents Nixon and Ford grappled with the problem of achieving "energy independence," and while subsequent administrations also have had energy on their agendas, Carter's efforts remain the most sustained and comprehensive to date. He managed to get several important elements of his energy program through Congress, including the creation of a Department of Energy focused on finding alternative energy sources.

The Carter presidency, however, was unable to reverse or even halt rising unemployment and inflation rates, a peculiar economic condition that became known in the '70s as "stagflation." This failure did much to dampen the appeal of his long-term energy plans. Though he tried mightily to build a national consensus around the need for a rational, long-term energy strategy, an American public preoccupied with its cost-of-living index wasn't listening.

Arguably the two most memorable events of Carter's four years in office were international in nature. Both occurring in 1979, one was a great success, the other a great humiliation. For his role in the Middle East peace process, President Carter received the Nobel Peace Prize. The historic agreements reached between Egypt and Israel in 1979 laid the framework for a peace process that continues through the present.

Carter's record with obtaining the release of American hostages held in Iran was not nearly so successful. A year of failed negotiations and an abortive rescue mission by U.S. Marines became an enormous political burden for his Administration. The hostage crisis, coupled with stagflation, were the issues that dominated the 1980 presidential race, one in which Carter lost to Ronald Reagan.

The importance of the Carter Presidency has been underestimated, and it is likely that his years in the White House will be reassessed in light of the energy crisis now confronting the United States. Carter's was the path not taken. Regardless, President Carter has shown the depth of his commitment to human rights and the alleviation of poverty during his twenty years after leaving the White House. Together with his wife, Rosalyn, he has been a tireless volunteer for Habitat for Humanity and other humanitarian organizations. Founder of the Carter Center in Atlanta, Jimmy Carter has been one of the best former presidents the country ever had.

# "THE ENERGY CRISIS IS REAL.
# IT IS WORLDWIDE"*

...I want to speak to you first tonight about a subject even more serious than energy or inflation. I want to talk to you right now about a fundamental threat to American democracy.

I do not mean our political and civil liberties. They will endure. And I do not refer to the outward strength of America, a nation that is at peace tonight everywhere in the world, with unmatched economic power and military might.

The threat is nearly invisible in ordinary ways. It is a crisis of confidence. It is a crisis that strikes at the very heart and soul and spirit of our national will. We can see this crisis in the growing doubt about the meaning of our own lives and in the loss of a unity of purpose for our Nation.

The erosion of our confidence in the future is threatening to destroy the social and the political fabric of America.

The confidence that we have always had as a people is not simply some romantic dream or a proverb in a dusty book that we read just on the Fourth of July. It is the idea which founded our Nation and has guided our development as a people. Confidence in the future has supported everything else—public institutions and private enterprise, our own families, and the very Constitution of the United States. Confidence has defined our course and has served as a link between generations. We've always believed in something called progress. We've always had a faith that the days of our children would be better than our own.

Our people are losing that faith, not only in government itself but in the ability as citizens to serve as the ultimate rulers and shapers of our democracy. As a people we know our past and we are proud of it. Our progress has been part of the living history of America, even the world. We always believed that we were part of a great movement of humanity itself called democracy, involved in the search for freedom, and that belief has always strengthened us in our purpose. But just as we are losing our confidence in the future, we are also beginning to close the door on our past.

In a nation that was proud of hard work, strong families, close-knit communities, and our faith in God, too many of us now tend to worship self-indulgence and consumption. Human identity is no longer defined by what one does, but by what one owns. But we've discovered that owning things and consuming things does not satisfy our longing for meaning. We've learned that piling up material goods cannot fill the emptiness of lives which have no confidence or purpose.

The symptoms of this crisis of the American spirit are all around us. For the first time in the history of our country a majority of our people believe

---

*James Earl Carter. 1979. Address to the Nation on Energy and National Goals, July 15, 1979, *Weekly Compilation of Presidential Documents* 15(29): pp. 1235–1241.

that the next 5 years will be worse than the past 5 years. Two-thirds of our people do not even vote. The productivity of American workers is actually dropping, and the willingness of Americans to save for the future has fallen below that of all other people in the Western world.

As you know, there is a growing disrespect for government and for churches and for schools, the news media, and other institutions. This is not a message of happiness or reassurance, but it is the truth and it is a warning.

These changes did not happen overnight. They've come upon us gradually over the last generation, years that were filled with shocks and tragedy.

We were sure that ours was a nation of the ballot, not the bullet, until the murders of John Kennedy and Robert Kennedy and Martin Luther King, Jr. We were taught that our armies were always invincible and our causes were always just, only to suffer the agony of Vietnam. We respected the Presidency as a place of honor until the shock of Watergate.

We remember when the phrase "sound as a dollar" was an expression of absolute dependability, until 10 years of inflation began to shrink our dollar and our savings. We believed that our Nation's resources were limitless until 1973 when we had to face a growing dependence on foreign oil.

These wounds are still very deep. They have never been healed.

Looking for a way out of this crisis, our people have turned to the Federal Government and found it isolated from the mainstream of our Nation's life. Washington, D.C., has become an island. The gap between our citizens and our Government has never been so wide. The people are looking for honest answers; not easy answers: clear leadership, not false claims and evasiveness and politics as usual.

What you see too often in Washington and elsewhere around the country is a system of government that seems incapable of action. You see a Congress twisted and pulled in every direction by hundreds of well-financed and powerful special interests.

You see every extreme position defended to the last vote, almost to the last breath by one unyielding group or another. You often see a balanced and a fair approach that demands sacrifice, a little sacrifice from everyone, abandoned like an orphan without support and without friends.

Often you see paralysis and stagnation and drift. You don't like it, and neither do I. What can we do?

First of all, we must face the truth, and then we can change our course. We simply must have faith in each other, faith in our ability to govern ourselves, and faith in the future of this Nation. Restoring that faith and that confidence to America is now the most important task we face. It is a true challenge of this generation of Americans....

We know the strength of America. We are strong. We can regain our unity. We can regain our confidence. We are the heirs of generations who survived threats much more powerful and awesome than those that challenge us now. Our fathers and mothers were strong men and women who shaped a new society during the Great Depression, who fought world wars, and who carved out a new charter of peace for the world.

We ourselves are the same Americans who just 10 years ago put a man on the Moon. We are the generation that dedicated our society to the pursuit of human rights and equality. And we are the generation that will win the war on the energy problem and in that process rebuild the unity and confidence of America.

We are at a turning point in our history. There are two paths to choose. One is a path I've warned about tonight, the path that leads to fragmentation and self-interest. Down that road lies a mistaken idea of freedom, the right to grasp for ourselves some advantage over others. That path would be one of constant conflict between narrow interests ending in chaos and immobility. It is a certain route to failure.

All the traditions of our past, all the lessons of our heritage, all the promises of our future point to another path, the path of common purpose and the restoration of American values. That path leads to true freedom for our Nation and ourselves. We can take the first steps down that path as we begin to solve our energy problem.

Energy will be the immediate test of our ability to unite this Nation, and it can also be the standard around which we rally. On the battlefield of energy we can win for our Nation a new confidence, and we can seize control again of our common destiny.

In little more than two decades we've gone from a position of energy independence to one in which almost half the oil we use comes from foreign countries, at prices that are going through the roof. Our excessive dependence on OPEC has already taken a tremendous toll on our economy and our people. This is the direct cause of the long lines which have made millions of you spend aggravating hours waiting for gasoline. It's a cause of the increased inflation and unemployment that we now face. This intolerable dependence on foreign oil threatens our economic independence and the very security of our Nation.

The energy crisis is real. It is worldwide. It is a clear and present danger to our Nation. These are facts and we simply must face them.

What I have to say to you now about energy is simple and vitally important.

Point one: I am tonight setting a clear goal for the energy policy of the United States. Beginning this moment, this Nation will never use more foreign oil than we did in 1977—never. From now on, every new addition to our demand for energy will be met from our own production and our own conservation....

Point two: To ensure that we meet these targets, I will use my Presidential authority to set import quotas. I'm announcing tonight that for 1979 and 1980, I will forbid the entry into this country of one drop of foreign oil more than these goals allow. These quotas will ensure a reduction in imports even below the ambitious levels we set at the recent Tokyo summit.

Point three: To give us energy security, I am asking for the most massive peacetime commitment of funds and resources in our Nation's history to develop America's own alternative sources of fuel—from coal, from oil shale, from plant products for gasohol, from unconventional gas, from the Sun.

I propose the creation of an energy security corporation to lead this effort to replace 2-1/2 million barrels of imported oil per day by 1990. The corporation will issue up to $5 billion in energy bonds, and I especially want them to be in small denominations so that average Americans can invest directly in America's energy security....

Point four: I'm asking Congress to mandate, to require as a matter of law, that our Nation's utility companies cut their massive use of oil by 50 percent within the next decade and switch to other fuels, especially coal, our most abundant energy source.

Point five: To make absolutely certain that nothing stands in the way of achieving these goals, I will urge Congress to create an energy mobilization board which, like the War Production Board in World War II, will have the responsibility and authority to cut through the redtape, the delays, and the endless roadblocks to completing key energy projects.

We will protect our environment. But when this Nation critically needs a refinery or a pipeline, we will build it.

Point six: I'm proposing a bold conservation program to involve every State, county, and city and every average American in our energy battle. This effort will permit you to build conservation into your homes and your lives at a cost you can afford.

I ask Congress to give me authority for mandatory conservation and for standby gasoline rationing. To further conserve energy I'm proposing tonight an extra $10 billion over the next decade to strengthen our public transportation systems. And I'm asking you for your good and for your Nation's security to take no unnecessary trips, to use carpools or public transportation whenever you can, to park your car one extra day per week, to obey the speed limit, and to set your thermostats to save fuel. Every act of energy conservation like this is more than just common sense—I tell you it is an act of patriotism.

Our Nation must be fair to the poorest among us, so we will increase aid to needy Americans to cope with rising energy prices. We often think of conservation only in terms of sacrifice. In fact, it is the most painless and immediate way of rebuilding our Nation's strength. Every gallon of oil each one of us saves is a new form of production. It gives us more freedom, more confidence, and much more control over our own lives.

So, the solution of our energy crisis can also help us to conquer the crisis of the spirit in our country. It can rekindle our sense of unity, our confidence in the future, and give our Nation and all of us individually a new sense of purpose....

In closing, let me say this: I will do my best, but I will not do it alone. Let your voice be heard. Whenever you have a chance, say something good about our country. With God's help and for the sake of our Nation, it is time for us to join hands in America. Let us commit ourselves together to a rebirth of the American spirit. Working together with our common faith we cannot fail.

Thank you and good night.

# 38
# Theodore J. Lowi (1931–   )

Cornell University professor of political science Theodore Lowi is widely cited for his critique of pluralism. Pluralist theory, whose roots extend back to Bentley's formulation of the group basis of politics, argues that American politics is a continual process of group interaction. Competition among groups provides a mechanism for conflict resolution. Competing groups check the power of the state and ensure accountability, and since all interests eventually benefit—at least some of the time—democracy is served. According to the theory, public policies at any given time represent an equilibrium point in the group struggle.

In his best known work, *The End of Liberalism*, Lowi delivered a devastating attack on pluralism, both as a theory and as an empirically grounded description of the policy-making process. Instead of interest group competition ultimately serving democratic ends, Lowi presents evidence that powerful groups have captured the entire political system, with the result that the state has become the handmaiden of those interests. His argument is similar to C. Wright Mills's earlier identification of a "power elite," but it is even more in the vein of Grant McConnell's *Private Power and American Democracy*, which contained one of the first formulations of the "iron triangle" phenomenon.

For Lowi, it is not so much a case of conscious manipulation of the political system by powerful interests, both in and out of government, as it is a case of politicians viewing interest-group politics positively—as the way things ought to be—rather than following James Madison's commentary, a necessary evil. In other words, the state has abrogated its power to speak with authority to its citizens; that authority now resides largely in the private sector. This is a grave development that has produced the present widespread crisis in public confidence in its governing institutions.

Lowi's solution to "interest group liberalism" is a return to "juridical democracy," a political process in which carefully thought-out proscriptive statutes guide public action under clear rules of law. According to Lowi, juridical democracy would reverse the current condition of providing broad delegations of power to administrative entities, which then enables powerful groups to capture the administrative apparatus in what scholars call the "captured agency phenomenon." A thorough reform of the legislative branch is essential, Lowi argued, in order to return to a republic of laws, and not of men.

# "THE WHOLE UNIVERSE IS COVERED BY THE EPA'S JURISDICTION"*

*Interest-Group Liberalism*
The frenzy of governmental activity in the 1960s and 1970s proved that once the constitutional barriers were down the American national government was capable of prompt response to organized political demands. However, that is only the beginning of the story, because the almost total democratization of the Constitution and the contemporary expansion of the public sector has been accompanied by expansion, not contraction, of a sense of distrust toward public objects. Here is a spectacular paradox. It is as though each new program or program expansion had been an admission of prior governmental inadequacy or failure without itself being able to make any significant contribution to order or to well-being. It is as though prosperity had gone up at an arithmetic rate while expectations, and therefore frustrations, had been going up at a geometric rate—in a modern expression of Malthusian Law. Public authority was left to grapple with this alienating gap between expectation and reality.

Why did the expansion of government that helped produce and sustain prosperity also help produce a crisis of public authority? The explanation pursued throughout this volume is that the old justifications for expansion had too little to say beyond the need for the expansion itself. An appropriate public philosophy would have addressed itself to the purposes to which the expanded governmental authority should be dedicated. It would also have addressed itself to the forms and procedures by which that power could be utilized. These questions are so alien to public discourse in the United States that merely to raise them is to be considered reactionary, apolitical, or totally naive.

Out of the emerging crisis of public authority developed an ersatz political formula that bears no more relation to those questions than the preceding political formula. The guidance the new formula offers to policy formulation is a set of sentiments that elevated a particular view of the political process above everything else. The ends of government and the justification of one policy or procedure over another are not to be discussed. The *process* of formulation is justified in itself. ...[I]t takes the pluralist notion that government is an epiphenomenon of politics and makes out of that a new ethics of government.

There are several possible names for the new public philosophy. A strong candidate would be *corporatism*, but its history as a concept gives it several unwanted connotations, such as conservative Catholicism or Italian

*Theodore J. Lowi. 1979. *The End of Liberalism: The Second Republic of the United States,* Second Edition, New York: W.W. Norton, pp. 50–56, 61–63, 119–120. Copyright © 1979, 1969 by W. W. Norton & Company, Inc. Used by permission from W. W. Norton & Company, Inc. Footnotes are omitted.

fascism. Another candidate is *syndicalism*, but among many objections is the connotation of anarchy too far removed from American experience. From time to time other possible labels will be experimented with, but, since the new American public philosophy is something of an amalgam of all of the candidates, some new terminology seems to be called for.

The most clinically accurate term to capture the American variant of all of these tendencies is *interest-group liberalism*. It is liberalism because it is optimistic about government, expects to use government in a positive and expansive role, is motivated by the highest sentiments, and possesses a strong faith that what is good for government is good for the society. It is interest-group liberalism because it sees as both necessary and good a policy agenda that is accessible to all organized interests and makes no independent judgment of their claims. It is interest-group liberalism because it defines the public interest as a result of the amalgamation of various claims. A brief sketch of the working model of interest-group liberalism turns out to be a vulgarized version of the pluralist model of modern political science: (1) Organized interests are homogeneous and easy to define. Any duly elected representative of any interest is taken as an accurate representative of each and every member. (2) Organized interests emerge in every sector of our lives and adequately represent most of those sectors, so that one organized group can be found effectively answering and checking some other organized group as it seeks to prosecute its claims against society. And (3) the role of government is one of insuring access to the most effectively organized, and of ratifying the agreements and adjustments worked out among the competing leaders.

This last assumption is supposed to be a statement of how a democracy works and how it ought to work. Taken together, these assumptions amount to little more than the appropriation of the Adam Smith "hidden hand" model for politics, where the group is the entrepreneur and the equilibrium is not lowest price but the public interest.

These assumptions are the basis of the new public philosophy. The policy behavior of old liberals and old conservatives, of Republicans and Democrats, so inconsistent with the old dialogue, is fully consistent with the criteria drawn from interest-group liberalism: *The most important difference between liberals and conservatives, Republicans and Democrats, is to be found in the interest groups they identify with. Congressmen are guided in their votes, presidents in their programs, and administrators in their discretion by whatever organized interests they have taken for themselves as the most legitimate; and that is the measure of the legitimacy of demands and the only necessary guidelines for the framing of the laws.*

It is one thing to recognize that these assumptions resemble the working methodology of modern political science. But it is quite another to explain how this model was elevated from a hypothesis about political behavior to an ideology about how our democratic polity ought to work.

*The Appeals of Interest-Group Liberalism*

The important inventors of modern techniques of government were less than inventive about the justifications for particular policies at particular times. For example, Keynes was neither a dedicated social reformer nor a political thinker with an articulated vision of the new social order. Keynes helped discover the modern economic system and how to help maintain it, but his ideas and techniques could be used to support a whole variety of approaches and points of view:

> Collective bargaining, trade unionism, minimum-wage laws, hours legislation, social security, a progressive tax system, slum clearance and housing, urban redevelopment and planning, education reform, all these he accepted but they were not among his preoccupations. In no sense could he be called the father of the welfare state. [Alvin H. Hansen]

These innovators may have been silent on the deeper justification for expanding government because of the difficulty of drawing justification from the doctrines of popular government and majority rule. Justification of positive government programs on the basis of popular rule required, above all, a belief in and support of the supremacy of Congress. The abdication of Congress in the 1930s and thereafter could never have been justified in the name of popular government; and, all due respect to members of Congress, they made no effort to claim such justification. Abdication to the Executive Branch on economic matters and activism in the infringement of civil liberties produced further reluctance to fall back upon Congress and majority rule as the font of public policy justification. Many who wished nevertheless to have majority rule on their side sought support in the plebiscitary character of the presidency. However, presidential liberals have had to blind themselves to many complications in the true basis of presidential authority, and their faith in the presidency as a representative majority rule came almost completely unstuck during the late 1960s and thereafter.

This is precisely what made interest-group liberalism so attractive. It had the approval of political scientists because it could deal with so many of the realities of power. It was further appealing because large interest groups and large memberships could be taken virtually as popular rule in modern dress. And it fit the needs of corporate leaders, union leaders, and government officials desperately searching for support as they were losing communal attachments to their constituencies. Herbert Hoover had spoken out eloquently against crass individualism and in favor of voluntary collectivism. His belief in this kind of collectivism is what led him to choose, among all his offers, to be Secretary of Commerce in 1921. And the experts on government who were to become the intellectual core of the New Deal and later Democratic administrations were already supporting such views even before the election of Franklin D. Roosevelt. For example,

> [The national associations] represent a healthy democratic development. They rose in answer to certain needs.... They are part of our representative system.... These groups must be welcomed for what they are, and certain precautionary regulations worked out. These groups must be understood and their proper place in government allotted, if not by actual legislation, then by general public realization of their significance. [Political Scientist E. Pendleton Herring]

After World War II, the academic and popular justifications for interest-group liberalism were still stronger. A prominent American government textbook of the period argued that the "basic concept for understanding the dynamics of government is the multi-group nature of modern society or the modern state." By the time we left the 1960s, with the Democrats back in power, the justifications for interest-group liberalism were more eloquent and authoritative than ever. Take two examples from among the most important intellectuals of the Democratic Party, writing around the time of the return of the Democrats to power in 1960. To John Kenneth Galbraith, "Private economic power is held in check by countervailing power of those who are subjected to it. The first begets the second." Concentrated economic power stimulates power in opposition to it, resulting in a natural tendency toward equilibrium. This is not merely theoretical for Galbraith, although he could not possibly have missed its similarity to Adam Smith; Galbraith was writing a program of positive government action. He admitted that effective countervailing power was limited in the real world and proposed that where it was absent or too weak to do the job, government policy should seek out and support it and, where necessary, create the organizations capable of countervailing. It should be government policy to validate the pluralist theory.

Arthur Schlesinger summarized his views for us in a campaign tract written in 1960. To Schlesinger, the essential difference between the Democratic and Republican Parties is that the Democratic Party is the truly multi-interest party:

> What is the essence of multi-interest administration? It is simply that the leading interests in society are all represented in the interior processes of policy formation—which can be done only if members or advocates of these interests are included in key positions of government.

Schlesinger repeated the same theme in a more sober and reflective book written after John Kennedy's assassination. Following his account of the 1962 confrontation of President Kennedy with the steel industry and the later decision to cut taxes and cast off in favor of expansionary rather than stabilizing fiscal policy, Schlesinger concludes,

> The ideological debates of the past began to give way to a new agreement on the practicalities of managing a modern economy. There thus developed in the Kennedy years a national accord on economic policy—a new consensus which gave hope of harnessing government, business, and labor in rational partnership for a steadily expanding American economy.

A significant point in the entire argument is that the Republicans would disagree with Schlesinger on the *facts* but not on the *basis* of his distinction. The typical Republican rejoinder would be simply that Democratic administrations are not more multi-interest than Republican. In my opinion this would be almost the whole truth.

The appeal of interest-group liberalism is not simply that it is more realistic than earlier ideologies. There are several strongly positive reasons for its appeal. The first is that it helped flank the constitutional problems of federalism that confronted the expanding national state before the Constitution was completely democratized. A program like the Extension Service of the Department of Agriculture got around the restrictions of the Interstate

Commerce clause by providing for self-administration by a combination of land-grant colleges, local farmer and commerce associations, and organized commodity groups.... These appeared to be so decentralized and permissive as to be hardly federal at all. With such programs we begin to see the ethical and conceptual mingling of the notion of organized private groups with the notions of local government and self-government. Ultimately, direct interest-group participation in government became synonymous with self-government; but at first it was probably a strategy to get around the inclination of the Supreme Court to block federal interventions in the economy.

A second positive appeal of interest-group liberalism...is that it helped solve a problem for the democratic politician in the modern state where the stakes are so high. This is the problem of enhanced conflict and how to avoid it. The contribution of politicians to society is their skill in resolving conflict. However, direct confrontations are sought only by so-called ideologues and outsiders. Typical American politicians displace and defer and delegate conflict where possible; they face conflict squarely only when they must. Interest-group liberalism offered a justification for keeping major combatants apart and for delegating their conflict as far down the line as possible. It provided a theoretical basis for giving to each according to his claim, the price for which is a reduction of concern for what others are claiming. In other words, *it transformed access and logrolling from necessary evil to greater good.*

A third and increasingly important positive appeal of interest-group liberalism is that it helps create the sense that power need not be power at all, control need not be control, and government need not be coercive. If sovereignty is parceled out among groups, then who is out anything? As a major *Fortune* editor enthusiastically put it, government power, group power, and individual power may go up simultaneously. If the groups to be controlled control the controls, then "to administer does not always mean to rule." The inequality of power and the awesome coerciveness of government are always gnawing problems in a democratic culture. Rousseau's General Will stopped at the boundary of a Swiss canton. The myth of the group and the group will is becoming the answer to Rousseau and the big democracy. Note, for example, the contrast between the traditional and the modern definition of the group: Madison in *Federalist* 10 defined the group ("faction") as "a number of citizens, whether amounting to a majority or minority of the whole who are united and actuated by some common impulse of passion, or of interest, *adverse to the right of other citizens, or to the permanent and aggregate interests of the community*" (emphasis added). Modern political science usage took that definition and cut the quotation just before the emphasized part. In such a manner pluralist theory became the handmaiden of interest-group liberalism, and interest-group liberalism became the handmaiden of modern American positive national statehood, and the First Republic became the Second Republic....

Evidence of the fundamental influence of interest-group liberalism can be found in the policies and practices of every Congress and every administration since 1961. The very purpose of this book is to identify, document, and assess the consequences of the preferences that are drawn from the new public philosophy. President Kennedy is an especially good starting point because his positions were clear and because justification was especially important to him. His actions were all the more significant because he followed the lines of interest-group liberalism during a period of governmental strength, when there was no need to borrow support from interest groups. But whatever he did in the name of participation, cooperation, or multi-interest administration, and whatever President Johnson did in the name of "maximum feasible participation" and "creative federalism," so did President Eisenhower and Presidents Nixon and Ford do in the name of "partnership." This posture was very much above partisanship, and that is precisely what makes it the basis of what we can now call the Second Republic. *Fortune* could rave its approval of the theory of "creative federalism," despite its coinage by Lyndon Johnson, as "a relation, cooperative and competitive, between a limited central power and other powers that are essentially independent of it...a new way of organizing Federal programs...[in which simultaneously] the power of states and local governments will increase; the power of private organizations, including businesses, will increase; the power of individuals will increase. Similarly, one of the most articulate officials during the Kennedy-Johnson years could speak glowingly of the Republican notion of partnership: "To speak of 'federal aid' simply confuses the issue. It is more appropriate to speak of federal support to special purposes...[as] an investment made by a partner who has clearly in mind the investments of other partners—local, state, and private."

In sum, leaders in modern, consensual democracies are ambivalent about government. Government is obviously the most efficacious way of achieving good purposes, but alas, it is efficacious because it is coercive. To live with that ambivalence, modern policy-makers have fallen prey to the belief that public policy involves merely the identification of the problems toward which government ought to be aimed. It pretends that through "pluralism," "countervailing power," "creative federalism," "partnership," and "participatory democracy" the unsentimental business of coercion need not be involved and that unsentimental decisions about how to employ coercion need not really be made at all. Stated in the extreme, the policies of interest-group liberalism are end-oriented but ultimately self-defeating. Few standards of implementation, if any, accompany delegations of power. The requirement of standards has been replaced by the requirement of participation. The requirement of law has been replaced by the requirement of contingency. As a result, the ends of interest-group liberalism are nothing more than sentiments and therefore not really ends at all....

*The New Representation: A Second Republic?*
If ambivalence toward government power is a trait common to all democracies, American leaders possess it to an uncommon degree. Their lives are dedicated to achieving it, and their spirits are tied up with justifying it. They were late to insist upon the expansion of national government, and when the expansion finally did begin to take place, it only intensified the ambivalence. *With each significant expansion of government during the past century, there has been a crisis of public authority. And each crisis of public authority has been accompanied by demands for expansion of representation.*

The clearest case in point is probably the first, the commitment by the federal government, beginning with the Interstate Commerce Act of 1887, to intervene regularly in the economic life of the country. The political results of the expansion were more immediate and effective than the economic consequences of the statutes themselves. The call went out for congressional reform of its rules, for direct election of senators, for reform in nominating processes, for reform in the ballot, for decentralization of House leadership, and so on. The results were dramatic, including "Reed's Rules" in House, direct election of senators, the direct primary movement, the Australian ballot, and the "Speaker Revolt." This is also the period during which some of the most important national interest groups were organized.

Expansion of government during the Wilson period was altogether intertwined with demands by progressives for reform and revision in the mechanisms of representation: female suffrage (Nineteenth Amendment), the short ballot, initiative, referendum and recall, great extensions of direct primaries, the commission form of city government, and the first and early demands for formal interest representation—leading to such things as the formal sponsorship of the formation of Chambers of Commerce by the Commerce Department, government sponsorship of the formation of the Farm Bureau movement, the establishment of the separate clientele-oriented Departments of Labor and Commerce, and the first experiments with "self-regulation" during the World War I industrial mobilization.

The Roosevelt revolution brought on more of the same but made its own special contribution as well. Perhaps the most fundamental change in representation to accompany expanded government was the development and articulation of the theory and practice of the administrative process.... Obviously the more traditional demands for reform in actual practices of representation continued. Reapportionment became extremely important; demands for reform produced the Administrative Procedure Act and the congressional reforms embodied in the 1946 LaFollette-Monroney Act. But probably of more lasting importance during and since that time has been the emergence of interest-group liberalism as the answer to the problems of government power. The new jurisprudence of administrative law is a key factor, to me the most important single factor. The new halo words alone indicate the extent to which new ideas of representation now dominate: *interest representation, cooperation, partnership, self-regulation, delegation of power, local option, creative federalism, community action, maximum feasible participation*, Nixon's *new federalism*, and even that odd contribution from the 1960s New Left—*participatory democracy*.

In whatever form and by whatever label, the purpose of representation and of reform in representation is the same: to deal with the problem of power—to bring the democratic spirit into some kind of psychological balance with the harsh reality of government coerciveness. The problem is that the new representation embodied in the broad notion of interest-group liberalism is a pathological adjustment to the problem. Interest-group liberal solutions to the problem of power provide the system with stability by spreading a *sense* of representation at the expense of genuine flexibility, at the expense of democratic forms, and ultimately at the expense of legitimacy.

Prior solutions offered by progressives and other reformers built greater instabilities into the system by attempting to reduce the lag between social change and government policy. But that was supposed to be the purpose of representation. Flexibility and legitimacy could only have been reduced by building representation upon the oligopolistic character of interest groups, reducing the number of competitors, favoring the best organized competitors, specializing politics around agencies, ultimately limiting participation to channels provided by preexisting groups.

Among all these, the weakest element of interest-group liberalism, and the element around which all the rest is most likely to crumble, is the antagonism of interest-group liberal solution to formalism. The least obvious, yet perhaps the most important, aspect of this is the antagonism of interest-group liberalism to law.... Traditional expansions of representation were predicated upon an assumption that expanded participation would produce changes in government policies expressed in laws that would very quickly make a difference to the problems around which the representation process had been activated. Since the "new representation" extends the principle of representation into administration, it must either oppose the making of law in legislatures or favor vague laws and broad delegations that make it possible for administrative agencies to engage in representation. This tends to derange almost all established relationships and expectations in a republic. By rendering formalism impotent, it impairs legitimacy by converting government from a moralistic to a mechanistic institution. It impairs the potential of positive law to correct itself by allowing the law to become anything that eventually bargains itself out as acceptable to the bargainers. It impairs the very process of administration itself by delegating to administration alien material—policies that are not laws and authorizations that must be made into policies. Interest-group liberalism seeks pluralistic government, in which there is no formal specification of means or of ends. In a pluralistic government there is, therefore, no substance. Neither is there procedure. There is only process....

*Environmental Protection: Intimations of Nixon*
Although President Nixon did cooperate with Congress in the drafting and the acceptance of the new and vast OSHA [Occupational Safety and Health Administration] and CPSC [Consumer Products Safety Commission] regulatory programs, his own approaches and preferences can be seen more directly through the Environmental Protection Agency actions and through wage-price controls. EPA was established in 1970 by executive orders issued by President Nixon. Through these actions President Nixon sought to consolidate several major programs in a single agency. EPA was then to do its job in a manner already established by OSHA and CPSC—by "setting standards consistent with national environmental goals." In other words, "EPA would be charged with protecting the environment by abating pollution." Nixon's concept of the agency was typical of the liberal approach. EPA would "monitor the conditions of the environment," "establish quantitative environmental base lines," and then "set and enforce standards for air and water quality and for individual pollutants." To do this, EPA would take

guidance from itself but could also encourage broader participation "through periodic meetings with those organizations and individuals interested in that regulatory package."

The whole universe is covered by the EPA's jurisdiction. Since pollution can come from anywhere, we must naturally equip our agency with power to cover anything and everything. How can anyone be against clean air or water? And let us, indeed, have it by 1976; and if not, then by 1986; if not by then, at least let there be satisfaction that authority was exercised on behalf of the people. It is as though there were a trade-off between pollution and the number of regulations concerning pollution. Congress knew nothing in the beginning and admitted it by mandating clean air and water to administrators to pursue entirely as they saw fit. And neither Congress nor the president has reviewed the substance of the thousands of standards and regulations emanating from EPA in order to determine whether there is any relation at all among these regulations or between them and the original legislative enactments. It seems that Nixon's main preoccupation was to be sure that he had a hand in environmental protection regulation, not that he wanted to restrain or to regularize it, or to make it more explicit, or to impose upon it the sense of justice that a strict constructionist might have had. Our experience with the Democrats of the 1960's, including the Democratic-dominated Congress, would have led us to expect little more from them. But the important point here is that the Republican administration did nothing different.

# DISCUSSION QUESTIONS

1. Governor Tom McCall worried about the impacts of tourism on his state. Discuss the kinds of negative environmental impacts that tourism and outdoor recreation can have on natural resources. Can these impacts be just as significant as the impacts associated with traditional resource extractive activities such as mining, timber, and grazing?

2. The environmental legislation passed in the 1970s relied heavily on "command-and-control," i.e., prescriptive standards that are set in law and bureaucratic agencies charged with ensuring compliance with standards. Command-and-control, however, has been widely criticized as ineffective and costly. Research what alternatives to command-and-control policies have been proposed and/or used.

3. Vine Deloria, Jr. describes the violence that accompanied Native Americans' political struggle for respect and equality. Cesar Chavez, on the other hand, told the president of the grape growers that he would consider his union movement a failure if it engaged in violence and terror tactics. Reflecting back upon Thoreau's night in jail, Frederick Douglass's escape from slavery, and Margaret Sanger's breaking of the Comstock laws, discuss protest tactics in current issues, e.g., logging in old-growth forests, Native American whale harvests, abortion, the environmental policies of the World Trade Organization, and wolf reintroduction. What are the limits of permissible protest? Is violence ever acceptable in a democratic society?

4. In answering his question, "What if I'm wrong?," Paul Ehrlich in effect advances what in legal circles is called the precautionary principle—i.e., under conditions of uncertainty take actions that are not irreversible and that leave the widest range of options for correction. Debate what might be the impacts of applying the precautionary principle to current issues such as climate change, ozone depletion, biodiversity, human cloning, and genetically engineered crops.

5. Garrett Hardin advanced the concept of "mutual coercion, mutually agreed upon." In a democratic state, how is that principle put into practice?

# PART VII

## "Things Fall Apart; The Center Cannot Hold"*

### CONSERVATIVE CHALLENGES AND LIBERAL

### COUNTER-ATTACKS, 1980–2001

Dissatisfaction with the government's performance in both economic matters and foreign policy characterized Americans' political attitudes in 1980, a presidential election year. In the 1970s the term stagflation had been coined to describe an economy which perversely combined high unemployment, low productivity, high energy prices, and spiraling inflation. On top of this lackluster economic performance, there were several affronts to America's national pride: The humiliating retreat from South Vietnam was still fresh in people's minds, the Organization of Petroleum Exporting Countries (OPEC) had the country over a barrel containing expensive crude oil, and, most painfully, 52 Americans were being held hostage in Iran by militant Muslims. President Carter's diplomatic and military rescue efforts proved unsuccessful, yet he persevered throughout 1980 to gain their release. He spent very little time campaigning for reelection. It would have made no difference, however, had he spent *all* of his time on the campaign trail. Americans were desirous of change, and that was exactly what the Republican candidate, California Governor Ronald Reagan promised them. Reagan handily won the election, and as a final insult to the outgoing administration, the hostages were released by the Ayatollah Khomeini on Reagan's Inauguration Day.

"Government is not the solution, it is the problem," the new President told Americans. From that point on, the Reagan administration proceeded to launch a conservative "revolution" that was premised on an earlier concep-

---

*William Butler Yeats. 1924. From the poem "The Second Coming."

tion of federal-state relations, one in which state and local governments wielded considerably more power than they had under New Deal and Great Society versions of federalism. Reagan once claimed that he wanted to be remembered as a "Roosevelt in Reverse"; in fact he is credited with having started a twenty-year effort at "reinventing government." The Reagan political philosophy has dominated the present era, to nearly the same degree as Theodore Roosevelt's progressivism, and Franklin Roosevelt's liberalism, dominated theirs. In order to understand the contemporary era, one must understand Reaganomics and the liberal backlash to it.

President Reagan's second inaugural address on January 21, 1985, provides an overview of his conservative philosophy of government. It also helps to explain his popularity, for he covered themes and issues that deeply resonated with a majority of Americans: Faith in progress and a better tomorrow for children; less reliance on government (especially the federal government) to solve problems; a strong national defense committed to spreading democracy throughout the world; an economy unburdened by excessive regulation; and an America poised for greatness in its third century of existence. No doubt the most important contribution Reagan made in his eight years in the White House—and it is evident in this address—was to lead boldly and fearlessly. In doing so he helped restore Americans' faith in themselves and in their society, but his strong stance on a number of domestic policies also created a whirlwind of protest. At some point in the 1980s governmental gridlock became a key characteristic of national politics.

Environmental policies and programs have been among the most divisive issues dividing liberals and conservatives during the last twenty years. When Reagan galloped into Washington from out of the West, he brought with him several leaders of the Sagebrush Rebellion (a movement seeking a reduction of the federal government's role in environmental regulation and the transfer of federal lands to states and private interests). The most prominent of the sagebrush rebels was Secretary of the Interior James Watt, but the Administrator of the Environmental Protection Agency, Anne Gorsuch, was a close second. She was the wife of another sagebrush rebel, Robert Burford, who headed the Bureau of Land Management during the initial Reagan years. At key departments and agencies—the EPA, the Agriculture and Interior Departments, and the Army Department holding jurisdiction over the Corps of Engineers—the order of the day was devolution, deregulation, and resource development.

The numerous laws passed in the '60s and '70s that considerably broadened the federal government's role in regulating air and water pollution, in overseeing the disposal and cleanup of toxic and hazardous wastes, in requiring long-range planning on the public lands, in protecting endangered species, in requiring environmental impact statements for all federal activities, and in managing the federal lands not exclusively for the benefit of business interests, became ground zero for the Reagan appointees. For example, at one point Secretary Watt told a congressional committee, "We have studied things for too long. It is time to get the nation moving again." Watt also was known for having said that the government suffered from "paralysis by analysis," and that he intended to do something about it. That "something" was to swing the pendulum back to the utilitarian, commodity-development side of the conservation movement. Watt's short but controversial tenure at Interior symbolized the conservative challenge to the environmental initiatives of the '70s; however, it, in turn, sparked increased activism by environmental interests—backlash to the backlash if you will. Membership in environmental interest groups soared during the '80s.

Although the Congress went along with some of the White House initiatives in resource and environmental reform, such as supporting huge increases in timber cutting on the national forests and in taking away management of the outer continental shelf (OCS) lands from the Bureau of Land Management, the attempts to turn back the clock on pollution control at the EPA had few supporters in the legislative branch. The liberal-conservative split on environmental policy first became evident over how the EPA was implementing the recently enacted statutes on clean air, clean water, and the Superfund program. It later extended to other resource areas. Members of Congress were not amused with the politicization of these popular pollution control programs, or with the evident foot-dragging that was going on within the agency. In fact, one of Administrator Gorsuch's aides, Rita Lavelle, was sentenced to a term in prison for violating federal law. In response to the Reagan Administration's hostility to the 1980 legislation that created the program for cleaning up toxic sites, Congress in 1986 passed the Superfund Amendments and Reauthorization Act (SARA), thereby strengthening and reiterating its support for the program.

That same year, however, Republicans and Democrats finally agreed to some long-overdue reforms of the water resources development programs of the Army Corps of Engineers. Many presidents, including Reagan's immediate predecessor, had tried to break the iron triangle of interests perhaps best described by Arthur Maass in his 1951 book, *Muddy Waters*. The close alliance among powerful congresspersons, the Corps, and local development interests produced countless projects of questionable national value, all at national taxpayer expense. Many observers thought it couldn't be done, yet President Reagan scored a significant political victory when Congress passed the Water Resources Development Act of 1986. For the first time in history, local and state beneficiaries of Corps projects would have to pay a portion of the costs—a system known as cost-sharing. The legislation also encouraged the Corps to broaden its mission to include environmental restoration; subsequent legislation has been even more insistent that the agency move away from a single-minded engineering and construction solution for all water-related problems. Movement into new missions has indeed developed within the agency, albeit slowly: Approximately 5 to 10 percent of the Corps' current budget is allocated to these new environmental restoration programs.

What Reagan did to change the Corps, President Clinton did in the 1990s to reform the federal government's other major water developer, the Bureau of Reclamation. The last major construction project of the Bureau—today considered a planning, service, and management agency—was the controversial Central Arizona Project. The Bureau now is experimenting with instream water flow regimes below Glen Canyon Dam on the Colorado River, it is investigating dam decommissioning, and it is engaged in a number of other environmental restoration programs. Overall, Reaganomics—

and the lack of available sites after a century of dam construction—have led to a significantly reduced federal role in water resources development, as the nation moves into the twenty-first century.

The judicial branch—long described as the "least dangerous branch" of the national government—also became transformed during the twelve years of Republican control of the White House. With the exception of a few high-profile cases, the judiciary, prior to the 1980s, had not been deeply involved in environmental policy making. No longer. The courts have become as much a battleground over environmental issues as are the legislative and executive branches. While proenvironmental organizations such as the Sierra Club had a longer history of using the courts to attain their objectives, the conservative appointments made by Reagan and President George Bush to the federal bench insured that those in the Sagebrush Rebellion and the property-rights movement would also get their views addressed. Several recent Supreme Court decisions, including *Lucas v. South Carolina*, have upheld property owners' complaints about regulatory "takings," (i.e., governmental controls that reduce property values to the extent that the results are considered a legal "taking," which constitutionally requires just compensation). At the same time, however, district and appellate courts have halted logging in old growth forests, and the Supreme Court in 2000 upheld Native Americans' water rights in the Southwest. There is no clear trend in court decisions over the past twenty years, other than the trend in the direction of judicial micromanagement of the policy-making process. In fact, scholars now speak of a judicial iron triangle of courts, agencies, and interest groups that rivals the congressional iron triangle. In today's litigious society, the courts exercise great power in shaping America's environmental agenda.

While federalism was undergoing an overhaul by conservatives in Washington, another significant trend emerged in the 1980s, that of globalization. The communications revolution picked up momentum with each passing year, and the world became increasingly smaller, if not in an absolute physical sense, certainly in a relative sense. More affordable air travel enabled increasing numbers of people to travel abroad. Individual computers with their attendant word and data processing programs became a staple in many households and mandatory in the business environment. The creation of the internet allowed people to communicate cheaply and virtually instantaneously with others halfway around the planet.

The globalization trend produced by these scientific and technological inventions has become evident in virtually every area of modern life: In the economic sphere, the rise of multinational corporations, world banks, world trade organizations, and the like has shifted economic power into a new realm; in the political arena, upheavals including the official close of the Cold War, the breakup of the Soviet Union, and the growing strength of the European Union have changed the world's geopolitical map and the distribution of power worldwide; and in the social and intellectual spheres, the cross-fertilization of culture and knowledge that is currently going on is breathtaking. Environmentalists in the '80s captured the essence of these dual movements—political decentralization and emergent transnationalism—in their powerful slogan, "Think globally, act locally." New organizations dedicated to doing precisely that sprouted up around the country like mushrooms after a rain. But these new groups weren't only representing liberal environmentalists. For almost every Center for Biological Diversity urging the federal government to undertake more resource preservation, there was a Shovel Brigade, whose members demonstrated for roaded access to lands they considered best managed by local, not federal, entities.

The emergence of new environmental issues during the '80s and '90s brought home to ordinary Americans, often in a dramatic way, the interconnectedness of the new world order. High on the list of public concerns were the condition of the air we breathe and the earth's atmospheric skin that protects all life. Although air pollution legislation had been in place since the 1950s, with increasingly stringent laws passed at regular intervals in the '60s and '70s, many people felt that pollution was becoming worse, not better. Barry Commoner, for example, in his 1992 book, *Making Peace With the Planet*, documented "the environmental failure" of American policy making that relied primarily on pollution *control* rather than pollution *prevention*. Other scholars and scientists, such as Dixy Lee Ray, vehemently argued against this view; in a reprise of the turn-of-the-century belief in progress and human ingenuity to deal with our collective problems, Ray excoriated "radical" environmentalists and ecoterrorists for their Luddite mentality. Monkey wrenchers Edward Abbey and Dave Foreman were high on her list of '80s political villains.

Nevertheless, a number of crises, beginning with the 1979 Three Mile Island nuclear plant near-meltdown, followed by the 1985 tragedy in Bhopal, India (when a Union Carbide plant blew up killing hundreds of Indians, sickening thousands of others, and contaminating the region with toxic chemicals), and finally the 1986 Chernobyl meltdown (whose effects still are being documented), captured people's attention both in the United States and elsewhere. They also considerably dampened enthusiasm for nuclear power. With a decision in 2000, Germany became the latest nation to phase out its nuclear power plants.

Added to these disasters and near-disasters was the most ominous of all: In the mid-1980s researchers in Antarctica documented what previous researchers had predicted, and what satellite data were transmitting. This was an alarming thinning of the ozone layer. The probable cause was chlorofluorocarbons (CFCs), which had been invented in the 1930s and patented under the trade names freon and styrofoam. They were everywhere in the developed world, from air conditioning units to disposable coffee cups. The depletion of the ozone layer was potentially so grave that collective action was quickly forthcoming. The historic Montreal Protocol, signed by those nations most responsible for the production and consumption of CFCs, was passed in 1987. It called for the worldwide elimination of these once-considered miracles of modern invention.

Although the Clean Air Act Amendments of 1977 were not updated during the eight years Ronald Reagan was in the White House, his vice-president and successor, George Bush, made air and water pollution legislation a priority. During the 1988 presidential race, responsibility for a polluted Boston Harbor became a national issue, as did America's beaches, which were fouled that summer by all sorts of industrial flotsam and jetsam. Proclaiming that he wanted to be the next environmental president, Bush also promised a "no net loss" wetlands policy during the campaign. Controversy over that policy has stalled revision of the Clean Water Act ever since. Neither the Bush nor the Clinton administrations was able to bring liberals and conservatives in Congress together to frame a new national wetlands policy.

Not to mention it was getting hotter. Climatologists—a newly emerging discipline—had documented a decade of higher than average temperatures, and they now began to speak more and more in terms of global climate change. A number of scientists hypothesized that global warming was produced, at least in part, by two centuries' worth of spewing industrial wastes into the atmosphere, thereby producing a greenhouse effect. Political action was called for, and the newly elected President Bush sent Congress in 1989 a comprehensive reform of the Clean Air Act. The revision, the Clean Air Act of 1990, contained provisions to attack air pollution both domestically and internationally. Ten years later, the EPA still is working on implementation of the controversial statute, while northeastern states, led by New York, and frustrated by years of delay, are suing midwestern states for noncompliance with the 1990 law.

At the same time, increased temperatures worldwide are being put in the earth's record book, and international meetings on global climate change, such as the Rio and Kyoto Conferences, are regularly held. In Washington, the United States Global Change Research Program operates out of the Executive Office of the President and provides a focal point for public and private research into what many think is the most urgent environmental problem of all: Climate change too rapid for most flora and fauna to adjust to. The celebrated biologist, E.O. Wilson, sounded alarm bells on this subject, and the causes and effects of biodiversity loss, in his important 1992 book, *The Diversity of Life*. If humankind keeps reproducing and consuming resources at the present rate, Wilson predicted, there will be a wave of extinction such as has not been seen in millions of years on this planet. The human species might well be included in this latest mass die-off. Biodiversity became another rallying point for environmental activism. Enter yet another new discipline: conservation biology, which is clearly prescriptive in its pursuit of biological diversity as a public policy goal.

Al Gore came at the problem not from a scientific perspective but from a political one. In his 1992 bestseller, *Earth in the Balance*, then-Senator Gore reached back into history to sketch out what the United States' response to the global environmental crisis ought to be: A plan of aid to developing countries and to the former states of the Soviet Union that is as selfless and generous as was the Marshall Plan of the 1940s. The book has been controversial, especially given Gore's role as Vice President in the Clinton Administration and his unsuccessful presidential bid. Nevertheless it gives voice to what many contemporary environmentalists believe needs to be done by the world's largest consumer of natural resources for the least well-off nations.

Although the current era has seen a significant increase in institution building at the transnational level, the results to date of the numerous international treaties, accords, conferences, and organizations dedicated to finding solutions for the deteriorating global commons have been meager. There are, of course, several reasons for such modest progress, including national sovereignty; but they must include recognition of the divisive nature of another feature of the contemporary period: the growing gap between rich and poor. Whether we are talking about rich versus poor nations, or rich versus poor classes within nations (including the United States), there are vastly different views about the nature of environmental problems and what to do about them. Getting agreement, for example, between the United States and the developing countries on limiting greenhouse gas emissions or on protecting tropical rainforests is virtually impossible given the present distribution of wealth worldwide. There presently exists not a single global environmental agenda, but several, each of which largely depends upon one's place on the world economic ladder.

The complex issue of the distribution of resources, whether in an international or domestic context, is exacerbated by the issue of race. In his second inaugural address, given on January 20, 1997, President Bill Clinton reminded Americans that "The divide of race has been America's constant curse." It was important that he pointed this out, because it has been easy to ignore the fact that the incredible economic success story of the decade has not raised all boats equally. In the affluent America of the 1980s and '90s— an era of economic transformation and political conservatism that is in many ways reminiscent of the 1880s and '90s—many groups feel left behind, left out, and even dumped upon. Those feeling most ignored by the new economy are the communities, and nations, of color. But white working-class men and women in the United States also have felt disadvantaged in the new world order of free trade agreements, huge trade deficits, and most favored nation status for China.

Among the most important contemporary voices raising issues of justice and equality is that of the sociologist, Robert Bullard. Over twenty years ago, Bullard began researching the impacts of pollution on poor, largely ethnic, neighborhoods in the South. In the 1980s the term environmental racism was created to describe what he and others found occurring in many of America's cities and towns. Environmental racism described local and statewide policy-making patterns that had the effect (if not the intent) of putting people of color at greater environmental risk than their Anglo neighbors. Bullard's important 1990 book, *Dumping in Dixie: Race, Class, and Environmental Quality*, challenged the prevailing notion that blacks and other ethnic minorities do not care about environmental issues. Of course they care, he argued, but their concerns are over living next to garbage dumps and chemical plants, and about having to drink polluted water or breathing foul air. They are less concerned with the mainstream environmental agenda, which includes such issues as expanding wilderness areas and controlling grazing on the public lands. In a passage that echoes Frederick Douglass's conception of the environment, one that links the social and natural environments, Bullard wrote that the environmental justice movement of the '90s must be as much about "protecting humans from the environment" as it is about "protecting the environment from humans." Recent efforts to create a "blue-green" political coalition of blue-collar workers and environmentalists in America and elsewhere exemplify what the environmental justice movement is about. It appears to be part of a larger political reform movement that a number of scholars, journalists, and politicians call neo-progressivism.

Although the present decade has witnessed phenomenal scientific breakthroughs—the human genome mapping project, for example—and has seen incredible success at "growing the economy," to use President Clinton's odd phrase, new environmental initiatives at the federal level have been few. It has been a period of governmental gridlock in Washington. As Jeffrey Berry documents in his 1999 book, *The New Liberalism*, environmental groups and their supporters in Congress have been very successful at checkmating the conservatives' reform agenda (which environmentalists label as "radical"). Strained relationships between the Clinton White House and the conservative, Republican-led Congress that emerged in the 1994 elections added to the gridlock. The nadir of that relationship occurred, of course, in 1998 when the House voted to impeach President Clinton; although the Senate did not vote to remove him from office, nevertheless the atmosphere between the two branches of government remained acrimonious. Such political bickering is not conducive to finding the common ground necessary for good environmental policy making.

However, the Clinton administration produced at least one major environmental initiative. Shortly after the embarrassing impeachment process, President Clinton launched his ambitious Lands Legacy Initiative which involved the liberal use of executive power to further protect existing federal lands from development. In a move similar to President Grover Cleveland's 1897 withdrawal from use of millions of acres of public domain lands—an action he also took just as he was about to leave office—Clinton used the 1906 Antiquities Act to create new national monuments throughout the West. Western legislators were enraged in 1897, and many were in 2000 as well. The administration's "roadless initiative" impacting some 43 million acres of Forest Service land that presently is roadless also added a lot of fuel to the political fires in the West. It is also testimony to the inability of the two branches of government to work together on environmental policies during most of the 1990s.

This is not to say that there hasn't been any progress made in environmental policy making. There has; but much of it has taken place behind the scenes. Within the federal bureaucracy there have been significant efforts at implementing ecosystem management and watershed planning. The Interior Department has initiated habitat conservation plans to smooth the conflict-ridden endangered species process. Agencies are investigating the removal of dams. They have experimented with using economic incentives rather than command-and-control rules, and with citizen-based, collaborative partnerships rather than expert-driven problem solving. Altogether, the reinventing government effort led by Vice President Gore has produced somewhat better interagency coordination; it streamlined and redirected a number of environmental programs to be more user-friendly; and it led to significant diversification of the federal workforce. But most of these incremental changes escape the public's attention. While important, they do not constitute grand new visions or bold initiatives.

In addition, a great deal of environmental action has been happening at the state, local, tribal, and regional levels, where new groups committed to working toward a sustainable future and finding compromises between economic growth and environmental protection are much in evidence throughout the country. The interest group society is alive and well in twenty-first-century America. As former Secretary of the Interior Stewart Udall noted at a recent conference on alternative dispute resolution, "One of the great expressions of our democracy is that when the government is lazy or fails to react, citizens don't just sit back and take it. They organize."

As James Madison first observed—and this observation was elaborated on by de Tocqueville, Bentley, Dewey, Lowi, Berry, and others—America is a pluralistic society and Americans an organizing people. As we move forward in time, voices that went unheard in earlier eras now are being heard in the state's environmental debates. New voices are added as we speak: With a wave of legal immigration in the 1990s that surpasses the previous record set 90 years ago, some 9 million immigrants from Asia, Latin America, the Middle East, and central Europe will in time surely enter the debate.

This must be viewed as a largely positive development in American democracy. But the present cacophony of voices heard in the environmental arena (not to mention other arenas) awaits political leadership that will transform noise into harmony. For this, too—strong national leadership that stresses our commonality in the midst of our great diversity—is a fundamental feature of American democracy. There is an unfinished environmental agenda in the United States which has many discrete components, but which perhaps can be reduced to these questions: What do we want to accomplish with all of our incredible wealth and bountiful nature? Spend, save, or share? And in what combination? Strong leadership is necessary to answer these questions.

The Gallup 2000 survey on the environment showed that even after thirty years of activism, environmental protection has strong public support. While not always the nation's top concern, the data suggest that environmental issues will not disappear from the public eye. But how do we reconcile this general, but often inchoate, public concern with the positions of increasingly strident and polarized interest groups, with the actions of political institutions such as Congress and the bureaucracy that are often consumed by their own agendas, and with a system of campaign finance that corrupts the nature of the political debate? Again, transforming leadership is essential to make the hard choices.

Americans are waiting for a voice to remake America, one which will bring greater social harmony out of the present political "chaos." A voice, if you will, that calls to the better angels of our nature. If that leadership doesn't emerge as a result of the 2000 election, it surely will sooner or later. A documented history of punctuated equilibrium—periods of quiescence and status quo politics followed by bursts of political creativity and action—is the basis for making that prediction. History teaches us that we must "Keep hope alive!"

# 39
# Ronald Reagan (1911–    )

Although Ronald Reagan did not enter public service until he was fifty-five years old, his political career had its roots much earlier in his life. His Irish American father was a New Deal liberal who was employed by the Works Progress Administration during the Great Depression. Ronald Reagan thus began political life as a Democrat, inspired by FDR.

His film career also began in the 1930s. Reagan served in the Army during World War II (but was stationed on the home front), and he became active in a number of Hollywood and film-industry organizations during the postwar period. He also starred in a number of "B" movies.

Elected in 1947 to the first of six terms as President of the Screen Actors Guild, Reagan testified during the infamous "Hollywood Ten" hearings held by the equally infamous House Committee on Un-American Activities (HUAC). In the 1950s, when national concern over the spread of communism was at its peak, Reagan abandoned liberalism for staunch Republican conservatism. From then on, a strong anti-communist stand became a hallmark of Reagan's political philosophy.

Having served two terms as Governor of California, from 1968 to 1976, Reagan successfully ran for the Presidency in 1980 against the incumbent Jimmy Carter. Just two months after his inauguration, he was nearly assassinated; his quiet courage in the face of this near-death experience gained him even greater popularity. It also helped him gain acceptance in Congress for his domestic program, termed Reaganomics. Founded on the theory of supply-side economics, the administration's spending cuts were quite the opposite of the Keynesian economics that underlay Roosevelt's New Deal and Johnson's Great Society liberalism. Its economic objectives were to stimulate economic growth and curb inflation, while at the same time reducing the role of the federal government in American life. Wherever possible, liberal social programs were dismantled or not implemented, public lands and water resources were opened for development, and decision-making authority shifted from Washington to state and local governments.

However, the Reagan Administration also increased federal spending for military and defense, which resulted in unprecedented budget deficits and a national debt that tripled during Reagan's eight years in office. His uncompromising foreign policy, especially vis-à-vis the "Evil Empire," as he called the Soviet Union, often is credited with bringing down the iron curtain and ending the Cold War.

Although Reagan sometimes appeared aloof and detached even from his own Cabinet, the "Great Communicator" was one of America's most popular presidents. A charming storyteller and gifted speaker, who peppered his speeches with optimism, patriotism, and the need to return to traditional values, Reagan hoped to "go down in history as the President who made Americans believe in themselves again." As befits an actor, he had a flair for the dramatic: He famously told the leader of the Soviet Union (and everyone else): "Mr. Gorbachev, tear down this wall!" After a decade of public disillusionment brought on by the Vietnam War, the Watergate scandal, the Iran hostage crisis, and poor economic performance, in his eight years in office Ronald Reagan succeeded in reassuring Americans that they still were a people with a unique destiny.

---

# "THE AMERICAN SOUND"

There are no words adequate to express my thanks for the great honor that you've bestowed on me. I will do my utmost to be deserving of your trust.

This is, as Senator Mathias told us, the 50th time that we, the people, have celebrated this historic occasion. When the first President, George Washington, placed his hand upon the Bible, he stood less than a single day's journey by horseback from raw, untamed wilderness. There were 4 million Americans in a union of 13 States. Today we are 60 times as many in a union of 50 States. We've lighted the world with our inventions, gone to the aid of mankind wherever in the world there was a cry for help, journeyed to the Moon and safely returned. So much has changed, and yet we stand together as we did two centuries ago.

When I took this oath 4 years ago, I did so in a time of economic stress. Voices were raised saying that we had to look to our past for the greatness and glory. But we, the present-day Americans, are not given to looking backward. In this blessed land, there is always a better tomorrow.

Four years ago, I spoke to you of a New Beginning, and we have accomplished that. But in another sense, our New Beginning is a continuation of that beginning created two centuries ago when, for the first time in history, government, the people said, was not our master, it is our servant; its only power that which we the people allow it to have.

That system has never failed us, but for a time we failed the system. We asked things of government that government was not equipped to give. We yielded authority to the National Government that properly belonged to States or to local governments or to the people themselves. We allowed taxes and inflation to rob us of our earnings and savings and watched the great industrial machine that had made us the most productive people on Earth slow down and the number of unemployed increase.

By 1980, we knew it was time to renew our faith, to strive with all our strength toward the ultimate in individual freedom, consistent with an orderly society.

We believed then and now: There are no limits to growth and human progress when men and women are free to follow their dreams. And we

---

*Ronald Reagan. 1988. Second Inaugural Address, January 21, 1985 in *Ronald Reagan: Public Papers of the Presidents of the United States 1985*. Washington, DC: U.S. Government Printing Office, Book I: pp. 55–58.

were right to believe that. Tax rates have been reduced, inflation cut dramatically, and more people are employed than ever before in our history.

We are creating a nation once again vibrant, robust, and alive. But there are many mountains yet to climb. We will not rest until every American enjoys the fullness of freedom, dignity, and opportunity as our birthright. It is our birthright as citizens of this great Republic.

And if we meet this challenge, these will be years when Americans have restored their confidence and tradition of progress; when our values of faith, family, work, and neighborhood were restated for a modern age; when our economy was finally freed from government's grip; when we made sincere efforts at meaningful arms reductions and by rebuilding our defenses, our economy, and developing new technologies, helped preserve peace in a troubled world; when Americans courageously supported the struggle for liberty, self-government, and free enterprise throughout the world and turned the tide of history away from totalitarian darkness and into the warm sunlight of human freedom.

My fellow citizens, our nation is poised for greatness. We must do what we know is right, and do it with all our might. Let history say of us, "These were golden years—when the American Revolution was reborn, when freedom gained new life, when America reached for her best."

Our two-party system has...served us...well over the years, but never better than in those times of great challenge when we came together not as Democrats or Republicans, but as Americans united in a common cause.

Two of our Founding Fathers, a Boston lawyer named Adams and a Virginia planter named Jefferson, members of that remarkable group who met in Independence Hall and dared to think they could start the world over again, left us an important lesson. They had become, in the years then in government, bitter political rivals in the Presidential election of 1800. Then, years later, when both were retired and age had softened their anger, they began to speak to each other again through letters. A bond was reestablished between those two who had helped create this government of ours.

In 1826, the 50th anniversary of the Declaration of Independence, they both died. They died on the same day, within a few hours of each other, and that day was the Fourth of July.

In one of those letters exchanged in the sunset of their lives, Jefferson wrote, "It carries me back to the times when, beset with difficulties and dangers, we were fellow laborers in the same cause, struggling for what is most valuable to man, his right of self-government. Laboring always at the same oar, with some wave ever ahead threatening to overwhelm us, and yet passing harmless...we rode through the storm with heart and hand."

Well, with heart and hand let us stand as one today—one people under God, determined that our future shall be worthy of our past. As we do, we must not repeat the well-intentioned errors of our past. We must never again abuse the trust of working men and women by sending their earnings on a futile chase after the spiraling demands of a bloated Federal Establishment. You elected us in 1980 to end this prescription for disaster, and I don't believe you reelected us in 1984 to reverse course.

At the heart of our efforts is one idea vindicated by 25 straight months of economic growth: Freedom and incentives unleash the drive and entrepreneurial genius that are the core of human progress. We have begun to increase the rewards for work, savings, and investment; reduce the increase in the cost and size of government and its interference in people's lives.

We must simplify our tax system, make it more fair and bring the rates down for all who work and earn. We must think anew and move with a new boldness, so every American who seeks work can find work, so the least among us shall have an equal chance to achieve the greatest things—to be heroes who heal our sick, feed the hungry, protect peace among nations, and leave this world a better place.

The time has come for a new American emancipation—a great national drive to tear down economic barriers and liberate the spirit of enterprise in the most distressed areas of our country. My friends, together we can do this, and do it we must, so help me God.

From new freedom will spring new opportunities for growth, a more productive, fulfilled, and united people, and a stronger America—an America that will lead the technological revolution, and also open its mind and heart and soul to the treasures of literature, music, and poetry, and the values of faith, courage, and love.

A dynamic economy, with more citizens working and paying taxes, will be our strongest tool to bring down budget deficits. But an almost unbroken 50 years of deficit spending has finally brought us to a time of reckoning. We've come to a turning point, a moment for hard decisions. I have asked the Cabinet and my staff a question and now I put the same question to all of you: If not us, who? And if not now, when? It must be done by all of us going forward with a program aimed at reaching a balanced budget. We can then begin reducing the national debt.

I will shortly submit a budget to the Congress aimed at freezing government program spending for the next year. Beyond this, we must take further steps to permanently control government's power to tax and spend. We must act now to protect future generations from government's desire to spend its citizens' money and tax them into servitude when the bills come due. Let us make it unconstitutional for the Federal Government to spend more than the Federal Government takes in.

We have already started returning to the people and to State and local governments responsibilities better handled by them. Now, there is a place for the Federal Government in matters of social compassion. But our fundamental goals must be to reduce dependency and upgrade the dignity of those who are infirm or disadvantaged. And here, a growing economy and support from family and community offer our best chance for a society where compassion is a way of life, where the old and infirm are cared for, the young and, yes, the unborn protected, and the unfortunate looked after and made self-sufficient.

Now, there is another area where the Federal Government can play a part. As an older American, I remember a time when people of different race, creed, or ethnic origin in our land found hatred and prejudice instilled in social custom and, yes, in law. There's no story more heartening in our history than the progress that we've made toward the brotherhood of man that

God intended for us. Let us resolve there will be no turning back or hesitation on the road to an America rich in dignity and abundant with opportunity for all our citizens.

Let us resolve that we, the people, will build an American opportunity society in which all of us—white and black, rich and poor, young and old—will go forward together, arm in arm. Again, let us remember that though our heritage is one of blood lines from every corner of the Earth, we are all Americans, pledged to carry on this last, best hope of man on Earth.

I've spoken of our domestic goals and the limitations we should put on our National Government. Now let me turn to a task that is the primary responsibility of National Government—the safety and security of our people.

Today, we utter no prayer more fervently than the ancient prayer for peace on Earth. Yet history has shown that peace does not come, nor will our freedom be preserved, by good will alone. There are those in the world who scorn our vision of human dignity and freedom. One nation, the Soviet Union, has conducted the greatest military buildup in the history of man, building arsenals of awesome offensive weapons.

We've made progress in restoring our defense capability. But much remains to be done. There must be no wavering by us, nor any doubts by others, that America will meet her responsibilities to remain free, secure, and at peace.

There is only one way safely and legitimately to reduce the cost of national security, and that is to reduce the need for it. And this we're trying to do in negotiations with the Soviet Union. We're not just discussing limits on a further increase of nuclear weapons; we seek, instead, to reduce their number. We seek the total elimination one day of nuclear weapons from the face of the Earth.

Now, for decades, we and the Soviets have lived under the threat of mutual assured destruction—if either resorted to the use of nuclear weapons, the other could retaliate and destroy the one who had started it. Is there either logic or morality in believing that if one side threatens to kill tens of millions of our people our only recourse is to threaten killing tens of millions of theirs?

I have approved a research program to find, if we can, a security shield that will destroy nuclear missiles before they reach their target. It wouldn't kill people; it would destroy weapons. It wouldn't militarize space; it would help demilitarize the arsenals of Earth. It would render nuclear weapons obsolete. We will meet with the Soviets, hoping that we can agree on a way to rid the world of the threat of nuclear destruction.

We strive for peace and security, heartened by the changes all around us. Since the turn of the century, the number of democracies in the world has grown fourfold. Human freedom is on the march, and nowhere more so than in our own hemisphere. Freedom is one of the deepest and noblest aspirations of the human spirit. People, worldwide, hunger for the right of self-determination, for those inalienable rights that make for human dignity and progress.

America must remain freedom's staunchest friend, for freedom is our best ally and it is the world's only hope to conquer poverty and preserve peace. Every blow we inflict against poverty will be a blow against its dark allies of oppression and war. Every victory for human freedom will be a victory for world peace.

So we go forward today, a nation still mighty in its youth and powerful in its purpose. With our alliances strengthened, with our economy leading the world to a new age of economic expansion, we look to a future rich in possibilities. And all of this is because we have worked and acted together, not as members of political parties, but as Americans.

My friends, we live in a world that's lit by lightning. So much is changing and will change, but so much endures and transcends time.

History is a ribbon, always unfurling. History is a journey. And as we continue our journey, we think of those who traveled before us.... Now...we see and hear again the echoes of our past: a general falls to his knees in the hard snow of Valley Forge; a lonely President paces the darkened halls and ponders his struggle to preserve the Union; the men of the Alamo call out encouragement to each other; a settler pushes west and sings a song, and the song echoes out forever and fills the unknowing air.

It is the American sound. It is hopeful, big-hearted, idealistic, daring, decent, and fair. That's our heritage; that's our song. We sing it still. For all our problems, our differences, we are together as of old. We raise our voices to the God who is the Author of this most tender music. And may He continue to hold us close as we fill the world with our sound—in unity, affection, and love—one people under God, dedicated to the dream of freedom that He has placed in the human heart, called upon now to pass that dream on to a waiting and hopeful world.

God bless you, and may God bless America.

# 40
# Dixy Lee Ray (1914–1994)

Washington State's first female governor (1977–1981), Dixy Lee Ray earned a reputation for her well-publicized positions on environmental issues, especially nuclear energy. Ray was a conservationist in the utilitarian tradition: She maintained a firm belief in progress and in humans' ability to solve problems through reason, science, and technology. Ray was educated as a zoologist and marine biologist, and taught at the University of Washington from 1947 until 1974. Much of her research was at the forefront of marine-related concerns, particularly those of the Pacific Northwest coastal habitat.

Ray's career included serving in a number of high-level positions. She was a consultant to the National Science Foundation's oceanography division, she served on presidential task forces on oceanography, and was Director of the Pacific Science Center in Seattle. In 1972, President Richard Nixon appointed Ray to the Atomic Energy Commission; she served as its chair from 1973 to 1975. During her tenure, which coincided with the creation of OPEC, Ray was instrumental in overseeing the expansion of nuclear power production in the United States. She promoted nuclear power as a necessary domestic energy source—an alternative to expensive imported oil. For several reasons, however, including the Three Mile Island near-disaster, that expansion proved to be short-lived.

After leaving the AEC she served as Assistant Secretary of State where she was involved with oceanography, international environmental issues, and related scientific affairs. She became Governor of Washington in 1977, serving one term.

Ray's support of the atomic energy industry often put her at odds with environmental groups, especially the antinuclear activists who emerged as a political force in the 1970s and '80s. Toward the end of her career she became a leading critic of the "deep ecology" movement, while she had muted praise for the mainstream environmentalists who were represented by such organizations as the Sierra Club and the Nature Conservancy. With Ray Guzzo she co-authored two well-known books: *Trashing the Planet* (1990) and *Environmental Overkill* (1993). Both books were scholarly elaborations of the political philosophy promoted by President Reagan in the 1980s. Ray's writings stressed free market environmentalism, the desirability of material progress, and the inevitability of change. She looked to science and technology for solutions to current environmental problems—the so-called "technological fix"—which some environmentalists think only adds to the problem. One of only a few women ever to have gained national stature on environmental issues, Dixy Lee Ray's voice serves as a counterpoint to the far more alarmist voices raised in the 1990s over the fate of the earth and of humankind.

# "FAUST'S SALVATION"*

Our nation, which, to me, is the greatest the human race has conceived, is just a bit more than 200 years old. We can expect an endless supply of problems; some people have doubts about our science, our technology, and the way we use our knowledge. We have some hopes and many fears. We must wonder a little about our age. How old are we, anyway?

Human society has been around a long time, but recorded history goes back only about 6,000 years. The earth has been around between four and five billion years, and every generation of human beings that lives on it thinks its problems are the worst and that humankind has never faced such difficulties before. Most of us believe that unless we solve our problems now, all will be lost.

It's sobering to dwell upon how long humans have survived in a frequently hostile environment. We don't have claws, talons, or fangs. We have no barbs or poison glands to protect ourselves. We don't even have any fur or feathers to keep us warm when the ambient temperature drops; indeed, in our birthday suits, we are ill-adapted to live anywhere, except in the rather warm tropics. Our eyesight is not so good as that of most birds; our hearing is less keen than that of almost all of the higher animals; and our sense of smell is nothing compared to that of most fish and mammals. We can be outrun on land and outswum in the seas.

Yet, with all these difficulties, we've made it somehow. We have managed to penetrate every ecological niche, and we are able to survive in every environmental climate and condition anywhere on earth.

No other species of higher life can do so. You don't find polar bears swimming in a tropical sea; cactus does not grow in a rain forest. Plants and animals have their own ecological and environmental niches, and they are restricted to them. What, then, are our advantages?

First, we have a brain—a brain the likes of which is not seen in any other higher animal. That brain is capable of abstract thought; that brain can solve problems. We have developed a means of communication through human language that so far exceeds communication among other animals as to be in a completely different category. We are learning a good deal more about animal language and animal communication, but to compare even that of the higher primates or of whales and dolphins to the language capabilities of human beings is to overlook the enormous diversity of expression, the implications and nuances of words in the thousands of languages that exist among human beings. Abstract thought and language lead to systematized thinking, which leads to learning, the highest activity human beings engage in.

*Dixy Lee Ray, with Ray Guzzo. 1990. *Trashing the Planet: How Science Can Help Us Deal with Acid Rain, Depletion of the Ozone, and Nuclear Waste (Among Other Things)*. Washington, DC: Regnery Gateway, pp. 159–166, 169–172. Reprinted with permission from Regnery Publishing Company, Inc. Footnotes are omitted.

Learning and teaching, the buildup of knowledge, the questioning of truth, the development of philosophical systems, the practical applications of ideas—these are the things that distinguish humans from all other living things. When we join thoughts, speech, and learning to the peculiar capability to walk on two legs—thus freeing our arms—and the development of dextrous hands, we have a physical form that is truly remarkable in the animal kingdom. These gifts give us the ability to manufacture tools and gadgets of all kinds. They give us the ability to create engines and machines that utilize non-living energy, making the muscle power of slaves and beasts of burden unnecessary in modern society.

It is through our technology that we have been able to fly far away from earth to learn, in truth, how precious it is. It is no coincidence that our awakening to the special nature of our world and to its uniquely balanced environment and its limitations coincided with our first glimpse of earth from outer space, through the eyes of astronauts, television cameras, and photographic equipment. It was through technology that we saw ourselves as we really are, alone on one living, precious globe in space, a human family dependent on the resources of our minds and of our home planet, Earth.

Considering what we humans have accomplished, what we've done to build the modern high-tech society in which we live, and how we've swarmed across the land and changed its face—at least in the temperate region—some critics appear to be fearful that we are now about to destroy nature itself.

Are they right?

Without doubt, humans have been hard on the environment in many discrete places. Whenever mankind has cleared land to build a city or to farm or to manufacture something, the naturalness of nature has been changed. From a longer perspective, civilizations have come and gone since antiquity. Sometimes, in areas that were once inhabited and then abandoned, nature has taken over. On a shorter time scale, it has been demonstrated again and again that areas once despoiled by pollutants can return to being a healthy abode for many species.

True, humans can be and have been destructive, but humans also learn. The ways to live in harmony with nature while maintaining a comfortable, even high-tech, lifestyle are far better understood today. And more and more they are being practiced. There is no reason to believe that, inevitably, everything will get worse.

But activist environmentalists charge that man has gone beyond having an effect on the immediate vicinity of his activities and is now damaging the entire planet. They say man's industrial activities are changing the composition of the atmosphere, presumably irreversibly, through increased production of $CO_2$ and other greenhouse gases. As already pointed out, until the predictions of human-caused, global atmospheric alterations can be accepted as certain, there must be a satisfactory explanation for the increases in greenhouse gases 300 years ago, 150,000 years ago, and in the geological past. And it must be established that the ozone-destroying chloride ion really does, in fact, come from CFC and not from any of a number of natural sources.

In the light of the enormous size of the atmosphere and the hydrosphere, and the colossal natural forces involved, it would appear that man's puny activities are being vastly exaggerated.

The fact is that weather will be what it is and that man's influence, if any, is trivial and relatively local. In the long term, climates, too, will change, as they have done in the past, determined not by man but by immense natural forces. Neither the sun nor the earth is immortal. Each will grow old and die. Inevitably, the sun will burn itself out, slipping first into that stage called a "red giant," where its size will become so huge that it will encompass the inner planets. Our earth will be swallowed up and cease to exist. Fortunately for us, the time scale for this is fairly long—about two billion years or so from now. That gives us a pretty good cushion of time to become better stewards of the environment. We are not ever going to control it on a worldwide scale.

Still, there are those who believe that we are threatening earth with intolerable stresses, born of just exactly those same things that have made us unique—human knowledge and technology. This belief finds expression in the modern environmental movement.

Now, aside from unrivaled success in obtaining favorable publicity for its positions, how is it that environmentalism became so successful? Part of the answer is fairly clear. There were two essential ingredients. One was national legislation that gave the activists access to the federal courts and standing before the law (the National Environmental Protection Act). In the last 15 years, more than 100 environmental laws have been passed. The other was the creation of many governmental agencies, including the Environmental Protection Agency, the Occupational Safety and Health Administration (OSHA), and the Nuclear Regulatory Commission.

Environmentalism, as we have come to know it in the waning years of the twentieth century, is a new and complex phenomenon. It is new in the sense that it goes far beyond the traditional conservation movement—be kind to animals, support good stewardship of the earth, and so on—a philosophy of nature that we have known from the past. It is complex in that it incorporates a strongly negative element of anti-development, anti-progress, anti-technology, anti-business, anti-established institutions, and, above all, anti-capitalism. Its positive side, if that is what it can be called, is that it seeks development of a society totally devoid of industry and technology.

As a movement, it is activist, adversarial, punitive, and coercive. It is quick to resort to force, generally through the courts or through legislation, although some of its more zealous adherents engage in physical violence (Earth First! and Greenpeace, for example). Finally, the environmentalist movement today has an agenda that goes far beyond a mere concern for nature, as shown by its links to and common cause with other leftist radical movements—such as are incorporated in the Green parties of Europe.

This is not to suggest that everyone who supports more responsible policies for cleaner air and water, who believes in restraining pollution, and who cares about how the earth's resources are used is a wild-eyed extremist. Far from it. The great majority of those who make up the membership of the Audubon Society, Sierra Club, National Wildlife Federation, Wilderness

Society, Nature Conservancy, and countless other groups are fine, decent citizens. They are honest, honorable supporters of a good, clean environment and responsible human actions. However, the leaders of some of their organizations—such as the Natural Resources Defense Council, Friends of the Earth, Earth First!, Greenpeace, Government Accountability Project, Institute for Policy Studies, and many others—are determinedly leftist, radical, and dedicated to blocking industrial progress and unraveling industrial society.

These activist leaders and spokesmen are referred to as "political environmentalists" to distinguish them from the rest of us, who believe that using scientific data, not scare tactics, is the correct way to deal with environmental issues.

Modern environmentalism arose in response to real and widely recognized problems, among them: growing human pressures on natural resources, accumulation of wastes, and increased pollution of land, air, and water. Remember, for example, accounts from Cleveland about the alarming condition of the Cuyahoga River, which flows through the heart of Cleveland's industrial corridor into Lake Erie and was once called the world's most polluted river. So many gallons of industrial and chemical waste, oil, and other flammables had been dumped into it over the years that the river actually caught fire and blazed for a time. The Cuyahoga has since been cleaned up, and so has Lake Erie.

Without question, by the 1960s it was time to curb the excesses of a throwaway society. It was time to face up to the fact that there simply wasn't any "away" to throw things any more; "vacant" land and open space were limited. It was also time to recognize that there is a human tendency to overuse a good product, whether it's a vitamin, antibiotic, fertilizer, pesticide, or wilderness. It was time to redress many environmental wrongs. But, perhaps inevitably, the movement has gone beyond correcting past abuses and now poses real obstacles to industrial and technological progress.

Under the slogan of protecting the environment, political environmentalists now oppose and cause delay in the construction of important facilities, even those that are obviously necessary and have wide support. It is now next to impossible and certainly far more expensive than in the past to build a sewage treatment plant, garbage incinerators, a power plant, a dam, or to open a new landfill. Industrial facilities, even when they are expected to produce useful commodities, hardly fare better. Liability for anything that might go wrong and the threat of litigation are effective deterrents used by political environmentalists against industry.

After achieving so much—establishing government agencies with oversight authority and regulatory power, armed with such laws as the National Environmental Protection Act, the Clean Air Act, the Clean Water Act, the Waste Management Act, and more than 100 other environmental laws—environmentalist groups apparently cannot leave well enough alone. They seem to be unable to let these laws and statutory agencies work to continue the significant progress of the last two decades. Instead, they press for ever more stringent and punitive controls. They continue to push for and insist on an unachievable pristine perfection, whatever the cost. Never mind that humans never survived without altering nature.

It is a fact that effluents no longer pour unchecked from the stacks and chimneys and waste pipes of industry. Open hearth furnaces and other industrial processes that depend on burning fuel have been largely replaced by electric furnaces and much of our foundry and smelting capacity has been shut down. Open burning of garbage no longer occurs and discharge of untreated sewage and waste water is becoming rare. It is certainly illegal.

Responsible timber companies have revised their logging practice and more trees are growing now than 50 years ago, an increase of more than three and a half times since 1920. Reforestation is a usual, not an occasional, practice. Coupled with modern agricultural procedures that require less land for food production, we now have at least as much wooded and forested acreage in America as existed in Colonial times and probably more.

So what do the political environmental extremists want? Instant ecological perfection? A return to the Garden of Eden? To be in control? To exercise power? To remake society according to their political philosophy?

Activist environmentalists are mostly white, middle to upper income, and predominantly college-educated. They are distinguished by a vocal do-good mentality that sometimes successfully cloaks their strong streak of elitism, which is often coupled with a belief that the end justifies the means and that violence and coercion are appropriate tactics. Political environmentalists are adept at publicizing their causes, at exerting pressure on elected officials and government agencies, and at using the courts of law to achieve their aims.

They also tend to believe that nature is sacred and that technology is a sacrilege. Some environmentalists appear to be in favor of taking mankind back to pantheism or animism.

The idea that nature is "pure" and the almost religious awe with which it is held seems to be a part of the attraction, the drawing power of the movement. This attitude appears to permeate the thinking of a great many persons who are members of the Sierra Club, Audubon Society, Wilderness Society, Friends of the Earth, and other groups. We can look upon it as a very sincere, if somewhat sophomoric, emotional response to legitimate worries about the environment.

The leaders of the political environmentalists compound this reverence for the purity of nature with scare stories of looming man-made catastrophe. They say that our environmental problems are so serious as to threaten the continuation of life on Earth—or, if that's not true, that we should at least pretend that it is....

The common threads of belief that seem to run through these opinions are Malthusian ideas of finite resources, limits to growth, forced population control, a distrust of human beings, a belief in the omnipotence of the State and its ability to control individual choice, and a rejection of science, technology, and industrialization. Does this represent the convictions of most Americans? No way!...

Ecoemotion and hysteria has also, of course, many adherents in Congress. Writing in *The International Herald-Tribune* under the title, "The Environment Indicts Our Civilization," Senator Albert Gore of Tennessee anticipates what he calls "an environmental holocaust without precedent."

If this were just political rhetoric, it could be dismissed. But Gore is serious. He calls for a series of global summit meetings to seek the "unprecedented international cooperation that the environmental crisis will demand."

Gore is supported by Frederico Mayor Zaragoza, director general of UNESCO, who said in Belgium in March 1989, that "the environment has to be addressed through global measures, but you need ways of enforcing them." The "ways" would be through a uniformed and armed United Nations "green force" equivalent to the blue-helmeted UN military peace-keeping force.

Senator Gore is not alone in his radical environmental stand. He is joined by many of his colleagues, including Senator Timothy Wirth of Colorado and Representative Claudine Schneider of Rhode Island. Representative Schneider has introduced a bill titled "Global Warming Prevention Act of 1989." It orders the United States government to take extensive tracts of land out of food production and cultivate sugar cane for ethanol to replace gasoline. On the international level, the Schneider bill calls for cutting off all aid to countries that propose any development other than those using "least-cost energy." It also directs that "priority shall be given to programs that enhance access of the poor to low-cost vehicles and efficient carrying devices, including access to credit for the purchase of bicycles, carts, pack animals, and similar affordable, non-motorized vehicles." How many citizens would agree that our tax money should be used to purchase draft animals?

We could hope that other members of Congress do not share this kind of environmental insanity, but 49 senators are co-sponsors on the bills introduced by Gore, Wirth, and Schneider.

...[W]hat can the common, everyday, sensible, taxpaying citizen do? Here are some suggestions:

First, a person can put pressure, individually and through groups, on members of the legislative branch, both state and federal, to refrain from acting precipitously on expensive "cures" for unproven environmental ills. Ask for evidence. It's public tax money that they are proposing to spend; it should not be wasted.

Second, don't succumb to the argument put forward by political environmentalists that action must be taken in advance of understanding the problem, "just in case." Keep in mind that they have a job or position to protect. Remember, the alarmists depend on continued crises, even if they are contrived, to keep themselves in business. Insist on facts.

Third, keep a sense of perspective. This old earth has been through a lot, including drastic climate changes, without any help from humans. It will continue to change. The earth has never been stable or remained the same for long.

Finally, humans cannot live on earth without altering it and without using natural resources. Our responsibility is to be good stewards of the environment and to remember that a well-tended garden is better than a neglected woodlot. It is demeaning beyond belief to consider mankind simply another species of animal, no better and no worse than wild beasts.

We human beings are what we are—imperfect but well-meaning and capable of improvement. We learn from mistakes. We have the ability to think rationally; and we should do so more often. We also have the gift to make conscious choices; and we should choose to pursue knowledge and understanding that will better the lot of all species on the planet.

In Goethe's *Faust*, Faust, jaded with every conceivable worldly experience, finally finds, in a land reclamation project, the contentment that has eluded him all his life.

Now it may seem strange that Faust should find his greatest happiness in a prosaic engineering project. But in nineteenth century Europe, the clearing of swamps had clear human benefits. (Swamps had not been graduated to the status of "wetlands," and no environmental impact studies were required.) Faust's soul was saved, not because he reclaimed land, but because, in Goethe's immortal words, "whosoever, aspiring, struggles on, for him there is salvation."

In this sense and in the knowledge that we who believe in technology are engaged in the struggle to improve the lot of every human being, we can still share Goethe's enthusiasm and have a taste of Faust's salvation.

# 41
# Robert D. Bullard (1946–    )

Sociology professor and head of the Environmental Justice Center at Clark Atlanta University, Robert Bullard published in 1979 one of the first studies to link demographics with the siting of toxic facilities in the United States. This work appeared three years before the Reverend Benjamin Chavis coined the phrase "environmental racism" to describe what minority groups perceived as a widespread problem, that of putting blacks and other communities of color at greater environmental risk than their white neighbors. Also in 1979, Bullard filed one of the first—albeit unsuccessful—environmental justice lawsuits under the Civil Rights Act of 1964.

In the 1990s Bullard helped plan the first National People of Color Environmental Leadership Summit in Washington, D.C. In addition to *Dumping in Dixie*, published in 1990, he is the author of several other books and articles detailing the environmental problems that people of color confront. Personally and intellectually, Bullard has been on the cutting edge of the environmental justice movement in America.

---

## "NO ENVIRONMENTAL JUSTICE WITHOUT SOCIAL JUSTICE"*

It is now time for people to stop asking the question, Do minorities care about the environment? The evidence is clear and irrefutable that white middle-class communities do not have a monopoly on environmental concern nor are they the only groups moved to action when confronted with the threat of pollution. Although a "concern and action gap" may still exist between blacks and whites, black communities are no longer being bullied into submission by industrial polluters and government regulators.

Clearly, a "new" form of environmentalism has taken root in America and in the black community. Since the late 1970s, a new grassroots social movement emerged around the toxics threat. Citizens mobilized around the antiwaste theme. These social activists acquired new skills in areas where they had little or no prior experience. They soon became resident "experts" on the toxics issue. The new grassroots environmentalists burst on the scene as "toxic busters." They, however, did not limit their attacks to well-publicized toxic contamination issues, but sought remedial actions on problems like "housing, transportation, air quality, and even economic development—

---

*Robert Bullard. 1990. *Dumping in Dixie*. Boulder, CO: Westview Press, pp. 103–114, 116–117. Copyright © 1990 by Westview Press. Reprinted by permission from Westview Press, a member of Perseus Books, L.L.C. Footnotes are omitted.

issues the traditional environmental agenda had largely ignored." Robert Gottlieb and Helen Ingram described the grassroots environmental movement as having the following traits:

- Focuses on equity and the urban industrial complex
- Challenges the mainstream environmental movement for its conservative tactics but not its goals
- Emphasizes the needs of the community and workplace as primary agenda items
- Uses its own self-taught "experts" and citizen lawsuits instead of relying on legislation and lobbying
- Takes a "populist" stance on environmental issues relying on active members rather than dues-payers from mailing lists
- Embraces a democratic ideology akin to the civil rights and women's movement of the sixties

Environmentalism, concern and action, has been too narrowly defined. Concern has been incorrectly equated with check-writing, dues-paying, and membership in environmental organizations. These biases no doubt have contributed to the misunderstanding of grassroots environmental movement in minority communities.

Black community activists in this new movement focused their attention on toxics and the notion of deprivation. When black community residents compared their environmental quality with that of the larger society, a sense of deprivation or unequal treatment emerged. Once again, institutional racism and discriminatory land-use policies and practices of government—at all levels—influenced the creation and perpetuation of racially separate and unequal residential areas for blacks and whites.

Institutional barriers have locked millions of blacks in polluted neighborhoods and hazardous, low-paying jobs, making it difficult for them to "vote with their feet" and escape these health-threatening environments. Mainstream environmentalists have been slow in recognizing these grassroots social activists as "environmentalists," mainly because of the way the problems are framed. Conversely, few black activists see themselves as environmentalists. Local problems are generally defined along equity lines as blacks see themselves fighting another form of institutional discrimination.

The environmental equity movement is an extension of the social justice movement. Environmentalists may be concerned about clean air, but may have opposing views on the construction of low-income housing in white, middle-class, suburban neighborhoods. Black residents have come to understand that environmentalists are no more enlightened than nonenvironmentalists when it comes to minority communities. But then, why should they be more enlightened? After all, we are all products of socialization and reflect the various biases and prejudices of this process. It is not surprising that mainstream environmental organizations have not been active on issues that disproportionately impact minority communities, as in the case of toxics, workplace hazards, urban and rural housing needs, and the myriad of problems resulting from the strains in the urban industrial complex. Yet, minorities are the ones accused of being ill-informed, unconcerned, and inactive on environmental issues....

Why were black organizations late in challenging the environmental imbalance that exists in the United States? There is enough blame to go around. Black organizations and their leaders have not been as sensitive to the environmental threat to minorities as they have been to problems in education, housing, jobs, drugs, and more recently the AIDS epidemic. In some cases, black leaders have operated out of fear of erosion of hard-fought economic gains by some environmental reform proposals....

Grassroots groups in black communities are beginning to take a stand against threatened plant closure and job loss as a trade-off for environmental risks. Job blackmail has lost some of its appeal, especially in those areas where the economic incentives (jobs, taxes, monetary contributions, etc.) flow outside of the black community. People can hardly be blackmailed over benefits they never receive from local polluting industry. Because of the potential to exacerbate existing environmental inequities, black community residents and their leaders are now questioning the underlying assumptions behind "risk compensation" as applied in minority and poor areas.

In their push to become acceptable and credible, many mainstream environmental organizations adopted a corporate model in their structure, demeanor, and outlook. This metamorphosis has had a down side. These corporatelike environmental organizations have alienated many grassroots leaders and community organizers (both black and white) from the larger movement—a complaint not unlike that of constituents who feel apart from their locally elected representatives in Washington....

Local community groups may be turned off by the idea of sitting around a table with a waste disposal giant, a government regulator, and an environmentalist to negotiate the siting of a toxic waste incinerator in their community. The lines become blurred in terms of the parties representing the interests of the community and those of business. Negotiations of this type fuel residents' perception of an "unholy trinity" where the battle lines are drawn along an "us versus them" power arrangement. Moreover, overdependence on and blind acceptance of risk assessment analysis and "the best available technology" for policy-setting serves to intimidate, confuse, and overwhelm individuals at the grassroots level.

Talk of risk compensation for a host community raises a series of moral dilemmas, especially where environmental imbalances already exist. Should risks be borne by a smaller group to spare the larger groups? Past discriminatory waste siting practices should not guide future policy decisions. For example, a "community saturated with facilities may have less impact sensitivity to a proposed project than might an area having few facilities." Any saturation policy derived from past siting practices perpetuates equity impacts. Facility siting becomes a "modern ritual for selecting victims for sacrifice...."

It is unlikely that the grassroots environmental movement will ever become a mass movement in the black community. However, there are clear signs that a small cadre of dedicated activists have taken up the "cause" of environmental equity. Few social movements can count on total support and involvement of their constituent groups. All social movements have "free riders," individuals who benefit from the efforts of a few. Blacks in the grassroots environmental movement have been and will probably remain wedded to their established social action organizations. After all, American society has yet to achieve a race-neutral state where these organizations are no longer needed. Black institutions still serve a special niche in society. Although the color barrier has been breached in most professional groups around the country, blacks still find it useful to have their own organizations. The predominately black National Bar Association (NBA), National Medical Association (NMA), National Association of Black Social Workers (NABSW), Association of Black Psychologists (ABP), and Association of Black Sociologists (ABS) are examples of race-based professional organizations. The chances are slim of having a mass movement of blacks flooding the ranks of mainstream environmental and conservation organizations.

Grassroots environmental organizations, whether in black or white communities, have the advantage of being closer to the people they serve and the problems they address. Future growth in the environmental movement is likely to come from the bottom up, grassroots environmental groups linking up with social action groups for expanded spheres of influence and focus....

Black communities do not have a long track record in challenging government decisions and private industries that threaten the health of their residents. Many of the organizations and institutions were formed as a reaction to racism and dealt primarily with social justice issues. The NAACP, Urban League, Southern Christian Leadership Conference, Commission for Racial Justice, and National Black United Front are some examples of these organizations. These organizations operated at the multistate level and had affiliates in cities across the nation. Few of these organizations, however, embraced an ideology that linked environmental disparities with racism. It is just recently that these organizations have begun to link environmental disparities to institutional racism. This linking of institutional racism with the structure of resource allocation (clean environments) has led black social action groups to adopt environmental equity as a civil rights issue, an issue well worth "taking to the street."

NIMBY [Not In My Back Yard] has operated to insulate many white communities from the localized environmental impacts of solid waste facilities while providing them the benefits of garbage disposal. NIMBY, like white racism, creates and perpetuates privileges for whites at the expense of people of color. Citizens see the siting question as an all-out war. Those communities that can mobilize political influence improve their chance of "winning" this war. Because blacks and other ethnic minorities remain underrepresented in elected and appointed offices, they most often must rely on indirect representation, usually white officials who may or may not understand the nature and severity of the community problem. Citizen redress often becomes a political issue....

Who are the frontline leaders in this quest for environmental justice? What role do outside elites play? The war against toxics in black communities has been waged largely by individuals indigenous to those black communities. Black grassroots community groups received some moral support from outside elites, but few elites were down in the trenches fighting alongside the toxic warriors. On the other hand, it was the ministers from the black churches and the activist leaders from the social action organizations (e.g., civic clubs, neighborhood associations, parents groups, etc.) who mobilized black community residents against the toxics threat. Few of these leaders identified themselves as environmentalists or saw their struggle solely as an environmental problem. Their struggle embraced larger issues of equity, social justice, and resource distribution. Black leaders and their constituents questioned the fairness of the decision-making process surrounding facility siting. People's perceptions are important factors in dispute handling. Gail Bingham noted:

> Although people's strategies for resolving environmental disputes may vary depending on their views about social conflict and the characteristics of a particular dispute, individuals and groups care about similar factors. They care about the outcomes and the extent to which it satisfies the real issues in disputes, as they see them. They care about the process—its fairness, its efficiency, and the opportunities it provides them for influencing a decision.

Most environmental disputes revolve around siting issues, involving government or private industry. Proposals for future sites are more likely to attract environmentalists' support than are existing sites. It is much easier to get outside assistance in fighting a noxious facility that is on paper than one that is in operation. Again, plant closure means economic dislocation. Because minority communities are burdened with a greater share of existing facilities—many of which have been in operation for decades—it is an uphill battle of convincing outside environmental groups to support efforts to close such facilities....

It makes a lot of sense for the organized environmental movement in the United States to broaden its base to include minorities, low-income, and working-class individuals and issues. Why diversify? As a participant in a Minority Roundtable of the Conservation Leadership Project held in the summer of 1989 in Seattle, I observed a host of reasons given by blacks, Hispanics, native Americans, and native Hawaiians for diversification. Some of the responses included:

- Minority voter blocs are forming convincingly in many regions of the country.
- The voting record of the Congressional Black Caucus is the most solid environmental record in Congress.
- The demographic shift toward more women and minorities in the workplace makes diversification both desirable and inevitable.
- Reacting positively to that demographic shift will demand and increase the sophistication of the mainstream environmental organizations.
- Diversity is ecologically and biologically correct.
- Diversity is ethically and morally correct.

- America's greatest asset is its human diversity, its multi-cultural heritage.
- Diversity broadens the perspective.

Diversification makes good economic and political sense for the long-range survival of the environmental movement. However, it is not about selfishness or "quota-filling." Diversification can go a long way in enhancing the national environmental movement's worldwide credibility and legitimacy in dealing with global environmental and development issues, especially in Third World nations....

The nation's major environmental organizations mirror the national picture of a severe underrepresentation of minority professionals at all levels. There is just a handful of minority environmental organizations in the country that have paid staffs. The Center for Environment, Commerce and Energy (CE²), based in the nation's capital, is just one of the few black environmental organizations. Norris McDonald, the president of CE², charged environmental organizations with making the same excuses as American corporations. Corporate recruiters' fallback position has been "they can't find blacks and other minorities." Or they halt their search after finding one minority—the we-have-one-minority (WHOM) syndrome—a malady commonly observed in corporate America and academia. However, McDonald has found something altogether different when advertising for minority interns. His office is routinely inundated with minority applicants vying for the few environmental internship positions he has in his organization....

There are a few encouraging signs pointing to a shift in the approach mainstream environmental organizations are using to diversify their constituency. Although still in an embryonic stage, The Environmental Consortium for Minority Outreach (TEC) is one of these programs. TEC was established by representatives from The Trust for Public Land, Human Environment Center, and the Group of Ten (i.e., the ten largest environmental organizations). Black environmentalist Gerry Stover of TEC and a participant in the Minority Roundtable in Seattle addressed the shortage of minorities in the environmental movement and the need for affirmative action:

> A major problem faced by all of the major environmental and conservation organizations in the United States today is the recruitment and retention of minorities for middle, senior, and executive level positions. Through the years there has been repeated verbal commitment to increased Affirmative Action efforts within our ranks, yet, for the most part, the results have been dismal.... The most commonly heard reasons for this situation are: (1) "The pool of qualified candidates is almost nonexistent." Or (2) "Recruiting takes time under normal circumstances. Recruiting minorities can be an endless task with limited or no results." Or (3) "Good minority candidates usually turn us down because of our salary levels or because of a lack of understanding of career potential within our organization."...

Nearly everyone can agree on the need for more minority leaders in the environmental and conservation movement. Enlarging this pool is not likely to be an easy or overnight task. TEC, however, cannot solve this acute shortage alone. Other institutions must pitch in and carry their share of the work, especially colleges and universities....

The environmental movement has proven that it can make a difference in the quality of life we enjoy in the United States. Environmentalists and conservationists alike wield substantial power and influence from city halls to the United States Congress. They also have a significant role in shaping the nation's development patterns, particularly when it comes to environmental impacts and land use.

The 1990s offer some challenging opportunities for the environmental movement to embrace social justice and other minority concerns. There can be no environmental justice without social justice. Population shifts and demographic trends all point to a more diverse America. It is time for the environmental movement to diversify and reach out to the "other" America—communities that have borne a disproportionate burden of the nation's pollution problem.

No segment of the population should have to bear the brunt of the nation's industrial pollution problem. Yet, institutional barriers still limit residential choices and mobility options for millions of minorities, working-class persons, and poor community residents. While much progress has been made in bringing blacks and other minority groups into the mainstream, all Americans do not have the same opportunities to escape the ravages of environmental toxins. Consequently, those communities that have the least economic means—minority communities are overrepresented in this group—have become victims of the toxic wars.

Environmental discrimination is difficult to prove—as is the case of other forms of discrimination—in a court of law. Nevertheless, there is mounting empirical evidence that minorities and low-income communities suffer disproportionately from facility siting decisions involving municipal landfills, incinerators, and hazardous-waste disposal facilities. Since risks generally increase with proximity to the noxious facilities, it is the poor and minority communities who are paying a high price in terms of their health.

Environmental equity and social justice issues are now being raised in this country and around the world. In keeping the narrowly defined concept of environmentalism, the larger movement is doomed to the charge of being an elitist movement that cares more about "protecting the environment from humans" than about "protecting humans from the environment."

# 42
# Edward O. Wilson (1929–    )

First distinguishing himself as an expert on insects, particularly ant communities, Harvard University naturalist E. O. Wilson has become the most visible and passionate spokesperson for biodiversity in the United States. His first major book, *The Insect Societies* (1971), laid the foundation for his controversial work in the field of sociobiology, an approach that examines the social behavior of humans and other animals from a predominantly biological perspective. Humans, the argument goes, behave in ways that are virtually indistinguishable from other animals. Wilson's extensive research, which won him two Pulitzer Prizes (one for *On Human Nature*, 1978, and one for *The Ants*, 1990), carefully and painstakingly examines the symbiotic relationship between human society and the biological world, or biosphere.

In one of his most respected books, *The Diversity of Life* (1992), Wilson argued that while biodiversity is a central feature of the world as humans have known it throughout their entire history on earth, today species and ecosystems are being exterminated at an unprecedented rate. Unchecked, this is bound to lead to a major catastrophe perhaps unparalleled in evolutionary history. While nature will recover, just as it has done at least five times previously after major events diminished life on earth, the millennia required for regeneration to take place makes no sense in humanity's timeframe. Moreover, there is no assurance, Wilson claimed, that the human species will not be included in the extinction process now underway.

If in fact humans are destroying the world's biodiversity, Wilson posits that their behavior can be explained by the very processes of natural selection that explain animal behavior. In the "nature" versus "nurture" controversy, Wilson comes down firmly on the side of biological determinism. There is, he argued in *Sociobiology: The New Synthesis* (1975), a biological basis for human aggression, for the most basic social conventions such as the taboo against incest, and for behavioral differences between males and females. Even the moral sense that must be called upon in order to protect other flora and fauna is, according to Wilson, a product of evolution. It is the moral sense, a biological trait, which gives humans the ability to not only save other creatures but themselves. Much of Wilson's argument recalls the work of the founder of modern psychology, Sigmund Freud, and the revolutionary nineteenth-century naturalist, Charles Darwin.

Wilson's work is controversial. Critics have called his arguments, especially his work on sociobiology, "shaky science." Some say that they are hearing a reconstituted Social Darwinism, which uses nature to justify established social orders, such as patriarchy.

Wilson's most recent controversial idea, set forth in *Consilience: The Unity of Knowledge* (1998), is that scholars must work toward a synthesis of the social and natural sciences, until *all* relationships are subsumed under the laws of physics. While many would agree that it is a laudable goal to link more closely these fields of inquiry, others question whether all knowledge will ever be reduced to a single unified physical theory.

# "THE AGE OF RESTORATION"*

The sixth great extinction spasm of geological time is upon us, grace of mankind. Earth has at last acquired a force that can break the crucible of bio-diversity. I sensed it with special poignancy that stormy night at Fazenda Dimona, when lightning flashes revealed the rain forest cut open like a cat's eye for laboratory investigation. An undisturbed forest rarely discloses its internal anatomy with such clarity. Its edge is shielded by thick secondary growth or else, along the river bank, the canopy spills down to ground level. The nighttime vision was a dying artifact, a last glimpse of savage beauty.

A few days later I got ready to leave Fazenda Dimona: gathered my muddied clothes in a bundle, gave my imitation Swiss army knife to the cook as a farewell gift, watched an overflight of Amazonian green parrots one more time, labeled and stored my specimen vials in reinforced boxes, and packed my field notebook next to a dog-eared copy of Ed McBain's police novel *Ice*, which, because I had neglected to bring any other reading matter, was now burned into my memory.

Grinding gears announced the approach of the truck sent to take me and two of the forest workers back to Manaus. In bright sunlight we watched it cross the pastureland, a terrain strewn with fire-blackened stumps and logs, the battlefield my forest had finally lost. On the ride back I tried not to look at the bare fields. Then, abandoning my tourist Portuguese, I turned inward and daydreamed. Four splendid lines of Virgil came to mind, the only ones I ever memorized, where the Sibyl warns Aeneas of the Underworld:

> The way downward is easy from Avernus.
> Black Dis's door stands open night and day.
> But to retrace your steps to heaven's air,
> There is the trouble, there is the toil…

For the green prehuman earth is the mystery we were chosen to solve, a guide to the birthplace of our spirit, but it is slipping away. The way back seems harder every year. If there is danger in the human trajectory, it is not so much in the survival of our own species as in the fulfillment of the ultimate irony of organic evolution: that in the instant of achieving self-understanding through the mind of man, life has doomed its most beautiful creations. And thus humanity closes the door to its past.

The creation of that diversity came slow and hard: 3 billion years of evolution to start the profusion of animals that occupy the seas, another 350 million years to assemble the rain forests in which half or more of the species on earth now live. There was a succession of dynasties. Some species split into two or several daughter species, and their daughters split yet again to

*Edward O. Wilson. 1992. *The Diversity of Life*. Cambridge, MA: The Belknap Press of Harvard University Press, pp. 343–351. Reprinted with permission from E. O. Wilson.

create swarms of descendants that deployed as plant feeders, carnivores, free swimmers, gliders, sprinters, and burrowers, in countless motley combinations. These ensembles then gave way by partial or total extinction to newer dynasties, and so on to form a gentle upward swell that carried biodiversity to a peak—just before the arrival of humans. Life had stalled on plateaus along the way, and on five occasions it suffered extinction spasms that took 10 million years to repair. But the thrust was upward. Today the diversity of life is greater than it was a 100 million years ago—and far greater than 500 million years before that.

Most dynasties contained a few species that expanded disproportionately to create satrapies of lesser rank. Each species and its descendants, a sliver of the whole, lived an average of hundreds of thousands to millions of years. Longevity varied according to taxonomic group. Echinoderm lineages, for example, persisted longer than those of flowering plants, and both endured longer than those of mammals.

Ninety-nine percent of all the species that ever lived are now extinct. The modern fauna and flora are composed of survivors that somehow managed to dodge and weave through all the radiations and extinctions of geological history. Many contemporary world dominant groups, such as rats, ranid frogs, nymphalid butterflies, and plants of the aster family Compositae, attained their status not long before the Age of Man. Young or old, all living species are direct descendants of the organisms that lived 3.8 billion years ago. They are living genetic libraries, composed of nucleotide sequences, the equivalent of words and sentences, which record evolutionary events all across that immense span of time. Organisms more complex than bacteria—protists, fungi, plants, animals—contain between 1 and 10 billion nucleotide letters, more than enough in pure information to compose an equivalent of the *Encyclopaedia Britannica*. Each species is the product of mutations and recombinations too complex to be grasped by unaided intuition. It was sculpted and burnished by an astronomical number of events in natural selection, which killed off or otherwise blocked from reproduction the vast majority of its member organisms before they completed their lifespans. Viewed from the perspective of evolutionary time, all other species are our distant kin because we share a remote ancestry. We still use a common vocabulary, the nucleic-acid code, even though it has been sorted into radically different hereditary languages....

Organisms are all the more remarkable in combination. Pull out the flower from its crannied retreat, shake the soil from the roots into the cupped hand, magnify it for close examination. The black earth is alive with a riot of algae, fungi, nematodes, mites, springtails, enchytraeid worms, thousands of species of bacteria. The handful may be only a tiny fragment of one ecosystem, but because of the genetic codes of its residents it holds more order than can be found on the surfaces of all the planets combined. It is a sample of the living force that runs the earth—and will continue to do so with or without us.

We may think that the world has been completely explored. Almost all the mountains and rivers, it is true, have been named, the coast and geodetic surveys completed, the ocean floor mapped to the deepest trenches, the atmosphere transected and chemically analyzed. The planet is now continuously monitored from space by satellites; and, not least, Antarctica, the last virgin continent, has become a research station and expensive tourist stop. The biosphere, however, remains obscure. Even though some 1.4 million species of organisms have been discovered (in the minimal sense of having specimens collected and formal scientific names attached), the total number alive on earth is somewhere between 10 and 100 million. No one can say with confidence which of these figures is the closer. Of the species given scientific names, fewer than 10 percent have been studied at a level deeper than gross anatomy. The revolution in molecular biology and medicine was achieved with a still smaller fraction, including colon bacteria, corn, fruit flies, Norway rats, rhesus monkeys, and human beings, altogether comprising no more than a hundred species.

Enchanted by the continuous emergence of new technologies and supported by generous funding for medical research, biologists have probed deeply along a narrow sector of the front. Now it is time to expand laterally, to get on with the great Linnean enterprise and finish mapping the biosphere. The most compelling reason for the broadening of goals is that, unlike the rest of science, the study of biodiversity has a time limit. Species are disappearing at an accelerating rate through human action, primarily habitat destruction but also pollution and the introduction of exotic species into residual natural environments. I have said that a fifth or more of the species of plants and animals could vanish or be doomed to early extinction by the year 2020 unless better efforts are made to save them. This estimate comes from the known quantitative relation between the area of habitats and the diversity that habitats can sustain. These area-biodiversity curves are supported by the general but not universal principle that when certain groups of organisms are studied closely, such as snails and fishes and flowering plants, extinction is determined to be widespread. And the corollary: among plant and animal remains in archaeological deposits, we usually find extinct species and races. As the last forests are felled in forest strongholds like the Philippines and Ecuador, the decline of species will accelerate even more. In the world as a whole, extinction rates are already hundreds or thousands of times higher than before the coming of man. They cannot be balanced by new evolution in any period of time that has meaning for the human race.

Why should we care? What difference does it make if some species are extinguished, if even half of all the species on earth disappear? Let me count the ways. New sources of scientific information will be lost. Vast potential biological wealth will be destroyed. Still undeveloped medicines, crops, pharmaceuticals, timber, fibers, pulp, soil-restoring vegetation, petroleum substitutes, and other products and amenities will never come to light. It is fashionable in some quarters to wave aside the small and obscure, the bugs and weeds, forgetting that an obscure moth from Latin America saved Australia's pastureland from overgrowth by cactus, that the rosy periwinkle provided the cure for Hodgkin's disease and childhood lymphocytic leukemia, that the bark of the Pacific yew offers hope for victims of ovarian and breast cancer, that a chemical from the saliva of leeches dissolves blood clots during surgery, and so on down a roster already grown long and illustrious despite the limited research addressed to it.

In amnesiac revery it is also easy to overlook the services that ecosystems provide humanity. They enrich the soil and create the very air we breathe. Without these amenities, the remaining tenure of the human race would be nasty and brief. The life-sustaining matrix is built of green plants with legions of microorganisms and mostly small, obscure animals—in other words, weeds and bugs. Such organisms support the world with efficiency because they are so diverse, allowing them to divide labor and swarm over every square meter of the earth's surface. They run the world precisely as we would wish it to be run, because humanity evolved within living communities and our bodily functions are finely adjusted to the idiosyncratic environment already created. Mother Earth, lately called Gaia, is no more than the commonality of organisms and the physical environment they maintain with each passing moment, an environment that will destabilize and turn lethal if the organisms are disturbed too much. A near infinity of other mother planets can be envisioned, each with its own fauna and flora, all producing physical environments uncongenial to human life. To disregard the diversity of life is to risk catapulting ourselves into an alien environment. We will have become like the pilot whales that inexplicably beach themselves on New England shores.

Humanity coevolved with the rest of life on this particular planet; other worlds are not in our genes. Because scientists have yet to put names on most kinds of organisms, and because they entertain only a vague idea of how ecosystems work, it is reckless to suppose that biodiversity can be diminished indefinitely without threatening humanity itself. Field studies show that as biodiversity is reduced, so is the quality of the services provided by ecosystems. Records of stressed ecosystems also demonstrate that the descent can be unpredictably abrupt. As extinction spreads, some of the lost forms prove to be keystone species, whose disappearance brings down other species and triggers a ripple effect through the demographies of the survivors. The loss of a keystone species is like a drill accidentally striking a powerline. It causes lights to go out all over.

These services are important to human welfare. But they cannot form the whole foundation of an enduring environmental ethic. If a price can be put on something, that something can be devalued, sold, and discarded. It is also possible for some to dream that people will go on living comfortably in a biologically impoverished world. They suppose that a prosthetic environment is within the power of technology, that human life can still flourish in a completely humanized world, where medicines would all be synthesized from chemicals off the shelf, food grown from a few dozen domestic crop species, the atmosphere and climate regulated by computer-driven fusion energy, and the earth made over until it becomes a literal spaceship rather than a metaphorical one, with people reading displays and touching buttons on the bridge. Such is the terminus of the philosophy of exemptionalism: do not weep for the past, humanity is a new order of life, let species die if they block progress, scientific and technological genius will find another way. Look up and see the stars awaiting us.

But consider: human advance is determined not by reason alone but by emotions peculiar to our species, aided and tempered by reason. What makes us people and not computers is emotion. We have little grasp of our true nature, of what it is to be human and therefore where our descendants might someday wish we had directed Spaceship Earth. Our troubles, as Vercors said in *You Shall Know Them*, arise from the fact that we do not know what we are and cannot agree on what we want to be. The primary cause of this intellectual failure is ignorance of our origins. We did not arrive on this planet as aliens. Humanity is part of nature, a species that evolved among other species. The more closely we identify ourselves with the rest of life, the more quickly we will be able to discover the sources of human sensibility and acquire the knowledge on which an enduring ethic, a sense of preferred direction, can be built.

The human heritage does not go back only for the conventionally recognized 8,000 years or so of recorded history, but for at least 2 million years, to the appearance of the first "true" human beings, the earliest species composing the genus *Homo*. Across thousands of generations, the emergence of culture must have been profoundly influenced by simultaneous events in genetic evolution, especially those occurring in the anatomy and physiology of the brain. Conversely, genetic evolution must have been guided forcefully by the kinds of selection rising within culture.

Only in the last moment of human history has the delusion arisen that people can flourish apart from the rest of the living world. Preliterate societies were in intimate contact with a bewildering array of life forms. Their minds could only partly adapt to that challenge. But they struggled to understand the most relevant parts, aware that the right responses gave life and fulfillment, the wrong ones sickness, hunger, and death. The imprint of that effort cannot have been erased in a few generations of urban existence. I suggest that it is to be found among the particularities of human nature, among which are these:

• People acquire phobias, abrupt and intractable aversions, to the objects and circumstances that threaten humanity in natural environments: heights, closed spaces, open spaces, running water, wolves, spiders, snakes. They rarely form phobias to the recently invented contrivances that are far more dangerous, such as guns, knives, automobiles, and electric sockets.

• People are both repelled and fascinated by snakes, even when they have never seen one in nature. In most cultures the serpent is the dominant wild animal of mythical and religious symbolism. Manhattanites dream of them with the same frequency as Zulus. This response appears to be Darwinian in origin. Poisonous snakes have been an important cause of mortality almost everywhere, from Finland to Tasmania, Canada to Patagonia; an untutored alertness in their presence saves lives. We note a kindred response in many primates, including Old World monkeys and chimpanzees: the animals pull back, alert others, watch closely, and follow each potentially dangerous snake until it moves away. For human beings, in a larger metaphorical sense, the mythic, transformed serpent has come to possess both constructive and destructive powers: Ashtoreth of the Canaanites, the demons Fu-Hsi and Nu-kua of the Han Chinese, Mudamma and Manasa of Hindu India, the triple-headed giant Nehebkau of the ancient Egyptians, the serpent of Genesis conferring knowledge and death, and, among the Aztecs, Cihuacoatl, goddess of childbirth and mother of the human race, the rain god Tlaloc, and Quetzalcoatl, the plumed serpent with a human head who reigned as lord of the morning and evening star. Ophidian power spills over into modern life: two serpents entwine the caduceus, first the winged staff of Mercury as messenger of the gods, then the safe-conduct pass of ambassadors and heralds, and today the universal emblem of the medical profession.

- The favored living place of most peoples is a prominence near water from which parkland can be viewed. On such heights are found the abodes of the powerful and rich, tombs of the great, temples, parliaments, and monuments commemorating tribal glory. The location is today an aesthetic choice and, by the implied freedom to settle there, a symbol of status. In ancient, more practical times the topography provided a place to retreat and a sweeping prospect from which to spot the distant approach of storms and enemy forces. Every animal species selects a habitat in which its members gain a favorable mix of security and food. For most of deep history, human beings lived in tropical and subtropical savanna in East Africa, open country sprinkled with streams and lakes, trees and copses. In similar topography modern peoples choose their residences and design their parks and gardens, if given a free choice. They simulate neither dense jungles, toward which gibbons are drawn, nor dry grasslands, preferred by hamadryas baboons. In their gardens they plant trees that resemble the acacias, sterculias, and other native trees of the African savannas. The ideal tree crown sought is consistently wider than tall, with spreading lowermost branches close enough to the ground to touch and climb, clothed with compound or needle-shaped leaves.

- Given the means and sufficient leisure, a large portion of the populace backpacks, hunts, fishes, birdwatches, and gardens. In the United States and Canada more people visit zoos and aquariums than attend all professional athletic events combined. They crowd the national parks to view natural landscapes, looking from the tops of prominences out across rugged terrain for a glimpse of tumbling water and animals living free. They travel long distances to stroll along the seashore, for reasons they can't put into words.

These are examples of what I have called *biophilia*, the connections that human beings subconsciously seek with the rest of life. To biophilia can be added the idea of wilderness, all the land and communities of plants and animals still unsullied by human occupation. Into wilderness people travel in search of new life and wonder, and from wilderness they return to the parts of the earth that have been humanized and made physically secure. Wilderness settles peace on the soul because it needs no help; it is beyond human contrivance.

Wilderness is a metaphor of unlimited opportunity, rising from the tribal memory of a time when humanity spread across the world, valley to valley, island to island, godstruck, firm in the belief that virgin land went on forever past the horizon.

I cite these common preferences of mind not as proof of an innate human nature but rather to suggest that we think more carefully and turn philosophy to the central questions of human origins in the wild environment. We do not understand ourselves yet and descend farther from heaven's air if we forget how much the natural world means to us. Signals abound that the loss of life's diversity endangers not just the body but the spirit. If that much is true, the changes occurring now will visit harm on all generations to come.

The ethical imperative should therefore be, first of all, prudence. We should judge every scrap of biodiversity as priceless while we learn to use it and come to understand what it means to humanity. We should not knowingly allow any species or race to go extinct. And let us go beyond mere salvage to begin the restoration of natural environments, in order to enlarge wild populations and stanch the hemorrhaging of biological wealth. There can be no purpose more enspiriting than to begin the age of restoration, reweaving the wondrous diversity of life that still surrounds us.

The evidence of swift environmental change calls for an ethic uncoupled from other systems of belief. Those committed by religion to believe that life was put on earth in one divine stroke will recognize that we are destroying the Creation, and those who perceive biodiversity to be the product of blind evolution will agree. Across the other great philosophical divide, it does not matter whether species have independent rights or, conversely, that moral reasoning is uniquely a human concern. Defenders of both premises seem destined to gravitate toward the same position on conservation.

The stewardship of environment is a domain on the near side of metaphysics where all reflective persons can surely find common ground. For what, in the final analysis, is morality but the command of conscience seasoned by a rational examination of consequences? And what is a fundamental precept but one that serves all generations? An enduring environmental ethic will aim to preserve not only the health and freedom of our species, but access to the world in which the human spirit was born.

# 43
# Albert Gore, Jr. (1948–   )

The son of an influential Democratic Senator from Tennessee, Albert Gore, Jr., entered politics in 1976 when he was elected to the first of four terms to the U.S. House of Representatives. He was elected U.S. Senator in 1984 and reelected in 1990. His second term was cut short in 1992, when Gore was selected as Bill Clinton's running mate, serving as his Vice President from 1993–2001. In the 2000 election he was the unsuccessful Democratic candidate for president, running against George W. Bush, the son of another famous politician, President George Bush.

During his political career, Al Gore has been notable for his interest in environmental issues and arms reduction. He played a key role in drafting the 1980 Superfund legislation, and he also was at the center of the 1982 congressional debate over the Reagan Administration's defense policy. Reagan's "Star Wars" idea, along with huge increases in the Defense Department budget, were, Gore argued, a destabilizing and ultimately dangerous foreign policy.

Just as he was about to be elected vice president in 1992, Gore published his best-selling book, *Earth in the Balance: Ecology and the Human Spirit.* Gore's argument is similar to that of E.O. Wilson's concerning the need for a regeneration of the moral spirit in order to heal the earth and protect its inhabitants. However, he took that argument into the political and practical realm by discussing concrete policies that the United States would do well to adopt in the coming decade, such as a global Marshall Plan. For a number of reasons, such an ambitious program of foreign aid and technology transfer to the most disadvantaged nations did not occur under the Clinton-Gore Administration. The poorest peoples and nations on Earth—many of which are in sub-Saharan Africa—made no progress in the 1990s. In fact, the AIDS epidemic and civil strife in the region are producing a human catastrophe of Holocaust proportions. A massive aid plan to avert this tragedy in the making awaits implementation by world leaders in the twenty-first century.

---

## "IT IS TIME WE STEERED BY THE STARS"*

Human civilization is now so complex and diverse, so sprawling and massive, that it is difficult to see how we can respond in a coordinated, collective way to the global environmental crisis. But circumstances are forcing just such a response; if we cannot embrace the preservation of the earth as our new organizing principle, the very survival of our civilization will be in doubt.

That much is clear. But how should we proceed? How can we create practical working relationships that bring together people who live in dramatically different circumstances? How can we focus the energies of a disparate group of nations into a sustained effort, lasting many years, that will translate the organizing principle into concrete changes—changes that will affect almost every aspect of our lives together on this planet?

We find it difficult to imagine a realistic basis for hope that the environment can be saved, not only because we still lack widespread agreement on the need for this task, but also because we have never worked together globally on any problem even approaching this one in degree of difficulty. Even so, we must find a way to join this common cause, because the crisis we face is, in the final analysis, a global problem and can only be solved on a global basis. Merely addressing one dimension or another or trying to implement solutions in only one region of the world or another will, in the end, guarantee frustration, failure, and a weakening of the resolve needed to address the whole of the problem.

While it is true that there are no real precedents for the kind of global response now required, history does provide us with at least one powerful model of cooperative effort: the Marshall Plan. In a brilliant collaboration that was itself unprecedented, several relatively wealthy nations and several relatively poor nations—empowered by a common purpose—joined to reorganize an entire region of the world and change its way of life. The Marshall Plan shows how a large vision can be translated into effective action, and it is worth recalling why the plan was so successful.

Immediately after World War II, Europe was so completely devastated that the resumption of normal economic activity was inconceivable. Then, in the early spring of 1947, the Soviet Union rejected U.S. proposals for aiding the recovery of German industry, convincing General George Marshall and President Harry Truman, among others, that the Soviets hoped to capitalize on the prevailing economic distress—not only in Germany but also in the rest of Europe. After much discussion and study, the United States launched the basis for the Marshall Plan, technically known as the European Recovery Program (ERP).

The commonly held view of the Marshall Plan is that it was a bold strategy for helping the nations of Western Europe rebuild and grow strong enough to fend off the spread of communism. That popular view is correct—as far as it goes. But the historians Charles Maier and Stanley Hoffman, both professors at Harvard, emphasize the strategic nature of the plan, with its emphasis on the structural causes of Europe's inability to lift itself out of its economic, political, and social distress. The plan concentrated on fixing the bottlenecks—such as the damaged infrastructure, flooded coal mines, and senseless trade barriers—that were impeding the potential for growth in each nation's economy. ERP was sufficiently long-term that it could serve as an overall effort to produce fundamental structural reorientation, not just offer more emergency relief or another "development" program. It was consciously designed to change the dynamic of the systems to which it extended aid, thus facilitating the emergence of a healthy economic pattern. And it was brilliantly administered by Averell Harriman.

Historians also note the Marshall Plan's regional focus and its incentives to promote European integration and joint action. Indeed, from the very beginning the plan tried to facilitate the emergence of a larger political framework—unified Europe; to that end, it insisted that every action be coordinated with all the countries in the region. The recent creation of a unified European parliament and the dramatic steps toward a European political community to accompany the European Economic Community (EEC) have all come about in large part because of the groundwork of the Marshall Plan.

But when it was put in place, the idea of a unified Europe seemed even less likely than the collapse of the Berlin Wall did only a few years ago—and every bit as improbable as a unified global response to the environmental crisis seems today. Improbable or not, something like the Marshall Plan—a Global Marshall Plan, if you will—is now urgently needed. The scope and complexity of this plan will far exceed those of the original; what's required now is a plan that combines large-scale, long-term, carefully targeted financial aid to developing nations, massive efforts to design and then transfer to poor nations the new technologies needed for sustained economic progress, a worldwide program to stabilize world population, and binding commitments by the industrial nations to accelerate their own transition to an environmentally responsible pattern of life.

But despite the fundamental differences between the late 1940s and today, the model of the Marshall Plan can be of great help as we begin to grapple with the enormous challenge we now face. For example, a Global Marshall Plan must, like the original, focus on strategic goals and emphasize actions and programs that are likely to remove the bottlenecks presently inhibiting the healthy functioning of the global economy. The new global economy must be an inclusive system that does not leave entire regions behind—as our present system leaves out most of Africa and much of Latin America. In an inclusive economy, for instance, wealthy nations can no longer insist that Third World countries pay huge sums of interest on old debts even when the sacrifices necessary to pay them increase the pressure on their suffering populations so much that revolutionary tensions build uncontrollably. The Marshall Plan took the broadest possible view of Europe's problems and developed strategies to serve human needs and promote sustained economic progress; we must now do the same on a global scale.

But strategic thinking is useless without consensus, and here again the Marshall Plan is instructive. Historians remind us that it would have failed if the countries receiving assistance had not shared a common ideological outlook, or at least a common leaning toward a set of similar ideas and values. Postwar Europe's strong preference for democracy and capitalism made the regional integration of economies possible; likewise, the entire world is far closer to a consensus on basic political and economic principles than it was even a few short years ago, and as the philosophical victory of Western principles becomes increasingly apparent, a Global Marshall Plan will be increasingly feasible.

It is fair to say that in recent years most of the world has made three important choices: first, that democracy will be the preferred form of political organization on this planet; second, that modified free markets will be the preferred form of economic organization; and, third, that most individuals now feel themselves to be part of a truly global civilization—prematurely heralded many times in this century but now finally palpable in the minds and hearts of human beings throughout the earth. Even those nations that still officially oppose democracy and capitalism—such as China—seem to be slowly headed in our philosophical direction, at least in the thinking of younger generations not yet in power.

Another motivation for the Marshall Plan was a keen awareness of the dangerous vacuum created by the end of the Axis nations' totalitarian order and the potential for chaos in the absence of any positive momentum toward democracy and capitalism. Similarly, the resounding philosophical defeat of communism (in which the Marshall Plan itself played a significant role) has left an ideological vacuum that invites either a bold and visionary strategy to facilitate the emergence of democratic government and modified free markets throughout the world—in a truly global system—or growing chaos of the kind that is already all too common from Cambodia to Colombia, Liberia to Lebanon, and Zaire to Azerbaijan.

The Marshall Plan, however, depended in part for its success on some special circumstances that prevailed in postwar Europe yet do not prevail in various parts of the world today. For example, the nations of Europe had developed advanced economies before World War II, and they retained a large number of skilled workers, raw materials, and the shared experience of modernity. They also shared a clear potential for regional cooperation—although it may be clearer in retrospect than it was at the time, when the prospect of warm relations between, say, Germany and England seemed remote.

In contrast, the diversity among nations involved in a Global Marshall Plan is simply fantastic, with all kinds of political entities representing radically different stages of economic and political development—and with the emergence of "post-national" entities, such as Kurdistan, the Balkans, Eritrea, and Kashmir. In fact, some people now define themselves in terms of an ecological criterion rather than a political subdivision. For example, "the Aral Sea region" defines people in parts of several Soviet republics who all suffer the regional ecological catastrophe of the Aral Sea. "Amazonia" is used by peoples of several nationalities in the world's largest rain forest, where national boundaries are often invisible and irrelevant.

The diversity of the world's nations and peoples vastly complicates the model used so successfully in Europe. Even so, another of the Marshall Plan's lessons can still be applied: within this diversity, the plans for catalyzing a transition to a sustainable society should be made with regional groupings in mind and with distinctive strategies for each region. Eastern Europe, for example, has a set of regional characteristics very different from those of the Sahel in sub-Saharan Africa, just as Central America faces challenges very different from those facing, say, the Southeast Asian archipelago.

Many of the impediments to progress lie in the industrial world.

Indeed, one of the biggest obstacles to a Global Marshall Plan is the requirement that the advanced economies must undergo a profound transformation themselves. The Marshall Plan placed the burden of change and transition only on the recipient nations. The financing was borne entirely by the United States, which, to be sure, underwent a great deal of change during those same years, but not at the behest of a foreign power and not to discharge any sense of obligation imposed by an international agreement.

The new plan will require the wealthy nations to allocate money for transferring environmentally helpful technologies to the Third World and to help impoverished nations achieve a stable population and a new pattern of sustainable economic progress. To work, however, any such effort will also require wealthy nations to make a transition themselves that will be in some ways more wrenching than that of the Third World, simply because powerful established patterns will be disrupted. Opposition to change is therefore strong, but this transition can and must occur—both in the developed and developing world. And when it does, it will likely be within a framework of global agreements that obligate all nations to act in concert. To succeed, these agreements must be part of an overall design focused on devising a healthier and more balanced pattern in world civilization that integrates the Third World into the global economy. Just as important, the developed nations must be willing to lead by example; otherwise, the Third World is not likely to consider making the required changes—even in return for substantial assistance. Finally, just as the Marshall Plan scrupulously respected the sovereignty of each nation while requiring all of them to work together, this new plan must emphasize cooperation—in the different regions of the world and globally—while carefully respecting the integrity of individual nation-states.

This point is worth special emphasis. The mere mention of any plan that contemplates worldwide cooperation creates instant concern on the part of many—especially conservatives—who have long equated such language with the advocacy of some supranational authority, like a world government. Indeed, some who favor a common global effort tend to assume that a supranational authority of some sort is inevitable. But this notion is both politically impossible and practically unworkable. The political problem is obvious: the idea arouses so much opposition that further debate on the underlying goals comes to a halt—especially in the United States, where we are fiercely protective of our individual freedoms. The fear that our rights might be jeopardized by the delegation of even partial sovereignty to some global authority ensures that it's simply not going to happen. The practical problem can be illustrated with a question: What conceivable system of world governance would be able to compel individual nations to adopt environmentally sound policies? The administrative problems would be gargantuan, not least because the inefficiency of governance often seems to increase geometrically with the distance between the seat of power and the individuals affected by it; and given the chaotic state of some of the governments that would be subject to that global entity, any such institution would most likely have unintended side effects and complications that would interfere with the underlying goal. As Dorothy Parker once said about a book she didn't like, the idea of a world government "should not be tossed aside lightly; it should be thrown with great force."

But if world government is neither feasible nor desirable, how then can we establish a successful cooperative global effort to save the environment? There is only one answer: we must negotiate international agreements that establish global constraints on acceptable behavior but that are entered into voluntarily—albeit with the understanding that they will contain both incentives and legally valid penalties for noncompliance.

The world's most important supranational organization—the United Nations—does have a role to play, though I am skeptical about its ability to do very much. Specifically, to help monitor the evolution of a global agreement, the United Nations might consider the idea of establishing a Stewardship Council to deal with matters relating to the global environment—just as the Security Council now deals with matters of war and peace. Such a forum could be increasingly useful and even necessary as the full extent of the environmental crisis unfolds.

Similarly, it would be wise to establish a tradition of annual environmental summit meetings, similar to the annual economic summits of today, which only rarely find time to consider the environment. The preliminary discussions of a Global Marshall Plan would, in any event, have to take place at the highest level. And, unlike the economic summits, these discussions must involve heads of state from both the developed and developing world.

In any global agreement of the kind I am proposing, the single most difficult relationship is the one between wealthy and poor nations; there must be a careful balance between the burdens and obligations imposed on both groups of nations. If, for example, any single agreement has a greater impact on the poor nations, it may have to be balanced with a simultaneous agreement that has a greater impact on the wealthy nations. This approach is already developing naturally in some of the early discussions of global environmental problems. One instance is the implicit linkage between the negotiations to save the rain forests—which are found mostly in poor countries—and the negotiations to reduce greenhouse gas emissions—which is especially difficult for wealthy nations. If these negotiations are successful, the resulting agreements will become trade-offs for each other.

The design of a Global Marshall Plan must also recognize that many countries are in different stages of development, and each new agreement has to be sensitive to the gulf between the countries involved, not only in terms of their relative affluence but also their various stages of political, cultural, and economic development. This diversity is important both among those nations that would be on the receiving end of a global plan and among those expected to be on the giving end. Coordination and agreement among the donor countries might, for example, turn out to be the most difficult challenge. The two donor participants in the Marshall Plan, the United States and Great Britain, had established a remarkably close working relationship during the war, which was then used as a model for their postwar collaboration. Today, of course, the United States cannot conceivably be the principal financier for a global recovery program and cannot make the key decisions alone or with only one close ally. The financial resources must now come from Japan and Europe and from wealthy, oil-producing states.

The Western alliance has frequently been unwieldy and unproductive when large sums of money are at stake. Nevertheless, it has compiled an impressive record of military, economic, and political cooperation in the long struggle against communism, and the world may be able to draw upon that model just as the United States and Great Britain built upon their wartime cooperation in implementing the Marshall Plan. Ironically, the collapse of communism has deprived the alliance of its common enemy, but the potential freeing up of resources may create the ideal opportunity to choose a new grand purpose for working together.

Still, a number of serious obstacles face cooperation among even the great powers—the United States, Japan, and Europe—before a Global Marshall Plan could be considered. Japan, in spite of its enormous economic strength, has been reluctant to share the responsibility for world political leadership and thus far seems blind to the need for it to play such a role. And Europe will be absorbed for many years in the intricacies of becoming a unified entity—a challenge further complicated by the entreaties of the suddenly free nations in Eastern Europe that now want to join the EEC.

As a result, the responsibility for taking the initiative, for innovating, catalyzing, and leading such an effort, falls disproportionately on the United States. Yet in the early 1990s our instinct for world leadership often seems not nearly so bold as it was in the late 1940s. The bitter experience of the Vietnam War is partly responsible, and the sheer weariness of carrying the burden of world leadership has taken a toll. Furthermore, we are not nearly as dominant in the world economy as we were then, and that necessarily has implications for our willingness to shoulder large burdens. And our budget deficits are now so large as to stifle our willingness to consider even the most urgent of tasks. Charles Maier points out that the annual U.S. expenditures for the Marshall Plan between 1948 and 1951 were close to 2 percent of our GNP. A similar percentage today would be almost $100 billion a year (compared to our total nonmilitary foreign aid budget of about $15 billion a year).

Yet the Marshall Plan enjoyed strong bipartisan support in Congress. There was little doubt then that government intervention, far from harming the free enterprise system in Europe, was the most effective way to foster its healthy operation. But our present leaders seem to fear almost any form of intervention. Indeed, the deepest source of their reluctance to provide leadership in creating an effective environmental strategy seems to be their fear that if we do step forward, we will inevitably be forced to lead by example and actively pursue changes that might interfere with their preferred brand of laissez-faire, nonassertive economic policy.

Nor do our leaders seem willing to look as far into the future as did Truman and Marshall. In that heady postwar period, one of Marshall's former colleagues, General Omar Bradley, said, "It is time we steered by the stars, not by the lights of each passing ship." This certainly seems to be another time when that kind of navigation is needed, yet too many of those who are responsible for our future appear to be distracted by such "lights of passing ships" as overnight public opinion polls.

In any effort to conceive of a plan to heal the global environment, the essence of realism is recognizing that public attitudes are still changing—and that proposals which are today considered too bold to be politically feasible will soon be derided as woefully inadequate to the task at hand. Yet while public acceptance of the magnitude of the threat is indeed curving upward—and will eventually rise almost vertically as awareness of the awful truth suddenly makes the search for remedies an all-consuming passion—it is just as important to recognize that at the present time, we are still in a period when the curve is just starting to bend. Ironically, at this stage, the maximum that is politically feasible still falls short of the minimum that is truly effective. And to make matters worse, the curve of political feasibility in advanced countries may well look quite different than it does in developing countries, where the immediate threats to well-being and survival often make saving the environment seem to be an unaffordable luxury.

It seems to make sense, therefore, to put in place a policy framework that will be ready to accommodate the worldwide demands for action when the magnitude of the threat becomes clear. And it is also essential to offer strong measures that are politically feasible now—even before the expected large shift in public opinion about the global environment—and that can be quickly scaled up as awareness of the crisis grows and even stronger action becomes possible.

With the original Marshall Plan serving as both a model and an inspiration, we can now begin to chart a course of action. The world's effort to save the environment must be organized around strategic goals that simultaneously represent the most important changes and allow us to recognize, measure, and assess our progress toward making those changes. Each goal must be supported by a set of policies that will enable world civilization to reach it as quickly, efficiently, and justly as possible.

In my view, five strategic goals must direct and inform our efforts to save the global environment. Let me outline each of them briefly before considering each in depth.

The first strategic goal should be **the stabilizing of world population**, with policies designed to create in every nation of the world the conditions necessary for the so-called demographic transition—the historic and well-documented change from a dynamic equilibrium of high birth rates and death rates to a stable equilibrium of low birth rates and death rates. This change has taken place in most of the industrial nations (which have low rates of infant mortality and high rates of literacy and education) and in virtually none of the developing nations (where the reverse is true).

The second strategic goal should be **the rapid creation and development of environmentally appropriate technologies**—especially in the fields of energy, transportation, agriculture, building construction, and manufacturing—capable of accommodating sustainable economic progress without the concurrent degradation of the environment. These new technologies must then be quickly transferred to all nations—especially those in the Third World, which should be allowed to pay for them by discharging the various obligations they incur as participants in the Global Marshall Plan.

The third strategic goal should be **a comprehensive and ubiquitous** change in the economic "rules of the road" by which we measure the impact of our decisions on the environment. We must establish—by global agreement—a system of economic accounting that assigns appropriate values to the ecological consequences of both routine choices in the marketplace by individuals and companies and larger, macroeconomic choices by nations.

The fourth strategic goal should be **the negotiation and approval of a new generation of international agreements** that will embody the regulatory frameworks, specific prohibitions, enforcement mechanisms, cooperative planning, sharing arrangements, incentives, penalties, and mutual obligations necessary to make the overall plan a success. These agreements must be especially sensitive to the vast differences of capability and need between developed and undeveloped nations.

The fifth strategic goal should be **the establishment of a cooperative plan for educating the world's citizens about our global environment**— first by the establishment of a comprehensive program for researching and monitoring the changes now under way in the environment in a manner that involves the people of all nations, especially students; and, second, through a massive effort to disseminate information about local, regional, and strategic threats to the environment. The ultimate goal of this effort would be to foster new patterns of thinking about the relationship of civilization to the global environment.

Each of these goals is closely related to all of the others, and all should be pursued simultaneously within the larger framework of the Global Marshall Plan. Finally, the plan should have as its more general, integrating goal **the establishment, especially in the developing world—of the social and political conditions most conducive to the emergence of sustainable societies**—such as social justice (including equitable patterns of land ownership); a commitment to human rights; adequate nutrition, health care, and shelter; high literacy rates; and greater political freedom, participation, and accountability. Of course, all specific policies should be chosen as part of serving the central organizing principle of saving the global environment.

# 44
# Jeffrey Berry (1948–    )

Jeffrey Berry is professor of political science at Tufts University. He is the author of numerous books and articles on American politics, including *The Interest Group Society* (1989) and *The New Liberalism: The Rising Power of Citizen Groups* (1999). Berry's research on pluralism and the continuing significance of interest groups in policy formation has earned him a national audience. His interpretation of American pluralist politics is largely positive, which sets his work apart from the more critical view argued by Theodore Lowi in *The End of Liberalism* (1979).

Berry's most recent research concluded that the "associational spirit" which so fascinated Alexis de Tocqueville in the early nineteenth century is alive and well in the new millennium. He found, however, that it is used more effectively today by liberals lobbying Washington policy makers than by conservatives. His widely read book provides an explanation as to why this is the case.

---

## "THE POWER OF ENVIRONMENTALISM"*

The question of how the Republican takeover of Congress affected the opportunities available to citizen groups of the right is just as pertinent for citizen groups of the left. When their allies lost control of the House and Senate, was the influence of the liberal groups seriously diminished? Research has shown that the access of citizen groups to the executive branch can be dramatically affected by a partisan switch in control of the White House. Mark Peterson and Jack Walker found, "When Reagan replaced Carter in the White House, there was a virtual revolution in the access enjoyed by interest groups in Washington." The executive branch is controlled by a single party, of course, whereas the minority party in Congress still exerts influence over the legislative process and still offers interest groups considerable access. Conservative groups were helped by the change in power, but there was no "virtual revolution" in access to Congress. What, then, was the impact on the liberal lobbies?

Traditional, material-oriented liberal groups were under siege during the 104th Congress. The controversial welfare reform bill was a catastrophic defeat for groups on the left that fought the legislation. Not only were they defeated by Republicans wanting to scale down the welfare state by pushing people off aid to families with dependent children (AFDC) and into the work

---

*Jeffrey M. Berry. 1999. *The New Liberalism: The Rising Power of Citizen Groups*. Washington, DC: Brookings, pp. 110–112, 114–117. Reprinted with permission from the Brookings Institution Press. Footnotes are omitted.

force, but they were abandoned by President Clinton, who signed the bill. Labor did win an important victory with the passage of the minimum wage increase, but the overall emphasis on budget cutting and shrinking government made it a terrible Congress for traditional, economic equality liberals.

In an evaluation of the liberal postmaterialist lobbies, the same approach should be taken as was used in examining the Christian right groups. Analysis will similarly be limited to one sector—in this case, environmental lobbies. Environmental groups are the largest and most prominent set of liberal citizen groups, just as the Christian right groups are the most visible and successful set of conservative citizen lobbies. Specifically, the groups' influence on agenda setting and the groups' success in getting their policies through Congress will be analyzed.

Not surprisingly, when the Republicans seized control the environmental groups immediately lost their influence over the agenda. GOP leaders and committee chairs were eager to work with their business allies to rewrite environmental statutes that various industries found onerous and unreasonable. The Contract with America reached out to business in a number of areas, but the most far-reaching plank was the Job Creation and Wage Enhancement Act. Among its many provisions, it required that agencies use cost-benefit analysis to justify any significant regulatory actions in the area of the environment, health, and safety. This radical proposal would have made it especially difficult for agency administrators to justify regulations to protect the environment since many of the benefits are aesthetic rather than economic. By itself the legislation promised to be a devastating setback to years of progress that environmental groups and liberal legislators had made in creating parks, preserving wilderness, and curbing pollution.

Beyond the Job Creation and Wage Enhancement Act, major revisions of the Clean Water Act, the Endangered Species Act, and the Superfund program, were also proposed. The environmentalists were further rocked when newspaper stories appeared revealing that corporate lawyers and lobbyists were rewriting the provisions of laws they didn't like and then giving their drafts to Republican committee staffers who were sticking them verbatim into proposed legislation. When the Senate Judiciary Committee took up its own measure to institute cost-benefit analysis, it turned the job over to attorneys from Hunton and Williams, a law firm with a large practice representing business clients with environmental problems. When Democratic staffers were briefed on the content of the legislation, it was Hunton and Williams lawyers who explained the bill's provisions to them. After Senator Slade Gorton (R-Wash.) undertook the job of overhauling the Endangered Species Act, the *New York Times* reported that he turned the job over to "lawyers who represent timber, mining, ranching and utility interests that have been most critical of the law." During oversight hearings by the House Resources Committee, lobbyist and former Representative John Rhodes (R-Ariz.) sat on the dais with Republican members of the committee. Rhodes was representing a client with an interest in the question before the committee.

Republican legislators responded to the criticism of their close relationship with business lobbyists by noting that their consultation with them was no different than the Democrats' consultation with environmental lobbyists when they were writing legislation. Ironically, the Republicans' delegation of legislative drafting to corporate lobbyists probably worked to the advantage of environmentalists. The adverse publicity not only helped to arouse public support for environmental protection but was a spur to organizing efforts and fundraising by the environmental lobbies. The outcry from environmentalists over the regulatory changes in the Job Creation and Wage Enhancement Act passed by the House caused Senator Dole to distance himself from the bill written by the Hunton and Williams lawyers. He never brought it up for vote. The House passed a rewrite of the Clean Water Act, but after environmentalists labeled it the "Dirty Water Bill," Dole ran from it as well, and the bill died without a vote in the Senate. When the rewrite of the Endangered Species Act was ready to come to the floor of the House, moderate Republicans sensed a looming public relations disaster, and their rebellion quashed the bill before any vote could be taken. A proposed rewrite of the Superfund law was easily beaten back by environmentalists. After ten months of bad publicity and legislative defeats, Speaker Gingrich threw in the towel on reforming the nation's environmental laws. Toward the end of the 104th Congress, the Republicans actually worked to pass some *pro*-environmental legislation.

A look back at the 104th Congress shows that the Republicans and their allied business groups overplayed their hand. As was the case with other strategic blunders by the Republican leadership in the 104th, a policy mandate was read into the election results where none existed. ...[T]he environmental lobbies, congressional Democrats and, occasionally, moderate Republicans, consistently defeated the efforts to weaken environmental protection statutes. Of the twelve bills highlighted by *Congressional Quarterly* as the most significant issues involving environmental policy in 1995–96, the pro-environmental side was the loser on only one and the winner on ten.

If the Republican-business proposals had been more moderate in their approach, they might have gotten half a loaf on some of these issues during the first six or twelve months of the 104th Congress. In the end, though, these legislative outcomes are not principally the consequences of faulty Republican strategy but instead reflect the power of environmentalism. Simply put, the environmental lobbies were successful because the public is strongly supportive of efforts to preserve the environment. At a time when the economy was buoyant, the GOP's bills designed to boost business turned out to be a tough sell. Environmental lobbies, aided by the press, had great success in framing the proposals as efforts to destroy apple pie and motherhood statutes like the Endangered Species Act and the Clean Water Act. Try as they did to frame the issues as "reforms," the Republican legislators and business lobbyists were never able to convince anyone but themselves that they were reformers.

Earlier, it was asked what difference it made when partisan control of Congress changes. For the formal agenda—the bills that committees take up—change makes a very big difference. It comes as no surprise that more probusiness legislation came onto the agenda and that the introduction of legislation favorable to the environment was sharply reduced. The Christian right also had much more success in getting hearings on its issues in the 104th than in the previous Congresses. The partisan change had much less impact on the legislative outcomes in the two areas studied. Despite the unusual nature of the 104th Congress, analysis of the effectiveness of liberal and conservative citizen groups reveals more continuity than change. Indeed, the findings for the 104th seem very much in line with the previous evaluations of the 1963, 1979, and 1991 sessions of Congress. The environmental lobbies continued to do well in the legislative process in 1995–96, though groups pushing for rights of women and minorities probably fared worse than usual. The Christian Coalition was certainly more visible on Capitol Hill than conservative citizen groups had been in the past, but the organization proved much less adept at legislative lobbying than at electoral politics. Few would have guessed at the outset of the 104th Congress that the biggest winners in that Congress would be the environmental lobbies, and the biggest loser would be the Christian Coalition....

Some might see this comparison of the Christian right and liberal environmental groups as evidence not so much of the failure of conservative citizen groups to capitalize on a great opportunity but as a cautionary tale about contemporary government. Isn't the real story that it has become harder to get anything at all done by the national government? Business lobbies were also disappointed by the 104th Congress and, unlike the Christian right, they have substantial support in both parties. It may very well be that the only reason the environmentalists did comparatively well is that it's much easier to defend existing statutes than to go on the offensive to try to get new ones enacted.

The basis of this argument is that American government has become increasingly fragmented over the years. Rising partisanship by legislators, Americans' increasing tendency to put one party in control of the White House and another in charge of one or both houses of Congress, and the growing numbers of interest groups active in Washington are all blamed for making policymaking much more difficult than in earlier times. Since this study has documented the growing success of liberal groups advocating quality-of-life concerns, the charge that interest groups have made policymaking more difficult merits close analysis. Different types of interest groups may be affecting the legislative process in different ways.

There are a number of reasons why the growth of interest group politics is seen as a cause of a decreasing capacity by Congress to address significant public policy problems. Some believe that the increasing number of lobbies has overloaded Congress with an avalanche of demands. Others believe that Congress has the capacity to meet such demands, but the growth of groups has created a crossfire of powerful organizations with contradictory policy preferences. Legislators may find that the least risky alternative is to do nothing. Still others say the growth of groups is not the problem. Rather the decline of our political parties has left a vacuum that powerful lobbies are only too happy to fill. Whatever the path of causation, agreement is substantial that interest group politics is making it ever more challenging for the political system to solve the nation's problems. As Washington journalist Kevin Phillips argues, "Washington is malfunctioning" because of "the enormous buildup and entrenchment of the largest interest group concentration the world has ever seen."

Thus, there may be something to the idea that today it is easier for interest groups to play defense than offense. Intuitively, it makes sense that in an era of greater conflict or weaker institutional capacity, lobbies would have an easier time blocking legislation than convincing Congress to pass new laws. The legislative process is full of opportunity for delay and obstruction. Political scientists have not conducted research with the offense and defense dichotomy in mind, but by trading the sports metaphor for one having to do with traffic jams, we find a relevant literature on legislative gridlock. Among other things, this research on gridlock has tried to determine if it is becoming more difficult to get important legislation passed. The best known of these studies, David Mayhew's *Divided We Govern,* found that divided control of government between Democrats and Republicans did not result in less important legislation being passed compared with periods when one party controlled both the White House and Congress. Substantial debate has occurred over how Mayhew and others have measured gridlock, but to date there is no convincing evidence that over time, as divided government became more common, Congress was afflicted by lower productivity.

Using the data from the 205 case studies, I looked at the specific charge that increasing numbers of interest groups have made legislating more difficult. With just three sessions of Congress, this study cannot answer the question of whether there is gridlock. But by making the unit of analysis the 205 hearings, the relationship of group participation to the passage of legislation can be tested. The computations specified the likelihood that legislation will pass when (theoretically) no groups participated and when ten groups participated. Under conditions where no groups participate, the probability of a bill passing is .66. When ten groups participate, the probability is .64, obviously a trivial difference in the likelihood of passage. Disaggregating the data by year, there were no substantial differences between no groups and ten groups in any of the three sessions of Congress. In other words, by 1991, when the growth of interest groups was said to have already debilitated the political system, getting legislation passed when there was a high level of interest group conflict was just as likely as when there was no interest group conflict.

Those who have written about gridlock or Congress's capacity to solve the nation's problems have often singled out citizen groups for particular blame. Not only have citizen groups added more demands on Congress— demands that are not easily met—but they are also said to be unusually contentious participants in policymaking. John Gilmour notes that these groups are difficult for legislators and other groups to negotiate with because citizen groups find it advantageous to be moralistic and uncompromising. Says Gilmour, "The language of moderation and compromise does not appear to generate many memberships." When the impact of citizen group participation on the likelihood of passage was calculated, however, it made no difference how many citizen groups were involved. In short, citizen group lobbying is unrelated to gridlock.

That the conservative citizen groups' poor showing in comparison to that of the environmentalists in the 104th Congress was due to their having to play offense is also questionable. That idea ignores the success of the liberal citizen groups when they were playing offense. If it is more difficult to get legislation passed than to defeat it, the same rules of the game apply to liberal lobbies. Liberal citizen groups and their allies in the House and Senate have been responsible for a torrent of legislation when they were on offense—that is, when the Democrats controlled Congress. Greater difficulty in playing offense didn't suddenly become the case in January 1995 when the Republicans took over both houses.

The performance of the conservative citizen groups can not be explained away by structural changes in American national government. The evidence for such a claim is weak. A more convincing explanation is that the conservative lobbies' disappointing record in the 104th Congress reflects strategic choices these organizations made about the allocation of their resources and their selection of issues.

# DISCUSSION QUESTIONS

1. Since the beginning of the environmental movement, there has been a running debate about the root causes of the nation's—and indeed the world's—environmental problems. Connect the positions of the authors in this section with those in earlier periods, including George Perkins Marsh, Margaret Sanger, Aldo Leopold, John Kenneth Galbraith, Garrett Hardin, Paul Ehrlich, and Barry Commoner. Which past authors best foretold the future?

2. Trace how the roots of the contemporary environmental justice movement, as described by Robert Bullard, can be found in the experience of minorities and the poor since the formation of the Republic. Recall the experiences, for example, of Frederick Douglass, the fictional Joads, Cesar Chavez, Martin Luther King, and Chief Seattle.

3. Discuss how the split between the rich and poor nations, and even between the rich and poor in wealthy nations such as the United States, may affect environmental issues in the twenty-first century. What can and should be done about these disparities? Compare and contrast the positions taken by Garrett Hardin and Al Gore.

4. At the beginning of the twenty-first century, America does indeed appear to have an "erosion of confidence" such as that described by Jimmy Carter and earlier by John Dewey. Whereas in 1965, 75 percent of Americans trusted their government, only 25 percent say they do today. Yet the economy is booming and the nation might also be described in President Reagan's words as "robust, vibrant and alive." What is happening in America to cause this disconnect?

5. Over the past thirty years, social movements have given political voice to groups that previously had scant political power. A fundamental question is whether the Constitutional structure, established in the late 1700s, is capable of effectively dealing with this great political diversity. What kinds of leaders, and what kinds of changes in law, policy, and institutions, might be necessary to bring harmony out of our present political chaos without sacrificing the gains made by those whose voices once went unheard?

# Selected Bibliography

## NOTE ON SOURCES

In the course of writing the section commentaries and authors' biographical sketches, we consulted a large number of primary and secondary sources. These include, but are not limited to: *Biographical Dictionary of Indians of the Americas*, James MacGregor Burns's biographies of Franklin Delano Roosevelt and his other work, *Contemporary Authors Online, Current Biography*, Mario DiNunzio's *Theodore Roosevelt: An American Mind, The Encyclopedia Americana*, Lois and Alan Gordon's *American Chronicle: Year by Year Through the Twentieth Century*, Henry F. Graff, ed., *The Presidents: A Reference History*, Howard R. Lamar, ed., *The New Encyclopedia of the American West*, Leonard Levy, et al., eds., *Encyclopedia of the American Constitution*, Peter B. Levy, ed., *100 Key Documents in American History*, the New York Public Library's *American History Desk Reference*, C. Wright Mills's *The Power Elite*, and Douglas Strong's *American Reform and Reformers: A Biographical Dictionary*. Needless to say, there are hundreds of excellent reference books and original sources for the material covered in this book; we consulted many of them in order to produce narratives that are as factually accurate and informative as possible.

For those who wish to do additional reading, we suggest the following works.

## FURTHER READING

Ambrose, Stephen E. 1996. *Undaunted Courage: Meriwether Lewis, Thomas Jefferson, and the Opening of the American West.* New York, NY: Simon & Schuster.

Andrews, Richard N.L. 1999. *Managing the Environment, Managing Ourselves: A History of American Environmental Policy*. New Haven, CT: Yale University Press.

Cawley, R. McGreggor. 1993. *Federal Land, Western Anger: The Sagebrush Rebellion and Environmental Politics*. Lawrence: University Press of Kansas.

Clarke, Jeanne Nienaber, and Daniel C. McCool.1996. *Staking Out the Terrain: Power and Performance among Natural Resource Agencies*, 2nd ed. Albany: State University of New York.

Cortner, Hanna J., and Margaret A. Moote. 1999. *The Politics of Ecosystem Management*. Washington, DC: Island Press.

Cronon, William.1983. *Changes in the Land: Indians, Colonists, and the Ecology of New England*. New York: Hill and Wang.

———. 1991. *Nature's Metropolis: Chicago and the Great West*. New York: W. W. Norton.

Darwin, Charles. 1859. *The Origin of Species*. London: John Murray.

Davis, Charles. 2001. *Western Public Lands and Environmental Politics*. 2nd ed. Boulder, CO: Westview Press.

DeSteiguer, J. E. 1997. *The Age of Environmentalism*. New York: WCB/McGraw Hill.

Fiorino, Daniel J. 1995. *Making Environmental Policy*. Berkeley: University of California Press.

Goldman, Eric R. 1977. *Rendezvous with Destiny: A History of Modern American Reform*. New York: Vintage.

Gottlieb, Robert. 1993. *Forcing the Spring: The Transformation of the American Environmental Movement*. Washington, DC: Island Press.

Gould, Stephen Jay. 1989. *Wonderful Life: The Burgess Shale and the Nature of History*. New York: W. W. Norton.

Hays, Samuel. 1959. *Conservation and the Gospel of Efficiency: The Progressive Conservation Movement 1890–1920*. Cambridge, MA: Harvard University Press.

Hofstadter, Richard. 1948. *The American Political Tradition: And the Men Who Made It*. New York: Vintage Books.

Ingram, Helen M. 1990. *Water Politics: Continuity and Change*. Albuquerque: University of New Mexico Press.

Jones, Charles O. 1975. *Clean Air: The Policies and Politics of Pollution Control*. Pittsburgh, PA: University of Pittsburgh Press.

Kaplan, Robert D. 1998. *An Empire Wilderness: Travels into America's Future*. New York: Random House.

Marx, Leo. 1964. *The Machine in the Garden: Technology and the Pastoral Ideal in America*. London: Oxford University Press.

McConnell, Grant. 1967. *Private Power and American Democracy*. New York: Alfred A. Knopf.

Merchant, Carolyn. 1984. "Women of the Progressive Conservation Movement: 1900–1916," *Environmental Review* 8(1): 57–85.

Nash, Roderick Frazier.1967. *Wilderness and the American Mind*. New Haven, CT: Yale University Press.

Paehlke, Robert. 1989. *Environmentalism and the Future of Progressive Politics*. New Haven, CT: Yale University Press.

Payne, Daniel G. 1996. *Voices in the Wilderness: American Nature Writing and Environmental Politics*. Hanover, NH: University Press of New England.

Press, Daniel. 1994. *Democratic Dilemmas in the Age of Ecology: Trees and Toxics in the American West*. Durham, NC: Duke University Press.

Putnam, Robert D. 2000. *Bowling Alone: The Collapse and Revival of American Community*. New York: Simon & Schuster.

Reisner, Marc. 1986. *Cadillac Desert: The American West and its Disappearing Water*. New York: Viking.

Richardson, Elmo. 1973. *Dams, Parks and Politics: Resource Development and Preservation in the Truman-Eisenhower Era*. Lexington: The University Press of Kentucky.

Robbins, Roy M. 1962. *Our Landed Heritage: The Public Domain, 1776–1936*. Lincoln: University of Nebraska Press.

Rogin, Michael P. 1975. *Fathers and Children: Andrew Jackson and the Subjugation of the American Indian*. New York: Alfred A. Knopf.

Smith, Henry Nash. 1950. *Virgin Land: The American West as Symbol and Myth*. Cambridge, MA: Harvard University Press.

Stegner, Wallace. 1953. *Beyond the Hundredth Meridian: John Wesley Powell and the Second Opening of the West*. Lincoln: University of Nebraska Press.

Stone, Christopher D. 1974. *Should Trees Have Standing? Toward Legal Rights for Natural Objects*. Los Altos, CA: William Kaufmann, Inc.

Truman, David B. 1955. *The Governmental Process: Political Interests and Public Opinion*. New York: Alfred A. Knopf.

White, Richard. 1991. *It's Your Misfortune and None of My Own: A New History of the American West*. Norman: University of Oklahoma Press.

Wilkinson, Charles F. 1992. *Crossing the Next Meridian: Land, Water, and the Future of the West*. Washington, DC: Island Press.

Yaffee, Steven Lewis. 1994. *The Wisdom of the Spotted Owl*. Washington, DC: Island Press.